D1554453

EUROPEAN HISTORICAL DICTIONARIES
Edited by Jon Woronoff

1. *Portugal,* by Douglas L. Wheeler. 1993
2. *Turkey,* by Metin Heper. 1994
3. *Poland,* by George Sanford and Adriana Gozdecka-Sanford. 1994
4. *Germany,* by Wayne C. Thompson, Susan L. Thompson, and Juliet S. Thompson. 1994
5. *Greece,* by Thanos M. Veremis and Mark Dragoumis. 1995
6. *Cyprus,* by Stavros Panteli. 1995
7. *Sweden,* by Irene Scobbie. 1995
8. *Finland,* by George Maude. 1995
9. *Croatia,* by Robert Stallaerts and Jeannine Laurens. 1995

Historical Dictionary of the REPUBLIC OF CROATIA

by
ROBERT STALLAERTS
and
JEANNINE LAURENS

European Historical Dictionaries, No. 9

The Scarecrow Press, Inc.
Metuchen, N.J., & London
1995

British Library Cataloguing-in-Publication data available

Library of Congress Cataloging-in-Publication Data

Stallaerts, Robert.
Historical dictionary of the Republic of Croatia / by Robert Stallaerts and Jeannine Laurens.
p. cm. -- (European historical dictionaries ; no. 9)
Includes bibliographical references.
ISBN 0-8108-2999-1 (alk. paper)
1. Croatia--Dictionaries. I. Laurens, Jeannine. II. Title. III. Series.
DR1507.5.S74 1995
949.72--dc20 95-3787

Manufactured in the United States of America
Printed on acid-free paper

DEDICATED

to

Mirko and Mihailo

CONTENTS

MAPS OF CROATIA

ACKNOWLEDGMENTS

This dictionary claims no originality in research results. It owes a great deal to most of the publications on the history of Croatia which are listed in the bibliography. We are especially grateful to the persons and institutions in Croatia and elsewhere with which we corresponded and which supplied us with ample data and advice. To single out some of them would be unfair to the rest.

We gratefully acknowledge permission to reproduce maps from the following sources: Dušan Bilandžić et al. (eds.), *Croatia between War and Independence,* 2nd ed. (Zagreb: University of Zagreb and OKC Zagreb, 1991); Mirjana Gross, *Počeci moderne Hrvatske* (Zagreb: Globus, 1985); Stanko Guldescu, *History of Medieval Croatia* (The Hague: Mouton De Gruyter, 1964).

EDITOR'S FOREWORD

The Republic of Croatia, to outside observers, is one of those new countries which resulted from the collapse of the former Yugoslavia. To its own people, however, it is a very old country which is finally getting another chance to forge a nation. The Croats trace their roots back many centuries and the depth of this resurgent nationalism helps explain why Yugoslavia split as it did and to some extent where it did. Of course, the demise was messy and remains so. But Croatia has returned and its people are trying to make a success of their new state despite often forbidding circumstances.

This *Historical Dictionary of the Republic of Croatia* is particularly useful in helping us understand what happened, why, and also what possible directions may be taken in the future, for it briefs us not only on today's Croatia but the various forerunners and even earlier origins. It mentions not only the former and present rulers and governing parties but the opposition then and now. Alongside the unsteady political superstructure it describes the more stable social, cultural and linguistic foundations. In addition to the Croats living in the new state, it considers those still outside as well as the minorities still inside and their respective problems. While hundreds of entries provide essential information, the chronology places events in a clearer framework and the bibliography directs readers to further sources of information.

Robert Stallaerts, who presents this broad panorama, has studied Yugoslavia and its components for two decades, including several years at the Institute for Economic Studies in Belgrade. He also attended courses in Dubrovnik and Zagreb, in present-day Croatia. More recently, in 1993, he worked as an interpreter at a humanitarian project in Savudrija. Stallaerts, who is a researcher at the Center for Ethics of the University of Antwerp, has written extensively on Yugoslavia and Croatia with special interest in the interaction between ethics and economics and the economics of self-management and participation. He was ably assisted by Jeannine Laurens who did post-graduate work at the Institute for Economic Studies in Belgrade and has published on the Yugoslav trade unions, self-management and delegate system.

Jon Woronoff
Series Editor

NOTE ON SPELLING

The Croatian language uses the Latin alphabet. However, some letters are marked by diacritical signs and indicate specific sounds. In domestic names and concepts, we have preserved the original spelling. The specific notations can approximately be summed up as follows:

c = ts	pronounced as in	"cats"
ć = tj		"tulip"
č = ch		"child"
đ = dj		"bridge"
š = sh		"shell"
ž = zh		"leisure"

In the alphabetical order of the dictionary, we have ignored the influence of the diacritical signs: e.g., c, ć and č are treated as equal.

The Cyrillic alphabet can easily be transcribed in the Croatian Latin version. This has been systematically done in the dictionary.

ABBREVIATIONS AND ACRONYMS

ARK	Antiratna Kampanja Zagreb - Anti-War Campaign Committee Zagreb
ARSH	Asocijacija Regionalnih Stranaka Hrvatske - Association of Croatian Regional Parties
AVNOJ	Anti-Fašističko Vijeće Narodnog Oslobođenja Jugoslavije - Anti-Fascist Council of the National Liberation of Yugoslavia
CCI	Croatian Cultural Institute - Matica Hrvatska (MH)
CHC	Croatian Helsinki Committee
CPY	Communist Party of Yugoslavia
DA	Dalmatinska Akcija - Dalmatian Action
DHK	Društvo Hrvatskih Književnika - Croatian Writers' Association
DM	Deutsche Mark - German Mark
EC	European Community
FTT	Free Territory of Trieste
GATT	General Agreement on Tariffs and Trade
HAZU	Hrvatska Akademija Znanosti i Umjetnosti - Croatian Academy of Arts and Sciences
HBNA	Herceg-Bosna Novinska Agencija - News Agency of the Croatian Republic of Herceg-Bosna
HČSP	Hrvatska Čista Stranka Prava - Croatian Pure Party of Rights

HDMS	Hrvatska Domovinska Stranka - Croatian National Party
HDS	Hrvatska Demokratska Stranka - Croatian Democratic Party
HDSP	Hrvatska Demokratska Stranka Prava - Croatian Democratic Party of Rights
HDZ	Hrvatska Demokratska Zajednica - Croatian Democratic Union
HGK	Hrvatska Gospodarska Komora - Croatian Chamber of Commerce
HINA	Hrvatska Izvještajna Novinska Agencija - Croatian News and Press Agency
HKBO	Hrvatska Kreditna Banka za Obnovu - Croatian Credit Bank for Reconstruction
HKDS	Hrvatska Kršćanska Demokratska Stranka - Croatian Christian Democratic Party
HKDU	Hrvatska Kršćanska Demokratska Unija - Croatian Christian Democratic Union
HMDS	Hrvatska Muslimanska Demokratska Stranka - Croatian Muslim Democratic Party
HMI	Hrvatska Matica Iseljenika - Croatian Homeland Foundation
HND	Hrvatski Nezavisni Demokrati - Croatian Independent Democrats
HNDL	Hrvatska Nacionalno-Demokratska Liga - Croatian National-Democratic League
HNK	Hrvatsko Narodno Kažalište - Croatian National Theater
HNS	Hrvatska Narodna Stranka - Croatian People's Party
HOS	Hrvatske Oružene Snage - Croatian Armed Forces
HPSS	Hrvatska Pučka Seljačka Stranka - Croatian People's Peasant Party
HR	Hrvatski Radio - Croatian Radio
HRTV	Hrvatski Radio i Televizija - Croatian Radio and Television
HSK	Hrvatsko-Srpska Koalicija - Croat-Serb Coalition
HSLS	Hrvatska Socijalna Liberalna Stranka - Croatian Social-Liberal Party
HSP	Hrvatska Stranka Prava - Croatian Party of Rights
HSS	Hrvatska Seljačka Stranka - Croatian Peasant Party

HTV	Hrvatska Televizija - Croatian Television
HUS	Hrvatska Udruga Sindikata - Croatian Association of Unions
HV	Hrvatska Vojska - Croatian Army
HVEP	Hrvatsko Vijeće Europskog Pokreta - Croatian Council of the European Movement
HVO	Hrvatsko Vijeće Obrana - Croatian Defense Council
IDS	Istarski Demokratski Sabor - Istrian Democratic Parliament
IMF	International Monetary Fund
IMRO	Internal Macedonian Revolutionary Organization
IRMO	Institut za Razvoj i Međunarodne Odnose - Institute for Development and International Relations
ISDRI	Interregional Network of Scientific Development Research Institutions
JAZU	Jugoslovenska Akademija Znanosti i Umjetnosti - Yugoslav Academy of Arts and Sciences
JNA	Jugoslovenska Narodna Armija - Yugoslav (People's) Army
JRT	Jugoslovenski Radio i Televizija - Yugoslav Radio and Television
KDM	Kršćanski Demokrati Međimurja - Christian Democrats of Međimurje
KNS	Kršćanska Narodna Stranka - Christian National Party
KOS	Kontra-Obavještajna Služba Jugoslovenske Vojske - Intelligence and Information Office of the Yugoslav Army
LCY	League of Communists of Yugoslavia - Savez Komunista Jugoslavije (SKJ)
MH	Matica Hrvatska - Croatian Cultural Institute
MUP	Ministarstvo Unutrašnih Poslova - Ministry of the Interior (term used for Croatian Police Forces)

NDH	Nezavisna Država Hrvatska - Independent State of Croatia
OTV	Omladinska Televizija - Youth Television
OZNA	Odeljenje za Žaštitu Naroda - State Security Administration
PHARE	Poland and Hungary Action for Restructuring of the Economy
RDS	Riječki Demokratski Savez - Rijeka Democratic Alliance
RSK	Republika Srpska Krajina - Serbian Republic of Krajina
SDF	Srpski Demokratski Forum - Serbian Democratic Forum
SDPH-SDP	Socijaldemokratska Partija Hrvatske-Stranka za Društvene Promene - Social Democratic Party of Croatia-Party of Democratic Changes
SDS	Srpska Demokratska Stranka - Serbian Democratic Party
SFRJ	Socijalistička Federativna Republika Jugoslavija - Socialist Federal Republic of Yugoslavia
SHDP	Stranka Hrvatskog Državnog Prava - Party of the Croatian State's Rights
SKJ	Savez Komunista Jugoslavije - League of Communists of Yugoslavia (LCY)
SNS	Srpska Narodna Stranka - Serbian National Party
SR	Srpska Republika - Serbian Republic
SRS	Srpska Radikalna Stranka - Serbian Radical Party
SSH	Stranka Socijalista Hrvatske - Socialist Party of Croatia
SSSH	Savez Samostalnih Sindikata Hrvatske - Association of Independent Unions of Croatia
SZUP	Služba za Zaštitu Ustavnog Poretka - State Service for the Protection of the Constitutional Order
UDBA	Uprava Državne Bezbednosti - State Security Administration

UN	United Nations
UNCIVIL	United Nations Civil Forces
UNPA	United Nations Protected Area
UNPROFOR	United Nations Protection Forces
VUS	Vjesnik U Srijedu - The Wednesday Magazine
YUTEL	Yugoslav Television
ZAVNOH	Zemaljsko Anti-Fašističko Vijeće Narodnog Oslobođenja Hrvatske - Anti-Fascist Council of the National Liberation of Croatia
ZNG	Zbor Narodne Garde - National Guard

CHRONOLOGY OF CROATIAN HISTORY

395	The Roman Emperor Theodosius dies. His Empire is divided into an Eastern and Western part. The frontier cuts the future "South Slav lands" into two spheres of influence along a line still disputed today.
Around 550	The Slavs cross the Danube and arrive on the Adriatic shores.
614	The Slavs conquer the ancient Roman town Solin near Split.
641	The Christianization of Croatia begins under the rule of Pope John IV, who was a native of Dalmatia. He sent Abbot Martin to the Croatian lands.
680	Pope Agathon concludes a treaty with the Croats.
800	Croatia is a Frankish vassal state; delegates are present at the coronation of Charlemagne.
845-864	Reign of Prince Trpimir.
852	Trpimir signs a document as *Dux Chroatorum.*
864-876	Reign of Domagoj.
878-879	Reign of Zdeslav.

879-892	Reign of Branimir as the first independent ruler of Croatia. Pope John VIII recognizes the Croatian national church and the Croatian nation.
892-910	Reign of Mutimir, first-born son of Trpimir.
910-928	Reign of Tomislav, son of Mutimir. He gave himself the title *Rex Chroatorum.*
925	Ecclesiastical Synod of Split.
935-945	Reign of Krešimir, son of Tomislav.
948-952	Constantine VII Porphyrogenitus of Byzantium composes *De Administrando Imperio.*
960-968	Krešimir II incorporates Bosnia into his kingdom.
969-997	Stipan Držislav, son of Krešimir, gained the support of Byzantium and bore the title *Rex Dalmatiae et Croatiae.*
997-1000	Civil war. Venetians seize Dalmatian cities.
1007-1018	Krešimir III regains Dalmatia.
1058-1076	Krešimir IV unifies Dalmatia, Bosnia and Croatia.
1074-1075	Composition of oldest surviving Croatian chronicle, *Kraljestvo Hrvata.*
1076-1089	Reign of King Dmitar Zvonimir, last strong ruler of Croatia.
1091	King Ladislas of Hungary invades Slavonia.
1102	The Pacta Conventa inaugurates a personal union between Hungary and Croatia.

1242	Bela IV issues the "Golden Bull" of the free town of Gradec (Zagreb).
1301	The Arpad line of Hungarian Kings dies out. Charles of the Neapolitan Angevins is chosen as Croatian King.
1389	The Turks defeat the Slavs and Albanians at the battle of Kosovo.
1409	King Ladislas sells hereditary rights over Dalmatia to Venice.
1463	The Turks conquer Bosnia.
1468	Turkish raids on Croatia.
1482	The Turks conquer Hercegovina.
1491	Maximilian I of Austria recognized as King of Croatia.
1493	The Turks defeat a Croatian army in the field of Krbava.
1526	The Turks defeat the Hungarians at Mohacs.
1527	The Croatian Sabor elects Ferdinand of Habsburg as their King.
1572	Execution of Matija Gubec, the leader of a peasant revolt.
1578	Military reorganization of the Vojna Krajina under Karl von Štajerska. Vienna administers the region without interference of the Croat Ban or Sabor.
1591	Croatians defeat Turks in the battle of Sisak.
1595	New victory of Croats and Austrians at Petrinja; the

	lands north of the Kupa are definitively saved.
1606	Peace Treaty between Austrians and Turks defines lasting frontiers.
1619-1637	Reign of Ferdinand II of Habsburg. The Vojna Krajina of Karlovac and Varaždin are administratively divided.
1683	Defeat of the Turkish army at Vienna.
1699	The Treaty of Karlovci liberates most of Slavonia and Croatia.
1712	The Croatian Sabor decides to sign the Pragmatic Sanction.
1797	Napoleon conquers Dalmatia.
1809	Creation of the French Illyrian Provinces which included Istria, Dalmatia and parts of Croatia.
1815	The Congress of Vienna returns all Croatian territories to Austria.
1832	Janko Drašković publishes a book that defends the Great-Croatian ideas. Illyrian should be the official language.
1835	Ljudevit Gaj publishes *Novine Horvatzke* and *Danica*, the first Croatian newspaper and literary magazine.
1842	The cultural institution Matica hrvatska is founded.
1843	Metternich forbids the use of Illyrian symbols.

1848	The Sabor decides on the restoration of the integrity of the Triune Kingdom of Croatia.
1848-1849	Ban Josip Jelačić saves the Habsburg regime from a Hungarian revolt.
1861	Austria dissolves the Croatian Sabor as it refuses cooperation in the central parliament.
1867	Creation of the Dual Monarchy by the Ausgleich (Agreement) between Austria and Hungary.
1868	The Croatian Sabor concludes the Nagodba with Hungary, obtaining some form of autonomy but Istria and Dalmatia remain under Austria, Slavonia under Hungary.
1873	Nomination as Ban of Ivan Mažuranić, who initiates a Croatian-friendly cultural policy.
1875	Revolt in Bosnia-Hercegovina.
1878	Victorious in the Russo-Turkish war, the Russians impose on the Turks the Treaty of San Stefano. The same year, the Great Powers react with the Conference of Berlin. Austria-Hungary is granted the right to occupy Bosnia-Hercegovina.
1881	The Vojna Krajina is reintegrated in the Croatian lands. Only Rijeka remains directly under Hungary.
1883	Following anti-Hungarian riots, the new Ban Karoly Khuen-Hédervary tries to fight rising Croatian nationalism.
1895	Young intellectuals, among them Stjepan Radić, are expelled after a riot against Hungarian rule. Many go to Prague and will be won for the Pan-Slavic movement.

1903	Riots force Hungarian-minded Ban Khuen-Hédervary to resign in favor of T. Pejačević.
1904	The Radić brothers found the Croatian Peasant Party.
1905	Croats and Serbs agree on a common Yugoslav policy in the Resolutions of Rijeka and Zadar.
1908	Austria-Hungary annexes Bosnia-Hercegovina. Serbia protests and gets support from the Pan-Slavic and Yugoslavian movement.
1912	Students strike in Zagreb and the Sabor is dissolved.
June 28, 1914	The young Serbian nationalist Gavrilo Princip kills Archduke Francis Ferdinand in Sarajevo. Austria-Hungary declares war on Serbia and in August World War I breaks out.
1915	A Yugoslav Committee is formed in London. It is headed by the Croat Ante Trumbić.
1917	The Declaration of Corfu is a joint statement of the Yugoslav Committee and the Prime Minister of the Serbian government, Nikola Pašić.
1918	A National Council takes over government functions in Zagreb. The Croatian Sabor proclaims independence from defeated Austria and adheres to a common South Slavic State.
December 1, 1918	Proclamation of the Kingdom of Serbs, Croats and Slovenes under the Serbian Karađorđević dynasty.
1919	In Belgrade, the Socialist Workers' Party of Yugoslavia is founded.

1920	The Socialist Workers' Party, now Communist Party of Yugoslavia (CPY), accepts the right of secession of non-Serbian lands. By the Treaty of Rapallo, Italy acquires Istria, Rijeka, Zadar and several Adriatic islands.
1928	A Serbian radical shoots S. Radić in the Belgrade parliament. Riots break out in Zagreb.
December 6, 1929	King Alexander installs a dictatorship. The name of the state is changed to Yugoslavia. Ante Pavelić, a member of the Party of Rights, founds the Ustaša movement.
October 9, 1934	Assassination of King Alexander in Marseille by Macedonian and Croatian separatists.
1936	Josip Broz Tito becomes the head of the CPY. The party henceforth follows a unitary line on the Yugoslav question.
1939	Dragiša Cvetković and Vladko Maček sign the Sporazum. Croatia becomes an autonomous Banovina within Yugoslavia.
April 6, 1941	The Germans attack Yugoslavia.
April 10, 1942	The Independent State of Croatia is proclaimed. Pavelić takes over the government.
November 29, 1943	The Second Session of the Anti-Fascist Council of the National Liberation of Yugoslavia (AVNOJ) decides on a federal organization for the future Yugoslavia.
March 7, 1945	In Belgrade Tito forms the provisional government of the Democratic Federation of Yugoslavia.
May 8, 1945	Fall of Zagreb.

1946	Trial of Archbishop Alojzije Stepinac.
1948	The Cominform conflict opposes Tito to Stalin. Yugoslav Stalinists - among them the Croat Andrija Hebrang - are purged.
1952	First step in the introduction of the Yugoslav system of self-management, mainly characterized by factory councils.
1954	Fall of the communist leader Milovan Đilas who started to plead for cultural and political pluralism.
1965	Great economic reform.
1966	Fall of the conservative centralist leader Ranković.
1967	Declaration on the status of the Croatian literary language.
1967-1972	The "Croatian Spring" claims economic, cultural and political autonomy. After long hesitation, Tito finally crushed the Croatian leadership.
1974	The new Constitution decentralizes major powers to the Republics and Autonomous Provinces.
May 4, 1980	Death of Tito.
June 1981	Street demonstrations, strikes and riots in Kosovo.
1982	The Kraigher Commission presents a proposal for a long-term stabilization program.
1986	Slobodan Milosević becomes President of Serbia and will put into practice a nationalistic memorandum presented the same year by the Serbian Academy of Arts and Sciences.

1987	The publication of the fifty-seventh issue of *Nova Revija* marks the beginning of the "Slovene Spring."
1988	The yoghurt revolution in Novi Sad brings supporters of Milosević to power.
February 1989	The UJDI - Yugoslav Association for a Democratic Initiative - is set up under the direction of Branko Horvat.
March 1, 1989	The HDZ - Croatian Democratic Union - is founded.
March 1989	The Croat Ante Marković becomes the President of the government of the Federation.
December 1989	The Eleventh Congress of the Croatian League of Communists proposes multiparty elections in April 1990.
January 1990	The Slovene and the Croatian delegations leave the Extraordinary Fourteenth Congress of the League of Communists.
February 1990	First the Slovenes and then the Croats withdraw their troops from Kosovo.
April 8, 22, 1990	The first multiparty elections in Slovenia result in victory of the opposition coalition DEMOS.
April 22 - May 6, 1990	Multiparty elections in Croatia give victory to Tuđman and his HDZ.
May 30, 1990	First session of the new multiparty parliament (Sabor).
June 6, 1990	The Assembly of the Knin Commune proposes creating a Community of the Communes of Northern Dalmatia and Lika.

August 17, 1990	Referendum on Cultural Autonomy of the Serbs of Kninska Krajina. They get the support of Serbia.
October 1, 1990	The Serbs in the Kninska Krajina proclaim their autonomy.
October 1990	Slovenia and Croatia present a "Model of a Confederation in Yugoslavia."
November 1990	The federal government invites the Constitutional Court to investigate the constitutionality of Slovene and Croatian laws.
December 3, 1990	The Minister of Defense of the Federation, Veljko Kadijević, threatens all who form paramilitary units.
December 21-22, 1990	The Croatian parliament accepts a new Croatian Constitution. Croatia is defined as a sovereign state.
December 23, 1990	Successful plebiscite on the independence of Slovenia. The right of secession within six months is proclaimed on December 26.
March 2, 1991	First incidents and shooting at Pakrac.
March 31, 1991	Incidents in Plitvice between Serbs and Croats and intervention of the army result in deaths.
April 8, 1991	Trial of the Croatian Minister Špegelj.
May 2, 1991	Deadly clashes between Croatian police forces and insurgent Serbs at Borovo Selo.
May 12, 1991	Referendum in Knin about political autonomy and adherence to Serbia.
May 15 - 17, 1991	The Federal Presidential Council does not elect the Croat Stipe Mešić as its new President.

May 19, 1991	Referendum on the sovereignty of Croatia in a Yugoslav confederation.
May 20, 1991	The European Community (EC) declares that future cooperation will depend on the maintenance of the unity of the country.
June 25, 1991	Declaration of Independence of Slovenia and Croatia.
June 27, 1991	Military intervention in Slovenia.
July 7, 1991	In Brioni, the EC mediates an Agreement on ex-Yugoslavia.
July 13, 1991	First open attack of the Yugoslav army on the Croatian forces near Vukovar in East Slavonia.
July 18, 1991	The Yugoslav army announces its intention to withdraw from Slovenia.
August 3, 1991	The Government of Democratic Unity is established in Zagreb by the agreement of eight parties represented in parliament.
August 25, 1991	The Yugoslav army and Serbian paramilitary organizations attack Vinkovci and Vukovar.
September 7, 1991	Opening of the EC Peace Conference on Yugoslavia in The Hague.
September 16, 1991	Bosanska Krajina becomes an autonomous Serbian region in Bosnia. Three other regions follow and fortify the strategic position of the Croatian Serbs.
September 25, 1991	The UN imposes an embargo on the transit of weapons to Yugoslavia.

	The Security Council unanimously confirms Resolution 271, concerning possible UN peace-keeping forces in Croatia.
October 7, 1991	The moratorium on the independence of Slovenia and Croatia comes to an end. In Zagreb, the presidential palace is bombed.
October 8, 1991	Cyrus Vance is appointed UN mediator in the peace talks.
November 18, 1991	Fall of Vukovar.
November 22, 1991	HSP leader Dobroslav Paraga is arrested in Zagreb.
December 13, 1991	Massacre at Vocin in Slavonia by Serb militiamen.
December 16, 1991	Genscher tells his EC colleagues that Germany will announce the recognition of Croatia on December 19.
January 3, 1992	The fifteenth armistice between the war parties is at last respected.
January 7, 1992	A Mig from the Yugoslav army shoots down a helicopter with UN observers above Varaždin.
January 15, 1992	The EC follows the advice of the Badinter Commission and recognizes Slovenia and Croatia.
February 6, 1992	Zagreb accepts the Vance proposal on the settlement of the war in Croatia.
February 15, 1992	Presidents Ćosić and Tuđman reach an agreement on the Vance proposal.

February 21, 1992	The UN Security Council adopts Resolution 743 on sending a peace-keeping force (UNPROFOR) to Croatia in execution of the Vance proposal.
February 28, 1992	Milošević declares before the Serbian parliament that the war is over.
February 29, 1992	A referendum is held on the independence of Bosnia-Hercegovina.
March 2, 1992	Bosnian Serbs in Sarajevo reject the independence of Bosnia-Hercegovina and take up arms.
April 6, 1992	The EC recognizes Bosnia-Hercegovina.
April 7, 1992	The US recognizes Croatia, Slovenia and Bosnia-Hercegovina.
April 27, 1992	Serbia and Montenegro form a new federation: New Yugoslavia.
May 15, 1992	The Security Council passes Resolution 752 on Bosnia-Hercegovina; any intervention - such as the Croatian military involvement - has to be stopped. In Croatia, UN troops take over the Baranja. Paramilitary organizations in the UNPROFOR area in Croatia are to be disarmed.
May 22, 1992	Admission of Croatia as a member of the UN.
May 27, 1992	The EC proposes a trade embargo against New Yugoslavia.
May 30, 1992	Resolution 757 of the Security Council introduces an embargo against New Yugoslavia. It urges Croatia to abandon any military involvement in Bosnia.

May 31, 1992	Milosević and his Socialist Party win the elections in Serbia.
June 2, 1992	The Secretary-General of the UN, Boutros Boutros-Ghali, presents a report and condemns irregular actions of both the Serbian and the Croatian armies.
June 8, 1992	The Security Council adopts Resolution 758 on the protection of humanitarian aid to Sarajevo. Ćosic is elected President of New Yugoslavia.
June 17, 1992	Bosnia-Hercegovina and Croatia sign an agreement on a Defense Alliance.
June 29, 1992	Resolution 761 admits use of force to break the blockade of the Sarajevo airport.
June 30, 1992	Resolution 762 installs a mixed commission to settle the question of the "pink zones" in Croatia.
July 3, 1992	Bosnian Croats constitute the autonomous region of Herceg-Bosna.
July 9, 1992	The Western powers send a military convoy into the Adriatic Sea to observe the embargo against New Yugoslavia.
August 2, 1992	Tuđman is reelected President with 56.7 percent of the votes. The HDZ wins the parliamentary elections.
August 3, 1992	The US State Department brings out a report on concentration camps in Bosnia.
August 7, 1992	Resolution 769 authorizes UNPROFOR to act as a customs and immigration authority in the UNPAs.
August 12, 1992	Tuđman forms his new government.

August 13, 1992	The UN Security Council adopts Resolutions 770 and 771 on military protection for aid and free access to camps. Belgrade recognizes Slovenia.
August 26, 1992	Opening of the Peace Conference in London under the chairmanship of John Major and Boutros Boutros-Ghali. Lord Carrington resigns and is replaced by Lord Owen.
August 27, 1992	The London Conference closes with programmatic statements to be put into practice by permanent negotiations in Geneva.
September 3, 1992	First session of peace talks in Geneva under the direction of David Owen and Cyrus Vance.
September 14, 1992	Security Council Resolution 776 on supplementary forces to protect humanitarian missions to Sarajevo.
September 22, 1992	The UN General Assembly excludes New Yugoslavia.
September 30, 1992	Tuđman and Ćosić agree to condemn ethnic purification and to stabilize relations between the two countries.
October 6, 1992	Security Council Resolution 779 extends the mandate of UNPROFOR and brings the Peruča dam and the Prevlaka peninsula under its control. Security Council Resolution 780 creates a commission to investigate war crimes in former Yugoslavia.
October 9, 1992	Security Council Resolution 781 decrees a no-fly zone above Bosnia-Hercegovina.
October 20, 1992	Tuđman and Ćosić open communication centers in Belgrade and Zagreb.

October 28, 1992	Mazowiecki presents a report on the violation of human rights and ethnic purification. The Security Council receives the Vance-Owen proposal on the future arrangement of Bosnia.
November 27, 1992	Croatia and the Republic of the Serbian Autonomous Regions of Bosnia-Hercegovina sign in Sarajevo an agreement on ending hostilities.
December 20, 1992	Milošević defeats Panić in presidential elections in Serbia.
December 27, 1992	In Geneva Tuđman and Izetbegović agree on the future constitutional construction of Bosnia-Hercegovina in the presence of Owen and Vance. Tuđman and Boutros-Ghali meet the same day on the same problem.
December 28, 1992	Tuđman and Ćosić talk in Geneva about Bosnia and the relations between Croatia and New Yugoslavia.
December 29, 1992	Panić is voted out of the parliament of New Yugoslavia.
January 2, 1993	Peace talks continue in Geneva on the Vance-Owen plan; the Bosnian leaders meet face to face for the first time.
January 4, 1993	The Croat Bosnian leader Mate Boban signs the Vance-Owen peace plan.
January 22, 1993	The Croatian army attacks the pink zone in the Maslenica area.
January 25, 1993	Security Council Resolution 802 condemns the Croatian attack in the Maslenica area and orders a truce.
February 5, 1993	Peace talks broken off on January 30 in Geneva are continued in New York.

February 7, 1993	Local and regional elections in Croatia.
February 19, 1993	Security Council Resolution 807 extends the UNPROFOR mandate until March 31.
February 22, 1993	Security Council Resolution 808 approves the establishment of an International War Tribunal to judge those responsible for war crimes in former Yugoslavia.
March 25, 1993	The Bosnian Muslim leader Alija Izetbegovic signs the Vance-Owen plan.
March 30, 1993	Security Council Resolution 815 extends the UNPROFOR mandate until June 30.
April 2, 1993	Cyrus Vance resigns as UN mediator and is replaced by the Norwegian Minister of Foreign Affairs Thorvald Stoltenberg.
April 6, 1993	Geneva Agreement between Zagreb and the Serbs of Krajina on the execution of Resolution 802.
April 8, 1993	"The Former Yugoslavian Republic of Macedonia" is accepted as a member of the UN.
April 16, 1993	Bosnian Croats attack the Muslim town of Jablanica.
April 18, 1993	Security Council Resolution 820 confirms sanctions against New Yugoslavia.
April 25, 1993	The EC Foreign Ministers reprimand the Croats for attacks in Bosnia and threaten sanctions. Tuđman mediates an agreement between Mate Boban and Alija Izetbegović.
April 29, 1993	The Bosnian Serb leader Radovan Karadžić conditionally signs the Vance-Owen plan in Athens.

May 6, 1993	The Parliament of the Bosnian Serbs rejects the Vance-Owen plan.
May 15-16, 1993	The Serbian Bosnians reject the Vance-Owen plan in their referendum.
May 22, 1993	In Washington, the US, Russia, France, Great Britain and Spain agree on a new international peace plan for Bosnia. It is immediately rejected by the Muslims.
May 25, 1993	Security Council Resolution 837 creates a War Crimes Tribunal for former Yugoslavia.
May 26, 1993	The Bosnian Croats reject accusations of ethnic cleansing in Mostar.
June 1, 1993	The New Yugoslavia Parliament votes president Ćosić out.
June 8, 1993	The Muslims conquer Travnik from their former allies, the Bosnian Croats.
June 14-15, 1993	Referendum in the Republic of Krajina of Croatia on union with the Serb Republic in Bosnia.
June 16, 1993	In Geneva, Tuđman and Milošević defend the division of Bosnia into three Republics along ethnic lines. The Vance-Owen plan is dead.
June 17, 1993	US President Bill Clinton declares he has given up his resistance to the creation of a Bosnian state along ethnic lines in three Republics.
July 1, 1993	The Frenchman Jean Cot replaces the Swede Lars Eric Wahlgren as head of the Blue Helmets.
July 5, 1993	President Tuđman declares he will not flatly decline talks with the Serbs on territorial corrections in the Dubrovnik and Prevlaka regions.

July 17, 1993	Agreement between Zagreb and Knin on security around the Maslenica bridge, the Zemunik airport and the Peruča dam, in line with the agreement of April 6 and Resolution 802.
July 19, 1993	Croatian Serbs shell Zemunik airport.
July 20-22, 1993	Croatian Serbs break off negotiations on Maslenica-Zemunik.
July 27, 1993	The first meeting of 17 Croatian opposition parties confronts a representative of the HDZ.
July 30, 1993	In Geneva the three parties conditionally agree on the principle of creating a Union of three Republics of Bosnia-Hercegovina. The Security Council requests that the Maslenica bridge be placed under UNPROFOR control.
August 1, 1993	The Krajina Serbs shell the Maslenica bridge.
August 4, 1993	The second meeting of 17 opposition parties decides to follow a common strategy against the politics of Tuđman and the government of the HDZ.
August 28, 1993	Solemn proclamation of the Croatian Republic of Herceg-Bosna in Gruda.
September 7, 1993	Tuđman insists on humane treatment of war prisoners in a public letter to Mate Boban.
September 9, 1993	The Croats take three villages from the Krajina Serbs near Gospić after continued shelling of the town of Gospić.
September 10, 1993	The Krajina Serbs shell Karlovac. Stoltenberg calls on Tuđman to stop the Medak offensive.

September 11, 1993	The Krajina Serbs shell a suburb of Zagreb.
September 12, 1993	The Krajina Serbs shell Jastrebarsko, Samobor and Kutina. They publicize a list with 50 targets. Tuđman announces a unilateral 24-hour armistice.
September 14, 1993	In Geneva, Tuđman and Izetbegović announce an armistice between Muslims and Croats in Bosnia. The Serbs shoot down a Croatian Mig 21.
September 15, 1993	An armistice is signed under UN mediation between the Croats and Krajina Serbs. The Croats will retreat from the villages conquered in the Medak.
September 16, 1993	According to the Serbian Press Agency, the Croatian army shells the Krajina headquarters of Knin.
September 17, 1993	The Krajina Serbs shell Zadar, Šibenik and Biograd.
September 18, 1993	UN officers report destructions and deliberate killings during the Croatian retreat from Krajina villages.
September 20, 1993	The journal *Erasmus* publishes an open letter of six intellectuals (among others, Ivo Banac and Vlado Gotovac) to President Tuđman demanding his dismissal.
September 22, 1993	The Croatian Defense and Security Council questions the extension of the UNPROFOR mandate in Croatia.
September 23, 1993	The Croatian government threatens in an ultimatum that UNPROFOR must leave before November 30, 1993.
September 26, 1993	Croatian refugees hold a protest meeting in Zagreb against UNPROFOR.

September 28, 1993	Tuđman requires a change in the UNPROFOR mandate before the UN General Assembly.
October 1, 1993	NATO decides to give air protection to UNPROFOR in Croatia if needed.
October 4, 1993	Security Council Resolution 871 extends the UNPROFOR mandate in Croatia for six months. The lifting of sanctions against New Yugoslavia are tied to a cooperative attitude of Belgrade in the Croatian problem.
October 7, 1993	UNPROFOR accuses the Croatian army of scorched earth tactics and cruelties during the offensive in Medak.
October 8, 1993	Tuđman presents his new proposals to resolve the crisis with the help of NATO during the Conference of the Council of Europe in Vienna. He is hostile to a global approach.
October 15-16, 1993	Second Convention of the HDZ. Tuđman remains President and reorganizes the HDZ.
November 1-2, 1993	Secret negotiations in Oslo between Zagreb and the Krajina Serbs are broken off.
November 2, 1993	In a spirit of national conciliation, Tuđman offers the Serbs in Croatia the status of ethnic community instead of national minority.
November 3, 1993	The UN declares that local Serbs refuse to allow experts to excavate a mass grave with the supposed remains of 200 murdered patients and personnel of the Vukovar hospital.
November 4, 1993	Zagreb and the Krajina Serbs sign an armistice for East Croatia.

November 5, 1993	The leader of the Bosnian Serbs, Momčilo Krajisnik, declares Bosnia-Hercegovina will be divided into three independent national states.
November 17, 1993	Opening of the War Crimes Tribunal for former Yugoslavia at The Hague.
November 20, 1993	Serbian and Croatian intellectuals - among them Manolić and Valentić - participate in a common dialogue in Zagreb.
November 29, 1993	The EC proposes to alleviate the sanctions against the Serbs in exchange for more territory in Bosnia and a *modus vivendi* in Croatia.
December 12, 1993	The first round of presidential and parliamentary elections in the Krajina is declared illegal by Zagreb.
December 22, 1993	The EC summons former Yugoslav leaders to appear in Brussels.
January 9, 1994	Tuđman and Izetbegović negotiate on a Croatian-Bosnian confederation at Petersburg near Bonn without results.
January 19, 1994	In Geneva, Tuđman and Milošević make a common declaration on the normalization of relations between Croatia and New Yugoslavia.
January 23, 1994	In the fourth round of the presidential elections in the Krajina, Milan Martić finally defeats Milan Babić.
January 26, 1994	Lieutenant General Sir Michael Rose takes over the command of UN forces in Bosnia.
January 28, 1994	An observer of UNPROFOR declares that 3,500 regular soldiers of the Croatian army participate in the battles of Central Bosnia.

February 2, 1994	Boutros Boutros-Ghali informs the Security Council on the presence of 3,000 to 5,000 Croatian soldiers in central and southern Bosnia.
February 3, 1994	The Security Council threatens Croatia with sanctions if it does not stop its intervention in Bosnia within two weeks. Croatian Ambassador to the UN Mario Nobilo declares that sanctions imply a renewal of the war.
February 4, 1994	Pope John Paul II summons Minister of Foreign Affairs Mate Granić to silence weapons in Bosnia.
February 7, 1994	Croatia and Slovenia sign agreements on mutual cooperation.
February 8, 1994	Mate Boban resigns.
February 9, 1994	NATO presents an ultimatum to the Serbs to withdraw heavy weapons from Sarajevo by February 20.
February 11, 1994	Mate Granić and Haris Siladjić adopt a joint declaration on a ceasefire in Bosnia within two weeks.
February 14, 1994	Tuđman pays an official visit to Romania.
February 17, 1994	The Russian envoy Vitaly Churkin convinces Serbs at Pale to stop strangling Sarajevo.
February 22, 1994	The non-aligned movement votes in favor of UN sanctions against Croatia.
February 25, 1994	The ceasefire goes into effect between Croats and Muslims in Bosnia.
February 28, 1994	NATO shoots down four Serbian planes defying the no-fly zone in Bosnia-Hercegovina. Tuđman pays an official visit to Albania.

March 1, 1994	In Washington, Mate Granić, Haris Silajdžić and Krešimir Zubak reach a preliminary agreement on a Muslim-Croatian federation in Bosnia-Hercegovina and a confederation of it with Croatia.
March 18, 1994	In Washington, the Constitution of the New Federation of Muslims and Croats and a Declaration on a Confederation with Croatia are signed.
March 22, 1994	Croats and Krajina Serbs meet in the Russian Embassy in Zagreb without immediate success.
March 30, 1994	Croats and Krajina Serbs sign a ceasefire going into effect on April 4.
April 1, 1994	The UN prolong UNPROFOR's mandate with six months.
April 6, 1994	Karadžić declares that he is prepared to talk about relations with the Muslim-Croatian Bosnian Federation on the condition of prior recognition of the Serbian Republic.
April 22, 1994	The Security Council and NATO impose an ultimatum on the Bosnian Serbs to withdraw from Goražde by April 27.
April 30, 1994	Stipe Mešić and Josip Manolić found the Croatian Independent Democrats (HND)
May 30, 1994	A new monetary unit - the kuna - is officially introduced.
June 8, 1994	The warring parties in Bosnia agree on an armistice of a month.
July 17, 1994	Presidents Franjo Tuđman, Alija Izetbegović and Suleiman Demirel issue a joint declaration at Brioni.

August 21, 1994	The Muslim government conquers the Bihać region and Fikret Abdić seeks refuge in the Croatian Krajina.
September 10-11, 1994	Pope John Paul II visits Croatia, but cancels his visit to Sarajevo.
September 15, 1994	Tuđman and Izetbegović discuss further arrangements of the proposed confederation.
September 23, 1994	Parliament passes a critical resolution on UNPROFOR and without major changes, it will be tolerated only 100 days more until January 10, 1995.
October 1, 1994	The Security Council passes Resolution 947 extending the mandate of UNPROFOR to March 31, 1995.
October 14, 1994	The IMF approves credits to Croatia.
November 9, 1994	The Krajina Serbs and Fikret Abdić attack the Bihać region.
November 11, 1994	The US announces not to control the arms embargo any longer.
November 18, 1994	The Krajina Serbs use napalm in the Bihać region.
November 19, 1994	The Security Council passes Resolution 958, allowing air strikes on Croatian soil with the consent of Tuđman.
November 21, 1994	NATO bombs Udbina, an air base of the Croatian Serbs.
November 27, 1994	Croatia threatens with intervention in the Bihać region.

December 2, 1994	Zagreb and the Croatian Serbs of the Krajina sign an agreement on economic matters.
December 15, 1994	Radovan Karađić invites former US President Jimmy Carter to Pale.
December 20, 1994	Carter mediates an armistice in Bosnia for four months.
January 11, 1995	Tuđman announces the decision not to extend the mandate of UNPROFOR in Croatia.

INTRODUCTION

Background

Croatia, a former republic of Yugoslavia, is a self-declared independent state since July 25, 1991. Its area is boomerang-shaped, one leg lying along the Adriatic Sea, the other in the Pannonian plain. On its western frontier lies Slovenia, in the north lies Hungary; in between the two legs lies Bosnia-Hercegovina. On the eastern side Croatia has a border line with Serbia and in the southeast with Montenegro, both united now in New Yugoslavia. The independence of Croatia was recognized by Germany on December 15, 1991, and by the European Community on January 15, 1992. On May 22, 1992, the Republic of Croatia was admitted to the United Nations, thus becoming a full member of the international community.

Croatia's area covers 56,538 sq. km. The Adriatic Coast is 1,778 km long, with 66 inhabited islands. A total of 4,784,265 residents were recorded in the Population Census of 1991. Of these 78.1 percent declared themselves to be ethnic Croats, 12.2 percent Serbs. Other minorities include mainly Hungarians, Italians and citizens of the other ex-Yugoslav republics. The population of Croatia is in some districts highly concentrated, especially in the large towns on the Adriatic and in Zagreb and Slavonia. Half of the Serb minority lives in the regions along the frontier with Serbia and Bosnia-Hercegovina. Especially the latter inhabitants of the earlier Vojna Krajina tended to form autonomous concentrations, controlling the militia and administration.

There are several geographic zones which were integrated into and separated from the country at different periods. On the other hand, regions now outside Croatia were sometimes seen as an integral part of the country. This is particularly the case with Bosnia-Hercegovina. Croatia now consists of Croatia proper, Slavonia, Istria and

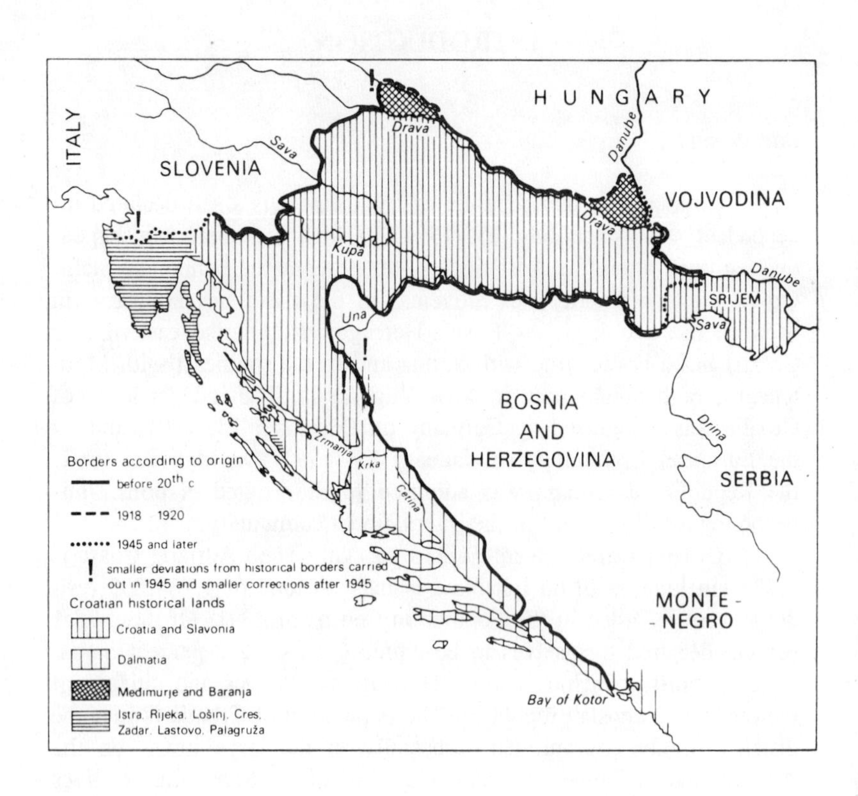

1. Borders of Croatia in 1991

Source: Dušan Bilandžić et al. (eds.), *Croatia between War and Independence,* 2nd ed. (Zagreb: University of Zagreb and OKC Zagreb, 1991). Reprinted by permission of Miroslav Krleža Lexicographic Institute.

Dalmatia. The earlier frontier region against the Turkish Empire, the Vojna Krajina, immediately came under Austria until the end of the nineteenth century.

Bordering on the Adriatic Sea, a large part of the country has a Mediterranean climate. Even the Pannonian plain enjoys a mild continental climate. The central mountain belt that links the Pannonian and Adriatic regions, the karst plateaus of Lika, Krbava and Gorski Kotar, endures harsher climatic conditions.

The gross national product of the Republic of Croatia exceeded in 1991 the sum of $14.2 billion. The various sectors contributed as follows: agriculture, forestry and fishing, 12.2 percent; manufacturing and mining, 32.3 percent; construction, 6.4 percent; trade, tourism and catering, 25.7 percent; transport and communications, 11.0 percent; crafts and other, 12.4 percent. In the generation of national product, the socially-owned sector still participated in 1990 with 87 percent. In 1992 exports reached a total of $4,597 million and imports amounted to $4,461 million. Traditionally the leading export industries are metal manufacturing (including shipbuilding), chemicals, timber and wood, textiles, leather products and petroleum products. More than 60 percent of exports and imports were transacted with developed countries, especially Italy and Germany. There was a considerable intake of foreign exchange from services and remittances from abroad.

The specific identity of the Croatian nation has been both advocated and denied on ethnic, linguistic and historical grounds. Some ethnic and historical arguments for both interpretations will be given in the section on history. Here we will try to explain something about the language puzzle.

The Declaration on the Croatian Language of 1967 states clearly and without reservation: Croatian is a separate language and has to be protected from the imperialistic intrusion of Serbian. There are clear differences in the vocabulary, morphology and grammar of the two languages. Some words are used in one and not in the other. Some grammatical constructions - especially verbal forms - are preferred in one language and not in the other. And there exist što-, ča- and kajkavian variants, according to the expression that is used for the word *what*. Serbian favors rigidly the što- variant; the situation is less clear in the Croatian language area. Related to this is the differentiation in e-, i- or ijekavian, depending on how an original "jat" sound was pronounced later. Serbian uses the harsh ekavian var-

2. Croatia in the Eighth to Ninth Centuries

Source: Stanko Guldescu, *History of Medieval Croatia* (The Hague: Mouton De Gruyter, 1964). Reprinted by permission of Mouton De Gruyter.

iant, while Croatian opts for the soft ije- pronunciation and writing. Supporters of the Croatian autonomous language theory have always stressed the specific characteristics and peculiarities of their language.

However, "Yugoslavists" have stressed the common origin of the Slavic languages and welcomed the attempts of the Illyrian school to create a common South Slav language. Students of the origins of the South Slav language dissent about the question of the common base of the South Slav language. Early documents seem to indicate a common base, but they are rare and display differentiations even at an early stage. Soon there appears a Croatian version of Old Church Slavonic with its own characteristics. Moreover, there is an intense discussion on the origin and use of the Cyrillic and the Glagolitic alphabet. The latter was used in Croatian areas, the former in the other South Slav regions. Both parties can find arguments for a common or a differentiated origin. Both languages soon developed their own particularities.

The attempt to create a common language for the South Slavs by the Illyrians can be called highly artificial. However, this can be said of any effort to create a standard language. Without doubt, the Illyrians acted under the influence of a romantic nationalist idea to unite the South Slavs. The South Slav languages must still have been standing close to one another for such an attempt to be successful. Under the communists, the difference between Croatian and Serbian was said to be no more than the difference between British and American English. We will simply close this short discussion with the observation that at the moment the need for their own Croatian standard language is strongly felt. Even a commission to change street names has been activated by the new regime.

History

The early history of Croatia tends to be mystified, as it has to play a justifying role in politics. Archeologists did considerable work, especially in the Adriatic area, but they could not mold various theories into a decisive structure.

A much debated question concerns the origin and ethnic nature of the Croats. There is some consensus on the fact that the Croatian tribes emigrated from the Caucasian regions and then crossed the Danube to reach the Adriatic Sea. But were they really Slavs, or can we consider them to be descendants of an Iranian Sarmatian tribe?

3. Croatia in the Tenth to Eleventh Centuries

Source: Stanko Guldescu, *History of Medieval Croatia* (The Hague: Mouton De Gruyter, 1964). Reprinted by permission of Mouton De Gruyter.

Are there Gothic influences and what was their relationship to other peoples such as the Alans and Avars? The discussion of this question is easily related to views on the formation of a national state and its ideological justification. Defenders of the Yugoslav idea - a common state for all South Slavs - generally defend the common origin of Serbs and Croats, their common language and the fact that differentiation was late and relatively unimportant. Croatian historians support the thesis that the Croats were a separate new tribe that functioned as an upper class above the Slavs who arrived earlier on the shores of the Adriatic.

There are four important sources reporting on the earliest history of the Croatians. The Byzantine historian Procopius of Caesarea, writing during the reign of Emperor Justinian the Great (527-565), described how the Slavs crossed the Danube around 531. Constantine Porphyrogenitus composed his *De Administrando Imperio* in the middle of the tenth century. According to him, Croats and Serbs asked his predecessor Emperor Heraclius (610-641) to settle in Dalmatia. Constantine declared that the "Slavs" invaded Dalmatia under Avar leadership. He further described in great detail how and why another army went to conquer Solin (near Split). This second eruption could have been the invasion of the Croats. Two other early commentators seem to confirm this thesis. The first is the Chronicle of the Priest of Dioclea, *Ljetopis Popa Dukljanina*. Earlier versions of the manuscript got lost and many passages were rewritten and filled in later. It also informs us about the Gothic influences on the Croatian people. A last source on the settlement of the Croats in Dalmatia - *Historia Salonitana* - was written by Archdeacon Thomas of Split around 1268. It also describes the Ostrogothic inroads into the Croatian lands and lends some support to the "Gothic" thesis on the origin of the Croats. As mentioned above, some "Yugoslav" historians attack the thesis that the Croats should have been a distinct ethnic group.

Once settled, the Croats constantly had to fight against the influence of the Byzantine Empire and the mainly Gothic invasions from the west. The Byzantine influence was still decisive in some coastal cities of the Adriatic, especially in the eastern part of what has been called "Red Croatia." This is the land south of the Cetina River. The Croat reign was firmly installed in "White Croatia" above the Cetina, while Frankish influence was dominant in "Pannonian Croatia." However, around 800, "White Croatia" was also a vassal state

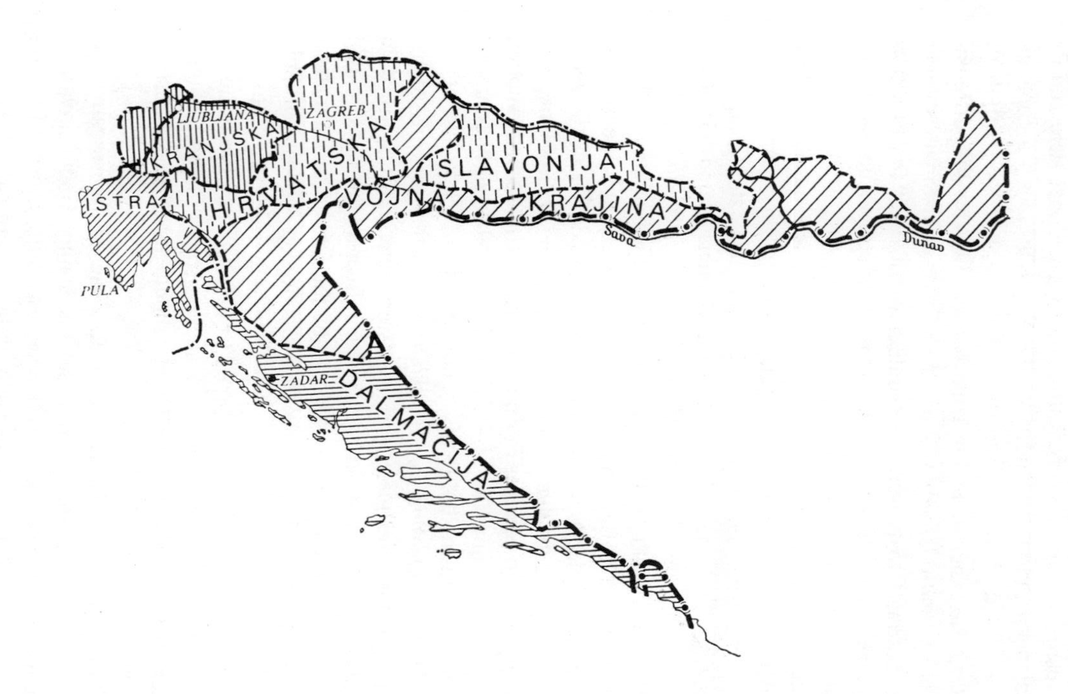

4. Croatia in the Mid-Nineteenth Century

Source: Mirjana Gross, *Počeci moderne Hrvatske* (Zagreb: Globus, 1985). Reprinted by permission of Mirjana Gross.

of Charlemagne. Croat subjects attended his coronation as Emperor in 800.

In 845 began the reign of Prince Trpimir. He was the founder of a dynasty that would bring the early medieval Croatia to its height of power. Trpimir signed a donation document with his title of *Dux Chroatorum*. Branimir (879-892) has been considered the first independent ruler of Croatia. Pope John VIII officially recognized the Croatian church and the Croatian nation. The strength of the reign and the territorial expansion provided enough reason for Tomislav to call himself *Rex Chroatorum*, King of the Croats. However this territorial expansion soon caused ecclesiastical difficulties, as is exemplified by the Synod of Split of 925. The national church with its liturgy in the Croatian language had to give way to the Latin clergy of the Dalmatian coastal cities. A new dynasty, the Krešimirovci, came to power. The greatest internal difficulties were at last surmounted by Krešimir II (960-968), who incorporated Bosnia into his kingdom. His follower, Stipan Držislav (969-997), gained the support of Byzantium and bore the title *Rex Dalmatiae et Croatiae*. When he died, civil war broke out and Venice took the opportunity to seize the Dalmatian cities. Around 1060 Krešimir IV succeeded in again unifying Dalmatia, Bosnia and Croatia. King Dmitar Zvonimir (1076-1089) acted as the last strong ruler of Croatia.

Politicians in the post-communist Croatian society tend to glorify this period of the early Croatian kingdom. In this case we can mention Branimir, Zvonimir and especially Tomislav. However, the idea of a national unified state could better be seen as a product of the romantic and nationalistic ideology of the middle of the nineteenth century. The Croatian medieval kingdom was based on a feudal system, where personalized and decentralized relationships were the rule, rather than strong centralized administration. For example, a king or ruler always bore the title of several regions that could easily change owners. Up to 1100, Hungarian influence had been growing to the point that the Croatian nobility deliberately chose to establish a personal union between Croatia and Hungary (Pacta Conventa). Earlier, the Hungarian King Ladislas had already invaded Slavonia. This initiated a long period of Hungarian domination on the Croatian scene. However, the Hungarians granted the Croats some autonomy in local administration.

The next mortal danger for Croatia and the Western world came from the east: the Turkish invasion. This is the cause of prob-

5. The Banovina of Croatia in 1939

Source: Dušan Bilandžić et al. (eds.), *Croatia between War and Independence,* 2nd ed. (Zagreb: University of Zagreb and OKC Zagreb, 1991). Reprinted by permission of Miroslav Krleža Lexicographic Institute.

lems lasting even today, as will be explained below. The South Slav peoples suffered a first blow at the famous battle of Kosovo Polje in 1389. The Ottomans conquered Bosnia in 1463. The first inroads within Croatia followed within five years. Hercegovina fell in 1482. In need of a strong protector, the Croats recognized Maximilian I of Austria as their King. Nevertheless, the Turks defeated a Croatian army in the field of Krbava. The Croats then elected Ferdinand of Habsburg as their King. His dynasty would govern most of the Croatian lands until the end of the First World War. The Austrians created an extended military zone between the regions dominated by the Turks and the lands they controlled. In fact, Croatia was to be divided into quite separate parts until the 1880s. For the first time, the Vojna Krajina received a special status. Much of the new population had fled from the regions occupied by the Turks. Among them were many orthodox Vlachs (later accepting the Serbian nationality) and Italians. The inhabitants got autonomy and prerogatives in return for their protective role against the Turks; they were not placed under the control of the Croatian nobility. In later times the military zone came under the direct military and administrative control of Austria. The Vojna Krajina is precisely the region where even today there live a majority of self-declared Serbs and where the rebellion against the Tuđman regime started.

The Croatian identity could not be restored until the middle of the nineteenth century. Half a century earlier, the French occupation helped to revive the ideal of unification. In 1805, the Dalmatian coast fell under French rule and, in 1808, the independent Republic of Dubrovnik was abolished. In 1809, Southern Croatia, Civil Croatia and the Military Frontier on the right bank of the Sava River became united in the Illyrian Provinces. However, after the retreat of the French troops, the regions returned to Austria. A strong movement for autonomy in Dalmatia resisted under the influence of Italy the unification with interior Croatia ("Croatia proper"). On the other hand, Hungarian nationalists eager to create a Great Hungarian State were hostile to the idea of an autonomous or independent Croatia. In 1827, they succeeded in having the Croatian Diet introduce the Hungarian language as a compulsory subject in higher education. The politically dominant circles in the Austrian Monarchy supported Croatia's political and territorial fragmentation. As a reaction against these forces, Croatian nationalist feeling and resistance began rising.

A first intellectual movement that organized the resistance against Magyarization and that worked for a general South Slav resurrection was the Illyrian movement. Its leader, Ljudevit Gaj, created the Illyrian language, meant to become the vehicle of all South Slav peoples. He published the first Croatian newspaper and literary magazine, *Novine Horvatzke* and *Danica*. The Illyrians got the support of part of the Sabor, the parliament of Zagreb. Around the same time, the Matica hrvatska was founded. This was a cultural institution that contributed greatly to awakening the national consciousness of the Croats. The Matica stimulated the study of Croatian ethnology and history, published books and promoted public libraries. Ten years earlier, Count Janko Drasković had defined the Croatian national program. He pleaded for a union of Croatia, Slavonia, Dalmatia, the Vojna Krajina, the region of Rijeka and Bosnia on the one hand and the Slovene regions, Kranjska, Koruška and Štajerska on the other. All this irritated the Hungarians, who founded a political party, an example immediately followed by the Illyrians. Accused of being Russophile, the use of Illyrian symbols was banned by Metternich.

The revolutionary year 1848 brought new hopes for the Illyrians. Metternich was dismissed, the Austrian Emperor guaranteed freedom of the press and a new Ban was appointed for Croatia. Ban Jelačić underwrote the Illyrian ideals and granted autonomy to the lower administrative levels of Croatia. The ties with Hungary were practically broken. The revolutionary Hungarians revolted against the Emperor in Vienna. Jelačić supported the Austrians and, with Russian help, the Hungarian uprising was crushed. A new Constitution defined a more favorable position for Croatia and the Croatian church no longer remained under the jurisdiction of the Hungarian bishopric. However, once the political situation in the Monarchy had been stabilized, a new period of Austrian absolutism set in.

Around 1861, three currents emerged in the Sabor of Zagreb. First, the old Hungarian party defended close cooperation with their homeland. The Illyrians pleaded for a united Croatia in a trilateral federation of equal partners with equal rights. A radical faction wanted total autonomy and independence. Out of this current grew the Party of Rights, with Starčević and Kvaternik as prominent figures.

In 1867, Austria and Hungary came to terms with one another again and signed the Ausgleich. The adjustment of the relations between Hungary and Croatia were left to the *Nagodba*, agreed on one year later. It was a retrograde document that again set precise limits to the autonomy of Croatia. Open rebellion by members of the National Party was followed by repression. A minor change of the document was accepted in 1869. It is in the shadow of this unfavorable document that Croatian political parties would strive in vain for more autonomy for Croatia until the First World War. The only, but important, achievement in this period was the administrative unification of all Croatian lands, with the exception of the region of Rijeka. It remained under the direct government of Hungary.

The Archduke Francis Ferdinand was assassinated in Sarajevo in 1914 by a member of a secret Serbian organization. Austria-Hungary declared war on Serbia. As a final result the Habsburg Monarchy collapsed. During the war, representatives of the Serbs and Croats had signed a document in Corfu to found a new state on the ruins of the old empires. Slovenia and Croatia were the demanding parties to a reluctant Serbian Prime Minister. The Slovenes and Croats had good reasons to press their brother Slavs into a union. First, they feared a resurrection of any Hungarian or Austrian construction. Second, social uprisings were imminent. The example of the Russian Revolution was fresh in their minds. Third, and most important, Italian forces were on their way to take part of the South Slav countries. During the war the allies had promised Italy some territorial compensations in this area. The Serbs were hesitating between Yugoslavia and Great-Serbia. They already had a long tradition as an independent state, their own army and central administration. They ultimately saw the new state as just a means of gathering all the Serbs into one country and only ceded when they got their King on the throne.

From the beginning opposite tendencies clashed in the new Yugoslavia. The Croats and Slovenes desired a federation with autonomy for its parts; the Serbs wanted a centralized country. Stjepan Radić, leader of the Croatian People's Peasant Party, protested against the new Constitution and was ultimately shot in the parliament in Belgrade in 1928. King Alexander installed his dictatorship and strengthened the central administration of his kingdom, now officially called "Yugoslavia." At last, political circles came to understand that common life in Yugoslavia would be impossible without some form of decentralization. The Croatian leader Vladko Maček and the Belgrade politician Dragiša Cvetković concluded an agreement, the *Sporazum*, that created an autonomous Croatian region, the Banovina. This solution could not really prove its usefulness, as the imminent world war distorted all relationships. The Nazis invaded the country and found Croatia eager to collaborate. They installed the Ustaša regime of Ante Pavelić in power and agreed on the creation of a nominally "Independent State of Croatia." During the war, it was especially the work of the Ustašis to convert, expel or murder some 600,000 Serbs living in Croatia. Consequently, at the end of the war the victorious partisans took revenge on the Croats in a massive slaughter and drove into exile a permanently hostile emigration. Memories of this clash are still exploited by the propaganda machines of present-day regimes. It motivates the Serbs in the Krajina Republic of Knin to call for an autonomous region.

Immediately after the war, the communists succeeded in controlling the destructive forces and installed a centralist regime. It was hoped that through economic development and the growth of a collective feeling of solidarity, nationality problems would wither away. The application of the idea of self-management left some space for autonomy on all levels of society. The economic reforms in the 1960s were accompanied by creeping political democratization. In 1966, a political breakthrough came within reach with the fall of Alexander Ranković, the conservative right-hand man of Tito. With *The Declaration on the Status of the Croatian Literary Language* of 1967 began the "Croatian Spring." Demands for cultural, economic and political autonomy were urged by means of public demonstrations, strikes and riots. Croatian political leaders - among them Savka Dabčević-Kučar and Miko Tripalo - backed some of the claims for more Croatian autonomy. In the early 1970s, Tito intervened and the Croatian political leadership resigned. However, it seems that the decentralizing forces were not at all defeated. Though official leaders were purged, the new Constitution of 1974 met most of the decentralizing demands. Croatia and other Republics obtained almost complete autonomy in all areas on the republican level. Federal decisions regarding matters of common interest were to be made by consensus with equal rights for all Republics. This Constitution laid the basis for the statehood of the Republics and Autonomous Provinces.

It is exactly this complete statehood that was demanded by rioting Albanians in 1981. At the same time, debt problems became pressing. Decentralized decision making made it possible for firms to conclude contracts for loans far above any reasonable level. Soft budget constraints, falling profitability and consumption of capital through wages and other collective advantages caused inflation and repayment problems. Political leaders now systematically blamed other Republics for the economic problems. Nationalism became rampant. Especially in Serbia, the economy was in danger of collapsing. Miloševic stimulated the national feelings by mass demonstrations in Kosovo, Vojvodina and Montenegro. He managed to reduce the autonomy of Kosovo and Vojvodina. In Novi Sad and Titograd, he purged resistant communist leaders through an anti-bureaucratic revolution. In Kosovo, he brought the government and civil services under Serbian control. In the League of Communists, he also pleaded for economic and political re-centralization. Slovenes and Croats declared their solidarity with the Kosovians and resisted any centralization of power in the Federation. At last, the Slovene and Croatian communists left the Extraordinary Congress of the League of Communists on January 20, 1990.

In the same year, elections in Croatia and Slovenia institutionalized the deep rift between the western and the eastern parts of the country. The opposition front was elected in Slovenia. In Croatia, the Croat-nationalist party of Franjo Tuđman obtained a majority. Yugoslavia split. Could it die without war? The answer depended on two opposite and irreconcilable views. Tuđman had always insisted that only the historical frontiers of the Republics could be the practicable and pragmatic frontiers of the new states. Milošević argued that all Serbs in every region had the right to chose whether or not they wanted to live in a Serbian state. About half of the 13 percent of Serbs in Croatia lived concentrated in frontier areas near Bosnia (in the Vojna Krajina and West Slavonia) and near Serbia (in East Slavonia). The Serbs of the Vojna Krajina organized a referendum and proclaimed autonomy. This was the start of a war between the Yugoslav army, Serbian militias and the Croatian army in the three regions. During the six-month war in 1991, at least 10,000 people died and the Serbs occupied about 30 percent of Croatia. Only agreement on intervention of the United Nations and the imposition of the Vance plan could stop the fighting and freeze the situation. The Vance plan for Croatia created UNPA zones, areas protected by the UN. These zones included several sectors, covering East and West Slavonia and the Krajina. In theory, UN troops had to disarm all militias in these areas and prepare the conditions for the return of the refugees.

There were also some "pink zones," territory conquered by the Yugoslav army without ethnic-Serbian population concentrations, especially south of the Krajina. Permanent Serbian provocations in these areas led to a new short-lived Croatian offensive at the end of January 1993. As a reaction, the Serbs in the Krajina brought back under their control the heavy weapons handed over to the UN under a previous agreement. A new agreement was concluded that possibly meant a setback in the long-term settlement of the problem. The Serbs in the Krajina were officially recognized as negotiating partners and this could be explained as some sort of official recognition of their statehood.

A second Croatian offensive in September 1993 intended to free the Gospić region from shelling. Following another agreement, UNPROFOR stepped in again to prevent further fighting.

Though Croatia was officially recognized by the European Community, the United States and the United Nations, so far the integrity of the full territory has not been achieved. On the other hand, there is permanent speculation about Croatian territorial ambitions in the south of Bosnia-Hercegovina. In April 1992, a referendum on the independence of the Republic of Bosnia-Hercegovina was boycotted by the Bosnian Serbs. The coalition of Muslims and Bosnian Croats could easily outvote the Serbs. The subsequent declaration of independence of the Bosnian-Hercegovinian state was followed by civil war, pitting Muslims and Croatian Bosnians against the Serbs. Soon, however, the Muslim-Croatian front cracked and an autonomous Herceg-Bosna under Croatian control was formed in the southern part of the new country. Official circles in Zagreb confirmed the recognition of the territorial integrity of the independent State of Bosnia-Hercegovina. But would local combatants respect these official proclamations?

The Vance-Owen plan for Bosnia-Hercegovina seemed to complicate the situation even more. The division into ten areas was most favorable to the Bosnian Croats and they were the first to sign it. It also strengthened them in the belief that they could and should operate as sole and absolute masters in the assigned areas. Armed clashes in the region of Mostar can be interpreted as ethnic cleansing by the Croat forces. The proposal that followed the Vance-Owen plan, an outright division along ethnic lines with the possibility of leaving the union within two years, gave perhaps too much and too little to Croatia. While Herceg-Bosna might join the mother country Croatia, the proposal could have adverse implications in the case of the Croatian Krajina. Applying the same principles as in the Bosnian case, the Krajina might easily end up within Serbia. First the Krajina would opt for a confederation with the other parts of Croatia, and later in a referendum grant itself autonomy or join the Great-Serbian State. Moreover, the necessary move in this direction has in reality already been made, though so far not publicly supported by Serbia. The threat of the Serbs in Croatia and in Bosnia to take seats in a common parliament crucially endangers the implementation of the Vance plan. And the occasional meetings of all Serbs in the Belgrade parliament functions as a real prefiguration of a Great-Serbia.

At the end of 1994, we were still a long way from a stable solution for the frontier and ethnic questions of the former Republics of Yugoslavia. This was particularly true in the case of Croatia. A sudden and unexpected turning point was NATO's ultimatum of April 9, 1994, to the Serbs to stop strangling Sarajevo. With some encouragement from the Russians, the Serbs left their positions. At the same time, American pressure on the Croats led to the restoration of the Croat-Muslim front. It was even agreed to form a Muslim-Croat federation in Bosnia, leaving behind the separate Croatian state Herceg-Bosna of Mate Boban. Moreover, the new federation in Bosnia-Hercegovina should later form a confederation with Croatia. The peace offensive was further supported by the Russians by bringing together the Krajina Serbs and the government of Zagreb. A ceasefire was signed on March 30, 1994, as a first step toward economic and political normalization. Even the Serb leader Karadžić now declared that he was prepared to talk about a general armistice and a political solution. It is, however, still far from clear how the long-term political demands of the Serbs will be reconciled with the Croatian and Muslim viewpoints.

THE DICTIONARY

AGATHON, POPE. Around 680, Pope Agathon and the Croatian Duke Borko made an agreement. The Croats (q.v.) promised that they would not attack the surrounding peoples. Probably the remaining Latin habitants of Dalmatia (q.v.) were first meant to profit from this arrangement. In return the Croats would receive God's protection and the support of St. Peter in case of a foreign invasion. According to the chronicler Archdeacon Thomas (q.v.), the agreement had been mediated by Archbishop John of Ravenna.

AGENCY FOR RESTRUCTURING AND DEVELOPMENT/ AGENCY ZA RESTRUKTURIRANJE I RAZVOJ. The main task of the Agency for Restructuring and Development of the Republic of Croatia is to foster the application of the Law on the Transformation of Socially-Owned Enterprises (q.v.). It defined transformation programs and provided supporting services. On behalf of the Croatian Fund for Development (q.v.), the Agency administers services to sell the shares that the Fund obtained through the transformation of enterprises. The Agency participates in studies on the development of particular branches of the economy, taking into account the strategic components of development, privatization (q.v.) and joint-venture investments of both domestic and foreign investors.

During the first phase of transformation, the socially owned enterprises could autonomously choose the model of transformation and the partners interested in investment. After June 30, 1992, a second phase of the transformation process began. The Agency itself then initiated the transformation of enterprises through new ownership relations and management organs. By November 20, 1992, the Agency for Restructuring and Development had made 910 approvals for intended enterprise transformations. The capital in enterprise shares amounted to approximately 9 billion DM.

In February 1993, new regulations were adopted that restricted the preference rights of the employees (present or former) of an enterprise to buy shares to 50 percent of the social capital, while the other part has to be obligatorily placed in the financial market for public sale. The Agency was integrated in the Fund for Privatization (q.v.).

Of 2,868 public enterprises that presented transformation programs, 2,210 or 77 percent received the approval of the Fund up until November 22, 1993. At that date, the transformation had already been accomplished by 1,805 enterprises, of which 1,621 had profited from the old regulations valid until February 1993. The Law obliges the Fund to place the shares obtained by the transformation on public sale. This usually happens through the stock market of Zagreb (q.v.). Until November 22, 1993, shares of 271 enterprises had been listed. The value of shares traded reached an amount of 23 million DM. The gains obtained are transferred to the national accounts. Partially, they can be used by the Fund for new investments.

AGRICULTURE AND FISHING. The policy towards agricultural development under the communist regime was one of slight discouragement. Private estates were limited to an area of 10 hectares, incentives for agricultural production were low because of regularly fixed prices and the possibilities of mechanization were poor. The percentage of the farming population within the total population has declined from 62.4 percent in 1948 to 15.2 percent according to the 1981 census.

The new government of President Tuđman (q.v.) has lifted the limitations on the size of farms and paid special attention to promoting the development of agriculture. Although Croatia still imports food, experts have assessed that it has the potential of producing more than enough to satisfy the needs of the population.

Of a total of 3,224,000 hectares of arable land, 63 percent are under cultivation: about 1,500,000 hectares are fields and gardens or 46 percent of the arable land, 400,000 hectares are meadows or 13 percent, 73,000 hectares are vineyards or 2 percent and 71,000 hectares are orchards, equal to 2 percent. The rest of the arable land includes 1,155,000 hectares of grazing land or 36 percent, 20,000 hectares (0.55 percent) of ponds and reed patches and 15,000 hectares (0.45 percent) of fish ponds.

Several factors make investment in agriculture attractive: the potential for the production and processing of agricultural products is only partially utilized; good opportunities exist for the production of healthy and ecologically safe food; and the possibility of developing fisheries in the Adriatic Sea.

The most important agricultural products for export are: livestock, wheat, beef, corn and fruits. Imported agricultural products are: oil seeds for light oils, livestock, coffee and fruits.

AHRENS, GEERT. Negotiator in the peace talks between the Zagreb authorities and the Krajina Serbs of Knin (qq.v.). On July 17, 1993, the conflicting parties reached a provisional agreement on an armistice in the regions of Maslenica, Zemunik and Peruča (qq.v.). The negotiations had to build on the earlier Geneva agreement of April 6, 1993 and Resolution 802 of the UN Security Council. The Croats would withdraw military forces brought in during the Maslenica offensive of January 1993, while the Krajina Serbs would place heavy weapons in the region under the control of UNPROFOR (q.v.). Security and freedom of movement on the Maslenica bridge, the Zemunik airport and the Peruča dam were to be guaranteed. UNPROFOR would take over military and police control in the region. At the end of the month, both parties claimed that the conditions had not been met by the other party. Hostilities resumed and the Maslenica bridge was bombed again by the Serbs of the Krajina.

ALBANIA (RELATIONS WITH). The relations of Croatia with Albania are good. Croatia traditionally supported the Albanian resistance in Kosovo against the Serbs and finds in Albania a natural ally.

During the visit of a delegation of the Albanian Ministry of Transport, it was agreed that as of September 1993 a regular maritime line should connect Rijeka (q.v.) with Drač.

ALBONA (REPUBLIC OF). The Miners' Republic of Labin in Istria (q.v.) lasted only for a few weeks. In 1920, Istria was ceded to Italy and fascist forces began harassing the radical leaders of the local miners. The union secretary Giovanni Pipan called to arms. The miners formed their Red Guards and seized control of the town of Labin. The Italian army suppressed the rebellion in April 1921.

ALEXANDER, KING see KARAĐORĐEVIĆ, ALEXANDER

ANGEVIN DYNASTY (1301-1382). The dynasty of the Angevins ruled over the Croatian lands from 1301 till 1382. The Kings were first faced with the task of establishing their authority in the crown lands. The rivalry between the Croatian families and their alliances with Venice was their second problem. The rise of the Serbian empire was a third problem. And, finally, the second King had no heir.

Charles Robert from Naples of the Anjou dynasty was presented in Zagreb (q.v.) as the new King by the Croat noble Pavle Subić. Subić recognized Charles Robert publicly as his sovereign and received in return the title of Ban (q.v.) of Croatia. While the King devoted his attention to strengthen his power in the Hungarian part of his kingdom, Subić reigned autonomously over Dalmatia (q.v.). In 1311, Subić attacked Zadar (q.v.) to take it back from the Venetians. He died the next year and was succeeded by his son Mladen II. The Venetians made use of internal rivalries between the Subić and Nelipić clan to seize Šibenik and Trogir. The Croatian nobility now appealed to King Charles Robert and he took the opportunity to invade Croatia with his army. To protect themselves against the King, the Nelipići accepted Venetian help. This allowed Venice to establish its authority in Split (q.v.) (1327) and Nin (1329). In 1331 Steven Dušan became King of Serbia and again the Croatian nobility appealed to the Venetians. This also weakened the position of the King in the question of the royal free towns. The Croat nobles asserted that these towns were no longer royal territory since the dynasty of the Arpads (q.v.) was extinct. Charles Robert died in 1342.

The second and last King of the Anjou dynasty was Charles Robert's son Louis I. He personally led an army of 30,000 men to the stronghold of the Nelipići, the fortress of Knin (q.v.). The Subić family on their turn invoked Venetian assistance to fight the King and their rival clan, the Nelipići. Despite the King's support, Zadar fell to the Venetians. Louis' brother, the King of Naples, was assassinated and consequently the Hungarian monarch concluded an eight-year truce with the Venetians in 1348.

Mladen III, a Subić, married the sister of the Serbian King Steven Dušan and brought a force of Serbians to his stronghold of Klis (q.v.). Other Croats and Hungarians prepared for a general war against the Serbs and the Subići of Klis. The fortress was conquered and Mladen III fell back on his old clan holding of Bribir. Steven Dušan died in 1355 and the Serb danger declined. In the next period all coastal cities accepted the Hungarian rule of King Louis. In 1358, Venice had to give up Zadar. The Hungarian King restored the Croat position in the Adriatic of the Croat national Kings.

In 1370, the King inherited the Polish throne. He had no sons, so he adopted Charles of Durazzo who functioned from 1371 until 1376 as Duke and Ban of Croatia and Dalmatia. A new Ban, Nikola Sec, served as Ban under Louis when Charles left for Naples. King Louis fell ill and died in 1382. His wife, Elisabeth Kotromanić of Bosnia, took over the reign of the kingdom.

ANTI-FASCIST COUNCIL OF THE NATIONAL LIBERATION OF CROATIA/ ZEMALJSKO ANTI-FAŠISTIČKO VIJEĆE NARODNOG OSLOBOĐENJA HRVATSKE (ZAVNOH). This Croatian regional section of the Anti-Fascist Council of the National Liberation of Yugoslavia (AVNOJ) (q.v.) was established at its First Session on June 13 and 14, 1943, at Otočcac and Plitvice. The first President of ZAVNOH was the poet Vladimir Nazor (q.v.). After the surrender of Italy in September 1943, the ZAVNOH made the decision to join Istria, Rijeka, Zadar (q.v.), and the islands to the Croatian state. In May 1944, following the declarations at the Second Session of the AVNOJ in Jajce on November 29, 1943, the ZAVNOH proclaimed the Federal State of Croatia an integral part of the Democratic Federation of Yugoslavia. In the Constitution of 1990 (q.v.), this decision was considered as contributing to the tradition and continuity of Croatian statehood. As such, the celebration in 1993 of the fiftieth anniversary of the ZAVNOH session was attended by high state officials such as Stipe Mesić, then President of the Sabor (q.v.).

ANTI-FASCIST COUNCIL OF THE NATIONAL LIBERATION OF YUGOSLAVIA/ANTI-FAŠISTIČKO VIJEĆE NARODNOG OSLOBOĐENJA JUGOSLAVIJE (AVNOJ). Especially the Second Session of this organ on November 29, 1943, has been of historical significance. The Council decided that the peoples of Yugoslavia should live in a federation of six republics: Serbia, Slovenia, Croatia, Bosnia-Hercegovina, Montenegro and Macedonia. Frontiers between the republics were considered to be of secondary importance and should be decided on later. Tito once said: "Frontiers do not exist to divide the republics and the people, but to unite them." Decisions of the AVNOJ were supposed to be first prepared and afterwards confirmed by its regional sections. In Croatia this organ was called the Anti-Fascist Council of the National Liberation of Croatia (q.v.).

ANTI-WAR CAMPAIGN COMMITTEE ZAGREB/ANTIRATNA KAMPANJA ZAGREB (ARK). The Anti-War Campaign Committee Zagreb was founded in the early summer of 1991. It is the hub of a network of various opposition, refugee, humanitarian, publishing and activist organizations. Activities include mediation among refugees, conflict resolution training, and public lectures and discussions. It is cosponsoring with Suncokret (q.v.) and other peace groups in Croatia and Yugoslavia a peace initiative in Pakrac, a town in the UN Protected Area divided by the frontline. It publishes *ARK-zin* magazine, a forum for opposition journalists and activists.

ARALICA, IVAN (1930-). Contemporary writer of historic novels. He is also a member of parliament and president of the Council for the Strategic Development of Croatia (q.v.).

ARBA see RAB

ARCHITECTURE. Many civilizations and peoples have passed along the shores of the Adriatic. Though war has always threatened and still threatens the cultural heritage, much of the rich architectural history of Croatia has been preserved.

Illyrian (q.v.) vestiges were largely destroyed by invaders. Examples of Ancient Roman architecture are still numerous, for instance Diocletian's palace in Split (q.v.), the arena built by

Vespasian and the Temple of Augustus in Pula and the remnants of Solin, which still give an impressive view of a complete Roman town. The Euphrasius Basilica in Poreč (q.v.) is a remarkable example of Byzantine art on Istrian soil.

Early Croatian Christian churches such as the one in Nin display typical Croatian architectural characteristics based on local original concepts. St. Donatus church in Zadar (q.v.), the biggest pre-Romanesque building on the Yugoslav Adriatic, is outstanding in form and construction. St. Jacob's Cathedral in Šibenik exemplifies the local interpretation of Renaissance and early Gothic canons. Several beautiful Renaissance and Baroque monuments were built in the old town center of Dubrovnik (q.v.): the Franciscan Monastery, Sponza Palace, Rector's Palace Court and Church of Our Savior.

Austro-Hungarian rule and the Counter-Reformation strongly influenced architecture in the Zagreb and Pannonian (qq.v.) regions. The colors of the official Maria-Theresian buildings - especially schools and fortifications - still dominate the villages, especially in Slavonia.

Modern architecture is exemplified by the complexes in Zagreb and Split.

ARKAN. Željko Ražnjatović-Arkan is the leader of a Serbian paramilitary formation. With his "tigers," Arkan fought and killed like a wildcat in eastern Slavonia (q.v.). He contributed to the ethnic cleansing of the region and the affirmation of the new Serbian Republic. Arkan's "tigers" still occupy frontline positions in eastern Slavonia and they also function as the personal guard of the president of the Serbian Republic of Krajina, Goran Hadžić (q.v.). During an internal rebellion of the Serbs in the village of Mirkovci just before the commemoration of two years of Serb rule on July 22, 1993, Milan Martić (q.v.), Interior Minister of the Serbian Republic of Krajina (q.v.), threatened to call upon Arkan and his troops to crush the local revolt. Arkan indeed appeared on the second anniversary of the Serb occupation of Mirkovci, but peace had already been restored. Early in October 1993, the gang of Arkan escorted then president of the Krajina Goran Hadžić into the Baranja (q.v.) and provoked an incident with Belgian Blue Helmets. He organized a massive campaign for the Serbian elections of December 1993, clearly in support of Slobodan Milošević.

ARPAD DYNASTY (1102-1301). The House of Arpad ruled from 1102 until 1301. According to tradition, the Hungarian dynasty acquired the Croatian lands by the Pacta Conventa (q.v.). Consequently, the Hungarian Arpad Kings took an oath to respect the rights of the land and the people of the Croatian-Dalmatian kingdom. The Arpad Kings used to place these lands under the rule of relatives and granted them the title of Duke of Croatia and Dalmatia.

The first Duke was Koloman's son, Stefan, and when he succeeded his father as King of Hungary, he appointed his own son Geza as Duke. The Duke had his seat most of the time in Knin, and later in Zagreb (qq.v.). The Duke appointed the Ban, called the Sabor (q.v.) together, headed the army and coined money.

After the death of Geza, the Byzantines invaded Dalmatia (q.v.) and held Croatia in their grip from 1168 to 1180. After the death of the Byzantine Manuel Comnenus in 1180, Croat-Hungarian sovereignty was restored but soon challenged by Venice. The eighth Croat-Hungarian King, Bela III, gave several *župe* (districts) in fief to reward the Croatian nobles in their struggle with the Venetians. This meant the introduction of the feudal system in Croatia.

In 1196, the Serbs invaded the country during the succession struggle following the death of Bela III. Andreas, his younger son, became Duke of Croatia and countered a Serbian invasion. In 1202, the Venetians made use of the passing of the Fourth Crusade to conquer Zadar (q.v.). Andreas promoted the growth of towns in Pannonian (q.v.) Croatia. In 1209, Andreas recognized Varaždin (q.v.) as a free royal city. Before then, only Sisak (q.v.) and Križevci had obtained that status. Until the end of the century Zagreb-Grić, Vukovar (q.v.), Petrinja, Samobor, Požega, Virovitica and Osijek would follow. Bela IV was the last King who had a separate coronation as King of Croatia and Dalmatia. Bela's reign was brutally disrupted by the Mongol invasion (q.v.) in 1241. It broke Arpad royal power and that of the Croatian great nobility as well in favor of the new developing towns. In 1242, Bela IV granted his "Golden Bull" (q.v.) to the free town of Zagreb-Gradec. The King and the Sabor came to an agreement that there would be two Bans, one for Slavonia (q.v.) and one for Croatia and Dalmatia. From then on, the two regions embarked on a widely divergent development which lasted for centuries. The bishopric of Zagreb would depend on the Hungarian See until the end of the nineteenth century. In 1248, Pope Innocent confirmed the right of the Croats south of the Kupa (q.v.) to use Glagolitic (q.v.) in church rituals. The use of the Glagolitic alphabet for administrative and literary purposes deepened the cultural rift between Dalmatia and Slavonia. At the same time, Slavonia became culturally and politically more and more integrated with Hungary. Dalmatia strived for political autonomy.

In 1270, the Croatian Sabor refused to recognize the successor of Bela IV, Stefan V. The same happened in 1272 to the son of Stefan, Laszlo the Cuman. The Sabor granted the title of hereditary Ban of Croatia to Pavle Šubić, a Croatian noble. He actually acted as the "king-maker." After some years of quasi-autonomous rule, Šubić accepted Charles Robert from Naples of the Angevin dynasty (q.v.).

ARTUKOVIĆ, ANTE. Minister of Interior under Ante Pavelić (q.v.) in the Independent State of Croatia (q.v.).

ASSOCIATION OF CROATIAN REGIONAL PARTIES/ASOCIJACIJA REGIONALNIH STRANAKA HRVATSKE (ARSH). The Association of Croatian Regional Parties brings together all regional parties, among others the Istrian Democratic Parliament and Dalmatian Action (qq.v.). In Opatija near Rijeka (q.v.), they accepted a common declaration on the regional organization of the Republic of Croatia *(Deklaracija o regionalnom ustroju Republike Hrvatske)*. Firstly, they asked for the recognition of all existing European documents that regulate the rights of local self-government and cooperation. Secondly, they rejected the Croatian construction of *županije* (q.v.) and opted for a system of six to eight larger regions. These regions would have the right to autonomous legislation and participation in the government of the central state. The unity of the state is expressed by a common defense, foreign policy, monetary unity and common state organization. This conception implies at least a federal system and is contrary to the existing Croatian Constitution (q.v.).

AUSGLEICH. This agreement signed in 1867 by Austria and Hungary created the Dual Monarchy of Austria-Hungary. The relations between Hungary and Croatia were left to be negotiated. They were regulated one year later by the Nagodba (q.v.). Vienna maintained direct control over the lands of Dalmatia and Istria (q.v.). Croatia itself remained closely bound to Hungary.

AUTONOMY. Regional forces in Croatia striving for autonomy reflect historical conditions. Several reasons for these tendencies can be found in contemporary Croatia. They originate from the lack of continuity of the common historical experience over the national territory. The centrifugal tendencies take different expressions. First, and most serious, the claims of the Krajina (q.v.) Serbs have evolved from cultural autonomy to outright political and territorial independence. But other regions also defend themselves from the centralist grip of the capital, Zagreb (q.v.). While still timid in Slavonia (q.v.), autonomist tendencies are more outspoken in Dalmatia (q.v.) - structured through the political movement Dalmatian Action (Dalmatinska Akcija) (q.v.) - and even very strong in the peninsula of Istria (q.v.). There the local political movement Istrian Democratic Parliament (Istarski Demokratski Sabor) (q.v.) has defeated the political monopoly of the Croatian Democratic Union (Hrvatska Demokratska Zajednica) (q.v.). Secondly, one has to keep in mind that Istria only joined Croatia and Yugoslavia after the Second World War. Previously, the region had been strongly Italianized by the Italian occupation.

There are two other basic reasons for discontent under Istrian politicians. Firstly, although Istria had not been directly damaged by the last Serbo-Croatian war, it nevertheless suffered from the economic recession, for instance through the fall in tourist revenue. Secondly, the further development of the privatization (q.v.) process could centralize decisions over Istrian resources in the state organs of Zagreb. The Istrian Democratic Parliament thus threatened not to apply in Istria centralistic laws made in Zagreb.

Though criticized for not going far enough, the new law on local self-government (q.v.) could strengthen the autonomist tendencies. Istrian politicians already asked for an autonomous status of Istria in the Republic of Croatia and constantly point to the model of "European regions." It is likely that the autonomist forces will continue expanding in the future and even be encouraged by Italian interests.

AVARS. Nomad people who invaded Dalmatia (q.v.) for the first time in 569. In 582, they captured Byzantine-held Pannonia (q.v.). They launched new raids in 592, 598, 600, 601, 602 and 611. In 626, they occupied Constantinople unsuccessfully. They were warriors said to be in close association with the Slavs and then disappeared from the historical records. Perhaps the Slavs were their slaves. This fits in with an observation of Procopius and other writers who characterized the Slavs as peaceful. Later on, Avars and Slavs mixed and were described as one people. The name Avar could have changed into *Havar* and then *Harvat*, close to the later Hungarian term *Horvat* for the Croats (q.v.) (now *Hrvati*, sing. *Hrvat*, in Croatian). This explanation of the name Horvat has not generally been accepted, but the close association between the two peoples is more than incidental.

- B -

BABIĆ, GORAN (1944 -). Born on the island of Vis (q.v.). Poet, playwright and novelist. He participated in editing the journals *Pitanja* and *Oko*. The journal *Most/The Bridge* published a selection of his translated poetry. He was criticized for his support of Stipe Šuvar (q.v.) and his *White Book*. Babić now lives and works in Belgrade.

BABIĆ, MILAN. Mayor of Knin (q.v.). Former member of the Communist Party and delegate at the Fourteenth Congress of the League of Communists (q.v.) in 1991. After the collapse of the Communist Party, he joined the Serbian Democratic Party (SDS) (q.v.). Assisting Jovan Rašković (q.v.), he became the second-ranking political leader in Knin. He transformed the resistance movement into a well-armed and highly motivated militia. Babić organized the referendum on political autonomy of the Knin region from August to September 1990, and defended the town with Milan Martić (q.v.) and Lazar Mačura against the Croatian militia. In so doing, he received assistance from the Yugoslav army. He became President of the self-proclaimed parliament of the Serbian Republic of Krajina (q.v.). Later on, Babić clashed with Milošević, when Belgrade seemed to retreat under pressure from the international community and refused (or at least postponed) a union with the Krajina. Babić refused to accept the Vance plan (q.v.) and was not eager to receive the UNPROFOR (q.v.) troops in the Krajina. Consequently, the parliament of the Republic of Krajina dismissed Babić as its President during its second session in Glina in favor of Milan Paspalj (q.v.). Babić tried to restore his position in the presidential elections of late 1993, but he lost them to his rival Milan Martić, who was backed by Milošević.

BADINTER ARBITRATION COMMISSION. The Badinter Commission was set up by the European Community (q.v.) in the autumn of 1991 and works within the framework of the Peace Conference on former Yugoslavia. It is composed of constitutional experts of five member countries and presided over by Robert Badinter of France. One of its first tasks was to work out the general criteria candidates should meet to be recognized as independent states. The Commission has given further advice to the EC concerning the concrete application of these criteria. It has arbitrated on questions concerning the economic and financial inheritance of former Yugoslavia. One major problem was the division of the rights and obligations of the National Bank of Yugoslavia after splitting into Republican National Banks. The New-Yugoslav government regards the judgment of the commission as only advisory and not at all final.

BAKARIĆ, VLADIMIR (1918-). He was born in Gorica in the vicinity of Zagreb (q.v.). He joined the communist movement in 1932 and was arrested and prosecuted several times. During the Second World War, he became Commissar of the General Headquarters and Partisan Detachments of Croatia. After the war, he became the Regional Head of the Communist Party in Croatia and a member of the Politburo. He was Prime Minister of the Government of the Socialist Republic of Croatia. Later he held the highest functions in the Federation: he was a member of the Presidency of the Central Committee of the League of Communists of Yugoslavia (q.v.) and of the Presidency of the Socialist Federal Republic of Yugoslavia. He became a theoretician of the economic aspects of the socialist system of self-management. During the Croatian Spring (q.v.), he defended a rather conservative position. Tito (q.v.) entrusted him with the continuation of the centralist line after the purges.

BAN. The Ban and the Sabor (q.v.) are considered to be the two typical and traditional institutions of Croatian statehood. Some historians connect the institution of the Ban with the supposed Persian descent of the Croats (q.v.). The title was used for the first time in Europe when the Croats arrived in the Balkans. Under King Petar Krešimir (q.v.), there were three Bans: one in Croatia proper meaning the counties of Lika (q.v.), Gačka and Krbava and the littoral, a second in Pannonian (q.v.) Croatia and a third in Bosnia. The Ban or Viceroy performed the highest executive duties in the Croatian state. Though the Pacta Conventa (q.v.) of 1102 recognized the authority of the Hungarian King, the position of the Croatian Ban and Sabor were not really affected. After 1538, the state organization of Slavonia (q.v.) and Croatia were unified in the sense that one Ban and one Sabor became the constitutional organs of both regions. On the other hand, Dalmatia had been sold to Venice and the hinterland was lost to the Turks.

With the establishment by the Austrians of the Military Border (q.v.), the Ban and the Sabor lost authority even over this Croatian territory. Compensation was later offered by the institution of a region called Banija (q.v.) that came under the direct jurisdiction of the Ban. The unfavorable trend was not wholly reversed until 1880, when the union of almost all former regions stood on the political agenda. The much honored Ban Jelačić (q.v.) played an important role in this unifying operation. Only Dalmatia (q.v.) remained under direct Austrian rule until 1918. The Kingdom of Serbs, Croats and Slovenes (q.v.) proclaimed on December 1, 1918, was politically and administratively characterized by strong centralization. The function of the Ban was revived during the Banovina Croatia (q.v.) established just before the Second World War.

BANAC, IVO (1947-). Born in Dubrovnik (q.v.). Professor of History at Yale University. Editor of the journal *East European Politics and Societies*. He received a prize for his study of the nationality question in Yugoslavia. In the autumn of 1993, he wrote an open letter to President Tuđman (q.v.) in the journal *Erasmus* together with five other Croatian intellectuals. They criticized his policy and asked him to resign.

BANIJA. Region south of Petrinja. When it was reconquered from the Turks at the end of the seventeenth century, it was placed under the direct jurisdiction of the Croatian Ban (q.v.) and therefore called Banija. Now, it is again a disputed region, as the Serbs want to integrate it in the autonomous region of the Serbian Repubic of Krajina (q.v.). It is theoretically under control of UNPROFOR (q.v.) as Sector North of the Krajina (q.v.).

BANOVINA CROATIA. The Banovina Croatia came into life through an agreement between the Serb Dragiša Cvetković and the Croat Vladko Maček, the so-called Sporazum. The decree of August 26, 1939, on the Croatian Banovina defined its territory, its competences and its organization.

The Croatian Banovina contained the Banovinas of Sava and Primorje and the districts of Dubrovnik (q.v.), Šid, Ilok, Brčko, Gradačac, Derventa, Travnik and Fojnica. Its capital was Zagreb (q.v.). So, along with the region around Zagreb, the Banovina covered Slavonia (q.v.), the Dalmatian coast and parts of Bosnia-Hercegovina. Within the competences of the Banovina were agriculture, trade, industry, mining, forestry, construction, social and health policies, sports, justice, education and local administration. All other fields remained under the national state organs in Belgrade. This was the case for national security and public order. Belgrade organized the secret information services and countered anti-state propaganda. In order to finance its obligations, the Banovina collected taxes and managed its budget autonomously.

Legislative competence was shared by the parliament (Sabor) of the Banovina and the King. Executive power was exercised by the Ban in the name of the King. The representatives of parliament were chosen by free and secret elections. Minorities had to be represented in parliament. The King appointed the Ban (q.v.). It was the prerogative of the Constitutional Court of the State to decide on the constitutionality of the laws of the Banovina and to arbitrate in conflicts of competence between the Kingdom and the Banovina.

BANSKI DVOR. The Court of the Ban in Zagreb (qq.v.), now the official residence of the President of the Republic of Croatia.

BARANJA. The region between the confluence of the Danube and Drava Rivers. Its main town is Beli Monastir. At its south frontier lies Osijek (q.v.).

After World War II, the region was administratively integrated in the Republic of Croatia because Croats (q.v.) were more numerous than Serbs and the region gravitated towards the city of Osijek. The area was further colonized by Croatian partisans and war veterans. Presently the question of how this has affected the character of the region is being disputed. Serbs from Belgrade argue that the colonization injected a Croatian influence, while Croatians complain of Serbinization, as the colonists should have originated mainly from the Krajina (q.v.).

The Baranja was invaded by the Serbs in August 1991. In execution of the Vance plan, the area got the status of United Nations Protected Area (q.v.). In March 1992, UN troops from Belgium and Russia were deployed and took control of the region. So far, UNPROFOR (q.v.) has not been able to restore the situation as it was before the war. Croatian refugees cannot return to their homes and it seems that this situation will not change soon. In October 1993, President Tuđman (q.v.) insisted at the UN Security Council that the UNPROFOR mandate be changed. This only provoked more hostility from the Serbs.

BAROMIĆ, BLAŽ (1450- ?). Born in Vrbnik. In 1493, he achieved the printing of a Glagolitic (q.v.) breviary in Venice. The following year, he initiated the first Croatian Glagolitic printing press in Senj (q.v.) and produced the first Glagolitic missal in Croatia.

BAŠČANSKA PLOČA. The Plaque of Baška is the oldest extant longer document written in Croatian Glagolitic (q.v.). It was found on the island of Krk (q.v.), a center of Glagolitic writing.

Even today, the Plaque cannot be precisely read and exactly dated. It is supposed to be from about 1100. It was part of the rood of the church of Saint Lucy in Jurandvor near Baška on the island of Krk. The Plaque contains information about the donation of land to the church by King Zvonimir (q.v.). The witnesses who guarantee the veracity of this act are Pribinež of Vinodol, Jacob of the Islands and the prefects Desimir of Krbava and Martin of Lika. "Whoever refutes this may be cursed by the Lord and the Apostles and the Evangelists and Saint Lucy." The text also mentions the name and actions of two Benedictine abbots. Abbot Držiha wrote the act and Abbot Dobrovit built the church "in the time of Prince Cosmas who ruled the whole district and it was then that the monastery of Saint Nicholas in Otočac was united with the church of Saint Lucy."

The language of the Plaque is a Croatian vernacular retaining only a few elements of Old Church Slavonic. It can be regarded as the starting point of Croatian literature (q.v.).

BEBIĆ, LUKA (1937-). Member of the House of Representatives and President of the Committee on Internal Affairs and National Security. Former Minister of Defense (1991).

BIĆANIĆ, RUDOLF. He was the Vice-Governor of the Interwar Yugoslav National Bank and was involved with the Yugoslav Government in Exile from 1941 to 1944. He is the author of the influential book *Ekonomska Podloga Hrvatskog Pitanja* (The Economic Basis of the Croatian Question) that described the economic position of Croatia in Yugoslavia.

BIOGRAD (NA MORU). Original Slav settlement between Zadar (q.v.) and Šibenik, the town where the late medieval Croatian Kings were crowned. In 1125, it was conquered and destroyed by the army of the Venetian Doge Domenico Michieli. It never recovered and lost its historical role.

BLEIBURG. Carinthian town near the Austrian-Slovenian border, symbol of the tragedy of the communist repression of the Ustaša (q.v.). At the end of the Second World War, the Ustaša regime collapsed and the Croatian army fled to Austria. It was disarmed by the Allies and handed over to the partisans. This was the beginning of a massacre among soldiers and civilians, particularly in the vicinity of Bleiburg and Maribor. Especially in emigration circles, Bleiburg became a place of pilgrimage and a symbol of Croatian suffering.

BOBAN, MATE. Leader of the Bosnian Croats. He founded the Community of Herceg-Bosna, the Croat-dominated part of Hercegovina. On April 19, 1993, he declared that this province should most probably become a part of Croatia, a consequence and not a cause of the non-existence of the state of Bosnia-Hercegovina.

BOBETKO, JANKO (1919-). General and head of the general command of the Croatian army. In January 1993, he led the action in the Maslenica (q.v.) area and in September 1993, the Gospić offensive (q.v.).

BOGOMILISM. The Bogomils rejected the Catholic and Orthodox canons of Christianity. Inspired by old Christian sources, they preached an original dualism similar to what can be found in some Persian doctrines. There is only scanty literary testimony about the spread of this heretical dualistic belief in Croatia. In a letter dated October 11, 1200, Pope Innocent III declared that the Bogomils of Dalmatia (q.v.) had fled to Bosnia, where Ban Kulin had accepted them wholeheartedly.

Known heretics were the brothers Aristodes and Matthias of Zadar (q.v.), painters and sons of a Greek father Zorobabal. Because of their preaching, they were banned from the town and went to Split (q.v.), another stronghold of Bogomilism. Here they obtained protection for some time, but were ultimately expelled again. The story repeated itself in Trogir.

The lapidation in 1085 of the Catholic Archbishop Raineri by the Kačići, the most famous tribe of the Neretvans (q.v.), is probably connected to the strong influence of Bogomilism in the region.

In 1221, the Pope sent his legate Acontius to pacify the same region. The inhabitants - pirates of Omiš and its environs - continued sporadic rebellions for ages.

In 1225, the Roman Catholic clergy in Split was unable to prevent the election to power of a Bogomil Duke, Peter, Duke of

Hum. Acontius was sent, put a ban on the town and closed the churches for more than a year.

BORDERS OF CROATIA. The question of the Croatian borders is a sensitive one. The country conquered its autonomy and independence in a period of crisis and conflict with the neighboring states.

The Croatian border is 2,028 kilometers long. The greater part belongs to Europe's oldest borders. This is particularly so in the segments running along the river Drava, which traditionally has been the dividing line between the Croatian and Hungarian state. Across the Drava, where the Croatian territory extends along the left bank of the river, the border also has a historical origin: it is the former Military Border (q.v.), a borderland which was gradually joined to civil Croatia after its dissolution in the period 1873-81. The border in Međimurje (q.v.) partly relies on the river Mura. It was finally fixed after World War I when Međimurje, formerly a part of Hungary, was included in the Kingdom of Serbs, Croats and Slovenes (q.v.). However, the inclusion of Međimurje in Hungary was questionable anyway because in the past it had been Croatian for considerable stretches of time. Notwithstanding efforts at Magyarization, the majority of the population has always been considered to be Croatian.

The border in the Baranja (q.v.) is one of the more recent segments of the Croatian-Hungarian border. It was first drawn in 1920, following the stipulations of the Peace of Trianon and has no historical precedents. The southern part of what was formerly the Hungarian district *(zupanija)* of Baranja was then included in the Kingdom of Serbs, Croats and Slovenes as the logical hinterland for the city of Osijek (q.v.). It was an ethnically mixed area, settled not only by Hungarians, but also by a considerable number of Croats (q.v.) and Germans and a smaller number of Serbs. It can be regarded as a division of territories between victors and losers of the First World War.

The Croatian-Slovene border is one of the old European borders. The border areas along the river Sutla, Mount Žumberak and the river Kupa (q.v.) follow lines which had divided the historical lands of Carinthia and Styria from Croatia for several centuries. The Slovene border of Međimurje also mostly corresponds to the earlier limits of the Croatian region, aside from several villages in the Međimurje municipality of Strigovo which were assigned to Slovenia when the borders were redrawn in 1945. The Croatian-Slovenian border in Istria (q.v.) was determined after the end of World War II, more precisely in 1954, when the provisional Free Territory of Trieste (FTT) was finally divided between Italy and Yugoslavia. The part of the FTT which had been occupied by Yugoslavia was divided between Croatia and Slovenia on the basis of ethnic criteria. In 1956, there was a small correction when some villages in the Buje municipality were joined with Slovenia.

The longest Croatian border is that with Bosnia-Hercegovina. Its position today resulted from the Ottoman occupation of Bosnia-Hercegovina. The western frontier follows the river Una and the northern the Sava, the historical borders of Croatia and Slavonia (q.v.) since the Peace of Karlovci (q.v.) was concluded in 1699 between the Austrian Emperor and the Turks. Following another war, the Treaty of Požarevac (q.v.) of 1718 corrected the eastern border by extending the Croatian territory eastward, whereby Croatia gained all of Srijem (q.v.). The Peace of Svistovo of 1719 was of particular importance for the Croatian-Bosnian border along the upper course of the river Una. After Croatia regained the greatest part of Lika (q.v.) in 1699, the treaty gave Croatia Kordun (q.v.) and the Lika Pounje area. In 1945, the border with Bosnia was partly changed in the Bihac region. The southern section of the border between Croatia and Bosnia-Hercegovina follows the demarcation line of Venetian Dalmatia (q.v.) and the Republic of Dubrovnik (q.v.) with the Turkish empire. It is identical to the Mocenigo line - which gave Venetian Dalmatia its final shape in 1718 - and the borders of the Ragusan Republic, fixed in 1699.

The present interruption of the Croatian territory at Neum goes back to the same time, when Bosnia-Hercegovina was given access to the sea. It was a concession of Dubrovnik to the Ottoman Empire. It is exactly in this place that the Bosnian President Izetbegović now wants a corridor to the sea for the Muslims.

The border of Croatia with Serbia is of a more recent date. In 1945, the communists decided to divide Srijem on an ethnic basis. Another part of the Croatian-Serbian border goes back to the old Croatian border with Hungary, reconfirmed with the

Peace of Karlovci when the Turks were forced to leave Slavonia and Srijem.

Croatia officially inherited the borders fixed by the Second AVNOJ (q.v.) Session that established the Socialist Federal Republic of Yugoslavia composed of six republics. However, most Croatian borders stem from an older period. Some politicians today see this as a historical legitimation for the existence of an independent state, just as some politicians already did a century ago. There can be discussions about the frontiers that have been changed by the communists. But these are minor disputes in comparison with the claims of the Serbs on ethnic grounds. Of course, even these ethnic frontiers at least partially have their historical explanations, for example, in the policy of the Austrians concerning the Military Border.

BOSANSKA POSAVINA. Border area in Bosnia around the Sava. According to the population census of 1991, in this region lived 138,741 Croats. In 48 villages the population consisted only of Croats. In a letter to the Croatian Sabor (q.v.) of September 1993, the representatives of Bosanska Posavina described the region as a cultural entity with a majority of Croatian people in Bosanski Brod, Bosanski Šamac, Brčko, Derventa, Doboj, Gradačac, Modriča, Odžak and Orašje. Croatians colonized Posavina 13 centuries ago. The Franciscan brothers have been present for seven centuries. Bosanska Posavina is a historical Croatian space as it was also a part of the Croatian Banovina (q.v.). These arguments were presented to prevent its transformation into Serb territory by the Owen-Stoltenberg plan (q.v.).

BOŠKOVIĆ, RUĐER JOSIP (1711-1789). Physician and philosopher. This native of Dubrovnik (q.v.) was a Jesuit and taught as a professor at a number of universities. He founded a large observatory in Milan and published on mechanics, optics, geophysics, astronomy, mathematics and philosophy. His most important work in the area of theoretical physics, *Philosophiae Naturalis Theoria* (Theory of Natural Philosophy), was published in Vienna in 1758. Specialists defend the opinion that this work has laid the foundations of modern atomic physics.

BOŠNJAK, BRANKO (1923-). Former philosophy professor of the University of Zagreb (q.v.). He was a member of the *Praxis* (q.v.) group. He specialized in the philosophy of religion.

BRAČ. Third largest of the Adriatic islands, lying just off Split (q.v.). It shared a common history with its neighboring island Hvar (q.v.). The archaic name Brattia probably stems from the Illyrian *Brentos* - green.

BRANIMIR. Pope John VIII wrote a letter to Prince Branimir, dated June 7, 879. The Pope recognized Branimir's "earthly power." This has been regarded as the first international recognition of the statehood of Croatia.

BRČIĆ, IVAN. Priest from Zadar (q.v.) and one of the leaders of the revival of Croatian knowledge of the Glagolitic (q.v.) tradition in the middle of the nineteenth century. His *Čitanka staroslavonskoga jezika* (Old Slavonic Reader, 1859) for the first time clearly differentiated between the original old-style oval shaped Glagolitic and the native Croatian angular lettering.

BREŠAN, IVO (1936-). Playwright. *The performance of Hamlet in the village of Mrduša Donja, commune of Blatuša* received the Sterijina Prize for a contemporary dramatic text at the Yugoslav theater festival of 1972.

BRIONI. Island group lying on the southwest point of Istria (q.v.) near Pula. It was a residence of Tito (q.v.) and transformed into a national park (q.v.). During the communist period and after, it functioned as a conference place where essential decisions were made. One of them was the deliberation on the Ranković (q.v.) case. It was also the place where the leaders of ex-Yugoslavia discussed their problems under the mediation of the European Community (q.v.) in 1991. (See also BRIONI AGREEMENT)

BRIONI AGREEMENT. Agreement reached on the island of Brioni (q.v.) under the mediation of the European Community (q.v.) between the ex-Yugoslav parties (July 7, 1991). The army accepted an armistice in Slovenia (q.v.), while Slovenia and Croatia withheld for three months any measures that would have furthered their independence.

BUDAK, MILE (1899-1945). Writer and Croatian representative in Berlin during Pavelić's Independent State of Croatia (qq.v.). He was again a subject of discussion when the Tuđman (q.v.) regime decided to honor him as a writer with a street name.

BUDIŠA, DRAŽEN (1948). A Zagreb philosophy student elected to the leadership of the Student Federation in 1971. He led a student strike in the Croatian Spring (q.v.). During the repression of the nationalistic movement, he was sentenced and put in jail. Under the Tuđman regime, he became the leader of the Croatian Social-Liberal Party (q.v.) and a member of Parliament. From August 1991 to February 1992, he was Minister without Portfolio in the Government of National Union (q.v.). In the presidential elections of August 2, 1992, Budiša became the most successful challenger of Tuđman (q.v.). While the President obtained 56.7 percent of the votes, Budiša ended up second with 21.8 percent, far in advance of the other candidates such as Savka Dabčević-Kučar and Dobroslav Paraga (qq.v.). In his testimony at the trial of Dobroslav Paraga in July 1993, Budiša cast doubt on the subversive character of the activities of the Croatian Party of Rights and the Croatian Armed Forces (qq.v.).

BUSINESS ASSOCIATIONS. The membership of the two most important Croatian business associations is legally compulsory.

Companies and individual businesspeople have their own and partly joint organization. A company *(poduzeće)* is an entity separate and distinct from its owners. The owners of the company are not personally liable for its debts, thus having limited liability. The status of the individual businessperson *(samostalni privrednik)* implies sole proprietorship, indicating a business operated by a person as his or her own personal property. This type of enterprise is an extension of individual ownership.

The Croatian Chamber of Commerce (q.v.) is the association of all companies such as manufacturing firms, banks, financial institutions, insurance organizations and work shops. They have to register their activity at the court and automatically become members of the organization. The number of registered companies in Croatia was around 40,000 at the end of 1992.

The Alliance of Associations of Independent Businessmen is an independent organization of associations and alliances whose aim is to promote the common interest of all independent businesspeople. It was reorganized in March 1992 by a new statute. In December 1992, about 70,000 individual businesspeople were registered. They have a common representation in the Croatian Chamber of Commerce. In addition, there are several regional associations.

Voluntary business associations act as representatives of certain professional groups or regional interest groups. Among the most prominent are the Club of Managers of Zagreb, Entrepreneurs' Club of the Bank of Zagreb, Croatian Managers' Association (CROMA), Association of Hotel Managers of Croatia, Croatian Association of Dealers in International Trade, Gold and Foreign Exchange (Forex), and others.

- C -

ČAKAVIAN. Variant of the Croatian language, an alternative to kajkavian or štokavian (qq.v.). According to the equivalent for the word *what*, the variants use the expressions što-, kaj- and ča-. This variant was spoken most on the Dalmatian (q.v.) islands.

CARITAS. Coordinating center in Zagreb (q.v.) for 11 Croatian branches of the local Catholic relief agency, operating through local parishes and through branches in Banja Luka, Mostar and Sarajevo. The activities include distribution of food, medical supplies and clothing. European branches supply funds that care for orphans, raped and abused women, and that contribute to the rebuilding of homes and schools.

CARRINGTON PLAN. Project proposed by Lord Carrington during the Conference of The Hague. The independence of Slovenia and Croatia would only be recognized as part of a general agreement on the future of ex-Yugoslavia. The relations between the new entities and the problem of minority rights should be settled first. The plan was presented at the fourth session of the Conference on October 4, 1992. (See also VANCE-OWEN PLAN)

CARTULARY OF ST. PETER'S ABBEY. The Benedictine monastery of St. Peter was built in the village Selo, present-day Sumpetar, County of Poljica, near Split (q.v.). The consecration of its church was performed in 1080 by Archbishop Laurence of Split. It came into being at the time after the Lateran Council of 1059, when the Roman Catholic Church was passing through a period of radical reforms. They were designed to reestablish its spiritual prestige and authority vis-à-vis the hereditary prerogatives of secular feudal rulers. A vigorous campaign was initiated to eradicate corruption, simony and the widespread practice among the clergy of all ranks of taking concubines or marrying. The founder of the church, Peter Crni (Black Peter), provided the monastery with land and a work force, and later the monastery's possessions increased with endowments from other sources. There is a record in the monastery cartulary of all these purchases, donations and law suits concerning various pieces of land. The monastery was probably destroyed by the Tartars during their invasion of Croatia in 1242, but its cartulary was preserved. The codex was written in Latin, mostly in Carolingian script. There also exists an epitaph of Peter Crni, alluding to difficulties probably between *glagolaši* (priests using the Croatian vernacular in service) and the Latin party.

CATHOLIC CHURCH. The Catholic Church welcomed Croatian independence in 1941. After the victory of the partisans, a difficult period began because the church was identified with the pro-Fascist Ustaša (q.v.) regime. Its Bishop Stepinac (q.v.) was put on trial in the autumn of 1946. He publicly declared that Croatians have the right to a national state and was apparently seen as the symbol of Croatian nationalism. Of course, the church was one and perhaps the only institution to gather anti-communist forces and to disseminate an ideology and practice of resistance. In 1952, the Vatican sent a harsh note to the communists and diplomatic relations were suspended. The promotion of Stepinac to Archbishop and head of the Croatian church could be explained as an outright declaration of war to the new regime.

In the 1960s followed a period of adjustment and relatively stable relations. The signing of the Vatican-Belgrade agreement in June 1966 more than symbolized this new era. It consecrated the new model of the Vatican's adjustment to new political and ideological realities. Though an interested participant, the role of the church in the Croatian Spring (q.v.) was not particularly impressive. The wish to maintain good relations with the authorities kept it from official revolutionary intervention. There was also a depoliticizing effect of the priority of the eschatological sphere.

Of course, the church welcomed the end of communism and political pluralism. Archbishop Kuharić (q.v.) has obtained a strong position with the new Tuđman (q.v.) regime. Meanwhile, the complete rehabilitation of Stepinac is underway, if not wholly accomplished. The "opposition" paper *Slobodna Dalmacija* (q.v.) published in 1992 a series praising the Archbishop and exonerating him from previous accusations. The Vatican recognized the new state of Croatia even before the EC countries, only preceded by Germany. After two years in power, the Croatian Democratic Union (q.v.) officially pursues a Christian-Democrat image and tries to benefit from the profile of a Christian-Democratic party in international affiliations.

CAVTAT. Town, 20 km south of Dubrovnik (q.v.). It was founded by the Illyrians (q.v.) and under Greek (Epidaurum) and Roman (Civitas) influence. When the Avars (q.v.) and Slavs devastated the town, its inhabitants fled to the little island Lave (Laus), the later Dubrovnik.

CENTER FOR PEACE, NON-VIOLENCE AND HUMAN RIGHTS. This Center in Zagreb (q.v.) engages in efforts to protect human rights, serves as witness of illegal actions against Croatian civilians and advocates the rights of minorities in Croatia. It publishes books on mediation, non-violent conflict resolution and conscientious objection, and translates reports by international human rights organizations into Croatian. With researchers in Ljubljana and Zagreb, the Center is conducting studies into the media's treatment of the war.

CENTER FOR WOMEN VICTIMS OF WAR. This Center in Zagreb (q.v.) provides psychological assistance, trauma recovery, humanitarian aid, financial support and information on health and legal problems to women refugees of the war in Bosnia-Hercegovina and Croatia - especially victims of rape - without regard to nationality. It also helps women to emigrate and provides financial aid and letters of guarantee. It establishes shelters for women with exceptional needs.

CENTRAL BUREAU OF STATISTICS OF THE REPUBLIC OF CROATIA/DRŽAVNI ZAVOD ZA STATISTIKU REPUBLIKE HRVATSKE. The Bureau annually undertakes about 220 statistical research studies on the territory of the Republic of Croatia. The Bureau checks, processes, analyzes and publishes data according to areas and branches of activity, as well as territorially by districts. Every year, the Bureau issues the *Statistical Yearbook*, about 40 documents on different areas of statistics. Every month the *Monthly Statistical Bulletin* contains data on current economic trends. More than 400 issues of the *Bulletin* are planned for the year 1993. These concise information sheets are designed to inform the interested public briefly and quickly about ongoing research. Theoretical and specialized statistical studies are published in the series Studies and Analyses. The *Statistical Yearbook of Croatia* and the *Monthly Statistical Bulletin* appear in an English version. The publication "Population According to Ethnic Group by Settlement" has an appendix in English.

CERVA, AELIUS LAMPRIDIUS see CRIJEVIĆ, ILIJA

CESAREC, AUGUST (1893-1941). Writer in the interwar period, firmly committed on social problems. He edited, together with Miroslav Krleža (q.v.), the journal *Plamen* (Flame). He was a victim of the Kerestinec (q.v.) case.

ČESMIČKI, IVAN (1434-1472). Janus Pannonius, Croatian humanist, writer of odes and epigrams in Latin.

CETINA. River ending in the Adriatic near Omiš (south of Split). In early historico-graphical writings, it is supposed to divide White Croatia (q.v.) in the north from Red Croatia in the south.

ČETNIK. Serbian nationalist. Supporter during the Second World War of the Serbian General Draža Mihailović. The word *četa* means military company or detachment. The *četniks* first fought against the German occupiers and obtained the support of the Western Allies. Later they turned against communist partisans and Croats (q.v.).

Nowadays the Croats use the term *četnik* as a general name for all Serbian nationalists. In Serbia, especially the paramilitary organization of Šešelj claims to be the heir of the Četnik movement of Draža Mihailović. The movement of Vuk Drašcović was identified as well with the *četniks* of Mihailović.

CHAMBER OF COMMERCE see CROATIAN CHAMBER OF COMMERCE

CHERSO see CRES

CHINA see PEOPLE'S REPUBLIC OF CHINA (RELATIONS WITH)

CHRISTIAN DEMOCRATS OF MEĐIMURJE/KRŠĆANSKI DEMOKRATI MEĐIMURJA (KDM). The Christian Democrats of Međimurje is a small regional Catholic party. The party is led by its President Vladimir Mesarić. It concluded an agreement on cooperation with the Croatian Christian Democratic Party (q.v.) and the Christian National Party (q.v.).

CHRISTIAN NATIONAL PARTY/KRŠĆANSKA NARODNA STRANKA (KNS). The Christian National Party is a small Catholic party that concluded an agreement on cooperation with the Croatian Christian Democratic Party (q.v.) and the Christian Democrats of Međimurje (q.v.).

CHRISTIANIZATION OF CROATIA. Every theory on the early history of the Croats (q.v.) is subject to a high degree of uncertainty and discussion. One is inclined to see the Christianization of the Croats as a process with various episodes.

Constantine Porphyrogenitus (q.v.) gives the honor to Emperor Heraclius (610-641) "sending priests from Rome and making bishops of them and christening the Croats." The Franciscan historian Mandić (q.v.) likewise defends the thesis that Christianization began as early as 640. In that year John of Solin (Ivan Solinjanin) was elected as the new Pope of Rome. In 641, he sent Abbot Martin to Dalmatia (q.v.) to set in motion the process of Christianization. On the other hand, in this and in some later periods, the Dalmatian towns were under the direct influence of the Byzantine Empire. It can be conjectured that the Emperor - who regarded himself as a representative of God on Earth - should not have remained passive in conversion policies.

Other historians consider the influence of the Frankish reign in the beginning of the ninth century as decisive. They argue further that a strong church organization in Dalmatia was introduced by Pope John X as late as 914 to 928. Perhaps another date should be remembered. In 879, Pope John VIII sent a letter to Branimir (q.v.). The Pope recognized Croatia as an autonomous state and stressed the return of the Croatian people to the mother church of Rome.

Moreover, there is a whole discussion on the role of the Slav apostles Methodius and Cyrillus (q.v.) in the Christianization of Croatia. Mostly it is related to the question of the introduction of Glagolitism (q.v.) and the use of the national language in church services.

Earlier historians stress the strong national Slavic character of the heritage of Methodius and Cyrillus and the opposition to the Latin party in the coastal towns under Byzantine influence. Recent work sees it more as a complementary process. The Byzantines could even have supported the national church movement, especially in the northern part of the Adriatic. Opposition to a national church would have come then mainly from the Patriarchate of Aquilea and the Pope.

CHRONICLE OF THE PRIEST OF DIOCLEA/LJETOPIS POPA DUKLJANINA. The Chronicle of the Priest of Dioclea (Duklja, Doklea or other variants) was written in the twelfth century in Latin. The manuscript has been translated into Slavic and then again into Latin by Marko Marulić (q.v.), though not literally. The oldest published version is the Italian translation under the title *Il regno degli Slavi oggi corrotamente detti Schiavioni* done by Mavro Orbini, a Benedictine priest from Dubrovnik (q.v.). A variant of the original Latin manuscript was published by Ivan

Lučić (q.v.) in Amsterdam: *De regno Dalmatiae et Croatiae libri sex*. The chronicle tells the story of Croatia and Dalmatia (q.v.) from near the end of the ninth century to the middle of the twelfth.

This early history of Croatia seems to suggest the existence of one Great Croatia, divided into Red and White Croatia (q.v.). The whole coastal region (Primorje) running from the Raša River in Istria (q.v.) to Drač in present-day Albania should have belonged to one Croatia, White or Red. In this interpretation, the Neretvan lands, Zahumlja, Travunja and Duklja (Doklea) were all parts of Red Croatia, sometimes called "High Dalmatia." The northern coastal region from Istria to Split (q.v.) is White Croatia or "Low Dalmatia." Only the interior, called Transmontania or Zagorje, was Serbian land containing a part of Bosnia to the west of the Drina and the state Raša (q.v.) (Serbia proper) to the east of it.

CIBALIA see VINKOVCI

ČIČAK, IVAN ZVONIMIR. During the Croatian Spring (q.v.), he was the first student elected Pro-Rector of the University of Zagreb without being a party member. As a victim of Tito's (q.v.) political repression, he sat in prison from 1971 until 1974. Later he worked as a journalist and became known for his critical commentaries in the journal *Danas* (q.v.). Under the Tuđman (q.v.) regime he preserved his critical and oppositional role. He left *Danas* when its editorial policy came under growing political pressure through a state privatization strategy. He acted as the President of the Croatian Helsinki Committee for Human Rights (q.v.).

CILIGA, ANTE (1898). Born at Šegotici near Pula. Student of philosophy and history at the Universities of Prague, Vienna and Zagreb. He joined the Socialist Party of Croatia in 1918 and participated in the Republic of Albona (q.v.) in 1921. From 1922 to 1925, he was Secretary General of the Communist Party of Croatia, and editor of its journal *Borba*. From 1926 to 1936, he stayed in Soviet Russia, the last years in Siberian concentration camps. On this experience, he wrote *The Russian Enigma* (London, 1940). Back in Yugoslavia, he was betrayed by the Communist Party of Croatia and thrown into the Ustaša (q.v.) concentration camp at Jasenovac. He survived and emigrated. In the 1970s, he was editing an emigrant magazine, *On the Threshold of a New Dawn.*

CITIES. The major Croatian cities are Zagreb (approximately 950,000 inhabitants), Split (200,000), Rijeka (200,000) and Osijek (160,000) (qq.v.).

CIVIC INITIATIVE FOR THE FREEDOM OF EXPRESSION/ GRAĐANSKA INICIJATIVA ZA SLOBODU JAVNE RIJEČI. Independent citizen's group founded by journalists, aiming to lessen state control of the media, and supporting free and independent journalism. The initiative monitors the legal situation, violations of the right to freedom and expression, and state pressure.

COMINFORM CONFLICT. Conflict between Stalin and Tito (q.v.) in 1948. Stalin accused Tito of nationalist tendencies and aspirations to lead a Balkan federation. Tito tried to defend his pure communist intentions, but finally broke away from the international communist movement. This process was accompanied by internal purges against orthodox communists. Several leaders were discarded and deported to Goli Otok, the Yugoslav Siberia. About 2,600 Croatian communists were sentenced. It was a very severe illustration of a revolution that "eats its children". Along with Bleiburg (q.v.), it remained one of the tightest taboo themes under the communist regime.

CONSTANTINE, THE PHILOSOPHER see CYRILLUS

CONSTANTINE PORPHYROGENITUS (905-959). He was born the second son of Leo VI and became Emperor of the Byzantine Empire in 913. He reigned with some interruption until 959. He wrote a book about the administration of the empire - *De Administrando Imperio* - dedicated to his son and giving him advice on how to handle the nations surrounding the Byzantine Empire.

Constantine was the first to have differentiated clearly between Croats (q.v.), Serbs and other peoples living on the shores of the Adriatic. He was also the first writer to mention the Croats by their own name. Earlier writers contented themselves with the general indication "Slavs" (Sclaveni, Slovenes). Constantine gave a mythological account of the descent of the Slavs and Croats and their arrival on the Adriatic. Five brothers Klukas, Lobelos, Kosentzis, Muchlo and Chrobatos (Croat), and two sisters (Tuga and Buga) led the Croats to their present homeland. According to Constantine, the Croats entered Dalmatia (q.v.) during the reign of Emperor Heraclius in the period 610-641.

Constantine's definition of the territory of the Croats on the Adriatic is far more restrictive than that in the Chronicle of the Priest of Dioclea (q.v.). Constantine spelled out in detail some other interesting events of Croatian history up to the mid-tenth century.

CONSTITUTION OF 1990. On December 22, 1990, a new Constitution of the Republic of Croatia was promulgated by all three chambers of the Croatian Parliament (q.v.).

The Republic of Croatia was established as the national state of the Croatian nation and a state of members of other nations and minorities who are its citizens: Serbs, Moslems, Slovenes, Czechs, Slovaks, Italians, Hungarians, Jews and others, who are guaranteed equality with the citizens of Croatian nationality and the fulfillment of ethnic rights in accordance with the democratic norms of the United Nations and the free world countries.

State power in Croatia is entrusted to three bodies: legislative (Parliament), executive (President and Government) and judicial.

The supreme head of the Republic is the President (q.v.), who is elected for a term of five years. According to the Constitution, the President appoints the Prime Minister and, on the proposal of the Prime Minister, other ministers of government. These appointments are subject to confirmation by the Chamber of Representatives.

Under the new Constitution, Parliament is the highest legislative body and consists of two chambers: the Chamber of Representatives, having between 100 and 160 members, and the Chamber of Counties.

CONSTITUTION OF 1974. This last basically communist Constitution integrated the amendments of the early 1970s. The autonomy of the Republics and the Autonomous Provinces was strengthened. Consultation and reconciliation procedures at the federal level were complicated and time-consuming.

CONSTITUTIONAL AMENDMENTS OF 1971. The 1971 amendments to the Constitution of the Republic of Croatia were very controversial. Supporters thought the statehood of the Republic should be reenforced and hence the amendments should be applauded. Especially controversial was the proposed First Amendment in which the rights of Serbs and other nationalities in Croatia were specified. "The Croatian nation *(narod)* in history through its historical aspirations, in community with the Serbian nation *(narod)* and nationalities in Croatia...realized in the national liberation war and socialist revolution its own national state - the Socialist Republic of Croatia....The Socialist Republic of Croatia is a sovereign national state of the Croatian nation *(narod)*, the state of the Serbian nation *(narod)* in Croatia, and the state of the nationalities that live in it."

Critics pointed out that in this formulation, the statehood of Croatia before 1918 was not recognized. But second and more important, the formulation implied that Croatia was not the national state of the Croats. It stated that Croatia was the state of Croats and Serbs.

In 1963, the Croatian Constitution did not mention the Serbs in Croatia as a constituent nation of the Republic. In 1971 this was now explicitly done in order to guarantee the rights of the Serbs in Croatia.

Though granting equal rights to the Serbs and other nationalities, the 1990 Constitution did not grant the Serbs the status of constituent nation of the Republic. Croatia is defined in this last Constitution as the historical state of the Croats.

CONSTRUCTION. After a period of very little domestic investment, the present situation in construction is one of surplus capacity in relation to the demand for construction services. Many construction enterprises have found work in foreign lands, especially developing countries. Implementation of the planned investment in the traffic infrastructure and construction of residential buildings in Croatia should revitalize these activities and increase their share of GNP.

COPYRIGHT. Croatia is a member of the Bern Convention for the Protection of Literary and Artistic Works of 1886, and has underwritten the Universal Copyright Convention of 1952, as well as the three main treaties on the protection of related rights: the International Convention for the Protection of Performers, Producers of Phonograms and Broadcasting Organizations of 1961 (The Rome Convention), the Convention for the Protection of Phonograms Against Unauthorized Duplication of 1971 (The Geneva Phonogram Convention) and the Convention Relating to the Distribution of Programs Carrying Signals Transmitted by Satellite of 1974 (The Brussels Satellite Convention). In the process of the establishment of an independent state in the fall of 1991, Croatia adopted a number of laws previously valid in the SFRJ. Croatia adopted with some modification the SFRJ Copyright Law of 1978.

CORVINUS, MATHIAS see KORVIN, MATIJA

COUNCIL FOR THE NORMALIZATION OF THE RELATIONS BETWEEN SERBS AND CROATS/DRŽAVNI ODBOR ZA NORMALIZACIJU HRVATSKO-SRPSKIH ODNOSA. A state organ where the government and representatives of the Serbs in Croatia meet and try to find solutions to the problems between the two ethnic communities. Only the Serbs living in Croatia who respect the authority of the Croatian government take part in these discussions. The negotiations with the Serbs of the Krajina (q.v.) take place under mediation of the UN. The President of the State Council is Josip Manolić of the Croatian Democratic Union (q.v.). Given the state of the relations between the Serbs and the authorities, a critic called the Council in the middle of 1993 a theater without a public. Some members of the Council such as Petar Vidaković are rather sceptical and openly pessimistic.

COUNCIL FOR THE STRATEGIC DEVELOPMENT OF CROATIA/VIJEĆE ZA STRATEGIJSKI RAZVITAK HRVATSKE. This Council was established in 1992 as an advisory organ to the Presidential Office. It is composed of 35 well-known academicians, businesspeople and politicians. The President of the Council is the writer Ivan Aralica. Its functioning came under attack in the press because of inactivity and lack of publicity.

COUNCIL OF EUROPE (RELATIONS WITH). Croatia is not yet a full member of the European institutions. So far, it has just received the status of special guest - members of the Croatian Parliament (q.v.) can attend the meetings of the European Parliament - and Croatia participates in the work of some intergovernmental commissions in the fields of education and culture. On December 10, 1992, the Council of European Ministers formally initiated the procedure that can lead to full-scale membership of Croatia. A commission should be set up to examine on the spot the functioning of a free press (q.v.) and democratic institutions and analyze the government's policy towards human and minority rights. However, in the middle of 1993, two reasons were given to slow down the formal procedure. In the first place, the problems related to the status of the UNPAs (q.v.) were not solved. Secondly, European countries started a campaign against Croatia condemning its role in Bosnia-Hercegovina. As a result, Croatia is not yet included in European association and co-operation programs, such as the PHARE program (q.v.). Minister of Foreign Affairs Mate Granić was invited to present the Croatian viewpoint at the conference of the member countries of the Council of Europe in Vienna in October 1993.

CRES. Second largest Croatian island near the eastern side of Istria (q.v.). It shares a common history with the nearby island of Lošinj. Cres was already settled in the Neolithic period. About 1200 B.C. it was colonized by the Illyrians (q.v.). At the end of the third century B.C., the Romans built on the channel between Cres and Lošinj the fortification of Absorus, present-day Osor. This name was sometimes used for the whole island. The Slavs occupied the island in the early seventh century and at times shared government with the Byzantines. In 842, it fell into the hands of the Saracens. In the early tenth century, it became a part of the national Croatian kingdom of King Tomislav (q.v.). During the following centuries the Venetians dominated the region. In 1815, the island came under the control of Austria. The Treaty of Rapallo in 1920 granted Istria and the surrounding islands to Italy. Cres finally joined Yugoslavia by the Treaty of Paris in 1947.

CRIJEVIĆ, ILIJA (1463-1520). Aelius Lampridius Cerva, Croatian humanist. Writer of neo-Latin poetry.

CRNIĆ, IVICA (1951-). Judge of the Supreme Court of the Republic of Croatia (1988-1992). Minister without Portfolio and Minister of Justice in the government of Prime Minister Nikica Valentić (q.v.).

CROAT-SERB COALITION/HRVATSKO-SRPSKA KOALICIJA (HSK). In 1905, two leading Croatian Yugoslavs Frano Supilo and Ante Trumbić (q.v.) met their Serbian fellow citizens living in the Habsburg empire and founded the Croat-Serb Coalition. They formed a further alliance with the Hungarian Independence Party led by Francis Kossuth, son of the Hungarian revolutionary Lojos Kossuth. From then on, the Hungarians supported the Croat-Serb Coalition against the Croatian nationalists in Croatia and Slavonia. In the last Croatian elections before the war in 1913, the Croat-Serb Coalition won the majority of seats in the Sabor (q.v.). The Croatian Serb Svetozar Pribićević (q.v.) was elected President of the Sabor.

CROATIA PROPER. Up until the First World War, the territory of present-day Croatia had been described as the Triune Kingdom of Croatia, Dalmatia and Slavonia (q.v.). The region around Zagreb and Varaždin (qq.v.) had then been called Croatia proper.

CROATIAN ACADEMY OF ARTS AND SCIENCES/HRVATSKA AKADEMIJA ZNANOSTI I UMJETNOSTI (HAZU). The Croatian Academy of Arts and Sciences was earlier a republican branch of the Yugoslav Academy of Arts and Sciences (q.v.).

CROATIAN ARMED FORCES/HRVATSKE ORUŽENE SNAGE (HOS). The Croatian Armed Forces was the paramilitary organization of the Croatian Party of Rights (HSP) (q.v.). Ante Prkačin, once the head of the general command of the HOS, declared before the court in the trial of Dobroslav Paraga (q.v.) that he did not know exactly what the abbreviation HOS meant. The *O* might stand for *oružene* (armed), *obrambene* (defense) or *oslobodilteljske* (of liberation). The paramilitary forces helped the Croatian National Guard and the Ministry of the Interior (MUP) (q.v.) in their fight against the Yugoslav army and the Serbian paramilitary organizations. Some HOS soldiers shocked a part of public opinion by openly wearing Ustaša (q.v.) symbols. The HOS displayed a tendency to launch uncontrolled armed actions. The MUP took measures to bring it under better control. Paraga and other leaders of the HSP were later brought before a military court on charges of terrorism and violation of the constitutional order. (See also CROATIAN PARTY OF RIGHTS)

CROATIAN ARMY. The regular armed forces of Croatia were created by a transformation of the Croatian National Guard. At first, regional territorial units and paramilitary formations such as the Croatian Armed Forces (q.v.), the military arm of the Croatian Party of Rights (q.v.), played a major role in the fighting. Later, a general headquarters was formed and autonomous forces were disciplined. By the beginning of 1993, the Croatian army consisted of five professional brigades and reserve forces, with a total of about 100,000 men. There is also a small navy. The forces' main need is aircraft. Of four Migs, one did not return in September 1993 during the Gospić offensive (q.v.).

CROATIAN CHAMBER OF COMMERCE. The Chamber of Commerce is a legal public establishment with the aim of defending the interests of its members and of the economy of Croatia. It has official organizational tasks and acts as a representative communication and negotiation party toward the government and the trade unions. The Chamber critically examines drafts and legal regulations. It attempts to reach the best pragmatic solutions and is engaged in negotiating collective agreements. The Croatian Chamber is a union of 11 regional chambers, each representing an industrial center: Zagreb, Split, Rijeka, Osijek, Zadar, Pula, Karlovac, Sisak, Varaždin, Gospić (qq.v.) and Bjelovar. The Croatian Chamber of Commerce also has representatives in most countries abroad. Here the first aim is to provide information and establish contacts with foreign business partners.

CROATIAN CHRISTIAN DEMOCRATIC PARTY/HRVATSKA KRŠĆANSKA DEMOKRATSKA STRANKA (HKDS). The Croatian Christian Democratic Party is a small Catholic party that concluded an agreement on cooperation with the Christian Democrats of Međimurje (KDM) and the Christian National Party (KNS) (qq.v.). Its presidency criticized the policy of Tuđman (q.v.) towards Bosnia-Hercegovina and the Serbs in the Krajina (q.v.).

CROATIAN CHRISTIAN DEMOCRATIC UNION/HRVATSKA KRŠĆANSKA DEMOKRATSKA UNIJA (HKDU). The elections of August 1992 not being very successful for these parties, the Croatian Democratic Party (HDS) and Croatian Christian Democratic Party (HKDS) (qq.v.) decided to unite in a Croatian Christian Democrat Union. However, some members of the HDS walked out before. Quite a lot joined the Croatian Democratic Union (HDZ) (q.v.) and some formed a new party of the Croatian Rights under the leadership of Ivan Gabelica. The regional sections of the HKDS of Međimurje and Opatija took their autonomy. The HDS totally merged in the HKDU, while the HKDS retained its identity. There is some competition to join Christian international organizations with the governing party HDZ increasingly assuming a Christian profile. The President of the Union is the former dissident Marko Veselica (q.v.).

CROATIAN COUNCIL OF THE EUROPEAN MOVEMENT/HRVATSKO VIJEĆE EUROPSKOG POKRETA (HVEP). The Croatian Council of the European Movement is a non-governmental and non-party organization that promotes the integration of Croatia in Europe. To that end, it organizes seminars and invites important Europeans, it holds exhibitions and disseminates publications on the Council of Europe, European Community (qq.v.) and other European institutions, with special attention to the role of Croatia therein. The Secretary of the movement is Ljubomir Čučić.

CROATIAN CREDIT BANK FOR RECONSTRUCTION/HRVATSKA KREDITNA BANKA ZA OBNOVU (HKBO). Following the presidential decree of June 9, 1992, on the proclamation of the Law on the Croatian Credit Bank for Reconstruction, this institution approves loans and projects contributing to the reconstruction of the Croatian economy if other financial institutions cannot intervene. On proposal of the government, the Sabor (q.v.) decides by a special decree the purposes for which the means assured by the Law on the Financing of Reconstruction are given without the obligation of repayment.

The Law on the Financing of Reconstruction defines the resources for the reconstruction of housing, economic, public or other objects damaged or destroyed by the war and for measures stimulating the development of the war-damaged regions. These projects are financed by physical persons, enterprises and other juridical persons, funds, banks and other financial organizations in proportion with their possibilities and interests. The citizens of the Republic contribute 2 percent of their net income, with the exception of pensioners and persons earning minimal wages or receiving social assistance. Resources are also collected including half of the proceeds of the sale of social enterprises, 10 percent of the money acquired by granting concessions for the use of natural resources or social goods, and other minor revenues. Also used for reconstruction are resources given as aid by other states, the proceeds of the final distribution of the balances of former Yugoslavia and war reparation payments. The Republic of Croatia guarantees a starting capital of one billion German marks and paid 10 percent in 1992. To collect further resources the bank will float bonds and accept credits.

The HKBO approves credits through other banks and financial organizations. Only exceptionally can the Management Board grant a credit to an end user. Among the 19 members of the Board are the Ministers of Finance, Development, Reconstruction, Industry and Energy, Agriculture, Forestry and Waterworks, Environmental Protection, Regional Planning and Housing, the Governor of the Central Bank, a Representative of the Council for the Strategic Development of Croatia, the Director of the Agency for Restructuring and Development (q.v.), the Director of the Croatian Fund for Development and the President of the Croatian Chamber of Commerce (q.v.). This Chamber also nominates four heads of industry.

Since its founding, the HKBO has taken over the main tasks of the Croatian Fund for Development as the financing of development plans and the management of regional planning. During the first year of its existence, the HKBO approved credits for a sum of about 106 million DM. The repayment term is five years and the interest rates only range from 3 to 5 percent (linked to a foreign exchange formula). The demand for loans far exceeds the possibilities of the bank and only the most pressing needs caused by the war can be satisfied. Most of the credits for infrastructure and housing have been awarded to Slavonia and Dalmatia (q.v.).

CROATIAN DEFENSE COUNCIL/HRVATSKO VIJEĆE OBRANA (HVO). The Croatian Defense Council is the military body of the Croatian Bosnians of Herceg-Bosna standing under the leadership of Mate Boban (q.v.). It received substantial help from the motherland Croatia. It first fought the Bosnian Serbs in alliance with the Muslims, but at a later time the allies engaged in fierce battles over the division of the remaining territories. In the center and west of Bosnia and especially around Mostar - claimed by the Bosnian Croats to become the new capital of Herceg-Bosna - both parties engaged in ethnic cleansing against each other.

CROATIAN DEMOCRATIC PARTY/HRVATSKA DEMOKRATSKA STRANKA (HDS). The Croatian Democratic Party is a Christian-Democratic opposition party whose president is Marko Veselica (q.v.). After unsuccessful elections, the party decided to merge with the Croatian Christian Democratic Union (q.v.).

CROATIAN DEMOCRATIC PARTY OF RIGHTS/HRVATSKA DEMOKRATSKA STRANKA PRAVA (HDSP). The party is one of the contemporary small parties that base their ideology of the historical state right *(pravaštvo)* on Starčević's (q.v.) ideas. The Croatian Democratic Party of Rights attacks, even before the courts, the Croatian Party of Rights (HSP) and Dobroslav Paraga (qq.v.) on the allegation that the HSP violates its own statutes and that Paraga takes decisions illegally. The leader of the party is Krešimir Pavelić, former secretary of the HSP. With the destitution of Paraga from the leadership of his own HSP, a tendency to unite all *"pravaši"* may set in.

CROATIAN DEMOCRATIC UNION/HRVATSKA DEMOKRATSKA ZAJEDNICA (HDZ). The Croatian Democratic Union was founded as a political movement in 1989 by Franjo Tuđman (q.v.) and his close assistants. Josip Manolić (q.v.) was the first President of the Executive Committee of the HDZ

(1989). Tuđman became the first President of the HDZ. The party held its First Convention in 1990. It obtained a substantial electoral victory in April 1990 and since then dominates the political stage. The HDZ renewed its legitimacy in the elections (q.v.) of 1992.

Some of the most influential national leaders of the HDZ are Franjo Tuđman, Stipe Mešić (q.v.), Josip Manolić, Josip Bojkovać, Vladimir Šeks (q.v.), Gojko Šušak (q.v.) and Vice Vukojević (q.v.).

There are three competing currents in the party. The right wing considers itself the authentic, original and "right" side of the HDZ that contributed most to the massive electoral victory of the party. It thinks it did not get the government posts it deserved since they were given to newcomers of the left and the "managing" side of the HDZ. The left accuses the right wing of being conservative, extremist and anti-democratic, advocating a policy that will govern Croatia by ideology and by force and that will bring the country into isolation. Some members of the HDZ argue that in the internal elections members of the right wing have always dominated. Others think that the lines of division in the party are not so clear. Probably this is true: the more party leaders come from far away from the center of Zagreb (q.v.), the more they are right-wing oriented. As long as the HDZ still dominates the political agenda, Croatian politics will crucially depend on the internal dynamics of the party.

At the beginning of September 1993, Stipe Mešić of the left wing and Branimir Glavas of the right wing openly fought a bitter duel in the press. The left-wing oriented Manolić threatened to leave or split the party. The party held a congress in the middle of October. Leaders announced the transformation of the HDZ from a movement to a real national party with a Christian-Democratic outlook.

At the Second Convention, the first significant move came from the right. The conservative county prefect Branimir Glavas had accepted an amendment that deprived members not elected in the presidency, but participating in the deliberations on behalf of their function, of their right of voting in that organ. As most left-wing figures (Mešić, Manolić) had a seat in the presidency, their political influence was contained. The most significant action came from President Tuđman himself. He presented his preferred list of candidates and completely recentered the party. The representatives of the extreme wings retired or were voted out. Tuđman so tried to close the ranks of the party on a center position. A new statute and party program were adopted, giving the HDZ a Christian-Democratic flavor. This move was not as radical as sometimes presented in the period before the Convention.

However, in the month of April 1994 both Presidents of the Houses of Parliament (q.v.), Mešić and Manolić, revolted and founded a new party, claiming to take away with them 16 members of parliament of the HDZ. This threatened the parliamentary majority of the HDZ in both Houses of Parliament.

CROATIAN ETHNIC GROUPS. The Croats (q.v.) consist of the Bunjevci and Šokci (many of them also live in Serbia and Hungary), Slavonci, Zagorci, Međumurci, then Croats in Bosnia-Hercegovina, Gorani, Istrijani (some are in Slovenia), Gradiščani (in Austria and Hungary), Dalmatinci, Konavljani, Bokelji (in Montenegro), Janjevci in Kosovo, etc. All these Croatian groups represent a richness of dialects, national costumes, habits and folk songs.

CROATIAN FUND FOR DEVELOPMENT/HRVATSKI FOND ZA RAZVOJ. The Fund was established as the financial intermediary to implement the Law on the Transformation of Socially-Owned Enterprises (q.v.). During the first phase of transformation, the socially-owned enterprises were free to choose a model of transformation of their ownership relations and management bodies. After the deadline of June 30, 1992, firms not being engaged so far in the transformation process came under the jurisdiction of the Croatian Fund for Development and the Pension Insurance Funds as new legal owners. The approach makes the Croatian Fund for Development a special kind of holding company in which the state is holding a dominant position.

The Croatian Fund for Development is obliged to put on sale all stocks or shares it gained by transformation of ownership. On the basis of a contract, the Fund can entrust the management of a company in a domestic or foreign person. The companies can be leased out by a public auction or by collecting public offers.

One of the functions of the Fund is to cofinance development programs. The Fund can finance a maximum of two-thirds

One of the functions of the Fund is to cofinance development programs. The Fund can finance a maximum of two-thirds of the total estimated value of investments, while the investor must provide at least 25 percent of the investment him- or herself. Both forms of credit and non-credit financing are possible, along with factoring services.

Other functions of the Fund are the establishment of a capital market and more even regional development.

CROATIAN HELSINKI COMMITTEE FOR HUMAN RIGHTS (CHC)/HRVATSKI HELSINŠKI ODBOR ZA LJUDSKA PRAVA. The Croatian Section of the Helsinki International Federation actively monitors human rights abuses and regularly presents reports on the situation in Croatia. Its President is Ivan Zvonimir Čičak (q.v.).

CROATIAN HOMELAND FOUNDATION/HRVATSKA MATICA ISELJENIKA (HMI). Cultural institution for contact with Croatian emigrants. It has always been considered to favor a strongly nationalistic policy.

CROATIAN INDEPENDENT DEMOCRATS/HRVATSKI NEZAVISNI DEMOKRATI (HND). Party founded at the end of April 1994 by Stipe Mešić and Josip Manolić (qq.v), the Presidents of the Houses of Parliament and founder-members of the Croatian Democratic Union (q.v.) (HDZ). The new party threatened the majority of the HDZ in parliament and through their position the dissidents could provoke a parliamentary crisis and new elections. The criticism of the new party mainly centers around three themes: the politics of Croatia towards Bosnia-Hercegovina, the status of Croatia as a Rights' state and the dominant position of President Tuđman (q.v.) in the Croatian system. Slavko Degoricija (q.v.) was a third important figure who left the HDZ for the HND.

CROATIAN MUSLIM DEMOCRATIC PARTY/HRVATSKA MUSLIMANSKA DEMOKRATSKA STRANKA (HMDS). The Croatian Muslim Democratic Party defends the interests of the Muslims in Croatia.

CROATIAN NATIONAL-DEMOCRATIC LEAGUE/HRVATSKA NACIONALNO-DEMOKRATSKA LIGA (HNDL). The Croatian National-Democratic League was founded at the beginning of 1993 by former HDZ politicians Ivan Vekić (q.v.) and Bosiljko Mišetić. It is a national, conservative party, seeing its priority as preserving the continuity of a (Great) Croatian state. As such, it adheres to the program of the *pravaštvo*, but not that of Starčević (q.v.) so much as that of today. According to its President Ivan Vekić, the League is supported mainly in the surroundings of Zagreb and in Dalmatia (qq.v.). At the end of 1993, the party took part in the ongoing negotiations with other factions to form a united Croatian Party of Rights.

CROATIAN NATIONAL PARTY/HRVATSKA DOMOVINSKA STRANKA (HDMS). One of the contemporary opposition parties that participated in the initiative of Drago Stipac (q.v.).

CROATIAN NATURAL HISTORY MUSEUM. The present Croatian Natural History Museum was founded in 1986. Its history goes far back into the past. There were already museums with natural history items in the second part of the eighteenth century, e.g., the Museum of Ivan Aletin in Dubrovnik (q.v.). Generally, these museums were the reflection of the interests of dedicated individuals, not of institutions, who collected rarities with great passion. As for the natural history items there were mainly preserved fish, reptiles, insects, birds, as well as plants, ferns and marine algae. The peak of the development of museums in Croatia took place in the nineteenth century. Even then, the main collectors were keen amateurs, but gradually the motives and criteria for collecting changed. All this is related to the beginnings of the Croatian Revival in the 1830s and the prevailing spirit of empiricism and scientism in Europe in general. With the establishment of natural history museums in Zagreb, Dubrovnik, Zadar (qq.v.) and other places, there was a strong tendency to show the flora and fauna of Croatia and its regions.

More concretely, the origin of the present Croatian Natural History Museum is situated in 1828 when the leader of the Croatian Revival Ljudevit Gaj (q.v.) requested the foundation of the Learned Society, i.e., the Yugoslav Academy of Arts and Sciences (q.v.), and the foundation of the National Museum in

Zagreb. In 1836 the Croatian parliament followed Gaj's suggestion to found these institutions. But the decisions of the Sabor (q.v.) remained temporarily unfulfilled because they were not confirmed by the central government in Vienna. In the meantime the natural history collection progressed under the protection of the Agricultural Society founded in 1842.

The National Museum really functioned as of 1846. In that year, the Croatian government bought and decorated a special palace where the Agricultural Society was installed with the museum collections, which were then opened to the public. Finally, in 1866, the central government in Vienna confirmed the existence of the growing institution and put it under the direction of the newly founded Yugoslav Academy of Arts and Sciences. Very soon the National Museum Departments were transformed into two distinct museums of natural history: the Croatian Zoological Museum led by the important paleomalacologist Spiridion Brusina and the Geological-Mineralogical Museum led by the geologist Georgius Pilar. After the death of Pilar in 1893, the great paleoanthropologist D. Gorjanović-Kramberger, who studied the Krapina Neanderthals, separated his Geological-Paleontological Museum from the other collections.

Thus, at the end of the nineteenth century, there existed three natural history museums in Zagreb: the Croatian National Zoological Museum, the Geological and Paleontological Museum and the Mineralogical and Petrographic Museum. This favored the independent development of the different natural history disciplines. This situation continued until the 1980s when a tendency arose for a new integration. In their full maturity, the museums were suited to making a new, relatively strong professional and scientific institution. The integration took place in 1986 when the United Croatian Natural History Museum was created. It is the national and central museum for natural history collections and museums in the Republic of Croatia. By a special decree, the Ministry of Culture legalized this function in 1993.

The Croatian Natural History Museum is an important exploration center. It gathers explorers for its projects and scientific programs. Its aim is to be a strong data base for Croatian zoology, geology, paleontology, mineralogy, petrography and botany. In the museum there are more than 2,500,000 natural specimens and about 35,000 titles of professional and scientific literature.

The Museum is a non-profit state institution financed by the Republic of Croatia and the City of Zagreb.

CROATIAN NEWS AND PRESS AGENCY/HRVATSKA IZVJEŠTAJNA NOVINSKA AGENCIJA (HINA). The Croatian News and Press Agency has its headquarters in Zagreb (q.v.).

CROATIAN PARTY OF RIGHTS/HRVATSKA STRANKA PRAVA (HSP). Today's Croatian Party of Rights can be traced back to the earlier party, better understood as the Party of the Historical Rights of Croatia. Ante Starčević (q.v.) was the father of the party and founder of its ideology. The historical rights refer to the moral and legal reasons that justify the independence and autonomy of Croatia. The theory stresses the continuity of the statehood of Croatia. In the course of history Croatia has always been an autonomous subject. It has deliberately chosen its destiny and alliances on its own terms. Any bond can be broken, if the conditions posed by the Sabor are no longer fulfilled. In the case of Habsburg rule, Croatia is considered to have been bound only by a personal union with the King. This union was freely chosen and this contract could be discontinued whenever the interests of Croatia so required. Concretely, this implied the virtual independence of Croatia from the Habsburg regime and especially Hungary.

Ante Starčević and Eugen Kvaternik (q.v.) defended this position more or less clearly in the Croatian Sabor (q.v.) as early as 1861. In 1871, Kvaternik organized an armed uprising against Austria and was killed in the rebellion. Ante Starčević chose a more cautious strategy and led his party to victory in the elections of 1884. However, due to Austrian and Hungarian resistance, the HSP could not fully realize its political program. After the collapse of the Habsburg Empire in the First World War, the radical Croatian-nationalist ideas were taken over by the Croatian People's Peasant Party (q.v.). Together with all other political parties, the Croatian Party of Rights was ultimately dissolved by King Alexander (q.v.) on January 6, 1929.

After the collapse of the communist regime, some intellectuals founded a new party under the name of Hrvatska Stranka Prava. Dobroslav Paraga (q.v.), President and leader of the new HSP, acknowledged the historical bonds with the older HSP from before 1929. He rejected any connections with the later Ustaša (q.v.) regime.

Soon, dissensions within the Croatian Party of Rights led to a split. The former secretary Krešimir Pavelić became leader of the Croatian Democratic Party of Rights (HDSP) (q.v.). Some other smaller parties appeared, all claiming to be reflections of Starčević's ideology. The HSP and Dobroslav Paraga appeared before the military court on the allegation of insubordination. Paraga was dismissed as President of the HSP. On September 17, 1993, the leaders of three parties, meeting in Kutina, began preparations for a new union on a broad common *pravaški* (Croatian Rights) program. The initiative came from the new leaders of the HSP, President Boris Kandare and Co-President Ante Đapić, who invited the leaders of the Croatian Pure Party of Rights (HČSP), Ivan Gabelica, and of the Croatian National-Democratic League (q.v.), Petar Badovinac and Bosiljko Mišetić. Later, other "state-building" parties, such as the Croatian Democratic Party of Rights, the Party of the Croatian State Rights (q.v.) and even the Croatian Democratic Union (q.v.) may join.

CROATIAN PEASANT PARTY/HRVATSKA SELJAČKA STRANKA (HSS). After the disintegration of the communist regime, the ideas and traditions of the Croatian People's Peasant Party (HPSS) (q.v.) were supposed to be continued by a new peasant party, the Hrvatska Seljačka Stranka (HSS). However, efforts to revive the party in the post-communist period were not too successful. Not until mid-September 1992 did party leader Drago Stipac (q.v.) feel that the new HSS was constituted and could work in continuity with the old Croatian People's Peasant Party. In the previous three years, four if not five parties had claimed to be the heirs of the HPSS. Another member of the presidency, Tihomil Rađa, maintained that the Croatian state could best be organized along the lines of Radić's (q.v.) own alternative design of the 1921 Constitution. Some new dissenters claiming they represented the ideas of the HPSS already appeared on the stage.

CROATIAN PEOPLE'S PARTY/HRVATSKA NARODNA STRANKA (HNS). The President of the HNS is Dr. Savka Dabčević-Kučar (q.v.). She was a progressive nationalist member and President of the Central Committee of the League of Croatian

Communists during the Croatian Spring (q.v.). After Karađorđevo (q.v.), she was forced to resign. Observers expected that she could have been a real sparring partner for the Croatian Democratic Union of Tuđman (qq.v.) in the first multiparty elections of 1990. However, the party failed completely and ended up in the 1992 elections in the fourth place with only 6 percent of the votes.

CROATIAN PEOPLE'S PEASANT PARTY/HRVATSKA PUČKA SELJAČKA STRANKA (HPSS). The HPSS was founded in 1903 by the brothers Ante and Stjepan Radić (qq.v.). Its declared goal was to further the interests of the Croatian peasants and to defend the autonomy of Croatia within a freely chosen federal union with the other peoples of Yugoslavia. Radić even had plans to set up an independent Croatian Peasant Republic. The party became the biggest political formation in Croatia during the interwar era. Except for a short period when party leader Radić was Minister of Education, it refused to cooperate with Belgrade. In November 1927, Stjepan Radić concluded an agreement with Svetozar Pribićević (q.v.), leader of the Independent Democratic Party, the party of the Serbs living in Croatia. This Peasant-Independent Democratic Coalition practiced systematic obstructionism in the National Assembly. Nationalist passions and ethnic tensions rose to the point that Radić was shot in Parliament by the Serb Montenegrin Puniša Račić (q.v.) during a tumultuous session on June 20, 1928.

Vladko Maček took over the leadership of the Peasant Party and refused any cooperation without a major change of the Constitution of the Kingdom. King Alexander (q.v.) abolished the parliamentary system and proclaimed a dictatorship on January 6, 1929. All activity of the political parties was banned and remained illegal until the assassination of the King in Marseilles on October 9, 1934. The party then repeated some years of fierce opposition under the regime of the new Regent. Finally, on August 20, 1939, Maček reached an agreement with the Belgrade politician Cvetković. The *Sporazum* granted autonomy to Croatia in the form of a self-administered Banovina (q.v.) inside Yugoslavia. This settlement of the Croatian nationality problem was undermined by the imminence of the Second World War. Already under pressure of Ustaša (q.v.) propaganda, some of the supporters of Maček's party criticized the project for not going far enough. At the beginning of the Second World War, the Independent State of Croatia (q.v.) was created and Maček was invited by the Germans to take power. He refused. He only agreed to call for benevolent neutrality towards the new Ustaša regime, led by the Ustaša *poglavnik* (head of state) Ante Pavelić (q.v.). The Croatian People's Peasant Party likewise opposed all cooperation with the communist partisans. The passivity of the HPSS led to its political downfall. At the end of the war, Maček emigrated to the United States, where he could write in peace his memoirs: *In the Struggle for Freedom*.

CROATIAN PHILOSOPHICAL SOCIETY/HRVATSKO FILOZOFSKO DRUŠTVO. The Croatian Philosophical Society publishes *Filozofska Istraživanja* and *Synthesis Philosophica* (q.v.).

CROATIAN RADIO/HRVATSKI RADIO (HR). Croatian Radio transmits its first program from Zagreb (q.v.) and has 55 regional radio stations. Its ideological evolution is similar to that of Croatian Television (q.v.). Many new local radio stations have sprung up and are broadcasting programs to local audiences. Each local community has a radio frequency at its disposal.

CROATIAN RADIO AND TELEVISION/HRVATSKI RADIO I TELEVIZIJA (HRTV). HRTV, the formerly public, self-managed radio and television organization of Croatia, was turned into a state-owned national television and radio organization. HRTV has three radio and two television national channels. HRTV's center is in Zagreb (q.v.). The structure of HRTV also includes five regional TV studios, which produce and transmit their programs within the programming scheme of HRTV. HRTV is governed by a Management Board, consisting of nine members of which six are there due to their function (Director General, Directors of Radio, Television, Transmission, Editor-in-Chief of Radio Programs and Editor-in-Chief of Television Programs) and three are elected by the employees of HRTV. The Management Board is in charge of capital, investments, development plans and programming, and makes decisions by simple majority. The Director General of HRTV is appointed by the Parliament (q.v.) for a five-year period. The Director General proposes the Directors of Radio, Television and Transmission, who are appointed by the government.

The HRTV Council appoints the Editors-in-Chief of Radio and Television. The HRTV Council is also the body in charge of influencing the programming policy and is supposed to take into account the preferences of the public. The HRTV Council has 25 members, 15 of whom are appointed by the Parliament (representing the power structure of the political parties) and 10 by various professional and other organizations. One member each is provided by the Association of Universities of Croatia, Croatian Academy of Arts and Sciences (q.v.), Matica hrvatska (q.v.), Croatian Writers' Association, Croatian Journalists' Association, Croatian Actors' Association, Croatian Musicians' Association, Catholic Church (q.v.), Serbian Orthodox Church and Islamic Community. The overall program guidelines for the national radio and television are specified in the Law on Croatian Radio and Television. One of the rules is a 20 percent restriction of advertising. HRTV's main source of income is license fees. In 1991, 83.6 percent of income came from license fees, 9.7 percent from advertising and 6.7 percent from other sources. (See also CROATIAN RADIO; CROATIAN TELEVISION)

CROATIAN REPUBLIC OF HERCEG-BOSNA/HRVATSKA REPUBLIKA HERCEG-BOSNA. The Croatian Republic of Herceg-Bosna was officially proclaimed on August 28, 1993. This region of Bosnia-Hercegovina existed informally much earlier as the Croatian ethnic entity under the leadership of Mate Boban (q.v.).

CROATIAN REPUBLIC UNION/HRVATSKA REPUBLIČKA ZAJEDNICA. An association of citizens who share ideas of the historical state rights of Croatia without officially adhering to one of the Croatian Rights parties.

CROATIAN SLAVONIC. Compared to Old Church Slavonic (q.v.), Croatian Slavonic is a common Slavonic influenced by Croatian vernacular in the fields of phonetics, morphology, syntax and, above all, vocabulary. This hybrid language was semiartificial in comparison with the ordinary language of the people.

It was used in acts of the church and in the Glagolitic (q.v.) literature.

CROATIAN SOCIAL-LIBERAL PARTY/HRVATSKA SOCIJALNA LIBERALNA STRANKA (HSLS). The party was founded in May 1989, even before the Croatian Democratic Union (HDZ) (q.v.) and the legalization of the multiparty system in December 1989. The President of the HSLS was Dražen Budiša (q.v.), a former dissident and as a student a leading figure in the Croatian Spring (q.v.). The HSLS developed into the second and most ambitious opposition party, though quantitatively its success in the elections remains far under that of the HDZ. The Social-Liberals participated in the Government of National Union (q.v.), in which Dražen Budiša obtained a ministerial portfolio. After the relative success in the new elections (q.v.), the Social-Liberals opted for a period of strong opposition. In 1993, the ideological leader of the party, Božo Kovačević (q.v.), declared that the party was on the point of switching to extra-parliamentary action, such as protest meetings in the streets. In the autumn of 1993, the party temporarily left the House of Representatives because its draft on the electronic media was not placed on the agenda of Parliament.

CROATIAN SPRING. The Croatian Spring was the national mass movement during the late 1960s and early 1970s. Three periods can be discerned.

First, and a pre-condition for the movement, was the breakthrough of communist reformers at the top of the League of Communists (q.v.) after the fall of Ranković (q.v.). From then on, intellectuals could cautiously express Croatian national interests.

Croatian writers and intellectuals set off the critical phase of the process by issuing the Declaration on the Croatian Language (q.v.) on March 17, 1967. This linguistic question quickly opened the discussion on the problematic relations between Belgrade and Croatia in general. The intellectuals and the Matica hrvatska (q.v.) now openly propagated nationalistic aspirations through publications and meetings. The party leadership of Croatia was divided into a conservative and a progressive wing. The Tenth Plenum of the Central Committee in January 1970 was marked by the affirmation of the national and progressive viewpoints. On the federal level, the Croatian party leaders paid at least lip service to legitimate Croatian interests. Among others, reforms in the economic, commercial and foreign exchange regime were urged. On November 22, 1971, the students and other groups went on strike.

Tito (q.v.) summoned the party leadership to Karađeorđevo (q.v.) and decided to break the resistance. The discussions ended with the dismissal of the progressive leadership of the Communist Party and the repression of the mass movement. The nationalist party leaders Dr. Savka Dabčević-Kučar, Miko Tripalo (q.v.) and Dragutin Haramija were forced to resign. Intellectuals and students were put on trial, sentenced and imprisoned. Among them were Dražen Budiša, Bruno Bušić, Ivan Zvonimir Čičak, Dr. Šime Đodan, Vlado Gotovac, Dr. Jozo Ivičević, Zvonko Kamarica, Ante Paradžik, Dr. Hrvoje Šošić, Ante Todorić, Dr. Franjo Tuđman and Marko Veselica. The cultural institution Matica hrvatska was banned in 1972 and did not make its reappearance until 1990. A new docile and conservative republican leadership was brought to power. However, on the institutional level, constitutional reforms were pushed through that responded to the nationalist aspirations and strengthened the power and statehood of the Republics. Most of the banned leaders of the Croatian Spring made a comeback under the Tuđman (q.v.) regime.

CROATIAN TELEVISION/HRVATSKA TELEVIZIJA (HTV). The Croatian Television functioned under the communist regime as the republic unit of the Yugoslav Radio and Television/Jugoslovenski Radio i Televizija (JRT). The federal institution supervised the regional stations and organized the exchange of programs. The first conflicts arose about a film sent by Belgrade to the Croatian Television that was subtitled in the Cyrillic alphabet, not in Latin as usual. The Croatian Radio and Television broke away from Belgrade during the change of the political climate and the electoral victory of the opposition. HTV is now said to be strongly under the control of the government and the Croatian Democratic Union (q.v.). This resulted in numerous disputes, even before the courts, between critics of the written press and Antun Vrdoljak, head of Croatian Television and HDZ Member of Parliament. (See also CROATIAN RADIO AND TELEVISION; TV MARJAN; YOUTH TELEVISION)

CROATIAN WRITERS' ASSOCIATION/DRUŠTVO HRVATSKIH KNJIŽEVNIKA (DHK). The earliest Writers' Association was founded in 1900. The present Croatian Writers' Association promotes the interests of its member writers. It organizes literary life and publishes the journal *Most/The Bridge*, a journal of translations.

CROATS. The name and origin of the Croats is a much debated theme. This debate is of course significant in the discussion about the justification of a Yugoslav or Croatian state.

National-Croat historians sometimes defend the thesis that the Croats were a non-Slavic people who invaded the Croatian lands when Slavs were already settled there. The origin of the Croat people would thus have an Iranian source. Scattered evidence has been collected in favor of this interpretation. The name of the Croatians had been found for the first time in an inscription on the Bogostan rock (Iran) dating from 520 B.C. It figured there written in cuneiform as *Harauvati*, one of the 23 peoples who recognized the authority of Emperor Darius. Other ethnic and linguistic characteristics of the Croatian people can be explained by the supposed Iranian origin. The clan and leadership organization of the Croatians (and their names) could be traced back to Iranian customs. But even specialists who defend these theories acknowledge an interaction with Slavic tribes during the migrations. However, when arriving on the Adriatic, the Croats would have formed a separate leading stratum on top of the Slavs who probably arrived earlier. This opinion can also be derived from the first more or less mythical traditions and sources on the arrival of the Slavs on the Adriatic.

Another interpretation rests on a confusion between Avars (q.v.) and Croats. In the sixth century, the Avars invaded Pannonia and Dalmatia (qq.v.). Probably they were accompanied by and ruled over Slav peoples. Ultimately the Avars were defeated by Byzantium and Charlemagne and seemed to disappear. One explanation is that their name changed from *Avar* to *Harvar*, and then to *Harvat*. This is close to the equivalent for Croatian, *Hrvat*.

To complicate matters, some defend the Gothic origin of the Croats. They point especially to the Glagolitic (q.v.) script that could be Gothic in origin.

Historians who favor the interpretation of a pan-Slavic settlement of the South Slav countries reject the theories about a separate origin of the Croats. The Croats were Slavs and the differentiation only came later when branches of the same people had settled on different territories.

No decisive answer can so far be given to this question. No clear ethnic lines can be drawn in a continuing process of migration, integration and assimilation of peoples and cultures. At most, one can ascertain a common history for a certain period of time in a certain area. In that way the development of a Croatian nation can be observed and defended. But in that way one can imagine a rationale for a South Slav state as well.

Numerous linguistic interpretations of the word Croat *(Hrvat)* and its variations have been presented. None of them has obtained firm corroboration by archeological findings, nor the consent of the scientific community.

CUSTOMS SYSTEM. On October 8, 1991, the new Customs Law and the Law on Customs Tariffs came into force. The Customs Law is based upon unrestricted exchange of goods. There are certain limitations for the purpose of protecting the domestic industry and the market.

Customs tariffs are in the range of 0 to 18 percent, with the majority of tariffs between 4 and 6 percent. For the time being, there are customs duties for smoothing the customs burden, 7.5 percent; a special duty on imported goods, 15 percent; and a 1 percent customs fee for record keeping.

Aside from other exemptions provided by the law, a foreign person can be exempted from paying customs duties on equipment imported on the basis of a foreign investment (q.v.) contract. Equipment imported by a domestic company and paid with foreign currency is also exempted from customs duties. There are three conditions necessary for this exemption: firstly, the foreign investment relationship must last for more than three years; secondly, the foreign investor's share must not be less than 20 percent; and last, there is an exception for gambling machines and amusement games.

A tariff concession based on the principle of "imports for the sake of exports" may be used by foreigners. The Customs Law provides the possibility of importing raw materials and semifinished goods without paying customs duties, provided that the imported goods would be used in manufacturing goods or providing services for export, and that the exporting takes place within one year at the latest after the goods entered the country. If the production should take more than a year, the time of export may be extended to three years. The value of the exports must be more than 30 percent higher than the value of the imported raw materials. The exports must be paid for in convertible currency.

CVIIĆ, KRSTO (1930-). Born in Nova Gradiška (Slavonia). Journalist and historian. Editor of the BBC World Service (1964-1969), journalist of *The Economist* (1969-1990) and editor of the periodical *The World Today* (1984-). In the autumn of 1993, with five other Croatian intellectuals he wrote an open letter to President Tuđman (q.v.). They criticized his policy and asked him to resign.

CYRILLIC ALPHABET. In the Balkans, language questions are always closely intermingled with state politics. It is not easy to draw the general lines of history on the basis of national schools that supply their own interpretations. The question of the origin of the Cyrillic alphabet is no exception. Older linguists supposed that the Cyrillic alphabet had been devised by St. Clement of Ohrid. More recent research assumes that he remained faithful to the Glagolitic (q.v.) tradition of Cyrillus and Methodius (q.v.). The invention of Cyrillic is now placed later and ascribed to Bulgarian Slavic apostles, working between 885 and 993. The oldest Cyrillic inscription has been found on the gravestone of Emperor Samuel of Bulgaria, erected by his parents and brother in the year 993. The close geographical and cultural ties of Bulgaria and its capital Preslav with the Byzantine Empire contributed to this new creation. The Cyrillic alphabet is a modification of the Glagolitic by the use of Greek uncials inasmuch as suitable corresponding letters could be found for the Slavic sounds.

In Bosnia and Dalmatia (q.v.) a variant to the Bulgarian original developed and was called "Bosanica."

The directive of the Tuđman (q.v.) regime to grant exclusivity to the Latin alphabet disregards this last historical development.

CYRILLUS. Cyrillus and his brother Methodius are called the Slav Apostles. Born in Thessaloniki to a Byzantine functionary as Constantine and Michael, they were also very well acquainted with the local Slavic dialect. Constantine was educated in the highest church circles of Constantinople and soon got the surname "The Philosopher." His brother Michael performed a high function in the Byzantine state administration, but soon went into a monastery. After other important state missions, Constantine was invited with his brother to take up a mission to Pannonia (q.v.), at the request of the King Rotislav and the Byzantine authorities. Rotislav wanted to counter the influence of the Frankish missionaries in Moravia. He asked the support of the Byzantines in the Christianization (q.v.) of his country in the Slavic language. After their stay and work in Rotislav's country, Cyrillus and Methodius were invited by the Pope in Rome and probably passed through Croatia. It is not clear whether and how their stay in Croatia influenced the local Christianization process and the use of the Slavic language in services.

The name of Cyrillus has been wrongly associated with the Cyrillic alphabet (q.v.), which had been devised by his followers in Macedonia or Bulgaria. It is more probable that Cyrillus used the Glagolitic (q.v.) alphabet, which according to some sources he created himself. Other historians maintain that the Glagolitic alphabet is much older and of local Croatian origin. At least, it is now believed that the followers of Cyrillus and Methodius contributed to the strengthening of the national Croatian church. Regular clashes with the Pope, the Patriarch of Aquilea and the Latin party in the coastal towns under Byzantine influence did not eradicate this national movement for ages.

- D -

DABČEVIĆ-KUČAR, SAVKA (1923-). Leader of the Croatian Communist Party during the Croatian Spring (q.v.) and victim of Tito's (q.v.) repression. In the post-communist period, she resumed her political ambitions and became President of the Croatian People's Party (q.v.). As this party did not obtain the expected success, she remained in the Parliament (q.v.) as a respected but marginalized politician. Her candidacy in the presidential elections of August 2, 1992, was also a failure. As a living example of the proper functioning of the opposition and the parliamentary system, Dabčević-Kučar was included in a mission under the guidance of the President of the Sabor, Stipe Mesić, to visit the Council of Europe (qq.v.) and to plead for the admission of Croatia as a full member.

ĐAKOVO. Town in East Slavonia (q.v.). The cathedral in Romanesque-Gothic style was erected by Bishop Josip Strossmayer (q.v.) in the middle of the nineteenth century.

DALMATIA, HISTORY OF. Dalmatia is a region along the Adriatic coast. It traces its name to the Delmata, an Illyrian (q.v.) tribe which conquered the northwestern part of the Balkans around 1000 B.C.

The Roman Province of Dalmatia was created in the year 10 A.D. by the division of the Province of Illyria into Pannonia (q.v.) and Dalmatia. It was still larger than the Dalmatia of later times, as it included a part of Istria (q.v.), Serbia, Bosnia, Montenegro and Albania. In 297 Dalmatia was divided into Dalmatia proper and Prevalitana.

After the decay of the Roman Western Empire, Dalmatia was overrun by the Goths. Odoacer ruled in 481 over Dalmatia, and later Theodoric. The Byzantines fought the Goths and the Slavs invaded the peninsula. During the reign of Empress Irene (797-802), the Franks conquered the greater part of Dalmatia. After the Peace of Aachen in 812, the towns of Dalmatia again came under the influence of the Byzantine Empire. When Vasilius I came to the throne in 867, Dalmatia became formally a *theme* (province) of Byzantium. In the second part of the ninth century, the Croat Trpimir dynasty (q.v.) began to assert their aspirations and power. In the next period, Tomislav (910-928), Drzislav (970-997) and Kresimir IV (1058-1073) (qq.v.) all integrated Dalmatia into their Croatian Kingdom.

A new period began in 1102 when Dalmatia as part of Croatia opted for a personal union with Hungary. However, in 1420, the Hungarian King Ladislas sold his hereditary rights to Venice, and Dalmatia became separated from inner Croatia for five hundred years. In 1797, by the Peace of Campo Formio, Dalmatia came under Austria and was conquered somewhat later by Napoleon (q.v.). It was incorporated in the Illyrian Provinces, a small prefiguration of the later Yugoslavia. After Napoleon's fall, Dalmatia returned under the direct rule of Austria until 1918.

Though there were some regional forces under the first and second Yugoslavia (q.v.), Dalmatia was never accorded the status of an Autonomous Province.

DALMATIA, LITERATURE OF. In the fifteenth and sixteenth centuries a new literary school arose in the cities and towns along the Dalmatian coast. They chose as their model the Renaissance and humanist literature of Italy and adapted it into a flourishing Croatian literature. Not surprisingly, most writers resided in Split or Dubrovnik (qq.v.), taking advantage of the prosperity of a wealthy class of educated merchants and landowners, and of the ample possibilities of international exchange. Especially Marko Marulić (q.v.) of Split and a whole school of writers of Dubrovnik brought Croatian literature to a height, comparable to other Western national cultures. (See also DRŽIĆ, MARIN; GUNDULIĆ, IVAN; MARULIĆ, MARKO)

DALMATIA, REGIONS OF. The geographic term *Dalmatia* covered different territories in different historical periods.

The region derives its name from an Illyrian (q.v.) tribe, the Delmata. The Roman Province of Dalmatia (q.v.) consisted of the territory between the river Raša in Istria (q.v.) and the river Mat in Albania. In the Byzantine period it was restricted to the towns and islands on which the Byzantine Empire exercised its authority - Zadar (q.v.), Trogir, Dubrovnik (Ragusa) (q.v.), Kotor, and the islands of Krk, Cres, Lošinj and Rab (qq.v.). Zadar remained over the centuries the seat of the authorities of Dalmatia. In the Middle Ages, Klis (q.v.), Knin and Biograd (q.v.) were other leading centers in Dalmatian Croatia. In 1409, King Ladislas (q.v.) of Naples sold his hereditary rights as King of Dalmatia to Venice. Venice became the master of the Dalmatian shores. After occupation by and various wars with the Ottomans, Dalmatia's territory was extended inland. At the turn of the eighteenth century, Dalmatia was conquered by Napoleon and included in the Illyrian Provinces (qq.v.). From 1814 to 1914, the greater part of Dalmatia came back under Austrian government. Around 1880

Dalmatia was united with Pannonian Croatia in the Kingdom of Croatia, Dalmatia and Slavonia (qq.v.).

Even today, autonomous regional forces play a role in everyday politics. The region has its own daily paper, *Slobodna Dalmacija (q.v.),* and various local political parties spoke up for greater autonomy. Dalmatian Action (q.v.) is the most successful regional political initiative. It has formed an association with the Istrian and other regional parties, Association of Croatian Regional Parties (q.v.).

DALMATIAN ACTION/DALMATINSKA AKCIJA (DA). Regional party that strives for the autonomy of Dalmatia (q.v.). The President is Mira Ljubić-Lorger (q.v.). The party is a member of the Association of Croatian Regional Parties (q.v.). (See also AUTONOMY)

DANAS. *Danas* (Today) was a more or less independent journal under the communist regime. As a follower of *VUS (Vijesnik U Srijedu* - The Wednesday Magazine) banned by the communists for being Croatian nationalistic, *Danas* grew into a respectable journal, sometimes highly critical of the communist regime. Under the new regime, the government closed it down for financial reasons. When it reappeared as *Novi Danas,* it was denied access to the distribution network. Ultimately, it was caught in the maze of the privatization policy and its board of directors was replaced by representatives of the Agency for Restructuring and Development (q.v.). It is now more or less loyal to the Tuđman (q.v.) regime, but it retains some of its editorial independence and is much more critical than is sometimes suggested abroad.

DE ADMINISTRANDO IMPERIO. Treatise written by Constantine Porphyrogenitus (q.v.) around 952. Especially in chapters 29 through 31, the Emperor wrote in detail about the descent and the arrival of the Croats (q.v.) on the Adriatic coast. He continued the history up to his time.

The Croats originally came from White Croatia (q.v.), a land whose position is not exactly defined but supposed to be on the other side of the Carpathians. A clan of five brothers - Klukas, Lobelos, Kosentzis, Muchlo and Chrobatos - and two sisters - Tuga and Buga - with their people arrived from White

Croatia in Dalmatia (q.v.) and found it under the rule of the Avars (q.v.). The Croats defeated the Avars and became the rulers of Dalmatia. The Byzantine Emperor Heraclius (A.D. 610-641) gave them his approval, or even invited them to occupy Dalmatia. Some Croats left the coast again and conquered Pannonia (q.v.). Later, the Croats had to bow temporarily to the Franks, but they could master them finally as well. The Croats became independent and asked to be Christianized by Rome.

Constantine presents an interesting picture of Croatia in the middle of the tenth century. He sketches both the internal organization in *županije* (q.v.) and the geographical relations with other Slavic settlements. Croatia stretched from the river Cetina (q.v.) along the Adriatic coast to the town of Labin in Istria (q.v.). Inwards, it reached further than the frontiers of Dalmatia (q.v.) and in the east, it bordered Serbia. Croatia was subdivided into 11 *županije*, which can be identified as Livno, Cetina, Imotski, Pliva, Pset, Primorje, Bribir, Nona, Knin, Sidraga and one unconfirmed, Nina. These regions fell under the immediate jurisdiction of the King. Three more Croatian *županije* stood under the authority of the Ban (q.v.): Udbina (Krbava), Lika and Otočac. The following peoples surrounded the Croats: the Serbs, Neretvans or Pagani, Zahumljans, Travunjans, Konavljans and Dukljans (q.v.). All the peoples living along the Adriatic coast with the exception of the Dukljans are described as Serbs. Also Upper-Bosnia is defined as Serbian land.

Passages on the role of some Byzantine Emperors are strikingly apologetic. Another shortcoming is the systematic interpretation of names by easy association. The names of the founders of the Croatian dynasty could likewise be interpreted as symbols for genealogical explanation. Much in the treatise remains unclear and confused, especially as some passages sum up earlier themes in a slightly different way. The chapters on the Dalmatian peoples are no exception. Specialists point to contradictions between chapter 30 and chapters 29 and 31, going so far as to suggest different authors. All in all, this treatise is an interesting but not too reliable early source on Croat history.

DECLARATION OF CORFU. On the island of Corfu, the South Slavs of the Habsburg Empire and the Serb government reached an agreement on the future organization of a new state of Serbs,

Croats and Slovenes. The new state would be a kingdom. The questions of the future state organization and the majority required in the constituent assembly would be settled later. The Corfu Declaration was signed on July 20, 1917.

At the end of the war, both parties would offer a different interpretation of the agreement and its implications for the organization of the new state. Trumbić (q.v.) voted in 1921 against the first Constitution of Yugoslavia (q.v.).

DECLARATION ON THE CROATIAN LANGUAGE. The 1967 Declaration on the position and name of the Croatian literary language marked the beginning of the Croatian Spring (q.v.). It was a document of Croatian cultural institutions that asserted the specific Croatian identity of the Croatian people through the right to their own language. In the existing communist setting, the Declaration could be interpreted as an open rebellion against the regime. Consequently the Declaration was condemned by top political circles. The main promoters of the Declaration, the prominent intellectuals and writers Dalibor Brozević, Miroslav Brandt, Ivo Franges, Ljudevit Jonke, Slavko Mihalić (q.v.), Vlatko Pavletić, Jakša Ravlić and Petar Šegedin were expelled from the party or lost their academic and social positions. This reaction of the regime set in motion a spiral of national demands, soon translated into a political program for an autonomous Croatia: the Croatian Spring.

DEFENSE AND NATIONAL SECURITY COUNCIL/VIJEĆE OBRANA I NACIONALNE SIGURNOSTI. This is a state organ presided over by President Franjo Tuđman (q.v.). Military advisors and prominent politicians have a seat in this body. The Council offers advice on national security questions. For example, at the beginning of September 1993, the Council rejected the extension of the UNPROFOR (q.v.) mandate in Croatia without changing the conditions. The conclusions of the Council are of the utmost political and diplomatic importance. They morally commit the Croatian government. The smooth functioning of the Council is one of the cornerstones of the presidential system. It is under constant attack by the critics of a strong presidential regime.

DEGORICIJA, SLAVKO (1931-). Born at Kompolje near Otočac. He participated in the Croatian Spring (q.v.) and was removed from his political functions. In 1991, he became a Member of Parliament (q.v.) and President of the Council of Communities. He assumed high posts in the Croatian Democratic Union (q.v.) and became Minister of Economic Reconstruction (1991-1992). He was reelected a member of the House of Representatives and appointed by the Croatian government to lead the negotiations with the insurgent Serbs of the Krajina (q.v.). He joined the Croatian Independent Democrats, when this party was founded by Stipe Mešić and Josip Manolić (qq.v) at the end of April 1994.

DEMOCRATIC ALLIANCE OF ALBANIANS IN CROATIA/DEMOKRATSKI SAVEZ ALBANACA U HRVATSKOJ. Contemporary party of the Albanians living in Croatia.

DENATIONALIZATION. The decree on the evidence of nationalized property of May 14, 1991, partially filled an electoral promise made by the governing as well as by the opposition parties. By this decree, the former owners and their heirs were invited to declare the loss of nationalized enterprises, houses, commercial buildings, land and movable property. The declarations were collected by the Governmental Board for the Coordination of the Denationalization and delivered to the Ministry of Justice. Under Minister Ivica Crnić, the results of an inventory were made public. By the autumn of 1993, the state had received 67,433 declarations from 25,059 persons. Most of them concerned the return of land, 49,229; houses and buildings came second, 14,438; there were 1,961 claims regarding movables and 1,805 regarding enterprises.

Of the 1,805 enterprises, 802 were located in the larger towns of Zagreb, Rijeka, Osijek and Split (q.v.), and most concerned industry (410) and trade (328). The 14,438 declarations on buildings contained claims on 16,189 business buildings and 29,414 living spaces. The heading of land mainly covered woods: 50,000 hectares under 267 claims. Agricultural land came second and building areas were requested by 109 persons.

Of the churches, the Catholic Church (q.v.) has delivered the most declarations (2,464), followed by the Serbian Orthodox

Church (1,702). The Evangelical Church with two and the Greek Orthodox Church with 26 claims make the list complete. The Catholic Church requested 1,181 houses, 1,490 parcels of agricultural land (26,000 ha), 186 parcels of building grounds (162 ha), and 164 woods (1,700 ha). The Serbian Orthodox Church requested altogether 3,200 ha of land. Together, the churches sought 10 percent of the claimed lands.

A political decision as to the applicable criteria was needed to start the real implementation of the process of denationalization. In September 1993, the government of Prime Minister Nikica Valentić laid down three principles. First, the denationalization must take place gradually. Second, the rights on denationalization of each category of property shall be regulated by a special decree. Third and most important, first will be returned all that can be given physically to the former owners or their heirs. This implies that there will be no financial compensation for nationalized property.

DESNICA, VLADAN (1905-). Born at Zadar (q.v.). Translator and short story writer. He is author of the novel *Proljeća Ivana Galeba* (The Springtime of Ivan Galeb, 1960).

DIADORA see ZADAR

DIMOVI, NEBOJŠA (1903-1993). Assistant Minister of Economic Affairs of the Yugoslav Government in Exile under Prime Minister Ivan Subašić (q.v.) during the Second World War.

DIOCLEA (DOKLEA, DUKLJA). Heart of so-called Red Croatia (q.v.). The region of Dioclea had been administratively separated from Dalmatia (q.v.) in 297 and became the autonomous province of Prevalitana. Historians remain divided about the exact location and its frontiers. Usually, Dioclea is associated with Bar, the supposed residence of the author of the Chronicle of the Priest of Dioclea (q.v.), within the territory of later-named Zeta or Crna Gora. Other authors point to Drač in Albania. Constantine Porphyrogenitus (q.v.) wrongly connected Dioclea with the name of Emperor Diocletian.

DOBROBIT. Organization of volunteers in Zagreb (q.v.) that provides psychological counselling to war victims as well as training for community and civic leaders to cope with the needs of the traumatized and to better integrate them into society. It maintains hotlines and guidance centers, organizes self-help groups and publishes pamphlets to reach those in need of psychological assistance. Dobrobit seeks to raise public awareness of the problems confronting war victims.

DOMAGOJ see TRPIMIR DYNASTY

DORA FOUNDATION. This foundation in Zagreb (q.v.) arranges sponsorships of refugee children. It also provides scholarships for refugee students and war victims and arranges exchanges that allow refugee students to travel to the United States or Western Europe to continue their studies.

DRAKULIĆ, SLAVENKA (1949-). Born in Sovinjak (Istria). Journalist and writer of novels. Participated in the feminist movement and criticized communist conditioning of everyday life *(How We Survived Communism)*. Under the Tuđman (q.v.) regime, she is critical of short-sighted nationalism *(Balkan Express)* and as such in the press is sometimes considered a persona non grata. She was forced to give up her cooperation with the Croatian weekly *Danas* (q.v.). Drakulić writes fiction in Serbo-Croatian and non-fiction in English. Her articles appeared in *The Nation, New Republic, The New Statesman* and *The Guardian*. She is a member of the American Pen Club.

DRAŠKOVIĆ, JANKO (1770-1856). Count Janko's "Dissertation" of 1832 gave a national political program to the Croats. He defended the union of all Croatian lands with an official national language and governed by the Ban (q.v.). In its early manifestation, this form of Illyrianism (q.v.) accepted the incorporation of the Croatian state into the federated Habsburg monarchy.

DRUŠTVO HRVATSKIH KNJIŽEVNIKA (DHK) see CROATIAN WRITERS' ASSOCIATION

DRUŽBA BRAĆA HRVATSKOGA ZMAJA see SOCIETY OF THE BROTHERS OF THE CROATIAN DRAGON

DRŽIĆ, MARIN (1508-1567). Renaissance writer from Dubrovnik (q.v.). In 1538 the Dubrovnik Senate awarded him a stipend that enabled him to travel to Sienna in Italy. He produced pastoral plays in verse (*Tirena,* 1548; *Venera i Adon*, 1550), where stylized shepherds and mythological characters such as Adonis and Cupid mixed with real Dalmatian peasants. He also wrote well-known comedies in prose such as *Dunde Maroje* (Uncle Maroje). Critics maintain that his comedies have never been equalled in Croatian literature. He has been compared to Molière. Držić's comedy *Skup* is based on Plautus's *Aulularia,* as was Molière's *L'Avare*.

DRZISLAV, STIPAN see TRPIMIR DYNASTY

DUBROVNIK. According to legend and early chroniclers, Dubrovnik was founded by refugees from the Roman city of Epidaurum, in present-day Cavtat (q.v.). Avars (q.v.) and Slavs destroyed this city in the seventh century. Dubrovnik was a small rocky island, separated from the mainland by a narrow channel. The island was called Laus, which means rock in Greek. The name was transformed later into Ragusa. The Slav name, Dubrovnik, refers to an oak forest - *dubrava*. In his book of 949, the Byzantine Emperor Constantine Porphyrogenitus (q.v.) mentions the migration of the people from Epidaurum to Laus.

Among the numerous monuments in the splendid city, outstanding is the Dominican Monastery with a beautifully sculptured atrium. The monastery was built in 1301 in the extreme eastern section of the old town.

Resisting many intruders, through force and diplomacy the city built on a long tradition of liberty and independence. Though the old town received the status of a UNESCO-protected heritage, it was shelled during the war at the end of 1992.

DUGI OTOK. The Long Island is 44 km long and lies just off Zadar (q.v.). It was already occupied by prehistoric humans. Illyrians (q.v.) and Romans settled on the island, followed by Slavs. From the tenth century, it belonged to religious groups in

Zadar. It was first recorded under the name of Pizuh and later it was called Insula Tilaga.

DUKLJA see DIOCLEA

- E -

EAST SLAVONIA. Eastern part of Slavonia (q.v.) whose main towns are Osijek and Vukovar (qq.v.). The larger part of the territory was conquered by the Serbs during the Serbo-Croat war of 1991 and became the Sector East under the control of UNPROFOR (q.v.).

ECONOMIC AND SOCIAL COUNCIL/GOSPODARSKO-SOCIJALNO VIJEĆE. A tripartite advisory organ that can be consulted by the government in the case of conflict between the parties concerned. Officially, the President of the Croatian Chamber of Commerce (q.v.), the representatives of the three largest trade unions and the authorities take part in these trilateral consultations on economic and social problems. It is the official policy of the government to reach consensus in the Council before drafts and proposals are presented to Parliament (q.v.).

ECONOMIC FACULTY OF ZAGREB. The Economic Faculty of Zagreb University (q.v.) is the oldest and now also greatest higher institution in the economic field in the Republic of Croatia.

The beginning of economic studies in Zagreb is related to the operation of the Technical High School founded on December 18, 1918. A course in economics was introduced in the school year 1919/20. The next year a decree founded the High School for Trade. In 1925, this High School began to work within the University structures. In 1947, it was officially transformed into the Economic Faculty of Zagreb University. In 1965, the uniform curriculum was diversified and specializations in economic sectors were introduced. The Zagreb Economic Faculty founded similar institutions in Split and Dubrovnik (qq.v.), and helped with the introduction of economic studies in Rijeka, Osijek and Varaždin (qq.v.).

In the academic year 1961/62, the Zagreb Faculty for the first time organized a cycle of postgraduate studies. Since then, this initiative has spread to all sectors of economic science. The Economic Faculty now counts 5,000 regular students, 400 postgraduate students and more than 100 researchers and scientists.

ECONOMIC INSTITUTE OF ZAGREB. The Economic Institute of Zagreb, founded in 1939, was the first of its kind in the southern part of Europe. According to a long tradition, the Institute developed its research along different lines of economics. At present, the fields of interest include macro-economic theory and policy, labor economics, monetary economics, public finance, international economics, regional economics and business economics.

ECONOMY see AGRICULTURE; CONSTRUCTION; GROSS NATIONAL PRODUCT; INDUSTRIAL PRODUCTION; INDUSTRY; LABOR MARKET; MONETARY POLICY; PRIVATIZATION; PUBLIC FINANCE; TAX SYSTEM; WAR DAMAGE

EDUCATION. Croatian education has mythical and religious origins. The Byzantine chronicler Emperor Constantine Porphyrogenitus (q.v.) wrote that the first Croatian school had been founded by Buga, one of the seven legendary brothers and sisters who led the Croats to their present homeland.

In 925, the Synod of Split suggested that parents should educate their sons for the priesthood. The first Croatian schools were closely associated with the monasteries, especially the Benedictine ones. Originally, these schools used Latin, but later on the Croatian language and the Glagolitic (q.v.) alphabet were introduced. The Glagolitic script was then retained for many years. The first elementary reader printed in Venice used this alphabet.

The Paulist order founded the first Croatian university. It functioned until Joseph II banned the order from Croatia in 1786. Four universities (Zagreb, Split, Osijek and Rijeka) are now in operation, containing 52 faculties for about 60,000 students. Seven hundred more students study at three Art Academies and 1,500 attend three High Schools. Two hundred secondary schools organize the instruction of 200,000 students and half a million pupils are educated in elementary schools.

The new regime announced major reforms in the schooling system. So far, other priorities kept government and Parliament from the necessary legislative work in this field. This will involve a deideologization of the school programs, the reintegration of the gymnasia, the reintroduction of religious education, and the shortening of the eight year cycle of elementary education to six.

The practical functioning of the school system was greatly disturbed by the war circumstances. Schools were destroyed, pupils, students and teachers emigrated from risky areas and instruction periods were sometimes radically shortened. Many refugee children displayed strong emotional and concentration problems, interfering with the normal educational process. (See also ZAGREB UNIVERSITY)

EKAVIAN. Variant of the Serbo-Croatian language in opposition to the i- and ijekavian (qq.v.) variants. Ekavian is the eastern variant of Serbo-Croatian usually spoken in Serbia and in some parts of Bosnia.

ELECTIONS. The first freely elected Croatian Sabor (q.v.) of the post-communist period was installed in May 1990. It was still organized according to the old socialist Constitution (q.v.). The Parliament (q.v.) had a complex tricameral structure. The election law operated on the principle of a two-ballot absolute majority and produced a significant disproportion between electoral results and party representation. So, in the elections of May 1990, the Croatian Democratic Union (HDZ) (q.v.) won 205 seats out of 349. With 42 percent of the votes, it was awarded 58 percent of the seats. The reformed communists running under the name of Social Democratic Party of Croatia (SDPH-SDP) (q.v.) came out of the elections as the largest opposition force. Dr. Žarko Domljan of the HDZ became President of the Parliament.

The Constitution (q.v.) adopted in December 1990 established a bicameral parliamentary structure. The main legislative chamber is the House of Representatives (Zastupnički Dom). The second chamber is the House of Counties (Županijski Dom) and is meant to express regional interests. This House can veto a law voted by the House of Representatives. If the motivation of the veto is accepted by the House of Representatives, the legislative procedure has to be started again from the beginning. The new electoral law, adopted in April 1992, provided for a combination of majority and proportional representation in the House of Representatives and majority representation in the House of Counties. The law reserves four seats in the House of Representatives for small minorities and provides for proportional representation of the Serbian minority.

The elections for the First Chamber were held on August 2, 1992, and the ruling Croatian Democratic Union confirmed its position with 43 percent of the votes. The Croatian Social-Liberal Party (HSLS) (q.v.) became its greatest challenger with 17.3 percent of the votes. The other opposition parties that exceeded the 3 percent threshold of votes needed to be represented in the national parliament lagged far behind: HSP (6.9 percent), HNS (6.5 percent), SDPH-SDP (5.4 percent) and IDS (3.1 percent). The members of the House of Counties could only be elected in a second round on February 7, 1993, as the First Chamber had to pass first the law on the new counties. Of the 54 registered parties in Croatia, 26 took part in this election. Beside the government party HDZ and the national opposition party, the Croatian Social-Liberal Party (q.v.), the regional Istrian Democratic Parliament (q.v.) obtained a remarkable success. Some minor doubt was cast on the results and democratic significance of the elections; the control commission was not constituted on the principle of multiparty representation.

EMIGRATION. The movement of Croats going abroad has always been considerable. Already in the Middle Ages, the permanent war with the Ottomans caused regular waves of migration. In our century, political emigration prevailed at the end of and immediately after the Second World War. Economic motives became more important in the 1960s and 1970s. However, during the whole period from 1940 to 1981, the numbers of persons emigrating remained more or less the same.

Period	Emigrants
1940-1948	192,000
1948-1953	68,000
1953-1961	124,000
1961-1971	63,000
1971-1981	100,000

In the last years of the communist regime, the Croatian emigration living abroad has stimulated the change of regime through large financial contributions to opposition parties and political lobbying for independence. After the fall of the old regime, many intellectuals and businesspeople returned to their home country. Funds from abroad are now used to solve the refugee problem and to support Croats in Bosnia.

EMPLOYMENT REGULATIONS. Labor regulations are stipulated by the Employment Act. The contract that employees make with an employer may not violate the collective agreement, which regulates the basic rights and obligations of employees and employers. Collective agreements are made between the authorized labor unions and chambers of commerce or with government institutions, depending upon the field of activity. The basic regulations that must be adhered to include a 42-hour work week, the opportunity for overtime work, a half-hour daily break, a minimum of 18 days paid vacation and the minimum wages.

ENERGY POLICY. The energy policy, essential to achieving the planned economic development of Croatia, is being implemented by two public enterprises, Hrvatska Elektroprivreda (Croatian Electric Power Supply) and INA-Industrija Nafte (INA-Petroleum). Of the total energy consumed, approximately 47 percent is from petroleum and petroleum derivatives, 22 percent from gas, 13 percent from hydro-energy, 7.5 percent from coal, 5.5 percent from nuclear energy with other sources accounting for 5 percent. Croatia imports 40 percent of the energy it requires.

The basic energy development policy is based upon supplying the necessary energy through the application of modern technical methods, taking into account the economy and ecology. Therefore, it is planned that by the year 2010 an extensive gas pipeline system will be completed, and projects are underway for the construction of several small hydroelectric plants.

EPIDAURUM see CAVTAT

ERDUTSKI SPORAZUM. Agreement concluded in the little town of Erdut on July 31, 1993, between the Krajina (q.v.) Serbs and the Croat authorities. The town lies east of Osijek (q.v.) near the frontier with the Vojvodina (a Serbian Autonomous Province) and is now occupied by the Serbs. (See also VOLLEBAEK, KNUT)

EUROPEAN COMMUNITY (RELATIONS WITH). Croatia enjoys trade facilities with European countries on the basis of an Agreement on Trade and Cooperation. In July 1993, the EC threatened to withdraw these prerogatives as a sanction against the Croatian policy towards Bosnia-Hercegovina. Thanks to the intervention of German Foreign Minister Klaus Kinkel, the EC Ministers of Foreign Affairs took no other measures than sending their President on a goodwill mission. The Croatian representatives at the EC argued that Croatia was already living under quiet sanctions before, as it was not allowed to take part in the PHARE program (q.v.). (See also COUNCIL OF EUROPE)

- F -

FERAL TRIBUNE. Satiric annex of the newspaper *Slobodna Dalmacija* (q.v.) and independent fortnightly after the privatization of the journal. *Feral Tribune* attracted much public attention through its harsh political satire. The paper published cartoons in which Tuđman (q.v.) has been compared with Milošević or identified with Stalin and Hitler. This latter cartoon could have insulted President Tuđman and led to prosecution based on articles 76 and 81 of the criminal code. A press conference of the Croatian Democratic Union (q.v.) was immediately followed by steps taken by the public prosecutor. This again raised the question of freedom of the press (q.v.), as in similar cases of Tanja Torbarina, Jelena Lovrić and Ivan Zvonimir Čičak (qq.v.).

FERDINAND, KING (1503-1564). Habsburg King of Bohemia who claimed the Hungarian throne after the death of King Louis II in the battle of Mohacs. The Croatian Sabor (q.v.) convened at the end of December 1526 in the Franciscan monastery in Cetin and agreed to elect Ferdinand King of Croatia on condition that he should provide military protection against the Turks. In a later session, the Sabor expressed the wish that the Kingdom of Croatia should be annexed to the Austrian hereditary lands. The Sabor in Slavonia (q.v.) and Hungary backed another candidate to the throne, Janos Zapolyai. This led to a civil war. The Habsburg dynasty continued to rule Croatia until the end of the First World War.

FILM. The first Croatian film was shot in 1919 and dealt with a great historical theme: the peasant uprising of Matija Gubec (q.v.). Another important production was made by Oktavijan Miletić in 1943: a reconstruction of the life of the composer Lisinki.

After the Second World War, the film industry was dominated by Socialist Realism. From this doctrine, the Zagreb School of Animated Film could easily escape and became world famous with films of Dušan Vukotić, Vatroslav Mimica, Joško Marušić and others.

Each year the film festival of Pula shows the new Croatian productions and awards its "Zlatna Arena" (Golden Arena).

FIRST YUGOSLAVIA. The Kingdom of Serbs, Croats and Slovenes under the Karađorđević dynasty (qq.v.) (1918-1941).

FIUME see RIJEKA

FOLK CULTURE. Croatia's natural and geo-political disunity over the centuries has resulted in distinctive ethnographic areas. According to Dr. Ivan Ivančan, there are four characteristic regions in Croatia: the Alpine, Adriatic, Dinaric and Pannonian regions. They show a specific identity and present numerous particularities in folk tradition. For example, folk costumes in the cold Dinaric area are made primarily with wool whereas the costumes in Pannonia (q.v.) make use of flax and hemp.

Folk dances accompanied by traditional instruments and the human voice are likewise differentiated by regional elements. For example, Dinaric music bears eastern influences. Adriatic vocal bands *(klapas)* developed a very special style of multivocal singing.

Some of the folk dances and customs have preserved certain cultural characteristics that reflect their period of origin. Interesting are the Carnival dances that have survived especially on the Adriatic coast. During *Poklade*, called *Mesopust* or *Karneval* in other parts of Croatia, a straw man that is burned at the end of the festivity as a symbol of winter or evil is usually dressed in Turkish clothes and has a dark painted face. Another typical dance is the Moreška, a knights' dance still performed on the island of Korčula. It shows a fight between the White King and the Moors and probably originates in a historic battle with the Saracens, the Arabs who served in the Turkish army. The Sinjska Alka is a game that goes back to 1715 when the Town of Sinj had to be defended against the Turkish invaders. Participants of the game must thrust a spear into a metal ring while riding on a galloping horse.

Sometimes, typical regional dances and ethnic expressions were forbidden by the occupiers. The Istrian Balun dance is a case in point. Sometimes, foreign traditions were introduced. Repressed forms and mixed culture are typical in Međimurje (q.v.).

It is unhappily true that traditional folklore and customs are nowadays rapidly disappearing and revived only for short periods at some special festivities.

FOREIGN DEBT. Though a member of the International Monetary Fund, Croatia cannot get a standby arrangement because of the war. The World Bank also postponed a scheduled loan of $124 million for political reasons. Croatia has no access to the foreign capital market and its external debt level is declining. The difficult economic situation and the lack of access to new capital led to a delay in debt repayment. On May 31, 1993, the Croatian foreign debt amounted to $2.554 billion. Most are long-term loans, $2.455 billion, only $99 million are short-term credits. Half of the debt has to be repaid to private banks ($1.254 billion), one-third to other governments ($738 million), and the remainder to the IMF ($38 million), international financial institutions ($337 million) and other suppliers ($88 million). Bonds matured but not repaid amount to $463 million for capital and $110 million for interest. This is two times as much as at the end of 1991.

Because of the depressed national product, the debt rate amounts to 30 percent, a sign of very high indebtedness. On the other hand, only 7 percent of the current intake of foreign exchange is used for the repayment of debt. Of course, this favorable indicator does not reflect the portion of matured debt that is not repaid.

Another problem not included so far is the inherited debt of the former federation. By the end of 1991, the total external debt of Yugoslavia amounted to $15.9 billion, out of which $15.1 billion were convertible currency debts and $0.8 billion nonconvertible currency debts. The former Yugoslav Federation's share in the total amount of debt was $3.1 billion. What is the share of Croatia? Until now there is no answer to this question. In the framework of the Conference on Former Yugoslavia, the Badinter Arbitration Commission (q.v.) has made proposals to spread the responsibilities over the former Republics of Yugoslavia. The government of New Yugoslavia considers the competence of the Commission to be only advisory and does not seem prepared to accept the proposed division of the former federal debt. The remaining $12.8 billion represent the debt of commercial banks and other entities which are located in specific Republics and can be allocated. The Republic of Croatia is responsible for $2.8 billion. A breakdown according to type of foreign creditor shows the following picture: commercial banks, $0.9 billion; governments, $0.8 billion; international financial institutions, $0.4 billion; other banks and institutions, $0.5 billion; suppliers, $0.2 billion.

FOREIGN INVESTMENT. The legal basis for the activity of companies, including those in which foreign capital is invested, has been established by the Constitution (q.v.) of the Republic of Croatia. As far as foreign investments are concerned the Constitution provides three essential guarantees: a) the rights acquired through the capital investment cannot be restricted either by law or by any other legal act; b) a foreign investor is granted free transfer of the profit; c) a foreign investor is granted free repatriation of the invested capital.

The legal framework for foreign investments in the Republic of Croatia is conceived in a way which provides for at least equal treatment of domestic and foreign investments. Foreign companies have a 50 percent tax reduction on their share of profits in comparison with domestic companies taxed at a rate of 40 percent, profits of foreign investors are only taxed at a rate of 20 percent.

Under the new company law, the ownership rights and the free management of such ownership has been acknowledged anew. While the enterprises in which foreign capital has been invested can be managed exclusively on the basis of the invested capital, excluding any form of self-management, such an attitude still does not apply to the socially-owned companies. Unless the investors agree otherwise, the participation in management is determined by the share of invested capital.

In principle, a domestic firm in which investments were made in foreign currency is not entitled to hold a foreign currency account for operating purposes, except in very special cases, such as funds for the execution of investment works abroad. The agreement on foreign investment must include a clause defining the time and method of conversion of the dinar portion of the profit which belongs to the foreign investor, as well as the exchange rate to be applied to such conversion.

The Ministry of Economy recorded the following flow of foreign investment during the year 1992 in German marks (DM).

Country	Amount (DM)
1. Germany	232,054,993
2. Switzerland	75,948,300
3. Austria	60,391,159
4. Italy	23,631,342
5. United States	12,188,983
6. Canada	8,216,271
7. Great Britain	3,398,326
8. Netherlands	1,450,995
9. France	978,472
10. Australia	152,191
11. Other Countries	9,129,759

As can be seen from the figures, by far the biggest share of foreign investment comes from Germany. Except for Switzerland, Austria and Italy, foreign investment in Croatia is negligible. The same was true in 1991. It has to be kept in mind that some of the foreign investment is made by Croatians abroad. The large Croatian colony in Germany certainly influences the German share.

FOREIGN POLICY. The first and primary goal of Croatia's foreign policy was the recognition of independence (q.v.). Once that goal was reached, the most urgent task was the reintegration of the temporally occupied regions in Croatia. A similar goal was the defense of the Croats in Bosnia and the support of Herceg-Bosna. A further goal was membership of the European Community (q.v.) and integration in the international order. In order to reach these primary goals of foreign policy, international diplomacy was deployed and priorities designed, picking some key alliances (e.g., with Germany [q.v.]) that however could not always be maintained as circumstances, especially in Bosnia-Hercegovina, seemed to oblige Croatia to follow its own course that was not always appreciated abroad.

FRANCE (RELATIONS WITH). France was, along with Great Britain (q.v.), one of the members of the European Community (q.v.) that resisted most strongly the early recognition of the independence (q.v.) of Croatia.

France had been historically a close partner to Serbia and it firmly advocated the preservation of the unity of Yugoslavia.

Ultimately, France put up with the EC decision to recognize the independence of Croatia on January 15, 1993, but this was only after consultation with a commission led by the French judge Badinter (q.v.). At the present time, relations with Croatia can still be characterized as cool and reserved.

This is also reflected in economic relations. In 1992, Croatia's exports to France only amounted to $57.8 million and imports to $71.8 million. This is respectively 1.3 percent and 1.6 percent of the country's total trade, taking the twelfth and eleventh positions in the range of trade partners.

FRANCIS JOSEPH I, EMPEROR (1848-1916). The Austrian Emperor established a strict centralist and absolutist regime. He also wanted to introduce German as the administrative and official language in Croatia. On the other hand, modernization laid the basis for economic development and an elementary school system was established. Under his reign, the Zagreb (q.v.) bishopric became independent from the Hungarian.

In 1859, Austria lost the war against France and Piedmont. The crisis of state finances obliged the Austrian monarch to temper absolutism and to grant concessions to the other regions of the Empire. The Constitution of 1860 recognized Croatian as the official language of Croatia.

FRANK, JOSIP (1844-1911). Inspired by the ideas of Ante Starčević (q.v.), Josip Frank founded the Pure Party of Rights (Čista Stranka Prava). He defended triadism; the Habsburg Monarchy must become a federation of three independent entities of which Croatia is one. He was intransigent towards the Serbs and gathered around his party the supporters of the Croatian national right.

FREE ZONES. The procedure of establishing and operating free zones is governed by the Law on Free Zones, passed on October 6, 1990. A free zone may be established by one or more juridical persons, either foreign or domestic. The user of a free zone may be a domestic or foreign juridical or physical person who has concluded an agreement with the free zone company. No customs or duties have to be paid on items imported into or exported out of the zone. The only charge is the 1 percent customs fee for record keeping. The goods manufactured and processed within the free zone may be distributed to the domestic market outside the free zone, according to the regulations on imports, upon the payment of customs and import duties on raw materials, manufacturing components and parts used in the production process. The user of the zone shall not pay taxes and levies, except for taxes on wages and salaries.

There are several free zones in the Republic of Croatia: Rijeka with the subzone Pula, Zadar, Split with the subzone Smokovik, Ploče with the subzone Metković, Osijek-Airport with the subzone Teina, Varaždin, Zagreb-Jankomir and Zagreb-Airport. Some of the zones are for the time being out of operation due to their location in war zones. (See also CUSTOMS SYSTEM; FOREIGN INVESTMENT; TAX SYSTEM)

FREEDOM OF THE PRESS. Article 36 of the Croatian Constitution (q.v.) guaranties the freedom of expression. This freedom can only be restricted by law in the interest of the security of the Republic and for the sake of the conduct of criminal proceedings. Article 38 states more precisely: "Freedom of expression shall specifically include freedom of the press and other media of communication, freedom of speech and public expression, and free establishment of all institutions of public communication." Censorship shall be forbidden and journalists shall have the right to freedom of reporting and access to information. The freedom of expression of thoughts as specified in Article 38 was in fact restricted for several months during the war, when the regulation on information activities during the war or in the case of imminent danger to the independence and unity of the Republic of Croatia was in force. This regulation aimed at precluding the publication of military information harmful to national security. It was sparingly used, and has known only one case: the confiscation of an issue of the weekly *Slobodni Tjednik*, clearly for publication of unlawfully obtained military information.

Article 23 of the Law on Public Information enacts the establishment of a Committee for the protection of the free press. A delegation of the Council of Europe (q.v.) visiting Croatia to report on this question could only remark that this Committee had not yet been installed. The foreign experts pointed further to the weak economic situation as a major threat to an independent press. In the second half of 1992, the boards of directors of several newspapers including *Vjesnik*, *Novi List* and *Slobodna Dalmacija* (qq.v.) were all replaced by the representatives of the government's Agency for Restructuring and Development (q.v.).

A tendency towards political monolithism endangers the free expression of criticism. At the time of the visit, the chief editor of the journal *Vjesnik* and the General Director of the Croatian Radio and Television were both representatives in Parliament (q.v.). However, Article 16 of the Law on Public Information says that a person enjoying immunity cannot be the main editor of a media organ. (See also PRESS)

FUND FOR PRIVATIZATION. This institution took over the functions of the Agency for Restructuring and Development (q.v.). The Fund is responsible for privatization operations, performing evaluation, revaluing, liquidation and other technical services.

- G -

GAJ, LJUDEVIT (1809-1872). Father of the Croatian National Revival and founder of the Illyrian movement (q.v.). In 1835, Gaj started publication of the periodical *Danica* (Morning Star). He was also a reformer of Croatian orthography. Gaj's new alphabet introduced diacritical marks to replace combinations of letters that had been used before: for example, he proposed to write č instead of ch.

GALBRAITH, PETER. First Ambassador of the United States to the Independent Republic of Croatia. He is known to show a highly benevolent attitude towards the new state.

GARIBALDI UNIT. Paramilitary formation of Italian volunteers deployed in the Velebit mountains north of Zadar (q.v.) by the Serb commander Captain Dragan. The Press Bureau Tanjug reported that numerous reconnaissance and sabotage actions behind the

Croatian enemy lines had been performed by this unit. Some of the participants believed that the territories that once belonged to Italy ought to be handed back to Italy. The unit tended to recruit among the descendants of Italian emigration circles who had left Istria (q.v.) between 1946 and 1954 and who were dissatisfied with the Osimo Agreement (q.v.).

GENERAL AGREEMENT ON TARIFFS AND TRADE (GATT). In November 1993, GATT accepted a proposal to start a working group that would examine the conditions for full membership of Croatia. Until then Croatia has the status of observer member. Admission to GATT could be the start of the full integration of Croatia in the international financial community. It would open the door to cooperation with the International Monetary Fund and World Bank.

GENEVA (DECLARATION OF). This document was signed on November 9, 1918, by the Yugoslav Committee and the National Council of Slovenes, Croats and Serbs (qq.v.) on the one hand and the delegates of the Kingdom of Serbia on the other. Both parties agreed to create a democratic federation, where the two sides should maintain their independence and form a common government on a parity base. Shortly after the signing, their home bases rejected the agreement. The National Council argued that its representatives had negotiated beyond their authority and the Serbian monarchy and political parties found their interests neglected.

GEOGRAPHIC REGIONS. There are three major geographic regions in Croatia.

1. The Pannonian (q.v.) and peri-Pannonian region. It enjoys a moderate continental climate and is crossed by the three major Croatian rivers: the Sava, Drava and Danube. It is the granary of Croatia, abounding in arable land and forests. Moreover, it contains oil and natural gas deposits, non-metals, thermal mineral springs and hydro-energy potential. Extensive parts of East and West Slavonia (q.v.) are now occupied by the Serbs and under UNPROFOR (q.v.) control.

2. The central mountain belt. It consist of the karst plateaus of Lika, Krbava and Gorski Kotar. It abounds in forests, grazing land, karst and water supplies.

3. The Adriatic coast with islands and hinterland. It has a Mediterranean climate and favors the tourism, shipbuilding and maritime sectors of the economy.

GERMANY (RELATIONS WITH). Germany has always been a supporter of the independence of Croatia. The country pushed the decisions of the European Community (q.v.) in this direction and even threatened to recognize the country unilaterally. It ultimately preceded the common EC decision to recognize the Republic on January 15, 1992.

Also on later occasions, Germany continued to defend Croatia in the European Community. When the British Minister of Foreign Affairs Douglas Hurd criticized the Croats because of their policy toward Bosnia-Hercegovina, Minister Klaus Kinkel took the defense of Croatia.

Mutual trade reflects the friendly relations between the two countries. In 1992, Croatia's exports to Germany amounted to $773.3 million and imports to $767.6 million, respectively 16.8 percent and 17.2 percent, the third and second positions in the range of trade partners.

GLAGOLITIC. The oldest Slavic alphabet. The name is derived from the verb *glagoljati* (to talk) and the word *glagoljaši* (the talkers), the priests who propagate the word. Cyrillus (q.v.) used the Glagolitic alphabet in his Christianization efforts. The so-called Cyrillic alphabet (q.v.) was only created by his followers. The Glagolitic alphabet is alternatively thought to be derived from a Latin, Frankish or Celtic model.

The first longer document in Croatian Glagolitic preserved until today is the *Baška Tablet* (Baščanska Ploča). It was written around 1100. It records the donation of a site by King Zvonimir to the Benedictine convent on the island of Krk (q.v.). The oldest Croatian Glagolitic manuscript is the *Glagolita Clozianus* originating from the eleventh century. It consists of fragments of a collection of sermons belonging to the Frankopan Dukes of the same island.

Specialists differentiate between the earlier tradition of "round" Glagolitic and the "angular" Glagolitic of the thirteenth century and later.

GLAS ISTRE. The Voice of Istria is a regional and independent newspaper edited in Pula. It is known for its critical stance on the central government.

GLAS KONCILA. The largest religious weekly in Croatia edited by the Catholic Church (q.v.). The publication also appeared under the communist regime. Its editor, the priest Živko Kustić, came under strong attack during the repression of the Croatian Spring (q.v.). In 1993, the 1,000th issue of *Glas Koncila* (The Voice of the Council) was published.

GLAS SLAVONIJE. The Voice of Slavonia. Regional and independent newspaper edited in Osijek (q.v.).

GOLDEN BULL. In 1242, the Hungarian King Bela IV granted Zagreb (q.v.), built on the hill of Gradec, the privileges of a free town. The *Zlatna Bula* (Golden Bull) sums up the rights and obligations in twelve articles.

1. When thieves or criminals rob the citizens in the territory of Hungary, Dalmatia (q.v.), Croatia or Slavonia (q.v.), the owner of the land on which they were robbed has to hand over the criminals or to compensate for what has been stolen, after it has been valued by wise people appointed by oath by their fellow citizens.

2. The citizens of the free town do not have to pay taxes anywhere in the kingdom.

Articles 3-6 fix penalties and punishment in case of offense and calumny, inflicting bodily harm, murder, theft between the citizens and from strangers and describe the way to proceed in crimes concerning money and violence.

7. The citizens freely choose the town judges and present them to us for confirmation. They can change them each year.

8. A citizen without natural heirs can freely grant his personal property to whomever he wishes; the immovables such as houses, building grounds, vineyards, agricultural land and service

buildings will be granted after consultation with his fellow citizens to his wife or relatives, but they cannot be taken beyond the competence of the town court, neither by him, nor by his wife or relatives. When a citizen dies without a will, and there is no wife or relatives, two-thirds of his possessions will be given to the poor and the town church by the wise men appointed by the council of citizens and one-third will be reserved for the town.

9. We stipulate that two days in the week, on Monday and Thursday, a festive market and each other day a normal market will be held.

10. The citizenry of the town has the following obligations: when the Hungarian wants to go to war in the Primorska region, in Koruško or in Austria, the citizens have to send 10 well-armored soldiers. Moreover, when the King has to go there, they have to grant the King for provision: 12 oxen, 1,000 breads and 4 barrels of wine. The Duke of Slavonia, if he is a relative of the King, has to be given half of these. And the Ban (q.v.), if he is in function - and not the Sub-Ban - has to be given 1 ox, 100 breads and 1 barrel, and this only once during his service. But all these obligations are not due in the following five years.

11. The citizens consented out of their free will to fortify Gradec with a big wall at their cost.

12. For the maintenance of the citizens living on the hill of Gradec, we have given the surrounding lands to them by decree of our loved and loyal Dionysius, Ban of All Slavonia....

We have confirmed this bull with our golden seal.

Done at Virovitica by the hand of Magistrate Benedict.

GOLDSTEIN, SLAVKO (1928-). Publisher and writer. Director of Liber University Press (1970-1983) and advisor of Cankar Publishing Press (1983-1992). Chairman of the Zagreb Jewish Association. President of the Croatian Social-Liberal Party (q.v.) (1989-1990). In the autumn of 1993, with five other Croatian intellectuals he wrote an open letter to President Tuđman (q.v.). They criticized his policy and asked him to resign.

GOSPIĆ OFFENSIVE. The second larger-scale offensive of the Croatian army in September 1993 on the Knin (q.v.) region. The Maslenica (q.v.) offensive of January 1993 was the first larger offensive of the Croatian army. Its aim was to restore order in the pink zone (q.v.) associated to the southern Knin region and to reassure regular communication lines between Dalmatia (q.v.) and Croatia. The United Nations Protected Areas (q.v.) and pink zones had been created after the six-month war in 1991 between the Krajina (q.v.) Serbs and Zagreb. The continuous shelling of the Maslenica and Gospić regions provoked a new Croatian offensive. However, critics noticed that reasons of domestic political strategy were not wholly absent in the timing of the new offensives. The Maslenica offensive set in shortly before parliamentary elections, while the Gospić offensive preceded an important internal Croatian Democratic Union (q.v.) party meeting.

The second offensive started on September 9, 1993, with an attack on the Medak region south of Gospić. The Croatian forces took three villages, Ćitluk, Divo Selo and Njegovina, in the pink zone of the UNPROFOR (q.v.) Sector South. The Krajina Serbs replied by shelling Karlovac (q.v.). A UN mediation campaign was set up and Stoltenberg summoned Tuđman (q.v.) to stop the offensive without delay. The fighting went on and the Krajina Serbs shelled Lučko (a suburb lying only eight km from Zagreb [q.v.]), Jastrebarsko, Samobor, Kutina and other places. The Krajina Serbs made public a list with 50 military targets, among them seven locations in Zagreb. The same day Tuđman announced a 24-hour armistice. On September 14, the Serbs shot down a Croatian Mig-21 which had attacked the region of Vrginmost. The next day, the contending parties signed an armistice under UN mediation. The Croatian army was to retreat from the villages conquered near Gospić and the zone come under the control of UNPROFOR. The shelling continued. According to the Krajina Press Agency (denied by the Croats), the Croatian army shelled Knin, the capital of Krajina, in the evening of September 16, 1993. As revenge, the Krajina Serbs shelled Zadar (q.v.), Šibenik and Biograd (q.v.). On September 18, 1993, UNPROFOR officers reported on destruction and deliberate killing during the Croatian retreat from the conquered villages. In the next days, the Croatian army even shot at Blue Helmets who evacuated victims from the Medak region. UNPROFOR Commander Jean Cot handed a protest note to the Croatian government. The Croats denied most of the facts and some of the arguments were accepted by UNPROFOR.

In the end, the armed conflict was extinguished slowly. Once more, the conflict did not degenerate into a generalized war between Serbia and Croatia. However, what was threatening was the fact that in this clash both parties used new weapons. The Serbs fired a Frog-7 surface-to-surface missile, and the Croats sent in Migs to attack the Serbian positions.

GOSPODARSKO-SOCIJALNO VIJEĆE see ECONOMIC AND SOCIAL COUNCIL

GOTOVAC, VLADO (1930-). Intellectual and writer. During the Croatian Spring (q.v.), he was editor of *Hrvatski Tjednik*, the influential weekly of the Matica hrvatska (q.v.). He was sentenced on the charge of being a "nationalist and separatist" and jailed from 1971 to 1974. Because of persistent contacts with Western emigrant circles and interviews with Western reporters, Gotovac was sentenced again on June 5, 1981, and given two years of prison and four years of denial of the right to public activity or publication.

During the Tuđman (q.v.) regime, he was elected a member of the House of Representatives for the Croatian Social-Liberal Party (q.v.). In the autumn of 1993, with five other Croatian intellectuals he wrote an open letter to President Tuđman. They criticized his policy and asked him to resign.

GOVERNMENT OF NATIONAL UNION. The government of national union was a coalition arranged on August 3, 1991, by the leading party, Croatian Democratic Union (HDZ) (q.v.), and led by Prime Minister Franjo Gregurić (q.v.). He was former Deputy Prime Minister in the HDZ government of Josip Manolić (q.v.). A coalition of nine parties was felt necessary to successfully cope with the circumstances of war and to secure the international status of Croatia. The government had 29 members, divided over three blocs. The leading party, HDZ, reserved for itself 12 seats giving access to important portfolios such as defense, reconstruction, health, labor, trade, agriculture and tourism. Independent technicians had been attracted to manage the departments of finance, culture, foreign affairs, traffic and information. Nine places were taken by the opposition parties. They got the posts of

Deputy Minister, Minister of Justice, Minister of Engineering and Minister of Industry and Energy.

Coalition partners fell away one by one in the course of the governing period. Difficulties with the Croatian Peasant Party (HSS) (q.v.) manifested themselves from the very beginning: the party already stepped out during the discussions on the formation of the Government of National Union. The next to leave was Vladimir Veselica, Minister for the Croatian Democratic Party (HDS) (q.v.). Rivalry in his party, especially between Vladimir and Marko Veselica (q.v.), contributed to his resignation. Dražen Budiša of the Croatian Social-Liberal Party (HSLS) (qq.v.) left the coalition because he could not take responsibility for decisions he had not participated in. His party declared the government had taken for granted too many presidential decisions. This is a real constitutional problem that threatens the quality of the democratic regime in Croatia. In view of the new elections, the government was finally reduced to three partners.

According to the Prime Minister, two main goals of the government coalition had nonetheless been reached: the official recognition of Croatia and the acceptance of its membership by the United Nations. The tasks still to be accomplished included the liberation of all territories within the internationally recognized frontiers, the return of all refugees to their homes, the reconstruction of the country, the transformation of socially-owned into private enterprises and the continuation of the democratization process.

GOVERNMENTS. Until the end of 1993, Croatia had consumed five governments that were led by Prime Ministers Stipe Mesić, Josip Manolić, Franjo Gregurić, Hrvoje Šarinić and Nikica Valentić (qq.v.).

GRAĐANSKA INICIJATIVA ZA SLOBODU JAVNE RIJEČI see CIVIC INITIATIVE FOR THE FREEDOM OF EXPRESSION

GREAT BRITAIN (RELATIONS WITH). Great Britain was, with France (q.v.), one of the members of the European Community (q.v.) that resisted early recognition of Croatia. It ultimately ratified the common decision of the European Community to recognize the Republic on January 15, 1992.

Even thereafter, relations with Croatia were far from smooth. Minister of Foreign Affairs Douglas Hurd threatened the Croats with sanctions just before the meeting of Ministers of Foreign Affairs of the European Community on July 17, 1993. Especially the attitude of Croatia towards Bosnia-Hercegovina was under attack. However, concrete measures at the meeting were discarded under the influence of the German Foreign Minister Klaus Kinkel who argued it was still too early for sanctions against Croatia.

Trade figures reflect the low profile relations. In 1992, Croatia's exports to Great Britain amounted to only $56.2 million, its imports to $64.5 million, respectively 1.2 percent and 1.5 percent, the thirteenth position in the range of trade partners.

GREGURIĆ, FRANJO (1939-). General Manager of INA, the largest Croatian petroleum company. Member of the House of Representatives for the Croatian Democratic Union (q.v.). He was Deputy Prime Minister in the government of Josip Manolić (q.v.). He became Prime Minister of the Government of National Union (q.v.), the coalition of nine political parties formed on August 3, 1991.

GRGUR NINSKI. Gregory of Nin was the most fervent defender of the movement for a national Croatian church using the Glagolitic (q.v.) language. He clashed with the Latin clergy of the church of Split (q.v.).

A Synod was called in Split in 925. Its resolutions were catastrophic for Gregory of Nin and his national Croatian church. It was first decided that the Croatian territory should again come under the jurisdiction of Split. The Apostle Peter himself had sent the saint Dujam to Salona and his relics were now held in Split. This gave the church of Split the title and authority of an archbishopric. The old church organization would be reintroduced and Nin suppressed. Moreover, preaching in Slavic language was forbidden, nor could new Glagolitic priests be consecrated. Even King Tomislav (q.v.), who supported the national church and Gregory of Nin, was threatened. His church would be banned.

Surprisingly, Pope John X did not give his consent to the resolutions of the Synod. The position of Gregory of Nin within Croatia was very strong and the Pope feared the negative consequences of a radical intervention. Moreover, under the threat of the Bulgars, Tomislav could seek an alliance with the Byzantines. But the Pope was successful in persuading the Emperor of the Bulgars to stop the war with Tomislav, and the Croatian King seems to have lost his independence. He withdrew his support of Gregory of Nin at a new Synod in Split in 928. All earlier measures against Nin and his national church were repeated. The use of the Glagolitic alphabet and Slavic language during church services was vigorously condemned. This time the Pope confirmed the decisions of the Synod. Gregory was summoned to obey the new hierarchy and disappeared from history.

The Glagolitic movement reappeared more than a century later as strong as ever. The Third Synod of Split had to be called in 1060. Especially directed against the popular Croatian clergy, a resolution said that priests with long hair and beards were forbidden entry into the church. Furthermore, the holy mass had to be celebrated in Latin or Greek. The Glagolitic alphabet introduced by Methodius (q.v.) was heretical and erroneous. The decisions of the Synod were imposed by force and led to a popular revolt during the reign of Petar Krešimir (q.v.).

GRIMANI. He formed with Mocenigo in 1817 the delegation of Venice, which concluded an agreement with Turkey. It stipulated that Venetian authority in Dalmatia (q.v.) should be extended inland. Since then, the borderline between Bosnia-Hercegovina and Croatia did not change any more on that portion.

GRLIĆ, DANKO (?-1986). Philosophy Professor of the University of Zagreb (q.v.). Member of the *Praxis* (q.v.) group. He was especially interested in the philosophy of aesthetics.

GROBNIČKO POLJE. The field of tombs is the place where in 1242 the Mongol invaders were defeated by the Croats. Croat intellectuals (e.g., Frano Supilo) held that here Western civilization was saved, as it would be a second time more than two centuries later by the Croatian battles against the Ottoman invader. (See also MONGOL INVASION)

GROSS NATIONAL PRODUCT. In 1990, the share of industry was approximately 40 percent, trade 16 percent, transport and communications 14 percent, agriculture 13 percent, building 7 percent, catering and tourism 5 percent. In the generation of national product, the socially-owned sector still participated in 1990 with 87 percent. (See also AGRICULTURE; INDUSTRY; TRADE)

GUBEC, MATIJA (?-1573). Leader of the Seljačka Buna or peasant uprising of 1573. On January 28, the peasants of the region of Stubica and Susjegrada organized a massive rebellion against their feudal lords. The peasants wanted to free themselves of taxes and obligations and planned to establish an independent peasant republic with Matija Gubec as their king. The rebellion spread over greater parts of the territory of Croatia and Slovenia. The domains of about 100 noblemen in 1,200 villages were affected. The peasant army grew to more than 15,000 men. On February 5, the army of the feudal lords crushed the peasant army. Matija Gubec was executed in Zagreb (q.v.) on February 15, 1573, wearing a crown of iron.

The Battle of Donja Stubica has been immortalized in 1939 by the painter Krsto Hegedušić (q.v.).

GUNDULIĆ, IVAN (1589-1638). Most famous Baroque writer of Dubrovnik (q.v.). He lived in the period of the Jesuit-led Counter Reformation. The theme of repentance was then fashionable in literature, as the title of one of his works testifies: Tears of the Prodigal Son (*Suze sina razmetnoga,* 1622). The drama *Dubravka* tells the story of his city. It is a hymn to the freedom of Dubrovnik.

Perhaps his greatest work is the epic poem *Osman* (1628). It describes the fierce battle of the Slavs against the Turks. The book was edited as a classic by the Matica hrvatska (q.v.), the nineteenth-century cultural institution of the Croatian romantic and nationalistic movement. Missing fragments were completed by Ban Ivan Mažuranić (q.v.).

GVOZD MOUNTAINS see PETROVA GORA

- H -

HADŽIĆ, GORAN. Serb leader of East Slavonia (q.v.). He was born in Pačetin near Vinkovci (q.v.). He became President of the Serbian Republic of Krajina (q.v.). He organized the referendum on the union of the Republic of Krajina with the Serbian Republic in Bosnia. He was accused by the Croatian authorities of subversion and conspiracy against the territorial integrity and security of the Croatian state. This did not prevent him from negotiating with the Croatian authorities in Geneva, though he once walked out when he was not treated with the honors reserved for the president of an officially recognized state. He was supported by Milošević against other Krajina leaders because he was inclined to accept the Vance-Owen plan (q.v.) for Bosnia-Hercegovina. At the beginning of September 1993, he declared in an interview with the Belgrade newspaper *Borba* that the Serbs in Croatia could no longer accept a confederation with Croatia, even if the constitution was changed and the Serbs were declared a constituent people of the Croatian nation. After the Croatian Gospić offensive (q.v.) in September 1993, the Serbian Democratic Party (SDS) of Knin (qq.v.) accused Hadžić of incompetence and demanded his dismissal. Nevertheless, he took part on behalf of the Krajina in the secret negotiations with Zagreb in Oslo at the beginning of November 1993.

HALLSTATT CULTURE. Early iron age culture. Characteristic for this period are the extensive remains of iron swords. They have been encountered massively in the Croatian soil.

HANŽEKOVIĆ, MARIJAN (1915-1993). Born at Požega. He worked at the Ministry of Foreign Affairs of the Kingdom of Yugoslavia from 1938 to 1941. As a member of the Croatian Peasant Party (q.v.), he was arrested and deported to the Jasenovac and Lepoglava concentration camps. When he left in 1943, he joined the partisans in the region of Moslavina. After the war, he worked in the Ministry of Finance and the Central Bank. In 1965, he became professor at the Economic Faculty (q.v.) of the University of Zagreb. He was a member of the Lexicographical Institute, the Economic Institute (q.v.) and the Institute for Public Finances in Zagreb (q.v.). He was the first

Minister of Finance in the Independent Republic of Croatia during the period 1990-1991 and a member of the Board of the Croatian National Bank (q.v.).

HEBRANG, ANDRIJA (1899-1949). Revolutionary among Tito's (q.v.) partisans. He was Secretary of the Communist Party of Croatia. At the end of the war, he had been accused of being a Croatian nationalist and was removed as Party Secretary. Nonetheless, after the war, he was appointed Minister of Industry and Chairman of the Economic Council and the Planning Commission. He opposed the proposal to forge industrialization with five-year plans on the Soviet model as long as the agricultural problem had not been solved. With the exception of Žujović (q.v.), he got no support in the government and he was succeeded by Boris Kidrić. In May 1948, Andrija Hebrang was accused of choosing the side of Stalin in the Cominform conflict (q.v.). He was arrested and died in prison under suspicious circumstances.

HEDERVARY see KHUEN-HEDERVARY, KAROLY

HEGEDUŠIĆ, KRSTO (1901-1975). Born in Petrinja. Painter and member of the Zemlja group (q.v.). He found his inspiration in the reality of the Pannonian (q.v.) villages. His collection of drawings entitled *Podravski Motivi* (Motives of Podravina), edited with a foreword of Miroslav Krleža (q.v.), shocked leading circles with its harsh vision of life in the villages. Krsto Hegedušić also showed his social commitment by painting in 1939 the peasant Battle of Donja Stubica (see GUBEC, MATIJA).

Hegedušić was the teacher of Ivan Generalić (q.v.) and adopted the typical "primitive" style of the Hlebina School (q.v.).

HEKTOROVIĆ, PETAR (1487-1572). Poet and landowner on the island of Hvar (q.v.). He recorded the folk songs sung by the fishermen in his play *Ribarje i ribarsko prigovaranje* (Fishing and Fishermen's Talk, 1568). This oral literature expressed itself in a variety of forms: lyric and epic poems, short stories, proverbs, riddles and counting, mocking and prayer songs. The language is the čakavian (q.v.) spoken at that time on the island of Hvar, more exactly the ikavian (q.v.) variant of the dialect. It also preserves typical grammatical forms for two-person actions, the dual number, and some other archaic forms.

HERMAN DALMATINAC. Herman Dalmatinac lived in the twelfth century. He was born in northern Istria (q.v.). He is known to be "the first Croat to attend the university of Paris." Actually, he was a disciple of Thierry de Chartres. Herman Dalmatinac won an impressive reputation as a translator and commentator of Arab and Greek scientific work in the fields of astronomy, philosophy and mathematics.

HISTORIA SALONITANA see THOMAS, ARCHDEACON

HLEBINA SCHOOL. School of painting deriving its name from the village of Hlebina, where Ivan Generalić was born and where the local painters of primitive art began to work in 1930. His style of painting is characterized by a total disregard of size and a simple expressive, so-called primitive way of drawing. The subject is the ordinary daily life in the village. This typical primitive art won worldwide recognition.

HOLJEVAC, VEĆESLAV. Partisan general and high communist party official. Former Mayor of Zagreb (q.v.), purged during October 1967 from the Central Committee of the Communist League of Croatia. He was accused of nationalistic deviations in his leadership of the Center for Croatian Emigrants, a quasi-governmental institution. Earlier, he had been under fire for being head of a commission that awarded prizes to two *Praxis* (q.v.) contributors.

HORVAT, BRANKO (1928-). Economist and politician. He worked a long time at the Institute of Economic Sciences (Institut Ekonomskih Nauka), the former Planning Institute of the Federation. He was the editor of the journal *Economic Analysis and Workers' Self-Management*. He was also a member of the Economic Institute (q.v.) of Zagreb.

Horvat has tried to unite democratic forces on a common platform, but without much success. He is highly critical of the economic policy of the Tuđman (q.v.) regime (as he was before of the communist). He advocates a sort of market socialism, a combination of social democracy and market economy. He founded and became president of the Social-Democratic Union (Socijalno-demokratska Unija). He organized a Balkan Conference with the primary aim of restoring cooperation between Yugoslav forces.

HORVATIĆ, DUBRAVKO (1939-) Poet, prose writer and essayist. He was editor of the magazines *Modra Lasta, Telegram* and *Hrvatski Tjednik* during the Croatian Spring (q.v.). From 1971 to 1990, he became of necessity a free-lance writer. Though stigmatized under the communist regime, he was awarded important literary prizes. Now he is finally becoming fully recognized. As Deputy President of the Matica hrvatska (q.v.), he entered into conflict with "his" President Vlado Gotovac (q.v.). He reproached Gotovac for being authoritarian and cited article 25 of the rules of the Matica that says that a leader of the institution should not be a leader of a party.

HOUSE OF COUNTIES/ŽUPANIJSKI DOM. Lower house of Parliament (q.v.). (See also ŽUPANIJA)

HRVATSKA AKADEMIJA ZNANOSTI I UMJETNOSTI (HAZU) see CROATIAN ACADEMY OF ARTS AND SCIENCES

HRVATSKA DEMOKRATSKA STRANKA (HDS) see CROATIAN DEMOCRATIC PARTY

HRVATSKA DEMOKRATSKA STRANKA PRAVA (HDSP) see CROATIAN DEMOCRATIC PARTY OF RIGHTS

HRVATSKA DEMOKRATSKA ZAJEDNICA (HDZ) see CROATIAN DEMOCRATIC UNION

HRVATSKA DOMOVINSKA STRANKA (HDMS) see CROATIAN NATIONAL PARTY

HRVATSKA IZVJEŠTAJNA NOVINSKA AGENCIJA (HINA) see CROATIAN NEWS AND PRESS AGENCY

HRVATSKA KREDITNA BANKA ZA OBNOVU (HKBO) see CROATIAN CREDIT BANK FOR RECONSTRUCTION

HRVATSKA KRŠĆANSKA DEMOKRATSKA STRANKA (HKDS) see CROATIAN CHRISTIAN DEMOCRATIC PARTY

HRVATSKA KRŠĆANSKA DEMOKRATSKA UNIJA (HKDU) see CROATIAN CHRISTIAN DEMOCRATIC UNION

HRVATSKA MATICA ISELJENIKA (HMI) see CROATIAN HOMELAND FOUNDATION

HRVATSKA MUSLIMANSKA DEMOKRATSKA STRANKA (HMDS) see CROATIAN MUSLIM DEMOCRATIC PARTY

HRVATSKA NACIONALNO-DEMOKRATSKA LIGA (HNDL) see CROATIAN NATIONAL-DEMOCRATIC LEAGUE

HRVATSKA NARODNA STRANKA (HNS) see CROATIAN PEOPLE'S PARTY

HRVATSKA PUČKA SELJAČKA STRANKA (HPSS) see CROATIAN PEOPLE'S PEASANT PARTY

HRVATSKA REPUBLIČKA ZAJEDNICA see CROATIAN REPUBLIC UNION

HRVATSKA REPUBLIKA HERCEG-BOSNA see CROATIAN REPUBLIC OF HERCEG-BOSNA

HRVATSKA SELJAČKA STRANKA (HSS) see CROATIAN PEASANT PARTY

HRVATSKA SOCIJALNA LIBERALNA STRANKA (HSLS) see CROATIAN SOCIAL-LIBERAL PARTY

HRVATSKA STRANKA PRAVA (HSP) see CROATIAN PARTY OF RIGHTS

HRVATSKA TELEVIZIJA (HTV) see CROATIAN TELEVISION

HRVATSKE ORUŽENE SNAGE (HOS) see CROATIAN ARMED FORCES

HRVATSKI FOND ZA RAZVOJ see CROATIAN FUND FOR DEVELOPMENT

HRVATSKI HELSINŠKI ODBOR ZA LJUDSKA PRAVA see CROATIAN HELSINKI COMMITTEE FOR HUMAN RIGHTS

HRVATSKI KNJIŽEVNI LIST. The Croatian Gazette was published in Zagreb (q.v.) during the period from April 1968 to October 1969. It was the first fully independent journal in Croatia following the Declaration on the Croatian Language (q.v.). The literary monthly had a significant influence on the Croatian national movement. It was published by the Association of Independent Writers, TIN. The name is an allusion to the writer Tin Ujević (q.v.). The editors wanted to stress the Croatian national heritage and local talent. An article on the use of language in the Yugoslav armed forces was the pretext for banning the journal.

HRVATSKI NEZAVISNI DEMOKRATI (HND) see CROATIAN INDEPENDENT DEMOCRATS

HRVATSKI RADIO (HR) see CROATIAN RADIO

HRVATSKI RADIO I TELEVIZIJA (HRTV) see CROATIAN RADIO AND TELEVISION

HRVATSKO FILOZOFSKO DRUŠTVO see CROATIAN PHILOSOPHICAL SOCIETY

HRVATSKO-SRPSKA KOALICIJA (HSK) see CROAT-SERB COALITION

HRVATSKO VIJEĆE EUROPSKOG POKRETA (HVEP) see CROATIAN COUNCIL OF THE EUROPEAN MOVEMENT

HRVATSKO VIJEĆE OBRANA (HVO) see CROATIAN DEFENSE COUNCIL

HRVATSKO ZAGORJE. Northwestern part of Croatia, lying at the foot of the mountains. The Zagorska Županija (q.v.) of the Middle Ages was smaller because part of its territory was included in the Varaždinska Županija.

HUMAČKA PLOČA. A twelfth-century tablet found near Ljubiški in Hercegovina. It is written both in Glagolitic (q.v.) and Bosnian (or Croatian) Cyrillic (q.v.). The latter alphabet, also called "Bosanica," is a specific form of Cyrillic.

HUMAN AND MINORITY RIGHTS. The Croatian Sabor (q.v.) endorsed in December 1990 all the documents of the Council of Europe (q.v.) concerning human rights and freedom of the press (q.v.), e.g., Council of Europe Resolution 428 (1970) with the Declaration on the Mass Media and Human Rights, Recommendation 834 (1978) Relating to the Dangers to the Freedom of the Press and Television, Recommendation R(81)19 with the Annex (1981) on the Access to Official Information, and the Declaration on Freedom of Expression and Information (1982).

The Constitutional Law on Human Rights and Freedoms and on the Rights of Ethnic and National Communities or Minorities in the Republic of Croatia (Ustavni zakon o ljudskim pravima i slobodama i o pravima etničkih i nacionalnih zajednica ili manjina u Republici Hrvatskoj) of 1991 pledges in its Preamble to "honor and protect national and other basic rights and freedoms of man and citizen." The law refers to all major international documents on that subject: UN Charter, Universal Declaration on Human Rights, International Covenant on Civil and Political Rights, International Covenant on Economic, Social and Cultural Rights, Final Acts of the Conference on Security and Cooperation in Europe (CSCE), Paris Agreement for the New Europe, and other documents of the CSCE relating to human rights, especially the Document of the CSCE's Copenhagen Meeting on the Human Dimension and the Document of the CSCE's Moscow Meeting on the Human Dimension, Council of Europe Convention on the Protection of Human Rights and Freedoms and the Protocols of the Convention, International Convention on the Elimination of All Forms of Racial Discrimination, Convention on the Prevention and Punishment of the Crime of Genocide, Convention on the Rights of the Child.

Croatian laws persuasively guarantee the protection of human rights. Practical application of these laws has proven much more difficult, especially in war circumstances and when faced with a large Serbian minority. It implies constant monitoring and evaluation of the current situation. The record encountered by visiting experts such as those of the Council of Europe is not wholly convincing. The Croatian Helsinki Committee for Human Rights (q.v.) came to similar critical conclusions.

HVAL APOCALYPSE. This missal of 1404 had been copied by a Bogomil heretic (q.v.) called Hval. It belonged to Duke Hrvoje Vukčić Hrvatinić of Bosnia and Split (q.v.) and has a full page picture of the lord in a suit of armor on a horse. It contains the "Apocalypse" or the "Revelation of Saint John the Evangelist."

HVAR. Larger island lying between Brač and Korčula opposite Split (qq.v.). Evidence of Neolithic habitation was found in some of the caves of the island. The Greeks founded their colony Faros on the location of present-day Starigrad. In 235 B.C., the island came into the hands of the Illyrian (q.v.) King Agron. In 219, it was conquered by the Romans. In the seventh century Slavs from the Neretva (q.v.) valley settled on Hvar. Byzantines, Venetians, Hungaro-Croatians, Austrians, French, Italians and others all took an interest in the island during later history.

- I -

IJEKAVIAN. Serbo-Croatian language variant in opposition to the i- and ekavian variants (qq.v.). It is the western variant of Serbo-Croatian or Croatian. It is most in use in Croatia.

IKAVIAN Serbo-Croatian language variant in opposition to the e- and ijekavian variants (qq.v.). It is the southern variant of Croatian and is spoken especially on the Adriatic islands.

ILIRSKA STRANKA see ILLYRIAN MOVEMENT

ILLYRIA. The Indo-European people known as the Illyrians settled in the Balkans around the tenth century B.C. Several tribes united in a kingdom with its center in Scodra, Shkodër in present-day Albania. Its last King Genthius surrendered to the Romans in 168 B.C.

ILLYRIAN MOVEMENT. Croatian national movement in the middle of the nineteenth century. It was initially a cultural movement, strongly influenced by the work of Ljudevit Gaj (q.v.). It developed later into a political party. It was influenced by German Romanticism with its emphasis on principles of language and nationality, by French political thought with its emphasis on the role of the state and by Pan-Slavism with its emphasis on the greatness and unity of the Slavs. Its cultural program had been given expression by Ljudevit Gaj and its early political ideas by Janko Drašković (q.v.). It strived for the unification of the Croatian lands and opposed Hungarian influence. When the Hungarians founded a political party in 1841, the Illyrians reacted with the foundation of the Illyrian Party (Ilirska Stranka). They sent many representatives to the Sabor (q.v.) but the Illyrian program was not successfully defended there. The name *Illyrian* was forbidden by the Austrian Emperor in 1843. The party renamed itself the National Party (q.v.).

The Illyrian movement can be seen as an early forerunner of the Yugoslav idea. The changing intellectual climate paved the way for a Serbian-Croatian coalition and the agreements on the creation of the Kingdom of Serbs, Croats and Slovenes (q.v.).

ILLYRIAN PROVINCES. Political unit, created by Napoleon (q.v.) during his domination from 1809 to 1814. It included the following previously Austrian lands: Carniola, West Carinthia, Gorica, Istria (q.v.), Dalmatia (q.v.) and Dubrovnik (q.v.). The regime tried to modernize and secularize the region. A sense of Slav unity and awakening national awareness remained after its dissolution. It manifested itself later in the Illyrian movement (q.v.).

ILLYRICUM. The Roman province of Illyricum stretched from the Drina in the south to Istria (q.v.) in the north and from the Adriatic to the Sava. Its administrative center was Salona (q.v.). Earlier there had been an Illyrian kingdom in the southern part with its capital in Scodra (Shkodër, Albania). Later, the Roman

Empire extended along the Danube valley and Illyricum was divided between the provinces of Dalmatia on the Adriatic and Pannonia (q.v.) in the interior. In 395 A.D. the Roman Empire was split after the death of Emperor Theodosius. The part south of the Drina belonged thereafter to the Eastern Empire and came under the administration of Byzantium.

ILLYRICUS, FLACIUS see VLAČIĆ, MATIJA

INDEPENDENCE. In May 1990, the Croatian Democratic Union (HDZ) (q.v.) won the first multiparty elections after the Second World War. A new Constitution (q.v.) was proclaimed on December 22, 1990. Article 140 reserved the right to take measures to defend the sovereignty of the Republic. In the referendum of May 19, 1991, the citizens of the Republic of Croatia confirmed by a majority of 94 percent the aspiration to live in a sovereign Croatia. On June 25, 1991, the proclamation of sovereignty and independence of the Republic of Croatia was officially read. In July 1991, the Yugoslav army invaded Croatia. The European Community (EC) (q.v.) mediated and all measures to concretize independence were frozen. No agreement on cooperation within the old Yugoslavia could be reached, so after three months Croatia decided to work out its own independence program. Germany (q.v.) and the Vatican were the first Western nations to recognize the independence of Croatia in December 1991. On January 15, 1992, upon advice of the Badinter Arbitration Commission (q.v.) operating within the framework of the Peace Conference for Yugoslavia, the EC countries recognized the Republic of Croatia within the borders of the former communist Republic. This was the beginning of worldwide recognition.

INDEPENDENT STATE OF CROATIA/NEZAVISNA DRŽAVA HRVATSKA (NDH). The Independent State of Croatia came into life on April 10, 1941, under the protection of the German invading powers. The Ustaša leader Ante Pavelić (qq.v.) returned from Italy and assumed power as *poglavnik* (head of the state). The new regime was rather well received by the majority of the Croats. Croatia's main leader, Vice-Premier Vladko Maček, resigned after the occupation and issued a statement advising that the situation be accepted peacefully. The largest party, the Croatian People's Peasant Party (q.v.), remained passive. Some of its leaders went abroad with the government, some others joined the Ustašis. Two-thirds of satellite Croatia's territory, including Zagreb (q.v.) and Bosnia, remained under direct German supervision; Dalmatia (q.v.) was occupied by Italy. So, in fact, neither the independence nor the integrity of the Croatian territory was achieved.

Still, Pavelić began a process of ethnic cleansing to make the state more purely Croatian. Orthodox Serbs, mostly concentrated in parts of Bosnia and in the old Military Border (q.v.), were either rebaptized, expelled or killed. A Serb rising in self-defense in the small towns was forcefully crushed. Peasants fled to the communist resistance movement, especially along the borders of Dalmatia. The role played by Catholic Archbishop Stepinac (q.v.) in the massive conversions of Orthodox Serbs is still very controversial. On May 9, 1945, the Yugoslav partisans entered Zagreb. A great number of Ustašis and other citizens who had sought refuge in Austria were handed over by the Allies to the partisans and were murdered at Bleiburg (q.v.).

INDUSTRIAL PRODUCTION. Industrial production started to fall even before the war broke out in 1991; it fell by 10 percent in 1990. This was primarily due to economic reforms implemented at the beginning of that year and to the loss of East European markets.

In 1991, industrial production further decreased by as much as 23 percent. A sharp drop in production occurred as a result of the war. War destruction considerably diminished production capacities. The war started in August-September 1991 and the consequent decline in economic activity is clearly visible. After the major military operations stopped at the beginning of 1992, production started to show slight signs of recovery. In 1993, that trend was again reversed and in April industrial production was only 58.4 percent of the prewar level. (See also INDUSTRY AND MINING)

INDUSTRY AND MINING. Industry and mining contribute the largest share to the gross national product (q.v.) of the Republic of Croatia. Six sectors dominate Croatia's industry.

The textile sector, including the manufacture of finished textile products as well as the manufacture of textile fiber and material, has the largest share in total industrial output. As a labor-intensive branch, it has great economic and social significance. Approximately 30 percent of textile production is exported to Europe and countries overseas. The strategy for the development of the textile industry anticipates, besides the necessary transfer of present state ownership to private hands, an expansion of commercial arrangements with the world, so that by establishing foreign enterprises, mixed ownership enterprises or contracts on manufacturing cooperation, it will be possible to ensure the renewal of manufacturing facilities and the introduction of modern technology.

The food industry is in second place regarding total industrial output, but if the manufacture of beverages, animal feed and tobacco production is added, it then becomes the most significant branch of industry.

The chemical industry represents the third most important industrial branch. The output of the chemical processing industry is slightly greater than that of the basic chemical industry. The strategy for the overall development of Croatia's chemical industry is directed toward adapting manufacture to contemporary ecological requirements.

The metal processing and machinery construction industries make nearly the same contribution to total industrial output. Approximately one-third of the output of machinery construction is exported. A basic problem is that the enterprises are not in a position to replace their equipment and purchase new technology, for which foreign capital is required. The present unfavorable position of the metal processing industry has been caused by a period of reduced demand due to the low level of domestic investment activities. Organizational changes and tie-ups with foreign firms are expected to restore the previous activity level.

The electrical industry is fairly diversified in terms of product assortment, ranging from light bulbs to generators. The development strategy for this branch anticipates, in addition to an eventual narrowing of the product assortment and acceleration in the development of electronics, the forging of links with internationally known enterprises with the goal of achieving an adequate development program for individual enterprises.

Shipbuilding is an important export-oriented branch. Exports made up around 12 percent of total Croatian exports for 1990. There are six large shipyards in Pula, Split (q.v.), Trogir, Kraljevica and Rijeka (two) as well as a number of smaller shipbuilding and repair plants for maintenance and remodelling. These installations produce all types of vessels, drilling platforms, tankers and warships. In addition, the manufacture of boat equipment, diesel engines, steel structures, loading and unloading equipment is developing. Since exporting began in 1956, Croatian shipbuilding has delivered 6 percent of the total world production.

Mining scores relatively low in the industrial activity of Croatia. (See also INDUSTRIAL PRODUCTION)

INFORMATOR. Economic journal edited in Zagreb (q.v.).

INSTITUTE FOR DEVELOPMENT AND INTERNATIONAL RELATIONS/INSTITUT ZA RAZVOJ I MEĐUNARODNE ODNOSE (IRMO). The Institute is an independent, non-governmental research organization engaged in the interdisciplinary study of developmental processes, international relations and cooperation. It was established in 1963 by the University of Zagreb and the Croatian Chamber of Commerce (q.v.). Since then its academic profile and research areas have gradually broadened. Beginning as the Africa Research Institute, the name was changed in 1970 to the Institute for Developing Countries in order to reflect new research interests and activities (e.g., Latin American culture and communications). As the Institute gradually moved towards interdisciplinary research into global developmental processes, European integration, and Mediterranean cooperation, it was again renamed in 1989 to the Institute for Development and International Relations (IRMO).

The Institute's principal objectives are the following: a) to contribute to the understanding of the complexities of developmental and transformation processes and changes; b) to participate in the international transfer of knowledge and in cooperation programs and projects; c) to provide assistance in formulating and implementing development and adjustment policies in different economic, social and cultural areas; and d) to engage in designing Croatia's national development, particularly by analyzing its economic and political position in the international environment.

Besides exploring methodological and theoretical issues of international development and international relations, the Institute carries out research on the means and practice of bilateral and multilateral international cooperation in the fields of economics, politics, science, environmental protection, culture and others.

IRMO's research activities are grouped into several programs: Macroeconomic Research, Resource Economics and Environmental Protection, European Studies and Culture and Communications. In the existing programs, emphasis has been placed on the systematic monitoring and analysis of Croatia's participation in world development and trade, especially within the framework of the European integration process. The Institute is open to new proposals for research and cooperation. The Institute's activities are financed on a program and project basis and supported by local and governmental funding bodies as well as a number of international organizations and foundations.

The Interregional Network of Scientific Development Research Institutions in Developing Countries (ISDRI) was founded by IRMO in 1983. The Institute is also the focal point of Culturelink, Network of Networks for Research and Cooperation in Cultural Development, established by UNESCO and the Council of Europe (q.v.) in 1989. The network gathers about 640 networks and member institutions from over 90 countries in all parts of the world.

Research is published in reports and periodical publications. *Razvoj/Development International* is the Institute's journal for the problems of socio-economic development and international relations. Started in 1986, the journal publishes quarterly in English, French and Spanish.

Culturelink is the bulletin of the Network of Networks for Research and Cooperation in Cultural Development. It is published in English four times a year. *Euroscope* is the newsletter produced by IRMO's European Documentation Center (IRMO-EDOC). It carries news about the European Community (q.v.), EC non-member states and the relationship between Croatia and the European Community. This publication is published in Croatian. *Svjetsko Gospodartstvo/World Economy* is a quarterly bulletin in Croatian, designed to inform about the major trends in the world economy and the world market, as well as about the position of the Croatian economy in this context.

INSTITUTE OF ETHNOLOGY AND FOLKLORE. At the end of the nineteenth century, ethnologic and folkloristic themes were already presented in lectures at the University of Zagreb (q.v.). A chair for ethnology was created in the Faculty of Philosophy in 1924. Its task was to teach and do research on the traditional cultures of the South Slav peoples. In recent years, specific Croatian ethnologic themes have come to the forefront with the creation of a special seminar in the academic year 1992/3.

The Institute of Ethnology and Folklore publishes a yearbook entitled *Narodna Umjetnost* (Folk Art). The two most important scientists in the field were Milovan Gavazzi (1895-1992) and Branimir Bratanić.

The Council for Ethnology of the Croatian (formerly Yugoslav) Academy of Arts and Sciences (q.v.) has edited about 50 volumes of the *Zbornika za narodni život i običaje južnih Slavena* (Anthology of the daily life and customs of the South Slavs).

INTERNATIONAL TRADE. During the 1980s Croatia always had a deficit in merchandise trade and interest payments. However, these deficits were always more than offset by a surplus on invisibles and workers' remittances. Specifically, Croatia traditionally ran a surplus in tourism and international transport. Croatia used to earn about half of the Yugoslav surplus in tourism.

The Croatian current account surplus disappeared in 1990 when the performance of tourism started to decline. Overvaluation of the domestic currency and unlimited sales of foreign currency to citizens greatly contributed to creating a deficit. Towards the end of 1990, workers' remittances also started to dry up. This was caused by the run on foreign currency accounts and the subsequent default of banks. A crisis of confidence in banks resulted and workers' remittances have no longer been channelled through Croatian banks.

The reason for the current poor export performance boils down to the fact that the country has gone through the war. Large parts of production facilities have been damaged or destroyed, transport has been cut by more than half and tourism is restricted only to the northern part of the coast.

Trade between Croatia and other countries increased from $6.34 billion in 1989 to $7.34 billion in 1990. Exports from Croatia amounted to $2.913 billion and imports reached $4.425 billion. The trade deficit in 1990 thus amounted to $1.51 billion. Compared to the previous year, exports increased by 3.7 percent and imports by 25.3 percent. The coverage of imports by exports decreased from 79.5 percent in 1989 to 65.8 percent in 1990.

The main export items were ships, machines, food, chemical products, electrical equipment and finished wood products. The main items imported by Croatia were oil and gas, machines and transport vehicles, chemical products and food. The major portion of Croatian exports goes to developed countries (61 percent) of which the European Community (q.v.) takes the lion's share (46 percent). The same is true regarding imports. The major trade partners receiving Croatian exports are Italy, Germany (qq.v.), United States, Hungary, Czechoslovakia, Netherlands, Iraq, Poland and Switzerland. The major suppliers are Italy, Germany, United States, Austria, Hungary, Czechoslovakia, Netherlands, Iraq, Poland and Switzerland. In 1990, Croatia recorded a trade deficit with Germany ($235 million), Austria ($152 million) and Hungary ($121 million).

In foreign exchange income, export of goods accounts for 32.5 percent, services for 30.5 percent and hard currency remittances from citizens abroad for 37 percent.

INVESTMENT. Investment activity fell to one-fifth of the prewar level. It has been stagnating at this low level since mid-1992, without showing any signs of recovery. The main cause of this decline is the high level of uncertainty resulting from the political situation in the country, high inflation rates, unresolved ownership rights and an unstable economic policy. (See also FOREIGN INVESTMENT)

ISLANDS. The largest Croatian islands are Krk, Cres, Rab, Brač, Hvar, Korčula, Pag, Vis, Lastovo (qq.v.) and Mljet. In total there are 66 inhabited islands and about ten times more uninhabited ones.

ISOLA LUNGA see DUGI OTOK

ISSA see VIS

ISTARSKI DEMOKRATSKI SABOR (IDS) see ISTRIAN DEMOCRATIC PARLIAMENT

ISTARSKI RAZVOD. Document of a boundary commission in Istria (q.v.), dated from 1275. It tried to establish the boundaries between the Patriarchate of Aquileia, the Principality of Pazin and the Republic of Venice. The original document disappeared but later extant copies in Glagolitic (q.v.) included interesting additions. Through the legal prescriptions, the social life of medieval Istria can be reconstructed.

ISTRIA. Large peninsula in the north of the Adriatic between the Bay of Trieste and the Bay of Rijeka. It is an extension of the limestone Dinaric Mountains.

The Illyrian (q.v.) tribe of the Histrians gave its name to the peninsula. Emperor Augustus (27 B.C.-14 A.D.) conquered Istria from the Illyrian tribes and used it as an outpost to launch campaigns into the Balkan peninsula. The river Rižana (North Istria) became the Roman frontier in 42 B.C., and the Raša in 12 B.C. Within two centuries, the frontier was replaced to present-day Rijeka (q.v.). The towns of Trieste, Poreč (q.v.) and Pula became administrative centers and got impressive architectural monuments, such as the Amphitheater in Pula. The classical period suffered an eclipse from the beginning of the fourth century.

Christianity appeared at the end of the third century. By 500 A.D. a marvelous example of Byzantine architecture was materialized in the Euphrasian Basilica in Poreč. At the turn of the sixth century, the Slavs penetrated Istria, and for 12 years (599-611) they ravaged the whole peninsula under the leadership of the Avars and Longobards. In contrast to the other nomadic peoples, only the Slavs took permanent residence in Istria. For some time, Istria was incorporated in the early feudal system of Charlemagne (788-814). During the ninth till the thirteenth centuries the lands of Istria were dominated by the Patriarchs of Aquileia and German feudal rulers. Then, during a long period, the region came under the influence of Venice until the fall of the Republic in 1797.

The Peace Treaty of Campo Formio annexed Venetian Istria to Austria. Soon after, Istria was conquered by Napoleon and incorporated in his Illyrian Provinces (qq.v.). After his defeat, Istria was returned to Austria. The period of absolutism oppressed peasants, mostly of Slav origin, and favored the merchandising and intellectual elite that spoke Italian or German. In 1846, there were in Istria approximately 135,000 Croats, 32,000 Slovenes and 60,000 Italians. However, in the elections of 1848, of five local representatives to the Vienna Parliament, four Italians and only one Croat were chosen. The Revolution of 1848 overthrew Metternich's absolutist rule and marked the end of the feudal regime. In 1853, the agrarian reform of Istria began. In 1861, a Regional Parliament was established. Due to the electoral system, Germans and Italians were again privileged. Croats and Slovenes reacted by developing a national political, social and cultural movement. Leftist workers' organizations were founded. The nationalistic antagonism was ultimately concentrated in the struggle between the political parties: the Italian National Liberal Party and the Croat-Slovene People's Party.

The dissolution of the Austro-Hungarian Monarchy in 1918 ended in the Italian occupation of Istria, confirmed by the bilateral agreement of Rapallo of November 12, 1920. This occupation brought a strong Italianization of Istria that lasted until the national liberation war. After the capitulation of Italy in September 1943, the Anti-Fascist Council of the National Liberation of Croatia (q.v.) decided to incorporate Istria in the Croatian state. However, a month after the Yugoslav army liberated Istria and Pula, the Yugoslav Executive was forced to sign an agreement in Belgrade on May 9, 1945. This stipulated that Istria would be temporarily divided into two zones: Zone A (Pula and Trieste) under the control of the Anglo-American army and Zone B under the control of the Yugoslav army. In Paris, on January 10, 1947, a Peace Treaty was signed with Italy. It came into effect in September of the same year, when Pula returned to Yugoslavia. The border in Istria between Croatia and Slovenia (q.v.) was only traced in 1954, when the provisional Free Territory of Trieste was finally split between Italy and Yugoslavia. In 1956, a small correction was made and some villages of Buje municipality were annexed to Slovenia.

ISTRIAN DEMOCRATIC PARLIAMENT/ISTARSKI DEMOKRATSKI SABOR (IDS). Main political party in Istria (q.v.), defending local and "green" interests of the Istrian peninsula. It has managed to defeat the political monopoly of the Croatian Democratic Union (q.v.). The IDS even threatened not to apply centralistic laws from Zagreb (q.v.) on the territory of the Istrian Province. Istrian politicians already asked for an autonomous statute of Istria in the Republic of Croatia and constantly point to the model of "European regions." The IDS has ultimately announced its wish to organize a referendum on the autonomy of Istria, a practice that reminds Zagreb of the referendum organized by the Knin-Serbs and that signalled the beginning of their self-declared independence. The government has heavily criticized the Istrian initiative. (See also AUTONOMY)

ITALY (RELATIONS WITH). Several problems remain pending with Italy. One concerns the Osim agreement: Croatia has asked for the renewed ratification of the agreement. This is bound up with compensation for the Italians who left Istria (q.v.) and lost their belongings. The leaders of the Istrian Democratic Parliament (q.v.) support these claims, indicating that the emigration could have affected 200,000 people. The problem is complicated by unpaid debts of former Yugoslavia to Italy: of $94 million of compensation for nationalized Italian real estate, only $16 million were actually paid. How can the remainder be divided between Croatia and Slovenia?

IVANIŠEVIĆ, KATICA. Born at Omišalj. Rector of the University of Rijeka and member of the House of Counties for the Croatian Democratic Union (q.v.). Elected President of this House on April 23, 1994, after the demission of Josip Manolić (q.v.).

- J -

JAGIĆ, VATROSLAV (1838-1923). Born in Varaždin (q.v.). Professor of Slavistics in Berlin, Petrograd and Vienna. Member of the Yugoslav Academy of Arts and Sciences (q.v.). Of his 600 writings, especially well-known are his contributions on Juraj Križanić (q.v.) and on the grammar of Slav languages. He was also an editor and commentator of old Slav texts: *Hrvojev missal, Zografsko evanđelije, Mariansko evanđelije, Kijevski listići, Bečki listići, Vinodolski zakon, Poljički statut.* In 1875, he founded the leading academic journal entitled *Archiv für slavische Philologie.*

JANUS PANNONIUS see ČESMIČKI, IVAN

JASENOVAC. Concentration camp during the Second World War where about 200,000 Serbs, Jews and Gypsies were murdered by the Ustašis (q.v.). The exact number of victims is disputed by both Serbs and Croats, but it is certain that the memory of these killings is used by Serb politicians to express their aversion to the Tuđman (q.v.) regime. During the Second Congress of the Croatian Democratic Union (q.v.) in the autumn of 1993, Tuđman proposed to commemorate all victims of the Second World War - the Ustaši included - at Jasenovac.

JELAČIĆ, JOSIP (1801-1859). Ban (q.v.) who did the most for the Croatian National Revival in the mid-nineteenth century. His statue had been removed by the communist regime but was put back with great ceremony by the Tuđman (q.v.) regime.

Ban Jelačić supported the Illyrian movement (q.v.) and was involved in the founding of institutions that stimulated the Croatian nationalist movement. At the request of the Austrian Archduke Francis Karl, Ban Jelačić suppressed the Hungarian revolt of 1848. In Croatia, serfdom and thus feudalism were abolished. Earlier, Jelačić had occupied Rijeka (q.v.) and proclaimed the Drava River and Međimurje (q.v.) integral parts of Croatia. By uniting most of the Croatian lands, he contributed strongly to the Dalmatian and Istrian movement (q.v.) for unification.

JUGOSLOVENSKA AKADEMIJA ZNANOSTI I UMJETNOSTI (JAZU) see YUGOSLAV ACADEMY OF ARTS AND SCIENCES

JURAJ MATEJEV DALMATINAC (?-1475). Born in Zadar (q.v.) and died in Šibenik. Architect and sculptor. He worked in various towns around the Adriatic. He constructed the Rector's Palace (Knežev Dvor) and erected the Minčeta Tower in Dubrovnik (q.v.). He built the church in Pag (q.v.) and the cathedral in Šibenik.

- K -

KAČIĆ-MIOŠIĆ, ANDRIJA (1704-1760). The Franciscan philosopher and writer was born at Brist in the Makarska region and passed the greater part of his life in the monastery of Zaostrog. He wrote a dissertation in 1752 on the philosophy of Duns Scotus. Four years later, he produced one of the most popular books of his time and after: *Razgovor ugodni naroda slovinskoga* (A Pleasant Discourse about the Slavic People). First published in 1756, it has been reprinted about 80 times. Its popularity can be partly explained by the patriotic feelings aroused by the book. In his third book, *Korabljica* (The Little Sailboat, 1760), Kačić-Miošić admonished his readers not be ashamed of their Croatian language. Even Adam could have spoken Slavic. The popularity and broad distribution of Kačić-Miošić's books contributed to the new štokavian (q.v.) standardization of the Serbo-Croatian language.

KAJKAVIAN. Variant of the Croatian language, an alternative to čakavian and štokavian (qq.v.). According to the equivalent for the word *what*, the variants of Croatian use the expressions što-, kaj- or ča-. The kajkavian variant has been spoken in the western part of the "Serbo-Croatian" language area on the border with Slovenia. Slovene itself is a Slavic language that uses the kaj-idiom.

KALEB, VJEKOSLAV (1905-). Born on the island of Murter near Šibenik. Prose and scenario writer. As an ex-partisan, he wrote on the war and on contemporary society in Croatia. His main work, *Divota prašine* (1956), has been translated as *Glorious Dust*.

KALLIA, TOMBSTONE OF. Tombstone with Greek inscription from the fourth century B.C., found on the island of Vis (q.v.). It is a testimony on the death of a Greek soldier, alluding to battles with the Illyrians (q.v.).

KANGRGA, MILAN. Philosophy Professor of the University of Zagreb (q.v.). Member of the *Praxis* (q.v.) group in the 1960s and 1970s. He was deeply inspired by the phenomenology of Heidegger and adopted some of his problem definitions and formulations. However, he remained convinced of the superiority of a creative interpretation of the philosophy of the young Marx.

KARAĐORĐEVIĆ, ALEXANDER (1888-1934). Prince Regent Alexander of the Serb dynasty of the Karađorđevići proclaimed on December 1, 1918, the creation of the Kingdom of Serbs, Croats and Slovenes (q.v.). The first period of parliamentary rule was characterized by permanent nationalistic tensions and ended in the murder of Stjepan Radić (q.v.). The King abolished the Constitution, prohibited parties and reorganized the administration of the country. Nationalist leaders and extremists emigrated, among them Ante Pavelić (q.v.). The Ustaša (q.v.) leader, in collaboration with the Macedonian secessionist movement IMRO, organized the assassination of the King in Marseilles in 1934.

KARAĐORĐEVIĆ, PAUL (1893-1976). Nephew of Alexander I, whose eldest son was only 11 when he was assassinated. Prince Paul became Regent of Yugoslavia in the period 1934-1941.

KARAĐORĐEVIĆ, PETAR II (1923-1970). Being only 11 when his father was assassinated, a nephew of his father, Prince Paul, became Regent.

KARAĐORĐEVO. This place near Belgrade is now associated with the symbolic end of the Croatian Spring (q.v.). The entire Croatian party leadership was summoned to gather in this residence of Tito (q.v.) on November 30, 1971. The goal was to purge the party leadership of its nationalistic elements. The meeting was immediately followed by the Twenty-first Session of the Presidium of the League of Communists of Yugoslavia (LCY) (q.v.). Though some of the claims of the Croatian mass movement were legitimate, the LCY had to remain the sole and leading force. Ideological unity and party discipline were needed. A week later Miko Tripalo (q.v.) resigned and Savka Dabčević-Kučar (q.v.) followed his example. It was the beginning of a vast purge of all members who had been labelled Croatian nationalists.

KARLOVAC. Karlstadt. Archduke Charles of Styria, Carniola and Carinthia decided to build a fortification where the Korana River flows into the Kupa (q.v.). Austrian royal engineer Matija Gabon started the execution of the project on July 13, 1579. The fortification was built as an ideal Renaissance town: a rectangular grid fortified by walls in the form of a star. For three centuries Karlovac functioned as a main center of the Military Border (q.v.).

KARLOVCI (PEACE OF). This Treaty of 1699 reversed the trend of expansion of the Ottoman Empire to the detriment of the Habsburg Empire. The Treaty followed upon the failure of the Ottoman siege of Vienna in 1683 and rewarded the Austrian military victories of Eugene of Savoy in the Vojvodina. The Peace Treaty was concluded in the town of Srijemski Karlovci near Novi Sad. The parties agreed that the new frontier between the two Empires should follow the river Tisa (Tisza) up to its confluence with the Danube and the river Sava up to the Una. This meant that the greater part of Srijem and Slavonia (q.v.) returned to the Habsburgs.

KARLOWITZ see KARLOVCI

KAŠIĆ, BARTUL (1575-1650). Jesuit, born on the island of Pag and living in Dubrovnik (qq.v.). In 1684, he published the first grammar of the Croatian language in Rome.

KAŠTELAN, JURE (1919-). Born in the village of Zakučac. His first collection of poems *Crveni Konj* (Red Horse, 1940) was seized by the police because of the revolutionary themes. Kaštelan introduced surrealism to Croatian poetry.

KERESTINEC. In the tragedy of Kerestinec in the summer of 1941, a number of Croatian communist leaders were murdered by the Ustaša (q.v.) regime. This offered Tito (q.v.) the occasion to reorganize the party in a "Stalinist" way.

KHUEN-HEDERVARY, KAROLY (1849-1918). Appointed Ban (q.v.) of Croatia by the Hungarian government, he ruled in a quasi-dictatorial manner from 1883 to 1903. He associated himself strategically with the Serb minority in Croatia and opposed all expressions of Croatian nationalism.

KIEV MISSAL PIECES. Fragments of a missal written in the Glagolitic alphabet during the tenth or eleventh century in Moravia or Bohemia and used in Croatia. They are preserved in Kiev.

KINGDOM OF CROATIA, DALMATIA AND SLAVONIA, TRIUNE. Traditionally, the kingdom of Croatia consisted of three parts: Croatia, Dalmatia and Slavonia. In its earliest history, Dalmatia was the focus of the kingdom. Later, this part of the kingdom came under the influence of Venice. Moreover, during a long period Slavonia was occupied by foreign peoples and only nominally belonged to the kingdom. Afterwards large parts of Slavonia were incorporated into the Military Border (q.v.) and remained separated from civil Croatia. In 1848, the Sabor in Zagreb (q.v.) urged that the unity of the Triune Kingdom of Croatia, Dalmatia and Slavonia be restored. This happened when the Military Border was finally abolished and the direct Austrian control lifted. Though the territorial integrity of the Kingdom only existed off and on in the course of history, most documents and King's titles use the expression "Triune Kingdom of Croatia, Dalmatia and Slavonia."

KINGDOM OF SERBS, CROATS AND SLOVENES/KRALJEVSTVO SRBA, HRVATA I SLOVENACA. Official name of the country of the South Slavs used since the proclamation of independence on December 1, 1918. The name refers to the idea of a federation of peoples as proposed in the Declaration of Corfu (q.v.) and in similar agreements made at the end of the war. Yugoslavists interpreted the name more strictly as the one people with the three names. In 1929, King Alexander (q.v.) centralized the administration and changed the name accordingly into "Yugoslavia." The 1943 Declaration of the Anti-Fascist Council of the National Liberation of Yugoslavia (q.v.) proclaimed Yugoslavia to be a Federation of Republics. It created three more Republics (Montenegro, Macedonia and Bosnia-Hercegovina) and two Autonomous Provinces (Vojvodina and Kosovo-Metohija). Though granted their own Republic, the Muslims did not get recognition as a nationality until 1967.

KLIS. Town and medieval fortress on a mountain pass dominating the peninsula of Split (q.v.). For centuries, the fortress was the bastion of defense against the attempts of the Turks to conquer the littoral region. It was the first stronghold of the Uskoks (q.v.).

KLJUIĆ, STJEPAN. Bosnian Croat, Croatian Democratic Union (q.v.) politician and former Croat representative in the Bosnian Presidency. During a meeting at Siroki Brijeg in the winter of 1992 and in presence of Stipe Mesić (q.v.), Kljuić was replaced by Mate Boban (q.v.) as leader of the HDZ (q.v.). The replacement was symbolic for the change of position of the Croats from a unitary state to a cantonization or even outright ethnic division of Bosnia-Hercegovina.

KNIN. Knin was once the seat of the last Croatian King, Petar Svačić. He was defeated by the Hungarians in 1097. In 1522, the Turks occupied Knin. The town was taken over by the Austrians in 1688. Kninska Krajina is sort of a Kosovo for the Croats. Just as the old Serbian homeland is now colonized by the Albanians, the old Croatian capital Knin is now occupied by the Serbs.

KOLAR, SLAVKO (1891-1963). Born in Zagreb. Writer. He joined the partisans in 1944, but was arrested by the State Security Administration (OZNA). He was accused of anti-Semitism and excluded from the Croatian Writers' Association (q.v.). As a writer, he is known for his humorous novels and short stories.

KOLOMAN, KING. First Hungarian King who became sovereign of the Croatian lands by the so-called Pacta Conventa (q.v.). By this procedure Koloman was chosen by the Croatian nobility as King of Croatia. In 1102, he was formally crowned at Biograd na Moru (q.v.). The greater part of the Kingdom of Croatia, Dalmatia and Slavonia (q.v.) remained until 1918 under the Hungarian or Austro-Hungarian dynasty.

Croatian political thinkers stressed the fact that this situation was deliberately chosen by the Croats (q.v.) and that it could be reversed if all implied conditions were not met by the monarchs. Modern historians cast doubt on the historicity of the so-called Pacta Conventa. Koloman had earlier invaded Croatia and Dalmatia by force and the Pacta Conventa could have been just a formal approval of this situation. (See also ARPAD DYNASTY)

KONAVLJE see TRAVUNJA

KONTURA. Croatian art magazine. It appeared for the first time in 1992. The second volume of 1993 presented a selection of articles on photography, young Croatian avant-garde art and art collectors.

KORČULA. Island in the mid-Adriatic archipelago between Split and Dubrovnik (qq.v.). It was colonized by the Greeks and by the Illyrians (q.v.). The Romans killed the local population in revenge for their pirate activities. Korčula was colonized again by the Neretvans (q.v.) and later by the Venetians. The town of Korčula (among others) is supposed to be the birthplace of Marco Polo. In the Second World War the island was occupied by the Italians. A considerable resistance movement developed on the island.

KORČULA CODEX. This codex in Latin dates from the second half of the twelfth century and came from a Dalmatian (q.v.) town. It contains a *Liber pontificalis*, a history of the Roman Popes, enriched with many details on Dalmatian and Croatian history. It is the oldest record of some Croatian historical facts, e.g., the coming to power of Petar Krešimir IV (q.v.). Pope Alexander II (1061-1073) heard that Krešimir, sovereign of the Croats, had murdered his brother Gojslav by a trick. The Pope sent a missionary, Mainardo, to discover if this was true. Mainardo was convinced by an oath, sworn by Krešimir and his 12 prefects, saying that he was not guilty of the crime. Thus he received back from the Pope the authority over his land.

KORDUN. Town in the former Vojna Krajina (q.v.), built as a fortification (cf. *cordon*) against the Turks. During the Serb-Croat war, the region around Kordun again became a disputed region.

KORVIN, MATIJA (1458-1490). Croato-Hungarian King, son of Janos Hunyadin. He got his nickname from the raven *(corvus)* in his coat of arms. He was chosen King when the Habsburg Ladislav V died without an heir. He succeeded in keeping the Habsburg lands united by centralistic measures and taxes, motivated by the Turkish threat. In the same year that Bosnia fell (1463), he conquered Jajce and kept the Turks out of Slavonia (q.v.) for another 50 years. He also took Senj (q.v.) and founded there the first military garrison in Croatia (1469). However, he lost the last Croatian island Krk (q.v.) (1480) and made enemies among the Croatian nobility who turned to Venice. The Croat Ivan Česmički (q.v.) was one of his advisers.

It was during his reign that Croatia began to be represented in the Hungarian parliament or diet and that Croatian internal affairs were discussed there as though the two kingdoms were a single entity.

KOSTAJNICA. Town on the river Una, with a fortification to defend the crossing. It was on the frontier with Turkish Bosnia, and only in 1688 did it definitely come into Austrian hands. It became one of the garrison towns of the Military Border (q.v.).

KOTRULJIĆ, BENKO (1416-1469). This diplomat of Dubrovnik (q.v.) is known as the first Croatian scientist. His work *On Trade and the Perfect Market* can be regarded as the first handbook on accounting.

KOVAČEVIĆ, BOŽO. Member of Parliament and Vice-President of the Croatian Social-Liberal Party (q.v.).

KOVAČIĆ, IVAN GORAN (1913-1943). Journalist and writer. He joined the partisans and was killed in a guerilla fight. His poem *Jama* (The Cave, 1943) is a passionate protest against war crimes.

KRAJINA see MILITARY BORDER; SERBIAN REPUBLIC OF KRAJINA

KRALJEVSTVO SRBA, HRVATA I SLOVENACA see KINGDOM OF SERBS, CROATS AND SLOVENES

KRANJČEVIĆ, SILVIJE STRAHIMIR (1865-1908). Born in Senj (q.v.). He was lifetime editor of the magazine *Nada* (Hope). In his poetry, he dropped the conventional motifs of love and patriotism and began writing meditative poetry, searching for the meaning of life. He introduced religious and cosmic themes, both lived and expressed in a personal and tormented way. Some critics consider his verses to be the peak of Croatian poetry.

KRBAVSKO POLJE. The field of Krbava is the Croatian Kosovo, the place where the Croatian nobility under guidance of Ban Emerik Derenčin lost its historic battle against the Ottomans on September 9, 1493. The battle was recorded by a contemporary writer, Priest Martinac (q.v.). Krbava lies near Lika (q.v.). The southern inland area of Croatia was left without protection and was soon to be occupied by the Ottomans.

KREŠIMIR IV (1058-1073). In 1069, King Krešimir gave the island of Moan to the Benedictine monastery of St. Krševan in Zadar (q.v.). The original document has not survived. The gift was later described in thirteenth century Gothic Latin. Even if the document is not authentic and made by the Benedictines to defend their property rights on the island, it contains interesting information on the genealogy of the Croatian ruler. (See also TRPIMIR DYNASTY)

KRIŽANIĆ, JURAJ (1618-1683). Born in Obrh in the region of Ozalj (near Karlovac). Križanić was one of the first strong supporters of the political union of Slav peoples. He condemned the division between the Eastern and Catholic Churches. During his second stay in Russia, he was persecuted for his critical views. He died in the army of the Polish King John III Sobiesky while fighting the Ottomans during the second siege of Vienna in 1683.

KRK. Northernmost and largest island in the Adriatic. The oldest Glagolitic (q.v.) inscriptions and manuscripts have been found here. In the thirteenth century, the use of Glagolitic was officially permitted by papal decree in the diocese of Krk. In the beginning of the sixteenth century, Glagolitic printing presses began to be in use here.

KRKA. River ending in the Adriatic. With the one along the Neretva (q.v.), its valley is the only natural connection with the lands of the interior.

KRLEŽA, MIROSLAV (1893-1981). He was the most important and influential Croatian writer of the first part of this century. He completed a diversified work of short stories, lyrics, novels, dramas and literary and social criticism. He directed several groundbreaking journals and remained controversial, even after his death.

Under the influence of expressionism and symbolism, he wrote the cycle *Hrvatski Bog Mars* (The Croatian God Mars, 1922). Educated in a military school and confronted with the reality of the war, he expressed his antiwar feelings in a very personal way.

Well read and translated are his three novels *Povratak Filipa Latinovicza* (The Return of Filip Latinovicz, 1932), *Na rubu pameti* (On the Brink of Reason, 1938) and *Banket u Blitvi* (Dinner in Blitva, 1938, 1939, 1964).

Different in style and character is his ballad on Petar Kerempuh *(Balade Petrice Kerempuha*, 1936). Here, he sings about the Croatian past in kajkavian (q.v.) peasant dialect.

During the period between the two world wars, he was the main editor of several literary journals that were soon prohibited by the authorities: *Plamen*, *Književna Republika* (1923-1927), *Danas* (q.v.) (1934) and *Pečat* (1939-1940). He engaged in some major encyclopedic and bibliographic projects. Krleža also played a key role in the so-called "conflict on the literary left," an interesting and important discussion on the eve of World War II. Krleža defended the freedom of the artist against any ideological constraint, however progressive it may be.

After the Second World War, he became Vice-President of the Yugoslav Academy of Arts and Sciences (q.v.) and editor of the Yugoslav encyclopedia. He continued writing and his plays were continually performed, e.g., *Zastave* (Flags, 1965).

Krleža remained controversial as he never fully adopted the dogmatic party line and occasionally even expressed himself as a Croatian nationalist: he signed the Croatian language declaration of 1967 and accordingly resigned from some official functions afterward.

The polemic about the "conflict on the literary left" has not lost its relevance. The same problems have been raised again by such non-conformist critics and writers as Pedrag Matvejević and Stanko Lazić (qq.v.). They have commented on and updated some of Krleža's views.

KRŠĆANSKA NARODNA STRANKA (KNS) see CHRISTIAN NATIONAL PARTY

KRŠĆANSKI DEMOKRATI MEĐIMURJA (KDM) see CHRISTIAN DEMOCRATS OF MEĐIMURJE

KUHARIĆ, FRANJO (1923-). Archbishop (1970) and Cardinal (1983) of the Catholic Church of Croatia with seat in Zagreb (q.v.). He participated in the Second Vatican Council (1964-1965). He published about religious themes and, as successor of Stepinac (q.v.), he wrote *Poruke sa Stepinčeva groba. Propovijedi u zagrebačkoj kathedrali na godišnjicu smrti kardinala Alojzija Stepinca, 10. veljače, od 1971-1990* (1990). (Messages from the Grave of Stepinac. Sermons in Zagreb Cathedral on the Anniversary of the Death of Alojzije Stepinac, February 10, from 1971 to 1990 [1990].)

KUKULJEVIĆ, IVAN (1776-1851). Writer and politician in the period of the Croatian Revival. He was the first to speak Croatian in the Sabor (q.v.) during his speech of March 2, 1843. He defended the use of Croatian as an official language.

KUPA. River passing through Karlovac (q.v.) and ending in the Sava near the town of Sisak (q.v.). The river marked the northwestern frontier with the Turkish Empire.

KVARNER (QUARNERO). Northern part of the Adriatic between Istria (q.v.) (Plomin, Opatija) and Dalmatia (q.v.) (Jablanac). The region includes the Kvarner islands of Cres, Krk, Rab and Lošinj (qq.v.).

KVATERNIK, EUGEN (1825-1871). Politician, collaborator and follower of the ideas of Ante Starčević (q.v.): on historical grounds Croatia has the right to constitute itself as an independent state. In the political context of 1860, this meant the autonomous union of all Croatian lands under the Habsburgs. Kvaternik's proposal to the King can be regarded as the beginning of the Croatian Party of Rights (q.v.). Ten years later, Kvaternik organized an open rebellion against the Austrian regime in order to achieve total Croatian independence. He was killed during the uprising in Rakovica (q.v.).

- L -

LABIN see ALBONA

LABOR MARKET. Employment in the social sector fell dramatically since 1990. Some 450,000 people have lost their job, which represents almost 30 percent of the pre-transitional employment level. On the other hand, employment in the private sector rose by some 60,000 people and has doubled. Moreover, there should be a rise of unofficial employment in the shadow economy. Namely, most private entrepreneurs are declaring only a fraction of their total employment to avoid taxes on employees. At the same time, unemployment first initially doubled - it rose by 140,000 until October 1992 - and then, surprisingly, started to fall. This is partly a consequence of the tightening of the regulations concerning who can be registered as an employed person. Moreover, not all who would like to work register as unemployed. Only about one quarter of registered job-seekers are receiving unemployment benefits. One more reason for the decline of unemployment is that many unemployed persons have found jobs in the shadow economy.

LADISLAS OF NAPLES. His father was Charles of Durazzo, enthroned as King of Hungary, but murdered at the court. The throne was claimed by his rival Sigismund of Bohemia. Ladislas himself was supported by the Croatian nobles and crowned as King in Zadar (q.v.) on August 3, 1403. In the same year, he returned to Naples and left the government of the Croatian lands to Hrvoje Vukčić Hrvatinić (q.v.). In 1409, Ladislas sold his hereditary rights over Dalmatia (q.v.) to Venice. Dalmatia remained under Venice until 1797.

LANGUAGE POLICY. All modern Slavic languages have their roots in Old Church Slavonic (q.v.). The codification of the language was needed for Christianization (q.v.). This was probably first done by Cyrillus (q.v.). He used the Macedonian variant of the Old Slavic language, spoken at Thessaloniki, and designed the Glagolitic (q.v.) alphabet. The so-called Cyrillic alphabet (q.v.) was probably developed half a century later by his followers in Macedonia or Bulgaria. Political developments and the use of the national language in religious services produced an early differentiation of Croatian Church Slavonic. The prosperity on the shores of the Adriatic, especially in Split and Dubrovnik (qq.v.), contributed to the development of a rich literature in vernacular Croatian. In the meantime, all over the country regional dialects prospered, mainly differentiating in the kaj-, ča- and štokavian (qq.v.) variants according to the equivalent for the word *what*. The Illyrians (q.v.) pleaded for uniformity in the South Slav language area, proposing the što- variant as standard. The Serb Vuk Karađić defended more or less the same idea. This development laid the basis for the creation of a common language in the Serbian, Bosnian and Croatian lands: Serbo-Croatian. Some linguists still deny its real existence in any period of history.

The Croatian Sabor (q.v.) of 1847 adopted Croatian as the official language for the Kingdom of Croatia, Slavonia and Dalmatia. In the spirit of reconciliation of all peoples of Yugoslavia, the communist regime adopted on December 10, 1954, the Novi Sad agreement on the common basis of the Serbo-Croatian language. At the beginning of the Croatian Spring (q.v.), on March 17, 1967, Croatian writers and intellectuals issued the Declaration on the Croatian Language (q.v.). This was followed by the rejection of the Novi Sad agreement on April 16, 1971.

The Tuđman (q.v.) regime has been favoring the differentiation and autonomy of the Croatian language. The publication of Croatian grammars and dictionaries banned under the previous regime has been stimulated with success. The officially professed tolerance towards the study and use of dialects other than štokavian points in the same direction.

LASIĆ, STANKO (1927-). Born in Karlovac (q.v.). Essayist and critic. Professor of Croatian literature (q.v.). He was editor of the periodicals *Croatica* (1970-1977) and *Književna Smotra* (Literary

Review, 1971-1975). He was a specialist of and received literary prizes for his work on Krleža (q.v.) and the "conflict on the literary left."

LASTOVO. Island, 13 km south of Korčula (q.v.). In the time of the Greek colonization, the island was known as Ladesta. In the bay of Ubli are Roman ruins. In the early Middle Ages, the island belonged to the Byzantines and as of the ninth century to the Neretvans (q.v.). Venetian, Zahumljan (q.v.) and a period of Croato-Hungarian rule followed. In 1252, it passed into the hands of Dubrovnik (q.v.) for ages. French, English and Austrians occupied it during shorter periods. The Rapallo Agreement attributed it to Italy. In 1943, the people of the island joined the partisan struggle.

LAW ON THE TRANSFORMATION OF SOCIALLY-OWNED ENTERPRISES. The Law on the Transformation of Socially-Owned Enterprises governs the transformation of ownership; it defines the way in which these enterprises in social ownership shall be converted into joint stock companies. The principal objective of the transformation is to ensure the restructuring of the enterprises and to intensify the entrepreneurs' activities on a market basis. The law was passed on February 5, 1991, and is considered to be the second most important act, after the Constitution (q.v.) of the Republic of Croatia.

The Law on the Transformation of Socially-Owned Enterprises provides the following guidelines. The discount rate granted to the employees purchasing shares in their own company is 20 percent plus 1 percent per each year of service in the company. Fifty percent of the shares issued at the current value of a company may be sold at the discount price. The unsold shares shall become the property of three funds: the Croatian Development Fund (q.v.), the Republic Fund for Pension and Disability Insurance of the Workers of Croatia and the Republic Fund for Pension and Disability Insurance of Private Farmers of Croatia. The first Fund will receive two-thirds of the unsold shares and the latter two funds will receive one-third of the unsold shares in the proportion of 70:30. The Fund will hand over the management of the company to the minority shareholders, and the latter will manage the company in accordance with the respective Articles of the Association. The fund will have to put on sale the shares thus acquired. At least 50 percent of the cash assets earned by the Croatian Development Fund will be reinvested in the same local district from which they have been generated. The nominal value of the shares that may be purchased by one person entitled to the discount is limited to the dinar equivalent of DM 20,000. The shares purchased by persons entitled to the discount may be paid in instalments over a period of five years.

The enterprises were given the possibility of carrying out the transformation under their own initiative until June 30, 1992. Thereafter the process was to be initiated and performed by the Agency for Restructuring and Development (q.v.) of the Republic of Croatia.

In February 1993, new regulations were adopted that restricted the preference rights of the employees (present or former) of an enterprise to buy actions up to 50 percent of the share capital, while the other part has to be obligatorily placed in the financial market for public sale. The Agency for Restructuring and Development was integrated in the Fund for Privatization (q.v.).

LEAGUE OF COMMUNISTS OF YUGOSLAVIA (LCY)/SAVEZ KOMUNISTA JUGOSLAVIJE (SKJ). Federal party organization under the Titoist regime. Until 1952, it was called Communist Party of Yugoslavia (CPY) (Komunistička Partija Jugoslavije, KPJ).

LEGAL SYSTEM. The Supreme Court is the highest judicial body of the state of Croatia. It comprises 15 members elected by the Chamber of Representatives. It shall ensure uniform application of the laws and the equality of citizens. The Constitutional Court consists of 11 judges elected in the same manner as the Supreme Court members and for the same period of eight years. The Constitutional Court decides on the conformity of laws with the Constitution (q.v.) and law. The Court also decides on conformity with the Constitution in the impeachment of the President.

LEXICOGRAPHICAL INSTITUTE MIROSLAV KRLEŽA/LEKSIKOGRAFSKI ZAVOD MIROSLAV KRLEŽA. The Lexicographical Institute is a scientific institution that produces the official national encyclopedias, bibliographies, biographies and other studies. The Institute was established by government decree of the then Federal National Republic of Yugoslavia on May 5, 1950. From its establishment until December 1981, the Institute was headed by the writer Miroslav Krleža (q.v.). The current publication program includes a new Croatian encyclopedia.

LIBURNIA. The lands of an Illyrian (q.v.) tribe, the Liburnians, who colonized the Adriatic coast between the rivers Rasa in the north (Istria) and Krka (qq.v.) (Skradin) in the south. The writer Kačić-Miošić (q.v.) calls Liburnia "a Croatian land" in his book *Korablijca* that was written in 1760.

LIJEPA NAŠA DOMOVINO. "Our Beautiful Homeland," opening words and title of the Croatian national anthem. It was composed in 1835 by Antun Mihanović-Petropoljski, an Austrian diplomat and Croatian patriot. It was set to music by Josip Runjanin in 1846. The song became popular at the end of the century and has now been constitutionally adopted as the Croatian national anthem.

LIKA. River and region at the inland foot of the Velebit mountains. Gospić on the Lika is the main town and center of the region. Fifteen kilometers south of Gospić lies Medak, the field of operations during the second Croatian offensive in the autumn of 1993. (See also GOSPIĆ OFFENSIVE)

LISINSKI, VATROSLAV see MUSIC

LISSA see VIS

LITERATURE, MODERN. Modern Croatian literature of the nineteenth and twentieth centuries can be divided into characteristic periods.

The Illyrian (q.v.) period covers the first half of the nineteenth century and is characterized by a romantic nationalist mood. Ivan Mažuranić (q.v.) was the most talented writer of this era.

The period of Realism follows in the second half of the nineteenth century. August Šenoa (q.v.) described contemporary life in Zagreb (q.v.) and Ksaver Galški focused on political dilemmas in the spiritual life of his heroes. In the same period, Silvije Strahimir Kranjčević (q.v.) created his autonomous poetic oeuvre.

The Croatian Moderna emerged from the late nineteenth century to the First World War. This literary movement thus appeared at the end of the period that was politically and culturally dominated by Ban Khuen-Hedervary (q.v.). The younger Croatian writers of this period were fascinated by modern French literature and rejected the previous romantic-Illyrian approach to literature. Literature had to become an expression of one's subjective state. The most prominent figures of this movement were Antun Gustav Matoš (q.v.), who opted for symbolism and expressionism, and Antun Branko Simić, who revolted against convention and traditionalism. These principles were also adhered to by Miroslav Krleža (q.v.).

Krleža was also the most prominent figure of the so-called "Interim" literature, produced between the two world wars. During the Second World War, Ivan Goran Kovačić (q.v.) wrote his famous poem *Jama* (The Cave).

Socio-realistic literature dominated for some time immediately after the Second World War. The main themes were the justification and glorification of the communist guerilla warfare and the values needed to construct a new communist society. Soon, however, moral dilemmas broke through the stereotypes.

The new contemporary literature, again both resuming the prewar currents and greatly influenced by the West, began appearing in the beginning of the 1960s and continues into the present. Ranko Marinković (q.v.) and Antun Šoljan were the two most gifted Croatian prose writers of the postwar period. Croatian literature is now fully integrated in world literature, as shown by the development of an interesting current of *Borgesovci* (followers of Borges, e.g., Goran Tribuson) and of literature of feminist or postmodern expression (Slavenka Drakulić, Dubravka Ugrešić [qq.v.]). Literature that finds its themes in Croatian history is currently back in vogue (Ivan Aralica). Poetry for its part followed its own development in the expression of strong personalities such as Jure Kaštelan, Ivan Slamnig, Vesna Parun, Milivoj Slaviček and Slavko Mihalić (qq.v.). Ivo Brešan (q.v.) was noticed for his dramatic work, e.g., a remarkable Hamlet adaptation to the Croatian environment. Ivo Frangeš, Aleksander Flaker and Stanko Lašić (q.v.) stand out as the most prominent critics of modern Croatian literature.

LJETOPIS POPA DUKLJANINA see CHRONICLE OF THE PRIEST OF DIOCLEA

LJUBIĆ-LORGER, MIRA (1953-). Born in Split (q.v.). Member of the House of Representatives. President of the party Dalmatian Action (q.v.).

LOCAL GOVERNMENT. Croatia was divided into 102 districts *(općine)* which are units of local self-management and also perform certain tasks of central government administration.

The 1990 Constitution (q.v.) specifies a different territorial division: districts should be units of local self-government, whereas groups of districts would make up counties - *županije* (q.v.) - functioning both as units of local government and as regional offices for the central administration. (See also LOCAL SELF-GOVERNMENT)

LOCAL SELF-GOVERNMENT. Article 128 of the Constitution (q.v.) guarantees citizens the right to local self-government. The right to local self-government implies the right to decide on needs and interests of local significance, particularly on regional development and town planning, organization of localities and housing, public utilities, child care, social welfare, culture, physical culture, sport and technical culture, and the protection and promotion of the environment.

Units of local self-government shall be communes or districts or towns. Their areas are laid down by law after the opinion of the inhabitants has been heard. (See also LOCAL GOVERNMENT)

LONDON (TREATY OF). By this secret treaty of April 15, 1915, the Entente powers tried to persuade Italy to declare war on Austria-Hungary. Italy's accession to the Allied side would be rewarded with a considerable extension of territory: Trieste, Istria (q.v.), northern Dalmatia (q.v.), Gorica, and a part of Carniola. This agreement was a real threat to the Croatian members of the

Yugoslav Committee (q.v.), especially Frano Supilo. If the Serbs made an agreement with the Allies or Italy, the greater part of the territory of the Habsburg Slavs was in danger. It weakened the Croatian position in the negotiations with the Serbs, who stood for a centralized state under the Serbian monarchy.

LORKOVIĆ, MLADEN. Minister of Foreign Affairs in the Independent State of Croatia (q.v.). Following the hardening of the Ustaša (q.v.) regime, Lorković was dismissed on September 1, 1944, and brought before a war tribunal for high treason. He allegedly had plans to take over the government in a conspiracy with the enemy.

LOŠINJ see CRES

LOVRIĆ, JELENA. Former journalist of the weekly *Danas* (q.v.). She was the first to be charged by the new regime under an article of the penal code concerning verbal offenses. This law was regularly used under the communist regime to silence dissidents. Lovrić had called Zdravko Mršić, the former President of the Agency for Restructuring and Development (q.v.), "Mister ten percent." She suggested in an article on the enterprise Dalmacija-Cement that Mršić had sought a commission of 5,000,000 DM to sign an agreement with Italian businessmen. Lovrić received a conditional sentence of six months imprisonment.

LUBOVAC, BRANKO. Deputy Prime Minister of the so-called Serbian Republic of Krajina (q.v.).

LUCIĆ, HANIBAL (1485-1553). Dalmatian poet born on the island of Hvar (q.v.). He wrote under the influence of the Petrarchan troubadour style, taken over by the Dubrovnik (q.v.) poets and the *začinjavci*, indigenous writers of religious poetry. His language is a mixture of his native čakavian dialect and of štokavian (qq.v.) elements from Dubrovnik writers. *Robinja* (The Slave Girl), his most important work, is the first Yugoslav play on the theme of liberation from Turkish captivity.

LUČIĆ, IVAN (1604-1679). Born in Trogir. He published *De regno Dalmatiae et Croatiae libri sex* (Sixth Book about the Kingdom of

Croatia and Dalmatia) in Amsterdam. He has been regarded as the founder of scholarly Croatian historiography and cartography.

- M -

MANDIĆ, DOMINIK (1889-1973). Franciscan priest, historian and writer. Born near Mostar in 1889, he entered the Franciscan order in 1906. He emigrated to the United States in 1952. He wrote on the early Christianization (q.v.) of Croatia and the medieval church in Bosnia-Hercegovina. He defended the view that Bosnia-Hercegovina is Croatian in origin and character. He opposed the interpretation of Constantine Porphyrogenitus (q.v.) according to which the territory of White Croatia is restricted to Croatia proper, while Red Croatia (qq.v.) was colonized by the Serbs. He made his own the version of the Chronicle of the Priest of Dioclea (q.v.), where Red and White Croatia appear as one large and indivisible Croatian area.

MANOLIĆ, JOSIP (1920-). Lawyer and politician. In 1941, he participated in the struggle of the partisans as leader of the communist youth organization of Croatia. He was removed from his leading position in the aftermath of the first Hebrang (q.v.) case. After the war, he held high posts in the Ministry of the Interior (MUP) and, from 1965, he was a Member of Parliament (q.v.). Because of his active role in the Croatian Spring (q.v.), he lost his mandate in 1971.

Co-founder of the Croatian Democratic Union (HDZ) (q.v.) and close collaborator of President Tuđman (q.v.), Josip Manolić was the first President of the Executive Committee of the HDZ (1989). He became Vice-President of the HDZ at its First Convention (1990) and Prime Minister of an HDZ government (1990-1991). He was elected a Member of Parliament in 1992. In 1993, he became President of the House of Counties (Županijski Dom). He was also President of the State Council for the normalization of relations between Serbs and Croats. In the autumn of 1993, he feared that the right wing of the party might take power and threatened to leave or split the HDZ. As a consequence of the Glavas amendment accepted at the Second Convention of the

HDZ, he lost his voting power and much influence in the party presidency.

Finally, he lost the confidence of the majority of his fellow party members in the House of Counties. During an internal meeting, with the exception of Josip Boljkovac and two other members, the HDZ faction voted for the replacement of Manolić as President of the House of Counties, declaring he clearly no longer belonged to the HDZ. Manolić himself feels that there exists a conflict with the party leadership and the President about three issues: the policy towards Bosnia-Hercegovina, the functioning of the rule of law and the running of the party. During the House of Counties session on March 25, 1994, Manolić refused to urgently put on the agenda the question of his own dismissal, referring to the internal rules of the House of Counties. He thereby provoked a minor parliamentary crisis. As the House of Counties has to give preliminary advice on certain questions, the work of the House of Representatives will also be partly paralyzed. Together with Mešić (q.v.), Manolić founded at the end of April 1994 a new party, the Croatian Independent Democrats (q.v.), which gathered 16 other members of parliament and became a threat to the parliamentary majority of the HDZ. (See also CROATIAN INDEPENDENT DEMOCRATS; PARLIAMENT)

MANUSCRIPT "RED I ZAKON." The manuscript "Order and Law," dated 1345, is the oldest existent Croatian text written in the Latin alphabet. It is a treatise on the acceptance of Dominican sisters into the nunnery. The manuscript is of first class historical-linguistic importance and also an important source for the study of the customs and mentality of the time. A similar manuscript in Croatian, *Regula Presvetog Benedikta* (Rule of the Most Holy Benedict), has a fragment that prescribes the way in which nuns were to sleep "each on her own pallet separately, candles to burn all night, and they must sleep clothed and girded with a belt or rope" (Katičić, *Two Thousand Years of Writing in Croatia,* 34).

MARIA THERESA (1717-1780). Maria Theresa reigned over the Austrian lands from 1740 to 1780. In 1767, she established a Croatian Royal Council (Consilium Regium). In 1779, she abolished the organ and passed its competencies to the Hungarian

Regency Council (Consilium Locumtenentiale). Both these measures impinged on the prerogatives of the Croatian Sabor (q.v.). The measures likewise reduced the competencies of the Ban (q.v.) to those of an executive officer of the Hungarian Council. This policy was in keeping with the centralistic and absolutist vision of the Austrian Empress. (See also PRAGMATIC SANCTION)

MARINKOVIĆ, RANKO (1913-1993). Born in Vis (q.v.). Novelist, dramatist and essayist. His novel *Kiklop* (Cyclops) and his short story *Ruke* (Hands) are believed to be milestones in Croatian literature. *Kiklop* was also performed with great success at the Yugoslav Theater Festival in 1977.

MARKOVIĆ, ANTE (1924-). Croat and last federal Prime Minister of ex-Yugoslavia. In March 1989, he took office with a program of economic reform and favored some form of confederation. When Slovenia (q.v.) decided to take over its frontiers, he was bypassed by a decision of the federal parliament to send in the army. In the elections he again defended a rational economic program and a peaceful transformation into a confederation, but was overcome by the success of the nationalistic forces. Only in Bosnia-Hercegovina and in Macedonia did he attain limited success. He was supported by the previous communist journal *Borba* and started YUTEL. In the end, he resigned, saying he could no longer take the responsibility for a federal budget that was largely used for war.

MARTIĆ, MILAN. First Interior Minister of the Serbian Republic of Krajina (q.v.) and head of the militia in Knin (q.v.), the most militant stronghold of the Serbian Krajina region. He became the rival of Milan Babić (q.v.) in the 1993-94 Krajina presidential elections. Backed by Slobodan Milošević, Martić finally defeated Babić in the fourth round after repeated reports of electoral irregularities.

MARTINAC, PRIEST. Member of the Lapčani clan of Lika (q.v.). He recorded the story of the battle of Krbavsko Polje (q.v.) in 1493 in a Glagolitic (q.v.) manuscript. He enlarged the observations with a general introduction on the Ottomans and compared the Turkish with the Mongol invasion (q.v.).

MARULIĆ, MARKO (1450-ca.1524). Poet from Split (q.v.), sometimes called "the father of Croatian literature." His most famous poem, *Judith,* was "composed in Croatian verse" *(Istorija svete udovice Judit u versih hrvatski složena*). Though the theme is biblical, Marulić sings about the battle of the Croats against the Turks and expressed patriotic feelings. He also wrote scientific treatises in Latin. His main philosophical and theological book *De Institutione Bene Vivendi Per Exempla Sanctorum* (On the Institution of Good Living Following the Example of the Saints) has been translated into many languages.

MASLENICA. Bay and strategic region near Zadar, uniting the northern part of Croatia (Croatia proper) with Dalmatia (q.v.). The Venetians already appreciated the advantageous position of the place. They wrote in a report of 1394 to the Senate: "more important than any other region, because it allows prevention of any invasion of the Dalmatian lands by those who want to conquer them."

The Krajina Serbs effectively succeeded in separating northern Croatia from Dalmatia, by bombing and destroying the communication network in this region. The border area was transformed into a pink zone (q.v.), theoretically under control of UNPROFOR (q.v.). This did not stop the air attacks of the Serbs.

On January 22, 1993, the Croatian army undertook a four-day campaign to protect the region. A new agreement was made. Border areas were placed under the control of UNPROFOR again, not without exacting some guaranties for the reconstruction of free communication lines. A new impressive project for a Maslenica bridge was drawn up and officially inaugurated by President Tuđman (q.v.). However, Serb shelling and shooting from the Krajina (q.v.) continued. (See also GOSPIĆ OFFENSIVE)

MATAVULJ, SIMO (1852-1908). Born in Šibenik. His stories describe Dalmatian (q.v.) life in detail.

MATICA HRVATSKA (MH). Croatian national cultural institution. Its aim is to further the Croatian national consciousness of the Croatian people by stimulating the study of the ethnic and cultural history of the Croats. It played an important role in promoting Croatia's own literature (q.v.) and science. It started the publication of Croatian journals and supported the public library movement. It was associated with the Illyrians (q.v.) who gradually transformed themselves into a Croatian national movement.

The idea of establishing the Matica hrvatska was first suggested by Ljudevit Gaj (q.v.) in 1829. The formal proposal drafted by Janko Drašković (q.v.) to start effectively with a company was accepted at a session of the Illyrian library council on April 11, 1842. The goal of the society was defined as encouraging the publication of the classics of Croatian literature - especially the great masters of Dubrovnik (q.v.) - and promoting the Croatian language (q.v.) in everyday life. Youth should be educated in a new spirit of national feeling.

The association started its activities by publishing the periodical *Kolo* (Circle). But in 1843, Vienna prohibited the use of Illyrian symbols and tried to suppress the activities of the Matica. However, the Matica succeeded in publishing a dictionary and literary classics such as *Osman* of the Dubrovnik master Ivan Gundulić (q.v.). From then on the activities of the Matica hrvatska followed the complexities of Croatian political life. It was subjected to Hungarian and Austrian pressure until 1918.

Between the two world wars, the political and cultural situation was difficult and its activities declined even more. The Matica vigorously protested against the dictatorship of King Alexander (q.v.) and succeeded during a short period in reassembling progressive writers under its banner. However, the conservative policy of the President of the Matica, F. Lukas, did much to estrange writers and cultural workers.

After the Second World War, the Matica slowly revived. Especially in the Croatian Spring (q.v.), it again stood at the forefront of the Croat nationalist movement. The Matica took the initiative of issuing the Declaration on the Croatian Language (q.v.) of 1967 and supported linguistic work that stressed the specific nature of the Croatian language. It stimulated the growing demands for economic and political autonomy of Croatia as well. Then, the repression of 1972 stifled most of its activities and put many supporters in jail. It now seems to be regaining strength under the Tuđman (q.v.) regime with a revival of Croatian nationalism and self-awareness.

MATKOVIĆ, MARIJAN (1915-). Born in Karlovac (q.v.), dramatist, poet and essayist. He was strongly influenced by Miroslav Krleža (q.v.) and gained recognition especially as a playwright. His creation *Vašar Snova* (The Fair of Dreams) won the Sterijina Prize for a contemporary dramatic text in 1958.

MATOŠ, ANTUN GUSTAV (1873-1914). Writer of essays, stories and poetry. He introduced symbolism in Croatian poetry.

MATTHIAS CORVINUS see KORVIN, MATIJA

MATVEJEVIĆ, PEDRAG (1932-). Professor of French and Slavic literature at Zagreb (q.v.) and Paris Universities. Essayist, critic and translator. He was awarded prizes for his work on Krleža (q.v.), the new poetry and Mediterranean culture. He joined the critical intellectuals under the Tuđman (q.v.) regime.

MAZOWIECKI, TADEUSZ. Special reporter of the Human Rights Commission, who regularly visited the regions of former Yugoslavia in order to evaluate the human rights situation. During his second stay, he was accompanied by the legal doctor Clyde Snow, who reported on his findings in Ovcara. Probably there lie the remains of more than a hundred male persons who were evacuated by the Serbs from the hospital of Vukovar (q.v.), tortured and murdered. On the other side, Croatian misconduct has been reported during the retreat from the Medak offensive.

MAŽURANIĆ, IVAN (1814-1890). "Illyrian" Ban (qq.v.) and writer. He was born in Novi Vinodol in the Croatian Primorje and grew up with the poetry of Kačić-Miošić (q.v.) and the folk songs of his region.

In 1848, he entered Croatian political life. Threatened by the Hungarian revolution of that year, Austria sought Croatian support and allowed the Illyrian movement to express its goals freely. Ivan Mažuranić became the leader of this movement. He was appointed Croatian Court Chancellor in 1861 and Ban in 1873.

During his reign, the National Party (q.v.) was in power. Liberal laws on the right of assembly and freedom of the press were approved. Judicial power was separated from the executive powers. Mažuranić also founded cultural institutions, e.g., in 1874, Zagreb University (q.v.) was opened. In 1878, Austria-Hungary occupied Bosnia-Hercegovina. Nevertheless, the Vojna Krajina (q.v.) - the traditional buffer zone against the Ottomans - was not returned to Croatia. In protest Mažuranić resigned as Ban of Croatia. When the National Party split into two wings, Mažuranić took the head of one faction.

Ivan Mažuranić was a writer as well. He shared the great intention of the Illyrian movement in this field: the creation of a common literary language, orthography and literature (q.v.). Between 1835 and 1848, Mažuranić published lyric poetry in Gaj's (q.v.) *Danica.* His poem *Smrt Smail-Age Čengića* (The Death of Smail-Aga Čengić, 1845) has been honored as the masterpiece of romantic national Croatian literature. Mažuranić worked through once more the theme of the Slav resistance against the Turkish oppressor. Mažuranić expressed the strong national pride and self-awareness of the South Slav peoples.

MEĐIMURJE. Plain between the Drava and the lower Mura in northern Croatia. It is a densely populated and rich agricultural area, whose main town is Čakovec.

Prehistoric settlement has been shown. Under Roman rule, the region was a part of Upper Pannonia (q.v.). Around 550, it was occupied by the Slavs and acquired its lasting Slav character. At the end of the eighth century, it was absorbed into Frankish Lower Pannonia. During the period 840-880, it was ruled by the Princes Pribina and Kočel. In 896, the Hungarians arrived. In 1094, King Ladislas (q.v.) founded the Zagreb bishopric and Međimurje was appended to it on account of the Slav language spoken in the region.

MENČETIĆ VLAHOVIĆ, ŠIŠMUNDO (1457-1483). Poet of Dubrovnik (q.v.), under influence of the Italian Petrarchists.

MESIĆ, STJEPAN (1935-). Last President of ex-Yugoslavia and afterwards President of the Croatian Sabor (q.v.).

Under the communist regime, he had been a Member of Parliament (1966) and Mayor of his birthplace, Orahovica. As a lawyer working for political freedom, he was imprisoned by the communist regime in 1971. He was a founder-member of the Croatian Democratic Union (HDZ) (q.v.). After the HDZ victory in the elections of May 1990, he was appointed Prime Minister of Croatia and then Croatian representative in the presidency of the Yugoslav Federation. As it happened to be the turn of Croatia to perform the duty of head of the presidency, Mesić had to take over this function from the Serb Jović in the session of May 15, 1991. However, the representatives linked to Serbia (Vojvodina, Kosovo, Serbia and Montenegro) blocked Mesić's election. Only when the war with Slovenia had started and the European Community (q.v.) intervened, could Mesić occupy his seat as President of ex-Yugoslavia. When federal Yugoslavia disintegrated further and then the war in Croatia between the army and the republican authorities intensified, Mesić resigned from his post of President of the Federation.

Following the 1992 presidential and parliamentary elections (q.v.) and the victory of the HDZ, Mesić was chosen President of the Sabor. He also had a seat in the presidency of the HDZ. With Josip Manolić (q.v.) he belonged to the so-called left wing of the HDZ. As a consequence of the Glavas amendment accepted at the Second Convention of the HDZ, Mesić lost his voting power and major influence in this body. In the spring of 1994, he came under pressure to resign as President of the House of Representatives, and just as Josip Manolić, he was urged to leave the presidency of a House of Parliament. Together with Manolić, he founded at the end of April 1994 a new party, the Croatian Independent Democrats (q.v.), which gathered 16 other members of parliament and became a threat to the parliamentary majority of the HDZ.

MEŠTROVIĆ, IVAN (1883-1962). Best known sculptor of Yugoslavia. Born in Vrpolje (Dalmatian Zagorje). He made statues of Croatian political and religious leaders such as King Kraljević Marko, Ban Josip Jelačić (q.v.), Bishop Josip Strossmayer (q.v.), the historian Franjo Rački (q.v.) and above all the Bishop Grgur Ninski (q.v.), who is still expressing his full authority in the middle of Split (q.v.). As a sculptor, Meštrović was most attracted by symbolism. He also played a major role in politics. He defended the Yugoslav idea in the Yugoslav Committee (q.v.). He even supported the King during his dictatorship proclaimed in January 1929. Meštrović ended in emigration defending the national Croatian cause. There is a museum devoted to his work in Split.

METHODIUS see CYRILLUS

MIHALIĆ, SLAVKO (1928-). Born in Karlovac (q.v.). Contemporary writer of criticism and poetry. As a journalist, he came to Zagreb (q.v.), where he worked as an editor and publisher. He was editor of *Most/The Bridge*, a periodical presenting Croatian literature (q.v.) in foreign languages. He was Secretary of the Croatian Writers' Association (q.v.). Mihalić's much praised poetry is intellectualistic with its own abstract lexicon. His work has been widely translated.

MILITARY BORDER/VOJNA KRAJINA. The Military Border was not just a line, but a whole area of entire districts and communities specially organized for war. Most aspects of life were subordinated to the needs of defense and the communities developed a distinctive character different from the civilian hinterland. The institution existed for more than 350 years and until today has lasting effects on the population and its mentality. It is one of the historical determinants of the contemporary Croat-Serb war on Croatian territory.

The Military Border arose as a buffer zone against the Ottoman aggression. Parts of the region came to live more or less spontaneously under the pressure of war circumstances. Early in the sixteenth century, the Croatian Military Border was then formally established by Ferdinand I (q.v.) of Austria. The Inner-Austrian estates requested him in 1522 to organize a defended zone in northwestern Croatia against the Turkish raids. Ferdinand used mercenary troops to garrison locations in Croatia and blocked temporarily the Turkish invasion routes. For financial reasons the mercenaries were later replaced by military colonists. Most of them were refugees from the territories in Bosnia-Hercegovina and Croatia occupied by the Ottomans. The military colonists received substantial social and economic privileges in their new locations in the Border. Settlers of Orthodox faith were given freedom of worship.

The Habsburgs established a special administrative statute and created two military districts. The area between the coast and the Sava River was called the Croatian Border (later the Karlovac [q.v.] Border) and the region between the Sava and Drava was called the Slavonian Border (later the Varaždin [q.v.] Border). In 1553 Ferdinand appointed a general officer to command both borders with full authority over civil and military matters. This appointment removed the borders from the jurisdiction of civil Croatian authorities and divided the land into a civil and military sector. The organization of the Military Border was further strengthened in 1579. Archduke Charles of Styria, Carniola and Carinthia built a fortification where the Korana River flows into the Kupa (q.v.). Karlovac was to function as the center of the Military Border. In 1630, Ferdinand II of Styria issued the *Statuta Valachorum* which emphasized and confirmed the military character of the Border.

When the last Ottoman offensive against Vienna was repelled in 1683, the Austrians advanced on the entire front line. The border moved southward to recover larger parts of Croatia-Slavonia. The Sabor raised forces and participated in the reconquest of the area between the Kupa and Una Rivers. The Croatian troops liberated the eastern part of this region as far as the Sava. Here the Sabor organized a third border district with the Ban (q.v.) as commander: Banija (q.v.).

A large number of Serbs arrived in the Military Border during the last decade of the seventeenth century. In 1689, the Austrian army had launched an offensive into Serbia, but the next year the Austrians were driven back across the Danube. They had been followed by the Patriarch of the Serbian Orthodox Church, Arsenius Crnojević, who was leading with him more than 30,000 families. The authorities settled most of the refugees in western Slavonia (q.v.), but the Serbs dispersed over the whole Military Border. Since then, Serbs predominate in the Karlovac and Slavonian Military Districts. In the Banal Border, they constituted more than half of the population and in the Varaždin Border, they formed a strong minority. In 1691 Emperor Leopold granted the Orthodox Church special rights exceeding the concessions offered by Ferdinand I. The Leopoldine patents gave the Patriarch extended rights. In 1712, Karlovac became the religious center of the Habsburg Serbs.

Around this time, the Ottoman military threat on the Christian West was extinguished. The Peace of Srijemski Karlovci (q.v.) of 1689 returned most of the Hungarian territory to the Emperor. The Treaty of Požarevac (q.v.) in 1718 resulting from the war of 1714-1718 completed the Habsburg conquest of Hungary. Even Šumadija, the Ottoman Province of Belgrade, was temporarily annexed. The Military Border had lost its primary function as a buffer zone against the Ottomans. The Austrians preserved the Military Border as a reservoir of legionnaires for their European wars. Soldiers of the Military Border fought everywhere in Europe.

From then on, the Military Border was more and more perceived as a nuisance to the development of normal trade relations with the Ottomans. Moreover, the maintenance of the Border was expensive and the authorities became unwilling to carry the financial burden. The Nagodba (q.v.) of 1868 defined Croatia-Slovenia as an integral part of the Hungarian kingdom. The agreement stipulated that Hungary would work for the reintegration of the Military Border into the Croatian state. On June 8, 1871, the Austrian Emperor signed a decree that gradually terminated the Croatian Military Border. In the same year, Croatian nationalists provoked a limited military revolt at Rakovica (q.v.). It was quickly mastered, but it convinced the Austrians to accelerate the dismantling of the Border. An imperial edict disbanded the last Border regiments on October 1, 1873. (See also SERBIAN REPUBLIC OF KRAJINA)

MINISTARSTVO UNUTRAŠNIH POSLOVA (MUP) see MINISTRY OF THE INTERIOR

MINISTRY OF THE INTERIOR/MINISTARSTVO UNUTRAŠNIH POSLOVA (MUP). The acronym MUP is the official name of the Croatian police forces.

MIROSLAV, KING. Croatian King who ruled in the period 945-949 after Krešimir I. He was a contemporary of Constantine VII Porphyrogenitus (q.v.). He notes that Miroslav was killed in a civil war by Ban Pribana and that in consequence Croatian power sharply declined. In this period Croatia lost the islands of Hvar and Brač to the Neretvans (qq.v.). (See also TRPIMIR DYNASTY)

MIROSLAV GOSPEL. The *Miroslavjevo Jevandjelje* was made in a scriptorium in Hum (now Hercegovina) for the Prince of Hum, a brother of the Serbian ruler Stefan Nemanja. It is written in Cyrillic (q.v.) and is famous for its beautiful miniatures and initials, probably done by a Benedictine monk from the Dalmatian coast. The scriptorium of Hum endeavored to replace the many manuscripts that had been burned during the anti-Bogomil (q.v.) campaign of Byzantium.

MIŠKIN, MIHOVIL PAVLEK. Writer and member of the Council of the Croatian Peasant Party (q.v.). He was sent to the concentration camp at Jasenovac (q.v.) on the establishment of the Independent State of Croatia (q.v.), where he died.

MISSAL OF 1483. First printed Croatian book, probably produced in Kosinje in the region of Lika (q.v.). It uses the Glagolitic (q.v.) alphabet. Its model is Prince Novak's Missal, now preserved in Vienna.

MODERNA see LITERATURE, MODERN

MONETARY POLICY AND INFLATION. Since the introduction of a separate currency - the Croatian dinar (CRD) - at the end of 1991, inflation has been the foremost concern of economic policy. Throughout the 1980s, Yugoslavia witnessed galloping inflation. This was, again, the situation even before the war broke out, and the war has increased inflationary momentum mostly through creating an enormous pressure on the budget. Along with the huge budget deficit, inflation was also fuelled with so-called selective credits. The selective credit policy consists of credit subsidies, i.e., soft loans, which commercial banks grant to certain sectors (foremost agriculture). These credits are refinanced by the central bank at below market interest rates. In the second quarter of 1993 selective credits - the worst example of socialist soft budget constraint practices - have been to some extent eliminated from the practice of the National Bank (q.v.) of

Croatia. The problem is, of course, that those sectors that have been beneficiaries will now pressure the budget, and in turn there will be a claim on the central authorities to monetize that deficit.

MONETARY UNIT. The Tuđman (q.v.) regime took over the Yugoslav dinar from the communists. The Croatian dinar was introduced at the end of 1991 to protect the country against imported inflation and the wild new printing of money in Belgrade. In 1993, the Croatian Parliament (q.v.) accepted the kuna as the new monetary unit. *Kuna* is the Croatian word for marten and refers symbolically to the primary means of payment in the early history of Croatia. The name was also used during the Second World War in the Independent State of Croatia (q.v.). The opposition in Parliament argued that the new currency unit could therefore harm the international image of Croatia. It was later revealed that the communist partisans in Bosnia-Hercegovina used the kuna as well.

MONGOL INVASION. In April 1241, the Mongol invaders defeated the Hungarian King Bela IV on the Sajo River near the present-day town of Miskolcz. The Croatian Duke Koloman, Bela's brother, fell mortally wounded. In the winter of 1242, the Mongols crossed the Danube and the Hungarian King fled first to Turopolje near Zagreb (q.v.) and then to the Adriatic coast. Fran Frankopan of Krk (q.v.), the Ban (q.v.) of Croatia and Dalmatia, called the Croat Župans (q.v.) to arms and defeated part of the Mongol army at Grobničko Polje near Rijeka (qq.v.). The Mongols returned to the east when they heard that the Great Khan had died in Asia. The Mongols had undermined the power of the Hungarian King and contributed in that manner to the complete feudalization of Croatia. Croatian nobles exercised their autonomous power on the devastated land. (See also ARPAD DYNASTY)

MOST/THE BRIDGE. The journal *Most/The Bridge* is published by the Croatian Writers' Association (q.v.). It is a journal of translations of Croatian literary work and criticism. Recent issues presented translations of Croatian historical work and essays.

MOVEMENT FOR PEACE. This organization based in Rijeka (q.v.) promotes peace by enhancing communications among national groups. It organizes peace rallies and cultural presentations, supports disarmament efforts, and publishes and disseminates pamphlets and brochures. It works with refugees, deserters and returning soldiers.

MUSEUMS see CROATIAN NATURAL HISTORY MUSEUM

MUSIC. Folk music has its roots in ancient times. However, this oral tradition has not left many material traces. The first written music on Croatian territory has been found to date from the eleventh century. Manuscripts of religious music were preserved in churches and monasteries. The first known composers on Croatian soil only appeared in the sixteenth century: Julije Slavetić and Ivan Lukačić (1587-1648), both from Šibenik, published motets.

Composers in the Adriatic region were in close contact with European - and especially Italian - musical developments and they followed the main trends in their work. Particularly interesting are a series of composers making creative use of the Croatian folk culture (q.v.).

The Illyrian (q.v.) movement stimulated musical creation in a nationalist Croatian spirit. Vatroslav Lisinski (1819-1854) is without doubt the greatest Croat composer of his time. He is also the author of the first modern Croatian opera *Ljubav i zloba* (Love and Malice, 1846). Ivan Zajc (1832-1914) organized musical life in Zagreb and composed the romantic heroic opera *Nikola Šubić Zrinski*.

The pianist Ivo Pogorelić is one of the best known contemporary Croatian performers.

- N -

NACIONALNI KONZORCIJ SRBA see NATIONAL CONSORTIUM OF SERBS

NAGODBA. The Croato-Hungarian Compromise of 1868 regulated the relations between the Kingdom of Dalmatia, Croatia and

Slavonia and the Kingdom of Hungary. The agreement reflected the continuing dominant position of Hungary over Croatia after the conclusion of the Ausgleich (q.v.). Although politically dependent on Hungary, the Croats retained some characteristics of their statehood and remained in a dominant position over the other Slav elements in the Empire. Croatia was politically acknowledged and preserved its independence in legislation, domestic administration, religious matters and education. Croatian was accepted as the official language in the Croatian civil service and in offices of the joint Imperial administration on Croatian soil. Croatian deputies could even speak Croatian in the Parliament in Budapest. The Croatian administration was headed by a Governor who was appointed upon the recommendation of the Hungarian Minister-President. Defense, finance, trade and transportation were joint affairs under Hungarian administration. Most of the state's income had to go to the Hungarian national treasury. Hungary retained the port of Rijeka (q.v.) under its direct control.

The Croato-Hungarian agreement caused great dissatisfaction among Croatian politicians. The National Party (q.v.) began fighting it bitterly. In 1871, Eugen Kvaternik (q.v.) of Starčević's Party of Rights (qq.v.) declared Croatia independent and organized an unsuccessful uprising. In 1873, after serious persecution of members of the National Party, the party leaders unwillingly consented to only a minor amendment of the agreement. The changes in the document were insignificant and the aspirations of the Croatian nationalists were blocked for years.

NAIVE PAINTERS. Typical Slavonian (q.v.) school of painters whose most appreciated representatives are Ivan Generalić, Ivan Lacković-Croata and Mijo Kovačić. (See HLEBINA SCHOOL)

NAPOLEON I BONAPARTE (1769-1821). Napoleon established the Illyrian Provinces (q.v.) by a Decree of October 14, 1809, that united all the lands conquered on Austria. Under the supervision of Governor Marshal August de Marmont a system of primary schooling was introduced. In 1813, the French troops withdrew from the Illyrian Provinces. Though short-lived, this experience would remain a reference point and source of inspiration for later generations to build a unified state of the South Slavs. (See ILLYRIAN MOVEMENT)

NARODNA BANKA see NATIONAL BANK

NARODNA STRANKA see NATIONAL PARTY

NARODNO VIJEĆE SLOVENACA, HRVATA I SRBA see NATIONAL COUNCIL OF SLOVENES, CROATS AND SERBS

NARONA. Roman settlement near present-day Metković, a town at the mouth of the Neretva (q.v.) in Hercegovina.

NATIONAL ANTHEM see LIJEPA NAŠA DOMOVINO

NATIONAL BANK. The National Bank of Croatia (Hrvatska Narodna Banka) was a republican branch of the Yugoslav National Bank. On December 22, 1991, the Croatian National Bank became independent when a decree came into force based on the Law on the Autonomy of the National Bank of Croatia, adopted by the Croatian government on October 8, 1991.

NATIONAL CONSORTIUM OF SERBS/NACIONALNI KONZORCIJ SRBA. The National Consortium of Serbs is an initiative of the Serbian National Party (SNS) (q.v.) to regroup all Serbs of Croatia - including those living in the United Nations Protected Areas and pink zones (qq.v.) - in one organization. Its purpose is to defend the interests of the inhabitants of Serb nationality and to define their status. The political, scientific and social autonomy of the participants is to be respected. Membership includes the representatives in Parliament (q.v.), the SNS, the Serbian Democratic Forum (q.v.), Orthodox institutions, the publishing house Prosveta, independent intellectuals and representatives of all other parties. A declaration of the Consortium about the questions of the political, historical and cultural status of the Serbs in the Republic of Croatia is to be discussed and accepted by consensus.

NATIONAL COUNCIL OF SLOVENES, CROATS AND SERBS/NARODNO VIJEĆE SLOVENACA, HRVATA I SRBA. It was founded at the end of World War I on October 5-6, 1918.

The Council did not accept a last offer of the Austrian-Hungarian monarchy to form a federation. The Croatian Parliament broke off all relations with Austria-Hungary on October 29, 1918, and proclaimed Croatia independent. It decided to join the State of Slovenes, Croats and Serbs. This state of the Slav peoples on the former Habsburg territory was not recognized by the international community, nor taken as an equal partner by the Kingdom of the Serbs. When Italy, in execution of the secret Treaty of London (q.v.), threatened to occupy major parts of Slovenia and Croatia, and when confronted with clear signs of internal social unrest, the National Council concluded an agreement with the Kingdom of Serbia on the unconditional unification of the two states.

NATIONAL EMBLEMS. The Tuđman (q.v.) regime has accepted some emblems that originated in the times of the early Croat kingdoms. They sometimes irritate the Serbs of the Krajina (q.v.), as they were also used during the Ustaša (q.v.) regime in the Independent State of Croatia (q.v.). The emblems are the tricolor flag (red, white and blue, arranged in this order perpendicularly to the staff) and the coat of arms (13 red squares and 12 silver squares arranged intermittently in a 5 times pattern). It is a very old symbol of Croatia resembling a red and white chess table. Historic tradition ascribes the use of the coat of arms to the reign of Stipan Držislav (q.v.) (969-997), whose status of King was officially recognized by the Byzantines. The use of the coat of arms was confirmed by fifteenth-century documents. It also appeared on a seal from the Charter that confirmed the election of Ferdinand I (q.v.) of Habsburg as the Croatian King at the town of Cetin in 1527. This old coat of arms crowned with the Zagreb, Dubrovnik, Slavonia, Istria and Dalmatia (qq.v.) coat of arms is the national symbol of the contemporary independent Republic of Croatia. The system of old national symbols will be further completed by the acceptance of kuna as the name for the monetary unit. *Kuna* means marten and it was used as a primary means of payment in the early history of Croatia. Money already carried this name in the Independent State of Croatia during the Second World War.

NATIONAL GUARD/ZBOR NARODNE GARDE (ZNG). The National Guard is one of the defense organizations of Croatia. It played a determining role in the first period of the Serbo-Croat war.

NATIONAL PARKS. Croatia possesses the following national parks (some of which are under the protection of UNESCO): the Kornati Islands, the Plitvice (q.v.) Lakes, Krka, Paklenica, the Island of Mljet, Risnjak and the Brijuni Islands.

NATIONAL PARTY/NARODNA STRANKA. The party united the Illyrian (q.v.) nationalists as a reaction against the formation of the party of the Hungarians in Croatia (Horvatsko-vugerska Stranka, founded in 1841). The party of the Croatian nationalists was therefore first called "Illyrian." King Ferdinand (q.v.) of Austria forbade the use of the name "Illyrian" in 1843 and the party was renamed Narodna Stranka - National Party. The party later split over the question of whether Croatia should have joint competences with Vienna. In 1863, Ivan Mažuranić (q.v.) formed the federalistic-oriented Independent National Party (Samostalna Narodna Stranka). This party wanted to make a compromise with Austria before Hungary did. It hoped in this way to avoid a joint diktat of the Crown and the Hungarians and thereby achieve Croatian national independence and territorial unity. However, this party lost the elections in 1865.

NATIONAL RIGHTS. Preservation of the rights of the minority forms a key problem in the legal and political life of Croatia. It is the special competence of the House of Counties to give the House of Representatives a prior opinion on the procedure for the enactment of the Constitution (q.v.) and the laws which regulate national rights. Laws which regulate national rights shall be passed by the House of Representatives by a two-thirds majority vote of all representatives.

NATIONALITY STRUCTURE. The nationality structure of the population is revealed by the population census. People simply have to declare themselves as belonging to a nationality. In the census of 1991, the following distribution was observed: Croats, 78.1 percent; Serbs, 12.2 percent; Yugoslavs, 2.2 percent; Muslims, 0.9 percent; Hungarians, 0.5 percent; Slovenes, 0.5 percent; Italians, 0.5 percent; and others, 5.2 percent. Altogether there are 26 minorities.

NAZOR, VLADIMIR (1876-1949). Writer, born on the island Brač (q.v.). At the end of 1942, when he was 66 years old, he joined the partisans along with the writer Ivan Goran Kovačić (q.v.). About this experience, Nazor wrote a diary and poems. In and after the war, he assumed government posts. (See also ANTI-FASCIST COUNCIL OF THE NATIONAL LIBERATION OF CROATIA)

NEIGHBOR, MY. A Christian humanitarian organization operating in Zagreb (q.v.). It provides assistance to some 20,000 families each month. It works for the repatriation of refugees and exiles by encouraging their involvement in the reconstruction of villages and the resumption of agricultural activities in war-ravaged areas. It publishes a newspaper about refugee affairs.

NERETVA. Main river in Hercegovina. The peoples who lived in this region in ancient times were called by Constantine Porphyrogenitus (q.v.) *Neretvans* or *Pagani* because they had not been baptized. Their land on the shores of the Adriatic at the mouth of the Neretva was surrounded by White Croatia and Zahumlja (qq.v.). Also, later in history, the inhabitants of the region preserved - not without reason - a reputation as free raiders and wild pirates.

NERETVANSKA KRAJINA. The Neretva (q.v.) region between the rivers Neretva and Cetina was first mentioned by Constantine Porphyrogenitus (q.v.) in the tenth century as *Pagani* or *Arenta.* This region was autonomous until the end of the eleventh century and famous for its pirates. They were in constant battle with Venetian ships and also attacked Dubrovnik (q.v.). Venetian and Croatian rulers paid tolls and taxes for free navigation in the region. In the second half of the twelfth century, they came under the dominance of Croatian rulers, especially the tribe *(plemen)* of the Kačići. Still, they continued their pirate activities and controlled the navigation on the Adriatic. In the year 1221, the Roman Curia offered the inhabitants of Omiš forgiveness for their sins if they would burn their ships.

NEWS AGENCY OF THE CROATIAN REPUBLIC OF HERCEG-BOSNA/HERCEG-BOSNA NOVINSKA AGENCIJA (HBNA). This news Agency has its headquarters in Međugorje.

NEXUS. Organization in Zagreb (q.v.) that coordinates medical and humanitarian aid from private donors for grassroots, small-scale initiatives in Croatia and Bosnia-Hercegovina. With an emphasis on personal contact between donors and recipients, Nexus checks to see that aid reaches its goal without being diverted to the black market, assesses the legitimacy of recipients' requests, and ensures that the aid is used effectively.

NEZAVISNA DRŽAVA HRVATSKA (NDH) see INDEPENDENT STATE OF CROATIA

NOVAK, SLOBODAN (1924-). Born in Split (q.v.). Short story and novel writer. Co-founder and editor of the literary periodicals *Krugovi* (Circles, 1952-1955) and *Forum* (1985-1987). His novel *Mirisi, zlato i tamjan* (Scents, Gold and Incense, 1968) has been adapted and presented at BITEF, the Belgrade Theater Festival, in 1974. Four feature films were based on his prose.

NOVAK, SLOBODAN PROSPEROV (1951-). Born in Belgrade. Professor of Croatian literature at Zagreb University (q.v.). As President of PEN-Croatia, he organized a meeting of PEN-International in a Dubrovnik (q.v.) that had just been devastated by war. In the autumn of 1993, he was criticized by the highest Croatian authorities for his independent and critical views on the situation in Croatia, presented in an introduction to a concert of the Zagreb Philharmonic Orchestra in Germany.

NOVI DANAS see DANAS

NOVI LIST. The New Paper is an independent regional daily edited in Rijeka (q.v.). It is an important source of information in a region where the ruling Croatian Democratic Union (q.v.) is weak. The newspaper is entirely owned by its employees after fighting off a government effort to impose a management board.

NOVI VJESNIK. The New Courier, a "daily for Democratic Croatia" *(Dnevnik za Demokratsku Hrvatsku)*, is the heir of the more than 50-year-old *Vjesnik*. The newspaper is thought to be financially and ideologically under the influence of the governing Croatian Democratic Union (HDZ) (q.v.). It cannot, however, be regarded as just a transmitter of HDZ ideology and has preserved a lot of editorial independence. The newspaper is edited in Zagreb (q.v.).

- O -

OLD CHURCH SLAVONIC. There are no remains of Croatian writing dating from earlier than the twelfth century. There is a debate on the question of whether the Apostle Cyril brought with him the Glagolitic (q.v.) alphabet, or whether he picked it up in Western Slavic areas. Notwithstanding the Byzantine influence, the Croatian church was under constant pressure from Rome to use the Western rites and Latin. The Split Synods of 925 and 1060 passed resolutions against the use of the Slavic liturgy. However many priests did not learn Latin and continued to use the Glagolitic Old Church Slavonic. This liturgical language came under the influence of the čakavian (q.v.) dialect spoken in daily life by the priests. The changes were accelerated after the Lateran Councils in the first half of the thirteenth century, when it was decided that a plurality of languages and rituals could be accepted in the Catholic Church on the condition that all liturgical texts should be revised in conformity with the Latin Vulgate. This stimulated translation activities and in Croatia a čakavian liturgical standard language was created under the influence of the spoken language.

Likewise, it was essential for the flowering of a čakavian secular literature in the fourteenth and fifteenth century. From the medieval period until romanticism, however, there is a lack of continuous tradition. The Glagolitic čakavian school, which had developed into a smooth and flexible literary language gradually died out. (See also GLAGOLITIC)

OMLADINSKA TELEVIZIJA (OTV) see YOUTH TELEVISION

OSIJEK. Main town of Slavonia (q.v.) on the right bank of the Drava. In the first century A.D., the Romans established the fortification of Mursa on the banks of the river. Emperor Hadrian gave it the status of *colonia* in 133. The Byzantine Emperor Constantine II defeated the Roman Emperor Magnentius in 351 near the village. During the great migrations at the end of the sixth century, the town was destroyed by the Avars (q.v.). A new settlement grew here in the tenth century. The name of Osijek was first encountered in 1196. In 1526, the town was taken by the Turks. After a campaign by Prince Eugene of Savoy in 1690, Osijek remained in Austrian hands under the name of Esseg.

OSIJEK CENTER FOR PEACE, NON-VIOLENCE AND HUMAN RIGHTS. Center located near the frontline of Serb-controlled Croatia. It seeks to ensure protection of human rights by monitoring abuses and through direct action, including use of "house sitting" teams to monitor homes of individuals (often Serbs) whose properties are at risk of illegal confiscation. It provides training in conflict mediation and public seminars on coping with war trauma, conscientious objection and human rights.

OSIMO AGREEMENT. Agreement signed on November 10, 1975, between Italy (q.v.) and Yugoslavia. It completed the Memorandum of Understanding from 1954 and settled definitively the frontier issues between the two countries. After the fall of communist Yugoslavia, Italy, Croatia and Slovenia (q.v.) entered a new round of negotiations on the ratification of this agreement. Minor territorial disputes and compensation demands of Italian refugees could revive the nationalistic animosity of earlier years.

OSOR see CRES

OWEN-STOLTENBERG PLAN. Global plan for Bosnia-Hercegovina of the mediators David Owen and Thorvald Stoltenberg. This plan was the next in line after the Vance-Owen plan (q.v.), once the latter had been rejected by the Bosnian Serbs in a referendum. The Owen-Stoltenberg plan is based on a division of Bosnia-Hercegovina along ethnic lines. Each of the three constituent peoples would get its own republic. Connections of strategic importance between dispersed areas or towards the sea would in principle be guaranteed. Sarajevo would be under United Nations and Mostar under European Community (q.v.) administration. The new compromise took for granted the reality of the Serb territorial gains during the Bosnian war. The plan granted the Serbs 52 percent of the territory, the Croats 17 percent and the Bosnians the remainder.

The recognition of the principle of ethnic division and the evident acceptance of the military fait accompli could have adverse implications for the solution of the Serb problem in Croatia. Tuđman (q.v.) found it necessary to publicly reject such a line of thought. He was nevertheless thought to agree with the ethnic division of Bosnia-Hercegovina under the influence of the Hercegovian lobby in his government, led by Minister of Defense Gojko Šušak (q.v.).

- P -

PACTA CONVENTA. Agreement reached between the Hungarian King Koloman (q.v.) and representatives of the 12 noble clans of Croatia. On the one hand, the authority of the King over Croatian lands was recognized. On the other, the Pacta defined the privileges and independence of the Croatian nobility towards the King. This agreement was later supplemented by further privileges granted by the King after 1102 to various Dalmatian (q.v.) towns. They determined their constitutional position, gave them certain privileges and freed them from obligations to provide accommodation for the King or to receive within their precincts Hungarians in the King's entourage, especially on the occasion of a coronation.

In the early period of this community between Croatia and Hungary, one can speak of a purely personal union. The Ban (q.v.) of Croatia, Dalmatia and Slavonia, though nominated by the King, enjoyed executive and juridical authority and convened the Sabor (q.v.) on his own initiative. Later on Hungarian political and administrative intervention would expand and cause permanent tensions and clashes between the two peoples. Austria would play an intermediary role, by directly intervening in some parts of Croatia. (See also AUSGLEICH; MILITARY BORDER; NAGODBA; PRAGMATIC SANCTION)

PAG. Long island off Karlobag and Zadar (q.v.). It is an important alternative route as the road along the coast and the Maslenica bridge are threatened by the Krajina (q.v.) Serbs. Pag was colonized by the Liburnians (q.v.) and the Romans. The Slavs arrived in the sixth century. In 1071, King Krešimir IV (q.v.) assigned the northern part of Pag to the church of Rab (q.v.) and the southern part to Zadar (q.v.). From 1409 to 1797, the Venetians held the island. In the town of Pag, Juraj Dalmatinac erected in 1443 the still existing parish church.

PAGO see PAG

PAINTING. As elsewhere in Europe, the earliest works of art in Croatia served religion. The oldest preserved frescoes in St. Michael's Church of Ston date from the eleventh century. In Byzantine or early Christian style, a painting shows the Croatian King who donates his church. A highly interesting "Danse Macabre" was painted by Master Vincent of Kastav in St. Mary's Church in Beram (Istria) around 1474. Madonna painting was popular in Dalmatia (q.v.). Blaž Jurjev (1390-1450) and Nikola Božidarević (ca. 1460-1517) developed their own style and use of color.

The Croats were also known for miniature painting. Both Julije Clović of Grižane (1491-1578) and Franjo Pestančić were official miniaturists at the Hungarian court. From the Renaissance on, Croatian painting along the Adriatic and in the Zagreb (q.v.) area followed the evolution of Central and Western European art.

After the Second World War, social realism was quickly followed by surrealism and abstract painting. Of particular interest in contemporary painting are the so-called "naive painters" (q.v.). The most known among them is Ivan Generalić of the Hlebina school (q.v.). This school developed out of the socially committed Zemlja group (q.v.).

PANNONIA. Region east of Zagreb (q.v.), now roughly identified with present-day Slavonia (q.v.). Pannonia became a province of the Roman Empire. First its western part was conquered in 35 B.C. and then its eastern part in 14 B.C., with the capture of Sirmium (present-day Srijemska Mitrovica). In about 106 A.D., Emperor Trajan divided the province into Pannonia Superior, the western and northern part, and Pannonia Inferior, the southern and eastern districts. In 297, Pannonia Superior was further divided by Diocletian into Pannonia Prima (north of the Drava and Mura) and Pannonia Ripariensisor Savia (south of the Drava and Mura with Siscia as capital); Pannonia Inferior was divided into Valeria (north of the Drava on the right side of the Danube) and Pannonia Segunda (south of the Drava with Sirmium as capital). The Romans had to withdraw from Pannonia after 395.

PANNONIAN CROATIA see WHITE CROATIA

PANNONIUS, JANUS see ČESMIČKI, IVAN

PARADŽIK, ANTE. He was elected President of the Student Federation of the Republic of Croatia during the Croatian Spring (q.v.) in 1971, although he was not a member of the Communist Party. He was put in jail during the repression of the movement. He was politically active again in the post-communist period. In 1991, he was deliberately shot at a barricade by Croatian national guards. Three of the four assassins were acquitted, but at the end of 1993 the trial was reopened.

PARAGA, DOBROSLAV. Politician, first and former President of the new Croatian Party of Rights (HSP) (q.v.). Paraga acknowledged the historical bonds with the HSP from before 1929, but he rejected any later connections with the Ustaša (q.v.) regime. However, his party supported a military section, the Croatian Armed Forces (HOS) (q.v.), whose members openly displayed Ustaša symbols. At first, the actions of this paramilitary group were highly successful and put great pressure on Tuđman (q.v.).

Paraga was prosecuted for an interview he gave the newspaper *Slobodna Dalmacija* (q.v.), published on January 18, 1992. He declared that Tuđman was a traitor because he signed the agreement of October 4, 1991, in The Hague. According to Paraga, this agreement implied the loss of Slavonia (q.v.). A passage that was agreed on during negotiations with the Serb community of East Slavonia (q.v.) should have been deleted in the official Croatian version. Paraga maintains that in doing so, Tuđman may have agreed to separate this region from Croatia and may have misled the patriots and Croatian fighters in East Slavonia. On the basis of these assertions, Paraga was accused of public offense to the President.

Paraga was later also accused of an attempt to overthrow the government by force. He was arrested but soon released. He participated in the second presidential elections without obtaining massive support. Thereafter, his militia, the HOS, moved to Bosnia-Hercegovina. In the summer of 1993, Paraga finally appeared before the military court on charges of attempt to overthrow the legal order. A long trial began and numerous officials appeared as witnesses. In the confused war climate of 1991, tendencies towards autonomy of the HOS had to be balanced against the need to defend the country against aggression and the lack of a clear organization of the defense forces.

In the autumn of 1993, Paraga was dismissed as HSP President by an extraordinary meeting of his party in Kutina. He was replaced by Boris Kandare and Ante Đapić as new HSP leaders.

PARENTIUM see POREČ

PARLIAMENT. According to the Constitution (q.v.) of December 1990, Parliament is the highest legislative body. It consists of two Houses: the House of Representatives (Zastupnički Dom) has between 100 and 160 national members; the House of Counties (Županijski Dom) (q.v.) represents regional interests.

Members are elected for a period of four years. Voting is by secret ballot. All men and women aged 18 years and older are entitled to vote and to run for office. A new electoral law was adopted in April 1992. It provided a combination of majority and proportional representation in the House of Representatives and majority representation in the House of Counties. The law reserved four seats in the House of Representatives for small minorities and provided for proportional representation of the Serbian minority. (See also ELECTIONS)

PARTY OF THE CROATIAN STATE'S RIGHTS/STRANKA HRVATSKOG DRŽAVNOG PRAVA (SHDP). One of the minor parties claiming to bring the correct interpretation of the ideas of Ante Starčević (q.v.). Its President is Nikola Bićanić. It participates in the integration discussions of the Parties of Rights.

PASPALJ, MILAN. President of the Parliament of the Serbian Autonomous Region of Krajina (Srpska Autonomna Krajina). Discarding the earlier President of the Parliament of the Krajina in Knin, Milan Babić (qq.v.), Milan Paspalj persuaded his Parliament in Glina to accept the Vance plan (q.v.). This happened on February 9, 1992, and fitted in with the political strategy of the Serbian President Slobodan Miloševič. At the time, he was threatened with sanctions by the international community and tried in vain to avert them.

PASSAROWITZ see POŽAREVAC

PAVELIĆ, ANTE (1869-1938). Croatian politician who endorsed the Yugoslav idea. In 1917, he became the leader of Starčević's Croatian Party of Rights (qq.v.) and supported the May Declaration, a manifesto of the South Slavic Club in the Vienna Reichsrat promulgated on May 30, 1917. This document called for unification of all lands in the Monarchy inhabited by Slovenes, Croats and Serbs. On October 5 and 6, 1918, delegates of Croatian, Serbian and Slovene parties founded the National Council of the Slovenes, Croats and Serbs. Ante Pavelić was made Vice-President of this body. On October 29, the Sabor (q.v.) accepted the proposal of Pavelić, Pribićević (q.v.) and others to declare independence from the Habsburgs and to transfer its powers to the National Council. On October 31, 1918, the National Council declared that the State of Slovenes, Croats and Serbs was ready to enter into a common state with Serbia and Montenegro. Pavelić supported the Unification Act of December 1, 1918, which effectively united the Kingdom of Serbia (and Montenegro) and the State of Slovenes, Croats and Serbs.

PAVELIĆ, ANTE (1899-1959). Lawyer and Croatian representative in the Belgrade Parliament. In 1929, he founded the Ustaša (q.v.) movement as a reaction against the dictatorship of King Alexander (q.v.). Together with the Macedonian separatist movement IMRO, he organized the assassination of the King in France. During the Second World War, he accepted the leadership of the Independent State of Croatia (q.v.) under protection of the Germans. The Ustaša regime and Pavelić were known for the cruelty of their anti-communist and anti-Serbian policy. At the end of the war, Pavelić fled abroad.

PEAKIĆ-MIKULJAN, MARIA (1943-). Writer. President of the Croatian Writers' Association (q.v.) (1985-1988). Director of the Publishing House of the Matica hrvatska (q.v.) (1988-1991). Member of the Central Bureau of the Croatian Democratic Union (q.v.).

PEJAČEVIĆ, LADISLAV (1824-1901). Ban (q.v.) of Croatia in the period from 1880 to 1883. He succeeded Ban Ivan Mažuranić (q.v.), who had resigned because the Vojna Krajina (q.v.) was not reintegrated into Croatia after the occupation of Bosnia-Hercegovina. In 1881, the Austrian government in Vienna made a concession and placed the Vojna Krajina back under the competence of Croatia. Problems with Hungarian nationalism provoked social unrest in Croatia and led to the appointment of a Royal Commissioner for Croatia. In 1883, the Hungarian-minded Karoly Khuen-Hedervary (q.v.) was appointed Ban.

PEOPLE'S REPUBLIC OF CHINA (RELATIONS WITH). On invitation of the President of the People's Republic of China, President Tuđman (q.v.) and a state delegation visited China from June 6 to 12, 1993. On this occasion, agreements were concluded on the promotion and mutual protection of investments, on cultural and educational cooperation, on maritime cooperation, and on consultations between the Croatian and Chinese Ministries of Foreign Affairs. The President of the People's Republic of China was invited to Croatia.

PERUČA. Dam on the Cetina River (q.v.). The Krajina (q.v.) Serbs conquered the construction and threatened to blow it up. The intervention of UNPROFOR prevented an ecological disaster.

PETROVA GORA. South of Karlovac (q.v.) and to the west of Topusko and Vrginmost lies the mountain chain Gvozd or Petrova Gora. The mountains separate the hinterland of Dalmatia from Croatia proper and Pannonian (qq.v.) Croatia. Peter's Mountain commemorates the name of Petar II Svačić, supposed to have been the last Croatian King. He fell in 1097 during the invasion of the

Hungarian King Koloman (q.v.). In 1102, the Croatian nobles formally accepted Hungarian rule by the Pacta Conventa (q.v.).

PETROVIĆ, DRAŽEN (? -1993). Born in Šibenik. Basketball player. He first played on his local team and then was transferred to a Zagreb team, Cibona. With both teams, he won the national Yugoslav competition. Then he left for Madrid and finally emigrated to the United States. He played for teams in Portland and New Jersey. A car crash in Germany marked the end of his life and the beginning of a legend.

PETROVIĆ, GAJO (1927-1993). Born in Karlovac (q.v.). Late Professor of Philosophy at Zagreb University (q.v.). Member of the *Praxis* group and long-time editor of the journal *Praxis* (q.v.). He defended a new interpretation of Marxism based on the philosophical works of the young Marx. His continuous radical criticism of the dogmatic ideology of the League of Communists of Yugoslavia (q.v.) led to an open conflict and the banning of the journal.

PHARE PROGRAM. The European Community supports the process of political and economic reforms in Central and Eastern Europe in several ways. The main instrument of financial and technical cooperation is the European Commission's PHARE program. The first program to be defined was the "Poland and Hungary Action for Restructuring of the Economy." Later, the program was extended to other Central and Eastern European countries. So far, Croatia has not been included for political reasons.

PHILOSOPHIC INSTITUTE OF THE UNIVERSITY OF ZAGREB. The Philosophic Institute was founded in 1967. Its first Director was Dr. Pedrag Vranicki. The Institute coordinates the philosophic research and organizes postgraduate studies.

It has a special mandate to do research in Croatian philosophy and to prepare publications, translations and critical editions of Croatian philosophers. In 1977, it merged with other sections into the Center for Historic Sciences, but in 1991 the Institute regained its autonomy. In its first period *Praxis* (q.v.) philosophers dominated the work of the Philosophic Institute. In recent times, and especially since 1991, the history of national Croatian philosophy has come to the forefront. The Institute publishes *Prilozi za istraživanje hrvatske filozofske baštine* (Contributions to the Research on the Croatian Philosophical Heritage) and *Studia historiae philosophiae Croaticae.*

PINK ZONES. Zones conquered by the Yugoslav army where there was not a majority of Serbs and which lie mainly around the Krajina (q.v.) enclave. Its area is estimated at 2,206 sq. km. Theoretically, they came under supervision of UNPROFOR (q.v.). In the region of Zadar (q.v.), the pink zones remained under constant pressure of the Serbian and Croatian parties. In 1993, permanent shelling from and over the zones twice led to an offensive of the Croatian army. (See GOSPIĆ OFFENSIVE; MASLENICA)

PIRKER, PERO. Mayor of Zagreb (q.v.) during the Croatian Spring (q.v.). He was forced to resign when Tito (q.v.) had all nationalist leaders removed.

PLITVICE. National park (q.v.) under UNESCO protection. It consists of 16 lakes linked with one another by overflows. It was Austrian officers who built the first accommodations for visitors. In 1893, the Society for the Development of the Plitvice Lakes was established in Zagreb. The area was declared a national park in 1928. It is one of the first regions that came under the control of the Serbs during the last Serb-Croatian war.

PLOČE. Port at the mouth of the Neretva River (q.v.). Though the town belongs to Croatian territory, President Tuđman (q.v.) agreed in the negotiations on the Owen-Stoltenberg plan (q.v.) to grant Muslims seaport facilities here. Mate Boban (q.v.) and the Bosnian Croats had refused to hand over the seaport Neum in Herceg-Bosna. Once Boban was removed from the negotiations between the Muslims and Croatia and an agreement was reached on a Muslim-Croat federation in Bosnia-Hercegovina and a confederation of this state with Croatia, the problem of seaport facilities for the Bosnians was automatically solved.

PLOMIN INSCRIPTION. The Glagolitic inscription from Plomin dates from the second half of the eleventh century. The inscription is accompanied by the relief of a male figure, most likely the pagan Silvanus. He is carrying a spring branch of green leaves. In early Christian times, he became equated with Sveti Juraj (St. George). Plomin lies on the east coast of Istria, halfway along the Rijeka-Pula road and opposite the island of Cres (qq.v.). The Romans built a fortification in Plomin and later a church dedicated to Sveti Juraj was built on that place.

PODRAVINA. Region in Slavonia (q.v.) along the Drava River.

POPULATION. According to the 1991 population census, Croatia counted 4,760,344 inhabitants. The population density amounted to 84.2 persons per square kilometer. However, population density differs greatly from region to region. Most densely populated is the region around Zagreb (q.v.) and the coastline along the Adriatic. In 1991, 54 percent of the population was concentrated in 204 urban settlements. Aside from the tradition of urbanization along the coast, industrialization played a significant role in the spatial layout of population density. The depopulation of the interior areas was accompanied by the low natural growth of the population. In 1990, the natural growth rate was only 0.7 percent. This stagnation has characterized Croatia's population growth since the Second World War. The birth rate continued to decrease from 25 per thousand at the beginning of the 1950s to 11 to 12 per thousand currently. In this period, the death rate stagnated between 9 and 11 per thousand. The infant mortality rate was very high immediately after World War II: about 100 per thousand infants; now it has dropped to 10 per thousand. (See also NATIONALITY STRUCTURE)

POREČ. Town on the eastern side of Istria (q.v.). The peninsula was colonized by an Illyrian (q.v.) tribe, the Histrions. In Roman times the town was known under the name of Parentium. After the fall of the Western Empire, the town was taken by the Ostrogoths. In 539, it came under Byzantine rule. In the middle of the sixth century, the Basilica Euphrasiana was built. It is the best preserved Byzantine cathedral on the Yugoslav coast. During the twelfth century, Poreč enjoyed a period of independence. In 1232, it came under the influence of the Patriarchs of Aquileia and, in 1267, the Venetians captured the town. After the fall of the Venetian Republic, Poreč came under the control of Austria. In 1918, Istria and Poreč were left to the Italians. In April 1945, Poreč was liberated by the partisans.

POSAVINA. Region in Slavonia (q.v.) along the Sava. It is a fertile plain and communications corridor.

POSAVSKI, LJUDEVIT. Knez of Lower Pannonia (q.v.) with seat in Sisak, he was the leader of a four-year rebellion against the Franks. The movement started in 819 and received support from the people of the surrounding regions of Carinthia, Carnolia and Timok. The Dalmatian Knez Borna, a vassal of the Franks, helped to crush the resistance and Ljudevit died in Dalmatia (q.v.).

POVALJSKA LISTINA. The Povlja parchment and the finely carved Povlja lintel prove that Cyrillic (q.v.) was in use on Brač (q.v.) in the early Middle Ages. One theory holds that this alphabet came from the Kingdoms of Dioclea and Zahumlja (qq.v.). It is composed of elements of the Greek alphabet adapted to the phonetic structure of the Slav language. An alternative theory attributes the invention of the alphabet to the followers of Cyrillus (q.v.) in Macedonia or Bulgaria. Still another theory considers it just as a development from Croatian Glagolitic (q.v.). In Croatia and Bosnia, the alphabet is now called Western (Bosnian or Croatian) Cyrillic or Bosančica. The use of Bosančica contradicts the statement that Cyrillic is exclusively Serbian. The Povlja are dated from around 1184.

POVELJA KULINA BANA. In this Charter of 1189, the Bosnian Ban (q.v.) Kulin granted privileges to the town of Dubrovnik (q.v.). He admitted free movement and tax-free trade on his Bosnian territory.

POŽAREVAC (TREATY OF). Treaty concluded in 1718 between the Habsburgs and the Turks. The agreement followed a victory of Prince Eugene of Savoy in 1715 at Petrovaradin (Vojvodina) and the occupation of Temesvar and Belgrade. The Habsburg Empire held Belgrade in its grip and expanded deeply into Serbia up to

Niš. This region and Belgrade were ceded again in 1739, but Slavonia and Srijem (q.v.) remained under the Habsburgs.

PRAGMATIC SANCTION. In 1712, the Croatian Sabor (q.v.) accepted the Pragmatic Sanction. It implied the recognition of Austrian hereditary rights on Croatia along the female line. The King of Austria, Charles III, could not sanction the document as long as Hungary had not been consulted. Only in 1723, the Hungaro-Croatian Diet adopted the Pragmatic Sanction. This opened the throne to Maria Theresa (q.v.).

PRAXIS. Journal of humanist Marxists who stressed the significance of the early humanist writings of Marx and pleaded for a creative adaptation of Marxism in the context of Yugoslav self-management. They clashed with the orthodox Marxist-Leninist interpretation of the official Communist Party officials. *Praxis* and its contributors were subjected to continuous criticism by these party officials, which included serious attacks by the Zagreb party organization and the Croatian Parliament in May and June 1966. Ultimately, in the spring of 1975, the printing and distribution of the journal was made impossible. The international edition of the journal was more or less continued by the journal *Praxis International*, edited abroad.

PRESIDENT. The President is elected by a majority vote of the voters for a term of five years. No one can be President more than twice. In accordance with the principle of the separation of powers, the legislative power is reserved for the Sabor (q.v.). However, Croatia has been described as a strong presidential regime. Presidential powers are broad and important, especially in defense, internal and international affairs. Along with the usual prerogatives of the head of the executive branch, formation of the government and preservation of the continuity of the working of legislative powers, the President has several special prerogatives. He is commander-in-chief of the armed forces. He shall appoint members of the National Defense Council and preside over it. He may, at the proposal of the government and with the counter-signature of the Prime Minister, after having consulted the President of the Parliament, dissolve the House of Representatives if it has passed a vote of no confidence in the government or if it has not approved the state budget within a month from the date when it was proposed.

In the performance of his powers the President of the Republic shall be assisted by a Presidential Council and other advisory and auxiliary bodies whose members shall be appointed and recalled by the President. The Deputy Prime Minister in the Government of National Union under Franjo Gregurić (qq.v.), Zdravko Tomac, remarked that the Croatian Constitution (q.v.) installs a half-presidential and no full-parliamentary regime. Especially the National Defense Council has been criticized by the opposition as constituting a danger to parliamentary democracy.

PRESS. The press under the communists gradually developed a rather varied landscape. Before and during the war, it helped to develop nationalist views along republican lines. The new strong regimes tried to bring the press under control, no less in Croatia than elsewhere in ex-Yugoslavia. The quality newspaper *Vjesnik* (q.v.) came under the influence of the new government and continued its life as *Novi Vjesnik* (New Courier) (q.v.). *Večernji List* (The Evening Paper) (q.v.) is a popular and more superficial evening newspaper. *Glas Istrije* (The Voice of Istria) defends regional interests. *Glas Slavonije* (The Voice of Slavonia) (q.v.) is fighting for its existence. The editors of *Slobodna Dalmacija* (Free Dalmatia) (q.v.) defended longest of all an independent course. It was ultimately brought under state control through a privatization strategy. *Novi List* (The New Paper) of Rijeka (q.v.) is a more or less alternative daily and *La Voce del Popolo* (The Voice of the People) (q.v.) represents the Italian minority.

Danas (Today) (q.v.), the best independent weekly under the communists, also came under government control through the same privatization policies. *Globus* is a rather sensational, nationalist weekly that nevertheless publishes interesting documents and stories. The same is even more true of *ST - Slobodni Tjednik* (The Free Weekly), which disappeared in the autumn of 1993. *Nedeljna Dalmacija* is a cultural weekly that was earlier associated with *Slobodna Dalmacija*. *Hrvatski List* (The Croatian Newspaper), an Osijek (q.v.) daily published from 1920 to 1945, was reinitiated in Zagreb (q.v.) on a weekly basis during August 1992 and is one of the rare existing independent papers. A group of editors of *Danas*, including Mladen Maloča, Dražen Vukov-Colić and Marinko

Čulić, started the new paper and they were joined by some journalists from *Globus*. *Arena* and *Vikend* (Weekend) are popular magazines edited in Zagreb.

The change of regime has been reflected in the publication policy of editing houses and institutions. Authors and viewpoints that were popular during the Croatian Spring (q.v.) and were then crushed by the communist regime now enjoy wide support and popularity. (See also FREEDOM OF THE PRESS)

PREVLAKA. Peninsula south of Dubrovnik (q.v.). In the autumn of 1991, the whole region was occupied by the Yugoslav army. The Konavle region and its airport have been destroyed by uncontrolled aggression and plundering. The Presidents of Croatia Tuđman (q.v.) and of New Yugoslavia Ćošić agreed on a truce and on the withdrawal of the Yugoslav army from the region by October 20, 1992. The area came under UNPROFOR (q.v.) supervision in application of Resolution 779 of the UN Security Council of October 6, 1992. In the summer of 1993, President Tuđman declared during a press conference that he would not reject negotiations with the Serbs on an exchange of territories. The Prevlaka area was implied.

In September 1993, an exchange of territories was incorporated as an element of the global peace plan for Bosnia-Hercegovina. Prevlaka would be given to the Serbs as their way out to the sea and Croatia would receive the hinterland of Dubrovnik. Soon a discussion arose as to whether the Bosnian Serbs or the Montenegrins should annex the peninsula. However, this quarrel was a bit premature. The peace plan was rejected by the Bosnian Muslims and the Croats tied an exchange of territories to a final settlement of the whole problem.

PRIBIĆEVIĆ, SVETOZAR (1875-1936). Leading Croatian politician of Serbian nationality. Leader of the Serbian Independent Party (q.v.). During Habsburg rule, he was a Member of Parliament in the Croat Sabor (q.v.) for the Croat-Serb coalition. He became the first Minister of the Interior under Prime Minister Stojan Protić of the Serbian Radical Party in the new Kingdom of Serbs, Croats and Slovenes (q.v.). Together with the new Prime Minister, the Serb and actual strongman of the regime, Nikola Pašić, Pribićević drafted the centralistic Vidovdan (q.v.) Constitution. Pribićević spent some years in the Yugoslav government, bitterly opposed by Stjepan Radić (q.v.), the leader of the main opposition party, the Croatian People's Peasant Party (q.v.). However, in 1925, Radić himself entered the government of Nikola Pašić. Radić resigned already in April 1926 and provoked the fall of Pašić.

In November 1927, Pribićević and Radić concluded an agreement that established the Peasant-Independent Democratic coalition. This led to an increased polarization and political instability in the Yugoslav Parliament. Pribićević had changed his political vision from a supporter of monarchy and unitarianism to a republican and a federalist. The Radić-Pribićević coalition practiced systematic obstructionism in the National Assembly. It ended with the shooting of Radić in Parliament on June 20, 1928. This brought the formal end of the parliamentary regime. After some fruitless consultations - in which Pribićević was also involved - the King assumed personal power on January 6, 1929. In the month of May 1929, Pribićević travelled to Belgrade to establish connections with the opposition. He was arrested and interned. In July 1931, he finally got a passport to Czechoslovakia. He never returned to Yugoslavia.

PRIVATIZATION see AGENCY FOR RESTRUCTURING AND DEVELOPMENT; FUND FOR PRIVATIZATION; LAW ON THE TRANSFORMATION OF SOCIALLY-OWNED ENTERPRISES

PRIVREDNA BANKA. This bank is the largest bank in the country with approximately one-third of the total banking business. The major shareholder of the Bank is the largest oil company, the INA holding company.

PRIVREDNI VJESNIK. The Economic Newspaper, edited in Zagreb (q.v.).

PROCOPIUS (? -565). Byzantine writer of a chronicle of the Gothic wars (534-552). As a secretary of the General Belisarius, he was a first-hand observer and contemporary writer. His book *De Bello* dealt with the wars of Emperor Justinian up to 554. Procopius is one of the first sources of ethnographic data on the Slavs. He described their outlook, housing, character, organization and religion. An account was given of the battles with the Romans around the Danube and the progression of the Avar (q.v.) and Slavic tribes to the Adriatic. Around 548, an army of Slavs crossed the Danube and kept killing, enslaving and plundering, as far as Epidamnus (Drač). Fifteen thousand Illyrians (q.v.) kept following the army, but did not dare to attack it.

PROMDEI BANKA. The Promdei Bank is the first private bank of Croatia. It was founded by Ibrahim Dedić, also owner of the Promdei holding company. This holding company consists of ten diversified enterprises which are shareholders of the Bank. The Bank has a license for Visa cards.

PUBLIC FINANCE. In the first years of its existence, the Republic of Croatia ran huge deficits. This was due, first, to the rapid growth of defense expenditures and other war-induced outlays (mainly transfers to refugees and expenditures for health care) and second, to the narrowing tax base. In addition, the social sector has been shrinking while the private sector was growing and this latter sector is characterized by widespread tax evasion.

Along with the army, to which about 35 percent of Croatian budget expenditures are allocated, the other major budget item is the losses of the big enterprises in industry, agriculture and public services that have to be heavily subsidized. About one quarter of budgetary expenditures go into covering losses of public enterprises.

The effect of measures to reduce the budget deficit, most notably the sale of state ownership (apartments and firms) and the issuance of so-called patriotic bonds, has so far been very limited.

PUSIĆ, VESNA (1953-). Professor of Sociology at Zagreb University (q.v.). In the autumn of 1993, together with five other Croatian intellectuals, she wrote an open letter to President Tuđman (q.v.). They criticized his policy and asked him to resign.

- Q -

QUARNERO see KVARNER

- R -

RAB. Island in Kvarner Bay between Pag and Krk (qq.v.). In the second century B.C. the Romans founded here a naval base that developed into a fortress city, cited as Arba by Plinius the Younger. The first official nudist beach in Yugoslavia was established in the "English Bay," named after King Edward VIII.

RAČIĆ, PUNIŠA (1886-1944). Serb nationalist Montenegrin. Representative in Parliament of the Radical Party. During a Parliamentary session in 1928, he shot down representatives of the Croatian People's Peasant Party (q.v.) and killed its President, Stjepan Radić (q.v.).

RAČKI, FRANJO (1828-1894). Theologian, historian and politician. He played a major role in the initial years of the Matica hrvatska (q.v.). He published many sources on the early history of Croatia. Franjo Rački was a Member of Parliament for the National Party (q.v.). He supported the idea of the South Slav union.

RADIĆ, ANTE (1868-1919). He founded the Croatian People's Peasant Party (q.v.) together with his brother Stjepan (q.v.). He acted more as the thinker and his brother as the leading politician of the party.

RADIĆ, STJEPAN (1871-1928). Founder and leader of the Croatian People's Peasant Party (HPSS) (q.v.). In his youth, he joined the Croatian nationalist students who were fighting the Habsburg Monarchy. In 1902, he became editor of the Zagreb newspaper *Hrvatska Misao* (Croatian Thought). In 1904, he founded the HPSS together with his brother Ante Radić (q.v.). The party succeeded in mobilizing the broad masses of Croatian peasants and developed into the most important political party of Croatia between the two world wars.

When, in 1914, the first Yugoslav state came into being, Radić was an advocate of a federal Yugoslav republic with autonomy for Croatia. He failed to win the backing of the Sabor (q.v.) for his republican ideas. In the constitutional elections of 1920, the HPSS obtained a majority in Croatia. However, Radić remained powerless on the Belgrade scene, where a royalist coalition had been formed. The Vidovdan (q.v.) Constitution was accepted and a centralist government installed. The same scenario was repeated in later elections. Radić did not give up his strong opposition to the King and his government, agitating sometimes more outside than in Parliament. On missions abroad, Radić sought but did not really find effective support for his plan to set up a Croatian Peasant Republic. For his unpatriotic behavior, he was imprisoned in 1924 and charged with high treason. However, the next year, he adopted a conciliatory profile and entered the government as Minister of Education. Two years later, he resigned and resumed his opposition role. He fell back on his earlier radical position and urged autonomy for Croatia in a federal Yugoslavia. In 1928, Radić was shot down in Parliament by a Serbian Montenegrin, Puniša Račić (q.v.). Radić died a few months later.

RADIO 101. News, cultural affairs and entertainment station for the central Zagreb (q.v.) area. It was very critical of the Tuđman (q.v.) regime. It withstood for some time efforts by the authorities to impose a pro-governmental editorial line. Now it has finally lost its independence and is state owned.

RAGUSA see DUBROVNIK

RAKOVICA REVOLT. The nineteenth-century revolt in Rakovica was one of the rare armed rebellions that sought to overthrow Habsburg rule in Croatia and wished to install an independent Croatia. On October 8, 1871, subversive activities were reported in the Ogulin Regiment of the Military Border (q.v.). The next day a revolt was under way in Rakovica. The main instigators were the nationalist followers of Ante Starčević, Eugen Kvaternik (qq.v.) and Ljudevit Bach. They seized the local armory and proclaimed the independence of a free Croatia with its own provisional government and a national army. The rebels did not gain much support. The rebellion was already crushed by the Austrians on October 12. The government troops took 63 prisoners and captured 194 rifles. Kvaternik and Bach were killed. However, this event had lasting effects: it convinced the Austrians that it would be better to abolish the Military Border.

RANKOVIĆ, ALEKSANDAR. Close aide and long-term Minister of the Interior in the Tito (q.v.) regime. Aleksandar Ranković organized the secret services in communist Yugoslavia and was known as a conservative hardliner. He opposed the liberal wing in the League of Communists of Yugoslavia (q.v.) and the liberal tendencies in Yugoslav society at the beginning of the 1960s. These were mainly rising in the more developed Republics of Croatia and Slovenia. Though as Vice-President considered to be the heir of Tito, he was ultimately removed in 1966. This meant not only a victory for the economic reformers, it also affected the occurrence of the Croatian Spring (q.v.).

RAŠA. River in southern Istria (q.v.), supposed to have been the frontier of White Croatia (q.v.) with Roman Italy. In earlier times, it was also the northern frontier of the territory colonized by an Illyrian tribe - the Liburnians (q.v.). The land on the other side of the river belonged to the Histrions. Sometimes, the inversion "Arsa" is used as the name of the river.

RAŠKOVIĆ, JOVAN. Psychiatrist and politician. Former leader of the Serbian Democratic Party (SDS) in the Kninska Krajina (q.v.). His first aim was to obtain cultural autonomy for the Serbs in the Krajina (q.v.). His negotiations with Tuđman (q.v.) in the summer of 1990 were not successful. In August and September 1990, he organized a referendum on political autonomy for the Krajina. Later, he was discarded by more radical leaders who wanted political independence for the Serbs in Croatia: Milan Babić and Milan Martić (qq.v.) took over the political and military organization of the Knin Serbs.

RAVENJANIN, IVAN. John of Ravenna. According to the chronicler Archdeacon Thomas (q.v.), John of Ravenna mediated an agreement between the Croats and Pope Agathon (q.v.) at the end of the seventh century.

RED CROATIA see WHITE CROATIA

RELIGION. According to the data of the population census, the inhabitants of Croatia declared themselves to be of the following beliefs: Roman Catholic, 76.5 percent; Serbian Orthodox, 11.1

percent; Islam, 1.2 percent; Protestant, 1.4 percent; Atheist, 3.9 percent; other and unknown, 6.9 percent.

RELJKOVIĆ, MATIJA ANTUN (1732-1798). Writer, born in the Slavonian (q.v.) village of Svinjar. He wrote under the influence of the Enlightenment. He published *Satir* (Satyr), a grammar, and a manual on sheep raising.

REPUBLIKA SRPSKA KRAJINA (RSK) see SERBIAN REPUBLIC OF KRAJINA

RICOV, JOJA (1929-). Born on the island Ugljan. Writer, editor of *Hrvatski književni list* (Croatian Literary Paper, 1968-1969). At the annual meeting of the Croatian PEN-Center, he criticized its president Slobodan Prosperov Novak (q.v.) for his speech in Munich.

RIJEČKI DEMOKRATSKI SAVEZ (RDS) see RIJEKA DEMOCRATIC ALLIANCE

RIJEKA. Strategic place in the bay of Kvarner (q.v.) in the upper northern Adriatic. The region was first settled by the Liburnians, an Illyrian (qq.v.) people. The Romans built the military base of Tarsatica at the mouth of the Rečina River. In the seventh century, the town was conquered by Avars (q.v.) and Slavs. They built the fortress of Trsat on the Roman ruins. The Slav name Rijeka can be found in documents from the thirteenth century. In the Middle Ages, the town was called Fiume. It is the Italian equivalent of Rijeka, also meaning "river." Until 1918, Fiume was the port of Hungary and stood under its immediate jurisdiction. Istria on one side and Dalmatia (qq.v.) on the other were under Austria. In 1918, Rijeka-Fiume was disputed by Italy and Yugoslavia and obtained an international statute. However, Italy invaded the region under the command of the poet Gabriel d'Annunzio. The Treaty of Rapallo of 1920 declared it a free city, but it was seized again by the Italians. After the Second World War, a plebiscite was held and Rijeka became the most important port of communist Yugoslavia.

RIJEKA DEMOCRATIC ALLIANCE/RIJEČKI DEMOKRATSKI SAVEZ (RDS). The Rijeka Democratic Alliance is a regional party and member of the Association of Croatian Regional Parties (q.v.). It opposes the so-called centralistic policy of the Croatian Democratic Union (q.v.) government in Zagreb. The President is Vladimir Smešny.

RITTER VITEZOVIĆ, PAVAO (1652-1713). Writer and forerunner of the Illyrian (q.v.) movement. He stressed the identity of language, way of life and common origin of the South Slavs and linked these ideas with the Croatian people. He constructed a great-Croatian theory on dubious grounds. However, he instigated followers to seek more acceptable arguments for his thesis. His main work *Croatia rediviva* was a protest against the Peace of Karlovci (q.v.), which still deprived the Kingdom of Croatia of its ancient territories. Since for him the name Croat (q.v.) embraced all Slavs, Vitezović divided the Slavic world into two parts: Northern Croatia, north of the Danube, and Southern Croatia, itself subdivided into White Croatia (q.v.), west of the Drina-Sava line including Slovenia, Dalmatia (qq.v.), Croatia and part of Hungary, and Red Croatia, east of it, including Serbia, Macedonia, Bulgaria and Thrace. His Pan-Croatianism was meant as both a historical reconstruction and a political project for the future. It was also a polemic against Venetian territorial pretensions.

RIVERS. Some of the biggest rivers flowing through Croatia are: the Sava (562 km in Croatia), the Drava (305 km), the Kupa (q.v.) (296 km), the Danube (188 km), the Bosut (186 km), the Korana (134 km), the Bednja (133 km), the Česma (123 km), the Una (120 km), the Vuka (112 km), the Dobra (104 km), the Glina (100 km) and the Cetina (q.v.) (100 km).

ROČKI ABECEDARIJ. In the Glagolitic (q.v.) alphabet the order of letters is of more importance than in the Latin alphabet for the letters not only indicate sound but also numbers. It was a common practice at the beginning of the thirteenth century to paint the alphabet on the wall of the church. An outstanding example of such an alphabet book is on the wall of the church St. Antony the Hermit in Roč.

ROLANDINUS. The medieval notaries had their own textbooks, collections of regulations and rules concerning their work. A copy of a book for notaries made in Bologna in 1277, Rolandino's book was owned by the Split (q.v.) scribe Petar in the fifteenth century.

RUKAVINA, IVAN. Commander of the general staff of the Croatian partisans. He was dismissed for insisting on the national question.

- S -

SABOR. The Croatian Parliament (q.v.) or Sabor is a body of elected representatives of the people and is vested with the legislative power in the Republic of Croatia.

Under the old regime, the Parliament consisted of three bodies: the Chamber of Associated Labor, the Chamber of Communes and the Socio-Political Chamber. Under the new regime, the Parliament has two bodies: the House of Representatives (Zastupnički Dom) and the House of Counties (Županički Dom). According to Article 71 of Constitution (q.v.) of December 22, 1990, the House of Representatives shall have no less than 100 and no more than 160 representatives. Citizens in every *županija* or county shall directly and by secret ballot elect three representatives to the House of Counties. The Law on the Županije has created 21 *županije*. The President of the Republic designates five more members. Ex-Presidents will also be seated after their term in this house. Representatives of the Croatian Sabor are elected for a term of four years.

According to the Constitution, there is a clear division of competences. The House of Representatives is the body that decides on laws and budget and that really bears the legislative power. The House of Counties has more of an advisory and controlling function. It discusses proposals before, and controls the legislative work after real decisions have been taken by the House of Representatives.

By the 1992 elections 138 representatives were chosen as members of the House of Representatives. The Sabor elected Stipe Mesić (q.v.) as its President.

SALONA (SOLIN). Salona was an Ancient Roman city near present-day Split (q.v.). It was destroyed by the invading Avars (q.v.) and Slavs, probably in 614 A.D. Its fall has been described in detail by Constantine Porphyrogenitus (q.v.). Impressive ruins can still be visited at the location of Manastarine.

ŠARINIĆ, HRVOJE (1935-). Prime Minister of the uniform Croatian Democratic Union (q.v.) government formed after the elections of August 2, 1992. Its first government session took place on August 13, 1992. Adviser to the President and Director of the Bureau of National Security. He directed secret negotiations with the Krajina (q.v.) Serbs in Norway at the end of October 1993. He summoned Marko Marković, journalist of *Slobodni Tjednik*, before the court on the charge of defamation.

SAVEZ KOMUNISTA JUGOSLAVIJE (SKJ) see LEAGUE OF COMMUNISTS OF YUGOSLAVIA (LCY)

SCULPTURE. Following the Slav invasion of the Croatian lands, functional sculpture was developed by local artists along specific and artistic lines. The ornaments of old Croatian churches show typical themes and forms, as for example the many reliefs of plaited ornamentation with three interwoven and highly stylized bands. Later on, this religious functional sculpture assumed greater size and autonomy. The portal of the Trogir cathedral made by Radovan is famous. Another example of local sculpture is the adorned capitals of the pillars of the Franciscan monastery in Dubrovnik (q.v.). Of particular interest are the *stecci*, the Bogomil (q.v.) tombstones that are found in Hercegovina and some southern parts of Croatia, especially around Dubrovnik.

Later Croatian sculpture has to a large extent followed the development of European styles. Ivan Mestrović (q.v.) was the most famous Yugoslav and Croatian sculpture. Early in his career, he was a master of Yugoslav symbolism, and later, he fell back thematically on his Croatian origins. Communist sculpture was characterized by some monumental commemorative works.

SECOND YUGOSLAVIA. Communist Yugoslavia. The second session of the Anti-Fascist Council of the National Liberation of

Yugoslavia (q.v.) in 1943 projected a socialist Yugoslav federation in succession to the monarchy.

ŠEKS, VLADIMIR. Croatian Democratic Union (HDZ) (q.v.) politician. He was one of the Deputy Prime Ministers in the government of Hrvoje Šarinić (q.v.) and Nikica Valentić. He increasingly represented the right wing of the party. He was one of the extreme leaders who retired at the demand of President Tuđman (q.v.) during the Second Convention of the HDZ.

SENIA see SENJ

SENJ. Town on the shores of the Adriatic in the bay of Kvarner between Rijeka and Zadar (qq.v.). Then called Senia it was a trading port in Roman times. It only became significant in the twelfth century when it became the see of a Bishop. The Croato-Hungarian King Matija Korvin (q.v.) granted Senj the privileges of a King's town. In 1526, it passed into the hands of the Habsburgs. At that time, numerous Uskoks (q.v.) fled before the Turks from the interior Bosnian lands and settled in Senj. War against the Ottomans and Venetians developed into piracy feared along the whole Dalmatian (q.v.) coast. It was even the cause of a war between Austria and Venice in 1615. Venice asked Vienna to silence the destructive activities of the Senj pirates. Vienna would or could not bring the local warlords under control. The Peace of Madrid of 1617 stipulated that the Uskoks should be deported from Senj to the region of Lika (q.v.) and Žumberak and their ships burnt.

Already in the tenth century, Senj was a center of Glagolitic (q.v.). The use of Glagolitic in the diocese of Senj was officially permitted by a thirteenth century papal decree. From 1493 to 1508, a Glagolithic press was printing in Senj.

ŠENOA, AUGUST (1838-1881). Poet, dramatist, critic, journalist and creator of the Croat historical novel.

ŠEPAROVIĆ, ZVONIMIR (1928-). Professor at the Faculty of Law of Zagreb University. Rector of the University (1989-1991). He was Minister of Foreign Affairs in the Government of National Union of Franjo Gregurić (qq.v.) (1991-1992). Afterwards, Šeparović became Croatia's Ambassador to the United Nations.

SERBIAN DEMOCRATIC FORUM/SRPSKI DEMOKRATSKI FORUM (SDF). The Serbian Democratic Forum is a movement of Serbs in Croatia that takes an intermediary position politically between the insurgent Serbs of the Krajina (q.v.) and the urban Serbs who are loyal to the Croatian government. The spokesman of the Serbian Democratic Forum is the Croatian Serb Milorad Pupovac.

SERBIAN DEMOCRATIC PARTY/SRPSKA DEMOKRATSKA STRANKA (SDS). The Serbian Democratic Party is the majority party of the Serbs in the Krajina (q.v.), founded as a successor of the Communist Party during the early months of 1990 in Donji Lapac near Knin (q.v.). The party suspended its relations with the Croatian Parliament (q.v.) on July 26, 1990.

SERBIAN INDEPENDENT PARTY/SRPSKA SAMOSTALNA STRANKA. Former party of the Serbs living in Croatia. It was founded in 1873 and first led by Pavle Jovanović and later by Svetozar Pribićević (q.v.). The Zagreb-based publication *Srbobran* was the party organ. The Serbian Independents advocated programmatically the union of Lika, Kordun, Banija, Dalmatia, Slavonia (qq.v.) and Bosnia-Hercegovina - all of which had a significant Serbian minority - with Serbia to form a Greater Serbia.

SERBIAN NATIONAL PARTY/SRPSKA NARODNA STRANKA (SNS). The Serbian National Party is the party of the Croatian Serbs in the urban parts of Croatia who are loyal to the Croatian state and government. Its Co-President Veselin Pejnović declared Croatia has been given the necessary legal infrastructure, but that the question is how to make it work for the Serbs loyal to the regime. How to bring about normal relations is the issue tackled in the SNS strategic document *Pravim i demokratskim sredstvima do trajnog mira* (Legal and Democratic Ways to a Stable Peace). In September 1993, the party's President Milan Đukić condemned the Gospić offensive (q.v.). In his view, violence would not bring a long-term solution to the Serbian problem in Croatia. At the same time, he declared that the Serbs in Croatia are more than just a minority.

SERBIAN REGIONS OF WEST SLAVONIA/SRPSKE OBLASTI ZAPADNE SLAVONIJE. A part of West Slavonia (q.v.) was conquered from Croatia by the Serbs in the war of 1991. In the beginning of 1992, it was placed under UNPROFOR (q.v.) as the Sector West. The Serbian Krajina (q.v.) of West Slavonia has its Parliament in Okučani. Its leaders were the Serbs Veljko Džakula, Dušan Ećimović and Mladen Kulić. They participated in peace talks with the Croatian authorities and concluded the Daruvar Agreement. After the Gospić offensive (q.v.) during September 1993, the hardliners of the Serbian Democratic Party of Knin (q.v.) demanded the dismissal and arrest of the three leaders. The Parliament of Okučani hardened its position as well and demanded the removal of UNPROFOR control posts in West Slavonia. It proposed that the government in Knin get a new name: Zapadna Raška or West Raška. Raška is the name for old Serbia.

SERBIAN REPUBLIC/SRPSKA REPUBLIKA (SR). Serbian Republic of the Serbian Bosnians in Bosnia-Hercegovina. Part of it has a frontier with the Serbian Republic of Krajina (q.v.) in Croatia. The leaders of the Krajina (q.v.) threatened to leave Croatia and to merge with the Serbian Republic of Bosnia-Hercegovina.

SERBIAN REPUBLIC OF KRAJINA/REPUBLIKA SRPSKA KRAJINA (RSK). The Serbian Republic of Krajina came into existence with the self-declared transformation of the Serbian Autonomous Region of the Krajina (q.v.). The statehood was symbolized by the opening of its own frontier passage with Hungary at Kneževo. The Republic's President Goran Hadžić (q.v.), its Prime Minister Đorđe Bjegović and its Minister of Foreign Affairs Slobodan Jarčević all defend the formal independence of the Serbian Republic of Krajina and the secession from Croatia. A merger with the Serbian Republic of Bosnia (q.v.) has been approved in a referendum, but the materialization of this plan seems to have been postponed under pressure from Belgrade.

The search for a new solution to the Krajina problem has to start from the observation that the Krajina is not homogeneous and that there are deep rivalries between the leaders of different regions. The leaders of West Slavonia, Veljko Džakula and Dušan Ećimović, were arrested because they reputedly held secret negotiations with Zagreb. After the Gospić offensive (q.v.), Hadžić was accused of incompetence by the Serbian Democratic Party of Knin (q.v.). During the meeting of the Krajina Parliament in Beli Manastir, Minister of Interior Milan Martić (q.v.) from Knin and Goran Hadžić from Slavonia (q.v.) accused each other of corruption and incompetence. Goran Hadžić and Slobodan Milošević (and Arkan [q.v.]) supported each other - earlier Milošević dropped Knin politician Milan Babić (q.v.). Milan Martić seemed to collaborate again for the time being with Knin Mayor Milan Babić and is allied to Vojislav Šešelj (q.v.).

One conceivable solution could be to divide the militant Knin region from West Slavonia with Banija and East Slavonia with Baranja (qq.v.). One can imagine that East and West Slavonia would be reintegrated in Croatia as autonomous regions and Knin would unite with the Bosnian Serbian Republic. In exchange, Croatia could perhaps get part of Hercegovina and better integrate its Dubrovnik (q.v.) region. In reality, this is perhaps already happening. Following a round of secret negotiations in Norway in 1993, an armistice for East Croatia was signed between the Krajina Serbs - Goran Hadžić was the negotiator - and the Zagreb government on November 4, 1993.

A further step toward relaxation was reached with the signing of an armistice between the Krajina Serbs and the Croatian government in the spring of 1994, following the reconciliation of Croatian and Muslim Bosnians and the Washington agreement on a federation in Bosnia and a confederation with Croatia. It was still unclear, however, whether this would also lead to a political solution of the Krajina problem.

ŠEŠELJ, VOJISLAV. Born in eastern Hercegovina. He was a sociologist and dissident under the communist regime. In the post-communist period, he became the leader of the Serbian Radical Party (SRS). He considered himself to be the heir of Draža Mihailović, the Serbian *četnik* (q.v.) leader during World War II. Šešelj's SRS established a paramilitary branch. In the spring of 1991 - even before the official proclamation of independence of Croatia - Šešelj's militia initiated provocative actions in Croatia. During the war, units were fighting in Vukovar (q.v.) and then dispersed themselves over all regions contested by the Serbs. His party grew into the biggest opposition and second party in Serbia. The Serbian President Slobodan Milošević more than tolerated the activities of the Šešelj groups. In the autumn of 1993, Šešelj withdrew his support of the Milošević government which in turn arrested several members of Šeselj's militia on charges of war crimes. Milenko Petrić and his gang were accused of murdering four Croats near Šid, a village in East Srijem (q.v.).

SEVDALINKE. Romantic love poetry of Bosnian-Muslim origin. This genre was also popular in Croat poetic circles in Hercegovina.

ŠICEL, BOŽIDAR. Lawyer from Zagreb (q.v.), Co-President of the Parliament of Bihać (West Bosnia). He is a Croat and lives in Cazin. He defended the option of Fikret Abdić to proclaim the region of Bihać autonomous under the name of "West Bosnia."

ŠIMIĆ, ANTUN BRANKO (1898-1925). Born in Drinovci, Hercegovina. His expressionistic collection of poetry *Preobraženja* (Transfiguration), written in an unconventional free style, marked the confirmation of the Moderna (q.v.) in Croatian poetry. Šimić freed himself later from expressionistic influences and embraced a more realistic poetry.

SIRMIUM see SRIJEMSKA MITROVICA

SISAK. Town on the confluence of the Sava and the Kupa (q.v.). Around 400 B.C. a concentration of Celts settled around the later Sisak. In the administrative reform of Emperor Diocletian in 297 A.D., Siscia became the capital of the Province of Savia, the part of Pannonia (q.v.) south of the Mura and the Drava. Sisak was also the capital of the Croatian Pannonian Prince Liutevit in the beginning of the ninth century.

In 1593 a decisive battle was fought near Sisak by the Austrian Emperor Rudolf and the Croatian Ban Thomas Erdödi against the Ottomans. It was a turning point in history. It was the beginning of a 13-year-long war, which ended with the first rollback of the Turks.

SISCIA see SISAK

SLAMNIG, IVAN (1930-). Born in Metković. Poet, story and novel writer, critic and literature theoretician. Member of the Croatian Academy of Arts and Sciences (q.v.).

SLAVIČEK, MILIVOJ (1929-). Born in Čakovec. Contemporary poet of ordinary daily life, writing in an easy, conversational style. Croatian Ambassador to Poland.

SLAVONIA. Presently an area in the eastern part of inner Croatia (Pannonia), usually subdivided into East and West Slavonia. The main towns in East Slavonia (q.v.) are Vukovar, Osijek and Vinkovci (qq.v.). West Slavonia includes Pakrac where some of the first war incidents took place. These regions are now Sectors East and West of UNPROFOR (q.v.). Between these zones, a greater part of Slavonia is still under the control of Zagreb (q.v.).

In the course of history, the term *Slavonia* changed its meaning frequently. At the end of the eleventh century when the Croatian peoples were joined under a Hungarian ruler, the term *Slavonia* referred to the greater part of the South Slav lands, including Bosnia and Serbia. During the Turkish conquest of a major part of the Croatian lands in the sixteenth and seventeenth centuries, the term designated the remainder of the Croatian lands which were free from Turkish rule or Venetian domination. In early modern times, Slavonia, comprising roughly the lands between the Sava, the Drava and the Danube, including the capital city of Zagreb, was nearly identical with inner Croatia of today. When, in the course of the early eighteenth century, the old Croatian territories were reconquered from the Turks, the term *Slavonia* was reserved for the eastern parts of the old Croatian lands, and even these territories were in the course of the eighteenth and nineteenth centuries divided between Croatia proper (q.v.) (also called Upper Slavonia) and Hungary. During the nineteenth and twentieth centuries, the term *Slavonia* had only a geographic, not a legal political meaning. Thus it referred only to the eastern parts of Croatia, within the boundaries of 1868.

SLOBODNA DALMACIJA. The Free Dalmatia is a daily paper edited in Split (q.v.). It first appeared on June 17, 1943, as the organ of the anti-fascist struggle of the people of Dalmatia (q.v.). The paper survived the communist regime and - so far - the transformations of the economy under the new regime. It is considered by some to be the only real opposition paper in Croatia. However, a new executive board has been imposed and asked journalists not to write any longer about certain subjects. Likewise, the humoristic annex of the paper, *Feral Tribune* (q.v.), has been under attack by the ruling party, the Croatian Democratic Union (q.v.). It is not clear what the outcome of these interventions will be, nor how serious the infringements of freedom of the press (q.v.) really are.

SLOVENIA (RELATIONS WITH). Though both Republics declared and fought simultaneously for their secession from the Yugoslav Federation and supported each other in this battle, there were also some minor problems that disturbed the honeymoon between Slovenia and Croatia. First of all, the Slovenes reproached the Tuđman (q.v.) regime for doing almost nothing to prevent Yugoslav troops from passing through Croatia to Slovenia after the proclamation of independence. On July 2, 1991, then Deputy Prime Minister Franjo Gregurić (q.v.) criticized the actions of the Yugoslav army in Slovenia but added that Croatian forces would not engage in armed operations against the Yugoslav army. Likewise, the Croats had cause to regard the attitude of Slovenia as rather apathetic once the Yugoslav army left Slovenia.

Frictions arose concerning the nationalization of property in the new states. The Croats accused the Slovenes of illegally keeping real estate in Croatia and of transferring industrial equipment to Slovenia. They threatened to seize the holiday resorts of Slovenian companies on the Croatian coast. At least one notable incident arose when the Croatian Army seized a Croatian holiday resort in Novigrad in the autumn of 1993. The Council for Refugees had requested the army's support to house new Croatian refugees from Bosnia. The Slovenian media blew up the case and the Croatian Minister of Foreign Affairs quickly apologized for the undiplomatic and illegal action.

There were also territorial disputes. The first frictions arose regarding the delimitation of the frontier region of Međimurje (q.v.). As state frontiers and cultural borders do not easily fall together, the usual practice is to mix languages during liturgical services in the church of the disputed small locality of Raskrižje. Though more than 70 percent of the population is Croat and Croatian cultural vestiges are easily certified, the communist authorities of 1945 attached the village to Slovenia. The region is now claimed by Croatia on ethnic grounds.

More serious and disruptive were the discussions about the frontier near the bay of Piran. The conflict lay bare the divergent views on the underlying basic principles of both parties. In the discussions of the bilateral technical commission on frontier issues, one party stuck to the registered frontiers of the communes, while the other defended the principle of natural frontiers. In the case in point, the river Dragonja in Piran Bay has more than one basin: its original course and several canalized ones. The discussion was not without practical importance because in the disputed area lie the Slovenian airfield of Portorož and some industrial salt fields. Moreover, the frontiers in the bay are of more than local interest to Slovenia because they may give access to international waters.

As a result of these conflicts, the signing of an agreement on friendly cooperation between Croatia and Slovenia has been postponed. The Slovenian Parliament blocked the procedure, arguing Croatia had to prove it earned Slovenia's friendship. Some politicians even claimed that signing an agreement would harm the image of Slovenia. At that time, Croatia was under attack from the international community for its policy towards Bosnia-Hercegovina.

At the beginning of 1994, tensions rose to new heights. Slovenia threatened to cut Croatia off from the Krško electric network because its unpaid bill has accumulated to 40 million DM. On the other hand, Croatia claimed it had not yet been compensated for the Croatian investments of about $1 billion in the Krško power station. Another bone of contention was the unsettled liabilities of the Ljubljanska Banka towards Croatian citizens and the interest to be paid on it. At the same time, no progress had been made in the Piran issue.

More difficulties are expected to arise in connection with the negotiations on the revision of the Osimo Agreement (q.v.) with Italy.

Despite this, the two new states have good reasons to maintain full cooperation in the economic field. Several agreements have been signed, especially on trade and transport. In 1992, Slovenia was still the main trade partner of Croatia. Croatia's imports from Slovenia amounted to $874 million, its exports to $1.1 billion or 20 percent and 24 percent respectively of total imports and exports.

SLUŽBA ZA ZAŠTITU USTAVNOG PORETKA (SZUP) see STATE SERVICE FOR THE PROTECTION OF THE CONSTITUTIONAL ORDER

SMIČIKLAS, TADIJA (1843-1914). Born in Reštovo in the Žumberak. He wrote *Poviest Hrvatska*, the history of Croatia in a "pragmatic" vein. It had to strengthen national Croatian awareness against the Hungarian cultural and political hegemony in the period of the Nagodba (q.v.). He became Professor of History at Zagreb University in 1882, a member of the Yugoslav Academy in 1883, President of the Matica hrvatska in 1889 and President of the Yugoslav Academy of Arts and Sciences (qq.v.) from 1900 to 1914. He edited a diplomatic codex of the Kingdom of Croatia, Dalmatia and Slavonia (q.v.) with source documents on the Middle Ages. In 1891, he published the book *Dvesto godišnjica oslobođenja Slavonije* (Two Hundred Years since the Liberation of Slavonia). He was twice elected to the Sabor (q.v.) on the list of the Independent National Party (q.v.) (1884-1887 and 1897-1902).

SOCIAL DEMOCRATIC PARTY OF CROATIA-PARTY OF DEMOCRATIC CHANGES/SOCIJALDEMOKRATSKA PARTIJA HRVATSKE-STRANKA ZA DRUŠTVENE PROMENE (SDPH-SDP). The SDPH-SDP is the successor of the Communist Party. Its leader and President Ivica Račan played an important role in the breakup of the communist system and the introduction of multiparty elections. At the first elections, it was strongly beaten by the nationalistic Croatian Democratic Union (q.v.). However, in August 1991, it participated temporarily in the Government of National Union (q.v.).

SOCIALIST PARTY OF CROATIA/STRANKA SOCIJALISTA HRVATSKE (SSH). Its President is Silvije Degen. Its program takes a position midway between the Western European socialists and the former communists. Contrary to expectations, it obtained no electoral success.

SOCIETY OF THE BROTHERS OF THE CROATIAN DRAGON/DRUŽBA BRAĆA HRVATSKOGA ZMAJA. This Society has adopted the name of the Ordo Equestris Draconis, an order founded in 1408 under the Croato-Hungarian King Sigismund. The Society of the Brothers of the Croatian Dragon was founded in 1905 by the historian Emilije Laszowski and the writer Velimir Deželić. Its concern was the study and preservation of the national cultural heritage. After the Second World War, its activities were prohibited and suspended. The Society revived under the Tuđman (q.v.) regime. The head of the order is Professor Juraj Kolarić, Dean of the Catholic Theology Faculty of Zagreb University (q.v.). The main projects of the Society include the reconstruction of architectural monuments, the publishing of Croatian literature and commemorative manifestations of historical-cultural events. The Society has erected a monument to the Croatian national anthem (q.v.) at Zelenjak. It will undertake a similar action for the commemoration of the 150th anniversary of the first speech in Croatian in the Sabor (q.v.) by Ivan Kukuljević (q.v.). The Society plans a "Kajkaviana Croatica" to present the Kajkavian (q.v.) culture to the broad public.

SOLIN see SALONA

ŠOLJAN, ANTUN (1932-1993). Born in Belgrade. He studied at the Faculty of Philosophy in Zagreb (q.v.) and lived and worked there as a professional writer. He is best known as a novelist. His books include *Luka* (The Port), *Drugi ljudi na Mjesecu* (Other People on the Moon) and *Prošlo Nevršeno Vreme* (Gone the Imperfect Time). He also wrote poetry, plays, essays and short stories and translated works from world literature. Critics called him the most significant Croatian writer of his generation.

ŠOŠIĆ, HRVOJE (1928). Born in Osijek (q.v.). Professor of Economy at Zagreb University. Member of the Initiative Board of the Croatian Democratic Union (q.v.). Deputy President of the Croatian Christian Democratic Party (q.v.). Member of the House of Counties of Parliament (q.v.).

ŠPEGELJ, MARTIN (1927-). General and Minister of Defense in the Government of Josip Manolić (q.v.). In the spring of 1991, the Minister was accused by the Yugoslav army of plotting an armed insurrection. He was judged *in absentia* on April 8, 1991, by a military tribunal in Zagreb (q.v.). His trial was interrupted by street protests. The Zagreb regime succeeded in hiding the General during the following months.

SPLIT. At the foot of Mount Marjan, there was a small settlement founded by Greek traders, called Aspalathos. The Roman Emperor Diocletian (245-313 A.D.) built his palace here. It still dominates the old town of Split. After Diocletian died, the Palace became state property, a refuge for Roman nobility who had fallen out of favor. In 424, Galla Placida, the daughter of Emperor Theodosius, was banished to the palace with her son Valerian. Marcellinus, who had proclaimed himself Emperor of Dalmatia, lived there in 461. Julius Nepos, dethroned by Odoacer, fled there. As Salona (q.v.) fell in 641, its inhabitants first fled to the islands and then to Split. The palace did not suffer much from the invasions of the Avars (q.v.) and Slavs. Split became the religious center of Dalmatia (q.v.). The Early medieval city developed under Byzantine rule and was briefly conquered by the Franks. The 925 and 928 Church Synods united the provinces of Dalmatia and Croatia. The region became the center of the early Croatian kingdoms. In 1075, the papal emissary crowned Zvonimir King of the Croats and Dalmatians. In 1105, Split recognized the sovereignty of the Hungarian Kings, retaining some autonomy on the basis of old municipal rights. This autonomy came to an end in 1420 under Venice. The fifteenth and sixteenth centuries were marked by significant humanistic activity. Split built a port terminal, custom house, and lazaretto and became the main port for exports on the Balkans. The war with the Ottomans brought its decline.

Marko Marulić (q.v.), the father of Croatian literature, was born, lived and wrote in Split. Emanuel Vidović, a forerunner of modern Croatian contemporary painting, was born and spent his life as a painter here. Other eminent citizens also lived in the city: Andrija Buvina, Archdeacon Thomas (q.v.), Juraj Dalmatinac, Ivan Lukačić, Tin Ujević (q.v.), Ivan Meštrović (q.v.), Vladimir Nazor (q.v.), among others.

Split is now the second largest city in the Republic of Croatia with 206,000 inhabitants. Because of its central position between the hinterland and the most populated Croatian islands (Brač, Hvar) Split has developed its transit and service functions. The University of Split counts a number of faculties and high schools: Faculty of Electrotechnics, Mechanical and Naval Engineering, Naval Faculty, Chemical and Technological Faculty, Faculty of Economics, Faculty of Law, Civil Engineering Faculty, Faculty of Natural-Mathematic Sciences and Education and a Department of the Medical Faculty from Zagreb. Among other cultural institutions, the Croatian National Theater is prominent with its activities in Split. Split organized several large international sports events: Mediterranean Games (1979), European Swimming Championships (1981), European Athletics Championships (1990). Quite a number of Split's representatives obtained internationally significant results: Đuđica Bjedov in swimming, Goran Ivanišević in tennis, Tony Kukoč in basketball.

Split's economy has lately suffered considerably because of the war through the destruction of traffic and business communications. Industrial branches with a positive record are rare exceptions. The economy has gone through a deep recession and it will require several years to recover. At the end of 1992, Split housed around 43,000 refugees and displaced persons from Croatia and Bosnia-Hercegovina.

Split is the capital of the Splitsko-Dalmatinska *županija* (q.v.).

SPOLETO, AIMONE VON. Duke, assigned by King Viktor Emmanuel III to become the King of the Independent State of Croatia (q.v.). "Tomislav II" refused and did not take up his functions.

SRIJEM. Due to the Treaty of Karlovci (q.v.) of 1699, this region belonged to Croatia after the Ottomans were forced out of Slavonia (q.v.). The borders of Croatia reached up to the point where the Sava flows into the Danube, namely Belgrade. The contemporary Croatian-Serbian border was drawn for the first time in 1945 and brought a division of Srijem. This division was decided, not without controversy, by the communist leadership of Yugoslavia in 1944/45. The border was drawn according to ethnic principles: eastern Srijem mainly settled by Serbs went to Serbia and was incorporated in the Autonomous Province of Vojvodina, the western part mostly settled by Croats went to Croatia. (See also SRIJEMSKA MITROVICA)

SRIJEMSKA MITROVICA. Town in Eastern Pannonia (q.v.), now called Srijemska Mitrovica or Srijem (q.v.). In Roman times, Sirmium was the capital of Pannonia Segunda. The Roman Emperors Aurelian, Decius, Claudius II and Probus were born here. In 582 the city was conquered by the Avars (q.v.). (See also SRIJEM)

SRPSKA NARODNA STRANKA (SNS) see SERBIAN NATIONAL PARTY

SRPSKA REPUBLIKA (SR) see SERBIAN REPUBLIC

SRPSKE OBLASTI ZAPADNE SLAVONIJE see SERBIAN REGIONS OF WEST SLAVONIA

SRPSKI DEMOKRATSKI FORUM (SDF) see SERBIAN DEMOCRATIC FORUM

STARČEVIĆ, ANTE (1823-1896). He has been called the father of the Croatian nation. He developed the theory of the Croatian historical state right. The Croats (q.v.) as a political nation have always existed and have the right to establish their own independent state. The conquest of a homeland has been historically determined by the arrival of the Croats in the sixth and seventh centuries. The Croat Kingdoms confirmed this fact. The acceptance of Hungarian and Austrian dynasties had been a deliberate choice. Croatia was only bound by a personal union that could be undone any time the monarch fell short of his obligations to the Croatian nation. This line of thought explains his resistance to Austrian absolutism and especially to Hungarian hegemony.

Starčević also defended a great-Croatian viewpoint. His colleague Kvaternik (q.v.) already used a broad notion of Croatia; it extended from the Alps to the Drina and from Albania to the Danube. Starčević pushed the frontier further to the east to the Serbian-Bulgarian border. According to him, there were only two Slavic nations: Croats and Bulgars. Slovenes were "highland" Croats, and Serbs did not really exist or were a religious Orthodox sect. The rulers of Dioclea (q.v.) and the Nemanjić dynasty were a Croat family. In any case, the Serbs and Slovenes did not have the right to a separate political territory.

In practical politics, the identity of the Serbs was recognized in Croatia inasmuch as they cooperated towards the construction of a Croatian state on the Habsburg territories. In contrast to his dogmatic colleague Kvaternik, Starčević stayed within the boundaries of political realism set by the Habsburg domination. His theory and political practice placed his followers before interpretation problems and in the course of history several parties claimed to be the true heirs of *Pravaštvo* (the theory of the historical state right). (See also CROATIAN PARTY OF RIGHTS; KVATERNIK, EUGEN)

START: NOVE GENERACIJE. Newly launched independent and critical fortnightly of politics of culture. It includes many journalists formerly with *Slobodna Dalmacija* (q.v.) before the government takeover.

STATE. Following the Western traditional concept of democracy, state power in Croatia has been incorporated in three bodies. Theoretically and constitutionally, there exist separate legislative (Parliament), executive (President and Government) and judicial organs. However, Croatia is known to have a strong presidential regime.

The supreme head of the Republic is the President (q.v.), who is elected for a term of five years. He has extensive power, especially in foreign policy and under war circumstances. According to the Constitution (q.v.), the President appoints the Prime Minister and, on proposal of the Prime Minister, other Ministers of government. These appointments are subject to confirmation by the House of Representatives.

STATE SERVICE FOR THE PROTECTION OF THE CONSTITUTIONAL ORDER/SLUŽBA ZA ZAŠTITU USTAVNOG PORETKA (SZUP). State body that watches and guaranties the constitutional order.

STEĆCI. The tombstones found in Hercegovina and interior Bosnia are sometimes claimed to be part of Croatian culture. Some archeologists think that the form of the typical tombstones - the *stećci* - can be traced back to ancient Roman examples. Others stress the importance of ornaments and figures, ascribed to the Bogomil (q.v.) tradition. The dualistic doctrine of the Bogomils is supposed to be of Bulgarian - Pop Bogomil - or even Iranian origin. This last theory fits the claims of some Croat-nationalist historians, who defend the Iranian descent of the "Croats" (q.v.). Other theoreticians see the Bogomil beliefs and the tombstones rather as a national expression of the autonomous Bosnian state church, at the crossroads of Eastern Orthodox and Western Roman Catholicism. The whole question has also been linked to the old discussions on the original population of Bosnia.

STEPINAC, ALOJZIJE (1898-1960). He became Bishop of Zagreb (q.v.) in 1937. His attitude during the Second World War is controversial. Some sources accuse him of full cooperation with the Ustaša (q.v.) regime, others say that he acted with reservations and had a moderating influence.

After the war the communist regime of Tito (q.v.) proposed that Stepinac establish an autonomous Catholic Church (q.v.), more or less independent from the Vatican. Stepinac and other Bishops answered in a letter of September 20, 1945, that the relations between the church and the state would primarily depend on the ending of the repression of the church. In his turn, Stepinac was arrested on September 18, 1946, and accused of cooperation with the Ustaša regime under the Independent State of Croatia (q.v.). On October 11, 1946, he was sentenced to 16 years of imprisonment and interned. At the end of 1952, Pope Pius I announced the election of the interned Stepinac to the College of

Cardinals. The communist regime broke off diplomatic relations with the Vatican.

Under the new Tuđman regime, Stepinac was posthumously rehabilitated. The Vatican even set up a commission to start the procedure to declare him a Saint.

STIPAC, DRAGO (1920-). Born in Busovača (Bosnia-Hercegovina). President of the Croatian Peasant Party (q.v.) in the post-Tito area. At the end of July 1993, Stipac took a special initiative. He gathered the leaders of 17 opposition parties to set out a common strategy against the politics of Tuđman and the government of the Croatian Democratic Union (q.v.). The opposition criticized especially the policy of Tuđman towards Bosnia-Hercegovina and Serbia. First, Tuđman's line of defending in Bosnia-Hercegovina the construction of a confederation and not a federation was dangerous for the Croats not living in the Croatian Community of Herceg-Bosna. Moreover, this model could inspire the international community to accept a similar attitude towards the Serbs of Croatia. Second, Tuđman was not firm enough during the negotiations with Milošević. He had not obtained any guaranties from the Serbs on the position of the Krajina (q.v.) in Croatia. However, the common initiative of the opposition forces remained informal and was short-lived.

ŠTOKAVIAN. Variant of the Croatian language, an alternative to kajkavian or čakavian (qq.v.). According to the equivalent for the word *what,* the variants use the expressions što-, kaj- and ča-. The štokavian variant was spoken in the eastern part (Serbia), the interior (Bosnia) and southernmost part (Dubrovnik) of the Serbo-Croatian language area.

Štokavian developed more or less into an accepted standard thanks to the flourishing cultural life and literature of Dubrovnik (q.v.). It was also chosen by the Illyrians (q.v.) to function as the uniting language of the South Slavs. The centralizing language policy in the Kingdom of Yugoslavia and during the communist period strengthened the position of štokavian. Under the recent Tuđman (q.v.) regime, a plurality of linguistic expression is respected with the reassessment of čakavian. At the same time, the promotion of the specific Croatian variant of štokavian is stimulated.

STRANKA HRVATSKOG DRŽAVNOG PRAVA (SHDP) see PARTY OF THE CROATIAN STATE'S RIGHTS

STRANKA SOCIJALISTA HRVATSKE (SSH) see SOCIALIST PARTY OF CROATIA

STRIKE (RIGHT TO). Article 60 of the Constitution (q.v.) of December 1990 guaranties the fundamental right to strike. It may be restricted in some branches of the public service.

STROSSMAYER, JOSIP JURAJ (1815-1905). Born in Osijek (q.v.). Bishop of Đakovo (q.v.). He studied theology at the University of Budapest and presented his doctorate in Vienna. He was a supporter of the Illyrian (q.v.) movement and adopted the idea of the national unity of all South Slavs. In 1848, he mediated between the Austrian Archduke Francis Karl and the Croatian Ban Josip Jelačić (q.v.) in order to put down the Hungarian revolt.

He was appointed Bishop of Đakovo on November 18, 1849. He believed in a reconciliation of Orthodoxy and Roman Catholicism. He became famous in international circles by a speech at the Vatican Synod held in 1869-1870, where he defended the position that the dogma of papal infallibility was a nuisance to the union of the Orthodox and Catholic Churches (q.v.).

He acted as founding father of Zagreb University (q.v.) and of the South Slav Academy of Arts and Sciences. He contributed large sums of money to the Art Gallery of Zagreb and laid the first stone of the Cathedral of Đakovo.

STUDIAE HISTORIAE PHILOSOPHIAE CROATICAE. This journal is the international edition of the periodical *Priloze za istraživanje hrvatske filozofske baštine* (Research into the Croatian Philosophical Heritage, 1975-). The yearly *Studiae historiae philosophiae Croaticae* is published by the Department of History of Philosophy of the Institute of Historical Studies of Zagreb University (q.v.). The first issue appeared in 1990 with contributions in English and German about the beginnings of philosophy in Croatia and some major thinkers and currents in the

Croatian philosophical tradition, such as Herman Dalmatinac, Marko Marulić (q.v.) and others.

SUBAŠIĆ, IVAN. Ban (q.v.) of Croatia in the period of the prewar Banovina (q.v.), 1939-1941. Prime Minister of the Yugoslav Government in Exile during the Second World War. Subašić made an agreement with Tito (q.v.) to abolish the prewar constitution of Yugoslavia and thereby paved the way for the communist regime.

SUNCOKRET/SUNFLOWER. This organization coordinates the grassroots relief work of international and domestic volunteers. It is concerned with the needs of refugees and displaced persons in Croatia and Bosnia-Hercegovina, primarily psycho-social needs and particularly those of children. It organizes educational and structured "free time" activities in 29 refugee camps, cultural art therapy and women's self-help groups.

SUPEK, IVAN (1915-). Participant in the communist resistance and member of the educational section of the Anti-Fascist Council of the National Liberation of Croatia (q.v.) (1943). Professor of Theoretical Physics at Zagreb University (q.v.) since 1946. Founder of the Ruđer Bošković Institute (1950). Though he occupied official positions in the communist regime, he was known to be an independent intellectual with heretical and oppositional views. He was elected Rector of Zagreb University during the Croatian Spring (q.v.) (1969). As such, he is still respected under the Tuđman (q.v.) regime. He is the President of the Croatian Academy of Arts and Sciences (q.v.).

Ivan Supek is a novel writer and playwright as well. He describes personal experiences in *U prvom licu* (In the First Person, 1965), *Heretik* (Heretic, 1968) and *Extraordinarius*. He participated in publishing the journal *Encyclopaedia Moderna*.

SUPEK, RUDI (1913-1993). Philosopher and sociologist at Zagreb University (q.v.). He was an editor of the journals *Pogledi* (Views) and *Praxis* (q.v.). Both were critical of the official communist bureaucracy and were censored by the authorities. Contrary to some of his colleagues, Rudi Supek contributed to the new journal *Praxis International* published abroad.

Along with theoretical studies, he produced a lot of sociological research on the practice of self-management. For this, he won international recognition. Together with Branko Horvat (q.v.) and Mihailo Marković, he published a basic reader on self-governing socialism.

ŠURBEK, DRAGUTIN (1946-). Table-tennis player. Repeated champion of Yugoslavia. He won the European Championship in 1968, 1970 and 1976, the World Championship in 1979 and more titles in pairs.

ŠUŠAK, GOJKO (1945-). Born in Široki Brijeg, Hercegovina. He emigrated to Canada and became the manager and owner of various enterprises. He was called back by Tuđman (q.v.) to lead the Ministry of Defense. He is said to favor the Hercegovian lobby and to support Mate Boban (q.v.), the Croat leader of the independent Community of Herceg-Bosna. At the Second Convention of the Croatian Democratic Union (q.v.) in the autumn of 1993, Šušak was chosen for the presidency of the party.

ŠUVAR, STIPE. Communist party leader of Croatia under the Tito (q.v.) regime. He was first a member of the Central Committee of the Communist Party in Croatia and became head of the League of Communists of Yugoslavia (q.v.) in Belgrade.

SYNOD OF SPLIT see GRGUR NINSKI

SYNTHESIS PHILOSOPHICA. Philosophical journal founded in 1986 and published in English, German and French twice a year in Zagreb by the Croatian Philosophical Society (q.v.). It is the international edition of the Croatian philosophical journal *Filozofska Istraživanja* (Philosophical Investigations, established in 1980-1981). The journal embraces a wide variety of philosophical and other related subjects - e.g., theology, world religions, natural sciences, psychology, law, politics, sociology, anthropology, literature, linguistics, history and so on. The primary purpose of the publication is to advance and nurture an atmosphere of philosophical pluralism as opposed to strict conformity to one particular school of thought. There is therefore a constant emphasis on continued dialogue. As such, individual thinkers from all over the world (Croats and non-Croats alike) are invited to contribute to the periodical by expressing their ideas and points of view. Back issues focused on subjects such as the philosophical-spiritual heritage of certain Slavic peoples, Ruđer Josip Bošković (q.v.), philosophy and religion, philosophy and literature, language and knowledge, contemporary philosophy of law, the multi-dimensionality of metaphor, philosophical terminology, philosophy in Latin America, Ancient Latin and Greek thought, and others.

- T -

TADIJANOVIĆ, DRAGUTIN (1905-). Born at Rastušje (near Slavonski Brod). Poet, editor and translator. His poetical work has been translated into many foreign languages.

TARSATICA see RIJEKA

TAX SYSTEM. *Taxes for personal income.* All citizens employed within the territory of the Republic of Croatia are taxpayers only if their total wages and other incomes exceed within a year's period the amount of three times the average annual wages in the Republic. The exceeding amount is taxed at rates ranging from 45 to 70 percent. A relatively small number of employed persons are effective taxpayers because, in addition to the large amount of untaxed income, citizens are entitled to other tax benefits. They can make deductions from total income for investments in objects of long-term useful value (including automobiles and household appliances) and for unemployed spouses. The same stipulations apply to the income earned by foreign citizens in the Republic.

Taxes and contributions deducted from wages. An employer contracts for the amount of net wages with an employee but must take into account tax liabilities which must be calculated and paid to relevant institutions. These tax liabilities include contributions to the pension fund, social and health security, education, etc. Tax and contribution rates are now so defined that gross wages are more or less twice the level of net wages, while contributions add another fourth.

Tax on business profits. The determination of the tax base is made in keeping with the Accounting Act and consists of the difference between total income and total expenditures. Income includes the following: a) business income from the sale of goods and services, grants, tax refunds, etc.; b) income from financing such as financial investment, interest, positive differences in the exchange rate, revaluation, etc.; c) extraordinary income from the sales of non-material and material investment, income from insurance, bonuses, income from penalties, prizes, write-off of claims by creditors, etc. Recognized expenditures include: a) all business expenditures such as material costs, depreciation, non-material costs, purchase value of goods and materials, gross workers' wages; b) finance expenditures such as interest, negative differences in the exchange rate, negative differences in the revaluation of effects, etc.; c) extraordinary expenditures such as unwritten-off value of material sold or disposed of and non-material investments, deficits, penalties, damages, write-offs of unpaid claims, etc. The rate of taxation on profits is 40 percent for domestic and 20 percent for foreign enterprises.

There are standard tax benefits for all enterprises and additional benefits for newly established firms. Enterprises are not required to pay taxes on the part of profits reinvested in the expansion or modernization of production facilities in their own or other enterprises. New enterprises do not pay taxes on profits generated in the first year of operations; in the second year, they enjoy a benefit of 50 percent of their tax liability; in the third year 25 percent. Newly established enterprises on islands, border and underdeveloped areas do not pay the taxes during the first two years of operation.

Sales tax. The second form of taxation which enterprises must comply with is sales tax on products and services. The tax must be included in the retail price of the product sold or service rendered. The retailer or service firm having made the sale is obliged to remit the amount of tax included in the price to the relevant agency. The tax rates for various products and services are stipulated by the Sales Tax Act. The rate varies from zero for basic products such as bread, milk and cooking oil to 60 percent for luxury products such as jewelry, perfumes and cosmetic products.

TELEVISION see CROATIAN TELEVISION; TV MARJAN; YOUTH TELEVISION

TESLA, NIKOLA (1856-1943). Born in Smiljan, near Gospić. He emigrated to the United States and became famous for his studies in the field of electricity and its applications.

THEATER. In the Middle Ages religious plays were performed in the major Dalmatian (q.v.) cultural centers. This was exemplified by a manuscript from the Tkon Anthology (q.v.). It contains a play in Glagolitic (q.v.) with stage instructions recorded in the margin.

Later on, Dubrovnik (q.v.) became the center of playwriting and performing with writers such as Lučić, Držić and Palmotić.

The Croatian National Revival had its center in Zagreb (q.v.). In 1840, the theater season opened with Ivan Kukuljević's (q.v.) nationalist play *Turci kod Siska* (The Turks at the Gates of Sisak).

Modern Croatian writers seem to be especially successful in producing comedies. Critical and satirical plays were also very popular, as was historical drama. Under the communist regime, symbolical and allegorical plays were performed along with more realistic productions.

Contemporary writers follow all the modern European trends. Avant-garde multi-media productions alternate with classical declamatory dramas.

THOMAS, ARCHDEACON (1200-1268). Author of the Chronicle *Historia Salonitana*, a history of the sub-bishopric of Salona (q.v.). The Archdeacon of Split (q.v.) wrote this work some time before 1268. The Chronicle relates the arrival of the Goths and Slavs in Dalmatia (q.v.) and the destruction of Salona. The Chronicle continues with the national history of the Croat kingdom and the choice of a Hungarian dynasty. Thomas' writings gave rise to the much disputed thesis on the Gothic origin of the Croats (q.v.). The source has been ascribed particular value when dealing with the church schism of the tenth century involving the religious centers of Nin and Split and when describing the Synods that were held to find a solution to the conflict.

TITO, JOSIP BROZ (1892-1980). On May 25, 1892, the future President of communist Yugoslavia was born at Kumrovec in the Croatian Zagorje. Croatia was still part of the Austro-Hungarian Empire. Broz's father was a native peasant and his mother came from Slovenia. Broz worked as a mechanic in small workshops. During the First World War, he served in the Austro-Hungarian army. He was taken a prisoner of war and transported to the Russian interior. When the Russian Revolution broke out, he was freed and joined the Red Guard. He was registered as a member of the Communist Party. Back in Yugoslavia, he continued his revolutionary work and spent some time in prison. In January 1939, Josip Broz was appointed General Secretary of the Yugoslav Communist Party. He was determined to put an end to the factional disputes and to give the party strong leadership.

From then on, Tito had a major voice in all the ensuing phases of the Yugoslav Revolution. His personal career was intimately bound up with the evolution of the communist cause. During the Second World War, he became commander in chief of the partisan armed forces. In 1943, the Second Session of the Anti-Fascist Council of the National Liberation of Yugoslavia (q.v.) established the second Yugoslavia as a federal republic consisting of six Republics. Tito had to make use of all his charisma to convince his comrade-partisans that all peoples of Yugoslavia should be granted equal rights. The partisan struggle ended with a complete victory for the communists. With the assistance of Russian and Western allies, Tito could form his first government on March 7, 1945. However, under pressure from the Allies, he had to share power with members of the government in exile. These politicians of the former Kingdom were completely neutralized and soon eliminated by the policy of the Communist Party.

More dangerous for Tito's government was the clash with the USSR. The Cominform conflict (q.v.) led to a break with Moscow. Tito's internal power base was threatened, but large-scale purges in the party restored order. An alternative ideology based on self-management was introduced in the beginning of the 1950s. Timid democratization of the regime threatened the party organization again from within. In 1952, Tito was forced to discard his closest aide and once Vice-President Milan Đilas. Another possible heir, Alexander Ranković (q.v.), dominated the

Ministry of the Interior and the Secret Police for years. He ultimately even controlled Tito himself. In 1966, Tito was obliged to discard his conservative comrade, then second in rank. After the fall of the hardliner Ranković, economic and political liberalization broke through and this threatened the party monopoly anew. The Croatian Spring (q.v.) and similar opposition movements in other Republics rose to an unexpected intensity. They were ultimately repressed by Tito at the beginning of the 1970s. Tito chose some former or young, second-class party leaders to restore the old order. At the same time, he pushed through constitutional reforms to take the wind out of the sails of nationalism. By granting more autonomy and self-government to the Republics, he hoped to reduce the level of conflict between the federal units. In the same way, he set up a federal presidency structure to ensure the continuity of the system after his death.

In international affairs, Tito profited from the rivalries of the two blocs during the Cold War and took a leading role in the movement of Non-Aligned Countries.

Tito died in May 1980 and the structures set up to ensure continuity functioned for a few years. Then, divergent aspirations could no longer be reconciled and the federal structure exploded.

TKON ANTHOLOGY. Tkon is a village on the island of Pašman near Biograd (q.v.). In the fourteenth century, the Benedictine monastery on the island became the base of Glagolitic (q.v.) worship. The scriptoria of the monastery produced the Tkon Anthology, a Glagolitic manuscript from the sixteenth century. It contains the play *The Passion of Our Savior* with detailed stage instructions.

TOMISLAV, KING (?-928). Croatian King, supposed to have governed from 916 to 928. Under his reign the Croatian kingdom expanded and reached its apogee. The Croatian kingdom comprised all the regions of great Croatia except Srijem (q.v.). (See also TRPIMIR DYNASTY)

TORBARINA, TANJA. Journalist. In the summer of 1991, she wrote three critical articles in the journal *Globus*. Antun Vrdoljak brought her before the court on the charge of public offense under Article 75 of the criminal code. The court in Zagreb (q.v.)

released Torbarina from the charge. The judge motivated his decision by declaring that she had been misled by her primary sources and that this sort of procedure was counterproductive for the image of Croatia.

TRADE UNIONS. Three national trade union organizations are officially recognized as the representatives of the workers and have seats in the Economic and Social Council (q.v.):
1. Hrvatska Udruga Sindikata (HUS)/Croatian Association of Unions. President is Berislav Berec.
2. Savez Samostalnih Sindikata Hrvatske (SSSH)/Association of Independent Unions of Croatia. President is Dragutin Lesar.
3. Konfederacija Nezavisnih Sindikata Hrvatske (KNS)/Confederation of Independent Trade Unions of Croatia. President is Mladen Mesić.

There are numerous sectoral and local organizations. One of the most important is the Koordinacija Službeničkih Sindikata (KSS)/Association of Unions in the Services. President is Krešimir Sever.

TRAVUNJA. Region between Zahumlja, Raša and Dioclea (qq.v.) with present-day Trebinje as its center. It is identified with Konavle by Constantine Porphyrogenitus (q.v.), though at this time the term was reserved for the coastal region.

TRIBAL ORGANIZATION. It is widely supposed that at the time of their arrival in Croatia, the Croats (q.v.) were organized in a *pleme*, a group of people bearing the same name and believed to have descended from a common ancestor. This tribe was composed of several clans *(bratstva or rodovi)*. Each of them comprised several families or communities of families. The territorial unity of a tribe was a *župa*. The chief of such a territory was the *župan*.

TRIBUSON, GORAN (1948-). Critic and writer of novels. Some are written in the so-called fantastic supernatural style of Borges.

TRIPALO, ANTE MIKO (1926-). Party leader and secretary. He represented and defended with Savka Dabčević-Kučar (q.v.) the progressive nationalist wing during the Croatian Spring (q.v.) and had to resign after Karađorđevo (q.v.). In the post-communist period, he resumed his political work as leader of the Croatian People's Party (q.v.).

TRIUNE KINGDOM OF CROATIA, DALMATIA AND SLAVONIA see KINGDOM OF CROATIA, DALMATIA AND SLAVONIA, TRIUNE

TRPIMIR DYNASTY (845-1074). The Trpimir dynasty is the first and only national Croat dynasty. In a charter of 852, the name of the Croat dynasty appears for the first time. Trpimir (845-864) is mentioned as *Dux Chroatorum*. At that time, the Arabs attacked the Byzantines and the Venetians who dominated the shores of the Adriatic. Trpimir took the opportunity to bring Zadar (q.v.) and other Byzantine possessions under his control. Moreover, he resisted a Bulgarian invasion in northeastern Bosnia. Consequently he was recognized as a strong and autonomous ruler of the Croatian lands. Trpimir had three sons. However, Domagoj, probably another relative, came to power. Domagoj repelled a new attack of the Venetians. He chose the side of the Frankish Emperor Ludwig II during the conquest of Bar from the Arabs and by this friendly diplomacy averted the Frankish occupation of the Dalmatian (q.v.) lands. The pressure of the Arabs on the Byzantine-dominated Dalmatian towns was exploited by the Croats and Neretvans (q.v.) to attack Venetian and Byzantine possessions.

Zdeslav (878-879), a son of Trpimir, came to power with the support of the Byzantines. The Byzantines ordered the Dalmatian towns and islands not to pay tribute to them, but to the Croatian *knez* (duke). Religious and political resistance to the Byzantines in the Croatian lands led to a rebellion against Zdezlav and he was replaced by Branimir (q.v.) (879-892). Croatia freed itself from the Byzantine yoke and became an independent country. Branimir got the support of the Pope of Rome and obtained the official recognition of the Croatian state. The youngest son of Trpimir, Muncimir (892-910), succeeded Branimir. Muncimir favored the introduction of the Glagolitic (q.v.) rite into the Croatian national church. He was the father of Tomislav (q.v.) (910-928). Muncimir sent his son to replace Prince Braslav in Pannonian (q.v.) Croatia when Braslav died. In that way, Dalmatia and Pannonian Croatia were for the first time united in a national Croatian state.

Tomislav successfully defended his region against the Hungarians. The Serbs and the lords of Red Croatia (q.v.) sought his protection. Mihailjo Višević of Hum (Hercegovina) acknowledged his suzerainty. Bosnia and Istria (q.v.) were under his control. In the meantime, the Bulgars also threatened Byzantium. The Byzantines formed an alliance with Tomislav and handed over to him their old Dalmatian *theme* (province): the towns of Split, Zadar and Trogir and the islands Osor, Rab and Krk (q.v.). This implied that the Croatian churches were no longer dependent on the patriarchate of Constantinople, but reverted to the Pope of Rome. In 925 and 928, religious strife between Grgur Ninski (q.v.) and the Bishop of Split was arbitrated by Synods called together by the Pope. Tomislav officially assumed the title of "King of Croats" and ruled over a territory that incorporated all great-Croatian lands except Srijem (q.v.). In 924, the Bulgars invaded Serbia. Tomislav granted asylum to the Serbian nobles in his land. When Simeon the Bulgar invaded Bosnia, Tomislav defeated his army and put the Serbian nobles back on their throne. Some Croatian historians saw the immigration of Serbs into Bosnia in this period as sowing the seeds of future clashes between the two peoples. Tomislav died around 928.

His heirs Trpimir (928-935) and Krešimir I (935-945) maintained the Croatian lands firmly under their control, except for the weakening of central authority over the Neretvans. Their pirate activities prefigured their later role in the history between Croats and Venetians. Krešimir's son Miroslav (945-949) acceded prematurely to power. The Ban Pribina provoked a rebellion against the young King and probably effected his murder. The Sabor recognized the rightful King Krešimir II, but Red Croatia opted for Pribina and the Red and White Croatian lands split once and for all. Ragusa (Dubrovnik) established its status of independent free town. The Serbs conquered part of Bosnia. Krešimir's son, Stipan Držislav (969-997), defeated Ban Pribana and tried to restore the old kingdom by skillful diplomacy. At the time of Držislav, the Bulgar state under Emperor Samuel strangled the Byzantines to death. In 986, the Byzantines recognized Stipan Držislav as "King of Dalmatia" in order to obtain his support. The Croat forces fought the Bulgars twice when Samuel invaded

Bosnia-Hercegovina and the hinterland of Zadar. A Croat-Byzantine fleet protected Dubrovnik (q.v.) against interference from Venice. After the death of Stipan in 997, the Croatian kingdom disintegrated. Byzantium and Venice took over the supremacy in the Adriatic.

Krešimir III (1000-1035), a son of Stipan Držislav, formally acknowledged submission to the Byzantines. He realized that he needed other allies and concluded a mutual defense pact with the Hungarians. Thanks to these friendly relations, Krešimir even acquired part of Sirmium (Srijem). The Croatian center shifted from then on northwards from Dalmatia to old Pannonian Croatia. Also Krešimir's son, Stipan I (1035-1058), maintained good relations with the Hungarians. Only under the reign of Petar Krešimir IV (q.v.) (1058-1073) was the old kingdom temporarily restored. Krešimir brought the Dalmatian towns back under his control. He called the Adriatic *nostrum Dalmaticum more* (Our Dalmatic Sea) when he granted the island of Maun to the cloister St. Krševan of Zadar in 1069. He took a pro-Latin orientation in church matters and was recognized by the Pope as "King of Croatia and Dalmatia." In 1066, Krešimir made a special grant to the monastery St. Mary in Zadar, where Ćika - probably his daughter - was a nun.

Petar Krešimir's son Stipan was soon replaced by the Ban (q.v.) of Pannonian Croatia, Dimitar Svinimir (1076-1089). He was married to Helen of Hungary, the sister of Laszlo who later acceded to the Hungarian throne. Svinimir and the Hungarians repelled a Carinthian army that invaded Pannonian Croatia. Svinimir was helped by the Pope to take the throne of all Croatian lands. In return, Svinimir firmly supported the Catholic Church. He built a basilica in Knin (q.v.). The story of his donation to the monastery St. Lucy in Baška on Krk (q.v.) has been engraved on the Baščanska Ploča (q.v.). In 1089, Pope Urban II called upon Svinimir to fight the Patzinak-Cuman nomads. Ban Petar Svačić of Dalmatia opposed this plan and Svinimir was mortally wounded during a meeting of the Sabor in Knin.

Between 1090 and 1092, a last insignificant heir of the Trpimir dynasty disappeared from the scene of history. The Hungarian King Laszlo took the lands north of the Gvozd in 1091. Around 1094, he founded the bishopric of Zagreb (q.v.). King Laszlo left his nephew Almos to rule the Slavonian territories when he went into battle with the Cumans. These nomads attacked Hungary at the instigation of the Byzantine Emperor Alexius Comnenus. Likewise, the Normans invaded the Dalmatian towns and islands. The Croatian nobles united around Petar Svačić (1093-1097). The new Croatian King expelled Almos from Slavonia and Dalmatia and Slavonia were together once more. In 1097, the Hungarian King Koloman (1095-1116), son of Laszlo, led his army against Petar Svačić and the Croatian nobles. Svačić fell on the battlefield in the Gvozd mountains (Petrova Gora - Peter's Mountains). Koloman pushed through to the Dalmatian shores and, in 1098, he took Biograd (q.v.) on the sea. In 1102, the Croatian nobles formally recognized the Hungarian monarch as the King of Dalmatia and Slavonia by the Pacta Conventa (q.v.). (See also ARPAD DYNASTY)

TRUMBIĆ, ANTE (1864-1938). Leading Croat in the Yugoslav Committee (q.v.). After the formation of the Kingdom of Serbs, Croats and Slovenes (q.v.), he voted against the Vidovdan (q.v.) Constitution of 1921.

TUĐMAN, FRANJO (1922-). General, historian and first President of Independent Croatia. He joined the communist resistance in 1941 and became a partisan General. After the war, he worked in the Ministry of National Defense and the Headquarters of the Yugoslav People's Army (1945-1961). Tuđman was the Director of the Institute for the History of the Labor Movement of Croatia (1961-1967) and Associate Professor of History at Zagreb University (1963-1967). He was a Member of Parliament of the Socialist Republic of Croatia (1965-1969). He was a member of the Managing Board of the Matica hrvatska (q.v.). For his role in the Croatian Spring (q.v.), he was sentenced to two years of prison on October 12, 1972. Acting as a persistent dissident, he got three more years of imprisonment and a five-year ban on public activity on February 20, 1981.

In 1989, at the beginning of the collapse of the communist regime, he was one of the leading founding members of the Croatian Democratic Union (HDZ) (q.v.) and elected President of the HDZ. The party won the first free elections in which Tuđman was chosen a Member of Parliament. The majority of the Sabor (q.v.) elected him in 1990 to be the first President of Croatia and neglected the demands of the opposition to organize direct presidential elections at that time. His mandate was confirmed and extended for a second term by direct presidential elections on August 2, 1992, in which Tuđman obtained 56.7 percent of the votes. During the HDZ Convention in the autumn of 1993, he was also reelected President of the HDZ for a second term.

TURKISH CROATIA. The land between the Vrbas and the Una Rivers, now northwestern Bosnia. During Turkish times, it was a frontier area occupied by the Turks between Croatia under Austria-Hungary and Bosnia under the Ottomans. It is the region around Bihać where the leader Fikret Abdić wanted to found an autonomous Muslim state independent from the government of Sarajevo.

TV MARJAN. Local independent television chain, transmitting from Split (q.v.).

TVRDKO, STIPAN (?-1391). Ban (q.v.) of Bosnia. His mother Jelena was a member of the Croatian Subić clan. He succeeded Stipan Kotromanić as ruler of Bosnia in 1353 and proclaimed himself King in 1377. The same year he led his army into Dalmatia and conquered Klis (qq.v.) and Ostrovica. In 1388, the Croatian Sabor (q.v.) appointed him King of the Croats. The rival army of the Hungarian King Sigismund and the invasion of Hum by the Ottomans hampered Tvrdko in building up his kingdom.

- U -

UGREŠIĆ, DUBRAVKA (1949-). Writer, Lecturer in Comparative Literature. Her novels have been translated into many languages, including *Štefica Cvek u raljama života* (In the Jaws of Life, 1978) and *Forsiranje Romana-reke* (Forcing the River-novel, 1988). Technically, she is perhaps the most "postmodernist" writer of Croatia.

UJEVIĆ, TIN (1891-1955). Poet. He has been known as an incurable bohemian and a sharp critic of everything that restrains the freedom of the human mind. One reviewer (Lavrin, *An Anthology of Modern Yugoslav Poetry,* 25) wrote about him in the following terms: "He was a questioner and seeker, tormented by nostalgia for the unattainable and by the ever present threat of inner disintegration."

UNCIVPOL. United Nations Civil Police, the civil branch of UNPROFOR (q.v.). Its members were supposed to become active in the Maslenica (q.v.) region, following peace negotiations led by mediator Geert Ahrens (q.v.) between Zagreb and the Serbs of Knin (qq.v.). During the Maslenica offensive of the Croats in January 1993, three villages with a Serb ethnic composition were conquered by the Croatian armed forces: Smoković, Islam Grčki and Kašić. In these villages a Serbian militia supervised by UNCIVPOL had to be installed according to point three of the agreement of July 17, 1993. The role of UNCIVPOL and UNPROFOR in the Croat-dominated surroundings of the region was unclear. Repeated hostilities and military bombing of the Maslenica bridge by the Serbs relegated the question of the civil arrangements to the background. The same happened earlier in the Baranja (q.v.) and other regions under the authority of UNPROFOR.

UNITED NATIONS PROTECTED AREAS (UNPA). These zones under the control of UNPROFOR (q.v.) were as large as 12,554 sq. km, or together with the pink zones, some 26 percent of the Croatian territory. The primary task of the force was to stop all hostilities and to place all heavy weapons under its control. Foreign militias were to be disarmed. Representative authority structures were to be built up and the conditions created so that the refugees could return to their homes.

Four sectors were occupied by UNPROFOR in Croatia: Sector East comprised East Slavonia with Vukovar, Osijek and Vinkovci (qq.v.); Sector West included West Slavonia with Pakrac; Sector North lay east and south of Karlovac with Banija and Kordun (qq.v.); and Sector South centered around Knin (q.v.). At the frontiers of the Sector South a pink zone (q.v.) has been created. (See also UNCIVPOL; UNPROFOR)

UNPROFOR. United Nations Protection Force. The main function of UNPROFOR in Croatia (UNPROFOR I) was to bring security to the regions conquered or occupied by the Serbs who no longer recognized the Croatian authority. They were basically the so-called Serbian Autonomous Regions (Srpske Autonomne Opštine) and their frontier zones. By underwriting the Vance plan (q.v.), Zagreb and Belgrade agreed that UN forces should take over military and security control in these regions. The protection forces had to normalize the covert or open war situation by supervising the agreed upon move of the Yugoslav army out of the regions and by disarming local militia. The action started in March 1992 in implementation of UN Security Council Resolution 743 of February 21, 1992. Only the first goal has been achieved so far: the Yugoslav army has withdrawn from the protected regions. Contrary to the agreement, the armed militia did not always leave and sometimes even obtained a more or less official status. Croat refugees who had been driven away were not allowed to return. Local authority structures - which according to the Vance plan were to reflect the ethnic composition of the region - have been taken over completely by the Serbs.

The situation has been complicated by the Bosnian war. Serbs conquered areas in Bosnia adjacent to the Vojna Krajina (q.v.) in Croatia and strived to unite both regions.

In a speech to Parliament on the occasion of the third year of functioning of the multiparty Sabor on May 30, 1993, President Tuđman (q.v.) argued that a six-month extension of the UNPROFOR mandate was only acceptable under the condition that within that period all the goals should be achieved. This implied a strengthening of the powers of UNPROFOR. If UNPROFOR's actions remained unsuccessful, Tuđman did not exclude the use of military force to restore the full integrity of the Croatian territory. A move in this direction occurred during the Gospić offensive (q.v.) of September 1993. However, the conflict died down temporarily. Tuđman repeated his conditions in the wake of a new six-month mandate of UNPROFOR. The Serbs should be disarmed, Croatian refugees return and all communications be restored. The UNPROFOR mandate in Croatia must be separated from its action in other parts of former Yugoslavia and the UNPROFOR occupation forces should move to the frontiers of Croatia with other states. Hostility towards UNPROFOR was now publicly manifested.

On September 26, 1993, refugees of the Croatian occupied regions held protest meetings against the laxity of UNPROFOR. The same evening, the Croatian army shot at Blue Helmets in the Medak region. The UNPROFOR commander handed a protest note to the Croatian authorities.

On the occasion of the extension of the UNPROFOR mandate, Tuđman began a diplomatic offensive to strengthen the activity of UNPROFOR in order to achieve the first projected goals of the agreement and the peaceful reintegration of the Krajina in the Republic of Croatia. In spite of Russian reservations in the Security Council, this demand was formally included in Resolution 871 of October 4, 1993.

The main resolutions of the UN Security Council regarding the UNPROFOR mandate in Croatia were the following: Resolution 743 (February 21, 1992), 762 (June 30, 1992), 769 (August 7, 1992), 779 (October 6, 1992), 802 (January 25, 1993), 807 (February 19, 1993), 815 (March 30, 1993), 847 and 871 (October 4, 1993).

UPRAVA DRŽAVNE BEZBEDNOSTI (UDBA). The UDBA, and previously the Odeljenje za Žaštitu Naroda (OZNA), was the State Security Administration which ran the secret security police in the communist system. It was very active during the Cominform conflict (q.v.) and subsequently until the fall of Alexander Ranković (q.v.). Later on, it remained known for its activities against emigrant movements.

USKOKS. Uskoks were the people who fled the Turks from various areas of Bosnia and Dalmatia (q.v.). They settled down especially around the fortress of Klis and later after its fall in 1537 at Senj (qq.v.).

USTAŠA. Croatian insurgent movement fighting the Yugoslav monarchy and state. The Ustaša organization developed out of discontent with the unitary administration and Serbian domination of the state between the two world wars. It was founded in 1929 as a reaction to the assassination of Stepan Radić and the dictatorship of King Alexander (qq.v.). Its manifesto was adopted on June 1, 1933. The basic starting points included the ethnic definition of the pure Croatian people and the historic right to a territory and an independent state. Moreover, all means were justified to further these aims, including armed struggle. Its main leader, Ante Pavelić (q.v.), fled abroad and organized the resistance in Italy. The Ustašis, in collaboration with the Macedonian secessionist movement IMRO, succeeded in assassinating King Alexander during his visit to France in 1934.

During the Second World War, the Ustašis took power under the protection of the German occupier. Ante Pavelić organized the repression and struggle against Serbian nationalists and communists. The Serbs who lived in Croatia were forced massively into Catholicism, death or exile. Around 700,000 people were affected. Memories of this holocaust reinforce the Krajina (q.v.) Serbs today in their resistance against the Tuđman (q.v.) regime. With the end of the Second World War and the collapse of the Ustaša regime, the Ustašis were repressed by the communist partisans. Many were killed near Bleiberg (q.v.) and Maribor. Some leaders such as Pavelić escaped abroad and formed resistance movements in exile.

- V -

VALENTIĆ, NIKICA (1950-). Lawyer and director of enterprises in the construction and petroleum industries. Under the new regime, he accepted high management functions and became Prime Minister of Tuđman's fifth government.

VALUN TABLET. Oldest known Glagolitic (q.v.) inscription in Croatia, carved in the middle of the eleventh century at St. Mary's church of Valun on the island of Cres (q.v.). It is bilingual Latin and Croatian and marks the family grave of grandmother Teha, her son Bratohna and grandson Juna.

VANCE PLAN. The Vance plan, agreed to by Belgrade and Zagreb, tried to define a solution to the problem of the Serb revolt in Croatia. A United Nations Protection Force (UNPROFOR) (q.v.) was installed to prevent further armed clashes and to restore previous living conditions. Zagreb envisaged the ultimate goal of the plan to be the integration of the territories in Croatia, while the Serbs seemed to use the plan as a vehicle to obtain autonomy in the long run. There were several sectors (UNPAs). Depending on the number, force and organization of the Serbs, the outcome could be different for the various regions. It also depended very much on the attitude of the Serbs in Bosnia. The Krajina (q.v.) was surrounded in the south by a pink zone (q.v.) near Zadar (q.v.). On January 22, 1993, the Croatian army started a four-day offensive here to liberate the Maslenica (q.v.) region. The government wished to restore the connection between the north of Croatia and hitherto isolated Dalmatia (q.v.). A new UNPROFOR agreement for the Maslenica area was signed by Zagreb and the representatives of the Krajina Serbs. However, on occasion, President Tuđman threatened to use force again, if the full integrity of the Croatian territory should not be restored by the end of a new six-month UNPROFOR mandate. But, already in the beginning of September 1993, continued shelling by the Serbs of the Maslenica bridge and the Gospić (q.v.) area led to a new offensive. The Tuđman army took three villages near Gospić and the Krajina Serbs began shelling more intensively Tuđman's Croatia, including a suburb of Zagreb (q.v.). (See also VANCE-OWEN PLAN)

VANCE-OWEN PLAN. Proposal first presented by Cyrus Vance and David Owen in October 1992 as a basic solution to the Bosnian problem. The Bosnian-Hercegovian state should not depart from the principle of central government, but the plan simultaneously respected the existence of the three ethnic communities, though dividing the country into ten provinces. Each nationality got three regions and Sarajevo would be a common area. The Croatian sphere contained the larger part of Hercegovina and a province in the north adjacent to Croatia. It was no surprise that the Croatian Bosnian leader Mate Boban (q.v.) was the first party to sign the plan on January 4, 1993. After some time, the Muslims accepted the plan under international pressure. Even the Bosnian Serb leader Karađic gave his conditional agreement, but ultimately the Bosnian Serbs rejected the plan in a referendum.

A threat of military intervention by US President Clinton was not really supported by the European powers. A new weaker program of action seemed to respect more closely the actual military and strategic situation. The Vance-Owen plan was dropped, or at least significantly altered. New negotiations led to a proposal that accepted the division into three ethnic regions bound by a loose confederal union. Even this new plan was not accepted by the Bosnian Serbs. (See also OWEN-STOLTENBERG PLAN)

VARAŽDIN. Chief town of Croatian Zagorje, north of Zagreb (q.v.). Varaždin is first mentioned in 1181. In 1209, it became a royal free town. Strongly fortified, the town withstood all assaults by the Turks and was never taken. From 1756 to 1776, Varaždin functioned as the capital of Croatia, the seat of the Ban (q.v.) who governed on behalf of the Austro-Hungarian crown. The King's Council (Hrvatsko kraljevsko vijeće) had its sessions here from 1767 until 1776.

VASVAR (PEACE OF). Peace concluded by the Austrians and Turks on August 10, 1664, at Vasvar (Eisenberg in Hungary). The commander of the main Habsburg forces, Count Raymond Montecuculli, defeated the Ottoman Grand Vizier Ahmed Kiuprili on the banks of the Raab in Hungary. The Ottomans had to flee back to Bosnia after a raid in Croatia and Hungary. Peace lasted for 20 years. However, the Ottomans retained their former Croatian territories and Vienna even agreed to pay a war indemnity. A secret clause granted the Turks free passage through Croatian territory to make war on Venice. Croatian nobles resented these stipulations. It was the background for the Zrinski-Frankopan conspiracy (q.v.).

VEČERNI LIST. The Evening News. A popular newspaper edited in Zagreb (q.v.) and most widely read in Croatia. Though in principle an independent newspaper, it is in general very loyal to the regime. It is the more popular twin of *(Novi) Vjesnik* (q.v.).

VEKIĆ, IVAN (? -   ). Former Croatian Democratic Union (HDZ) (q.v.) politician. He was Minister of the Interior in the government of Franjo Gregurić (q.v.) and President of the Socio-Political Council of the Croatian Parliament (q.v.). After three years he broke with the HDZ to become Co-President of a new minor conservative party, the Croatian National-Democratic League (q.v.).

VESELICA, MARKO (1936-). Former leader of the Communist Party and Professor of Political Economy at Zagreb University (q.v.). During the Croatian Spring (q.v.), Veselica manifested himself fully as a Croatian nationalist. He was a member of the Managing Board and the Executive Committee and President of the Economic Commission of the Matica hrvatska (q.v.). He was arrested at the end of 1971 and sentenced in 1972 to seven years of imprisonment. On April 24, 1981, he was again sentenced to 11 years of prison because of his dissident views and his contacts with emigrant circles.

Under the Tuđman regime (q.v.), he acted as President of the Croatian Democratic Party and Croatian Christian Democratic Union (qq.v.). He was the first President of the Society of Political Prisoners.

VIDOVDAN. The day of June 28. In South Slav history, this day acquired a special significance. It was the day of the battle of Kosovo Polje in 1389, the assassination of Habsburg Archduke Franz Ferdinand (q.v.) in 1914 and the first Constitution of Yugoslavia in 1921.

VIENNA FRAGMENTS. Fragments of the oldest Croatian Glagolitic (q.v.) missal, written in the twelfth century and now preserved in Vienna. According to the historian Jagić, it represents a transition between the Old Church Slavonic writing of Cyrillus (qq.v.) and Methodius and the native Croatian Glagolitic that flourished along the Dalmatian coast and the nearby islands from the twelfth century on.

VIJEĆE OBRANA I NACIONALNE SIGURNOSTI see DEFENSE AND NATIONAL SECURITY COUNCIL

VINKOVCI. Town in East Slavonia (q.v.), near Srijemska Mitrovica. Known as Cibalia in Roman times, it was the birthplace of the Roman emperor Valentine.

During the last war, the town was captured by the Serbs on July 22, 1991. Just before the second anniversary of this Serb occupation, a local peasant revolt with some military support was silenced by threat and persuasion.

THE VINODOL LAW CODE/VINODOLSKI ZAKONIK. Vinodol - the wine valley - is located on the northern part of the Croatian coast. After the settling of the Croats in this region, in the sixth or seventh century, the villages of Vinodol grouped together in a loose confederation. When, after 1225, King Andrew II of Hungary gave the valley to Vid, the Count *(Knez)* of Krk, the semi-autonomy that the Vinodol community enjoyed eroded. The main function of the Vinodol Law Code was to legitimize the feudal relationship that had developed between the Counts of Krk, Vinodol and Modruš and the population of the valley. The Statute of Vinodol, drawn up on January 6, 1288, regulated contracts, private property and inheritance and other institutions of civil law. Scholars have pointed out that there are traces of old Slavic tribal law in the Code, for example the payment of wergeld *(vražda)* to the relatives of a murdered man. The Code was originally written in a thirteenth-century čakavian (q.v.) dialect. Only a complete manuscript of the fifteenth century has been preserved.

VIS. Island of 90 sq. km in the Middle-Dalmatian archipelago lying opposite Split (q.v.). Located at the edge of Croatian territory, it boasts a remarkable history. The island had already been colonized in the Neolithic period. The Illyrian Liburnians (q.v.) occupied Vis around 1000 B.C. and in the sixth or fifth century formed a state under King Jonij. The tyrant Dionysius the Old of Syracuse conquered the island in the fourth century and founded his colony Issa. Issa was later an autonomous town which coined its own money and established colonies at Trogir and Lumbarda (Korčula) (q.v.). In the second half of the third century B.C., it became dependent on Rome. Ancient Vis was destroyed during the great migrations. In the early Middle Ages, the island of Vis came under the influence of the Byzantine Empire and then under Croatia. When King Ladislas (q.v.) sold his hereditary rights over Dalmatia (q.v.), Vis went to Venice in 1420. After the fall of Venice, the island passed into the hands of Austria (1797-1805), France (1805-1811), England (1811-1814) and Austria again (1814-1918). At the end of a short Italian occupation (1918-1920), Vis reverted back to Croatia, now incorporated in Yugoslavia. During the Second World War, Vis was occupied by the Italians again, but in the autumn of 1943, it became the main sea base and headquarters of the partisan army until the liberation of Belgrade.

The island is an important center of viniculture and agriculture (q.v.). The fishing industry is built around its main port, Komiža.

VITEZOVIĆ see RITTER VITEZOVIĆ, PAVAO

VJESNIK. *Vjesnik* (The Courier) was the main quality newspaper of Croatia under the communists. It has now come through a privatization strategy under the indirect influence of the new government and continues its life as *Novi Vjesnik* (New Courier) (q.v.). Though loyal to the regime, especially in its editorials, it preserves some critical distance and also reports on the initiatives of the opposition.

VLAČIĆ, MATIJA (1520-1575). Mathias Flaccius Illyricus was a prominent Croatian protestant. He resided mostly in Germany. His *Clavis Scripturae Sacrae* (Key to the Holy Scriptures) has been considered a precursor of modern hermeneutics and "Magdeburg Centuries" provided a documentary basis for the study of church history and a new level for theological discussion.

VOCE DEL POPOLO (LA). The Voice of the People is a newspaper in Italian edited in Rijeka (q.v.) for the Italian minority in Croatia and Slovenia (q.v.).

VOJNA KRAJINA see MILITARY BORDER

VOJNOVIĆ, IVO (1857-1929). Writer. Born in Dubrovnik (q.v.), he described in his work the decline and fall of his native town (Trilogy of Dubrovnik).

VOLLEBAEK, KNUT. Norwegian diplomat and assistant to the Co-Chairman of the International Peace Conference at Geneva. He was a negotiator in the peace talks between the Krajina (q.v.) Serbs and Croats. He obtained the signing of the Erdutski Sporazum (q.v.). Following another round of secret negotiations in

Norway in the beginning of November 1993, an armistice for East Croatia was agreed upon between the Krajina Serbs and the Zagreb government.

VRANICKI, PEDRAG (1922-). Philosophy Professor of Zagreb University. Rector of Zagreb University (1972-1976). Member of the *Praxis* group.

VUČEDOL. Archeological site on the Danube located east of Vukovar (q.v.). It stems from the early and middle Bronze Age culture that produced elaborate clay animal models, for example the "Vučedol dove."

VUKČIĆ HRVATINIĆ, HRVOJE (ca. 1350-1416). Duke of Split (q.v.) and Bosnia, born in Jajce. He was an ally of King Ladislas of Naples (q.v.) who was fighting his rival for the throne, the Hungarian King Sigismund. Ladislas was crowned in 1403, but soon left the Dalmatian and Bosnian lands under the rule of Vukčić. The Duke of Split continued to fight the Hungarian King Sigismund. Vukčić called for the support of the Turks and defeated Sigismund's army in 1415. This in fact opened the Croatian lands to further invasions from the Ottomans.

The Hval missal (q.v.) - made in Split at the order of Duke Vukčić and containing his portrait - is one of the most precious Croatian manuscripts preserved until today. Vukčić Hrvatinić had himself been for some time a member of the Bogomil (q.v.) church. In Jajce, his coat of arms can be seen on the entrance of his fortress.

VUKOJEVIĆ, VICE (1936-). Born in Veljaci (Ljubuški, Hercegovina). Croatian Democratic Union (HDZ) (q.v.) politician, Member of the House of Representatives. He is said to be a hardliner and with Vladimir Seks (q.v.) the leader of the right wing of the HDZ. He withdrew his candidacy for an important function after a speech by President Tuđman (q.v.) at the Second HDZ Convention.

VUKOVAR. Town in East Slavonia (q.v.) on the Danube. The word *vuk* means wolf; it is also the name of a river. *Varoš* means city.

The site was already colonized in prehistoric times. The Vučedol (q.v.) culture spread through the whole area. Grave finds indicate habitation during Illyrian (q.v.) and Roman times. The great migrations brought the Avarian (q.v.) and Slav peoples to this region in the sixth and seventh centuries. When, in 846, Prince Pribina of Lower Pannonia received from the Franks 100 villages under their authority, he probably established his seat in Vukovar. In the tenth and eleventh centuries, the country had been united to the other Croatian lands on the Adriatic, particularly under King Tomislav and Petar Krešimir IV (qq.v.). *Vukovar* as the name of the town is first recorded in the beginning of the thirteenth century as the seat of the *županija* (q.v.). Vukovar was at that time declared a free town, implying it was already an important center for a long time. In Hungarian-Croatian times, Vukovar developed further as a typical Slavonian town around its fortification. It obtained its privileges from King Koloman in 1231 as a free town. At that time, there lived along with Hungarians and Slavs large numbers of "Germans" (Saxons, Teutons). Only the towns of Varaždin (q.v.) and Perna had received this status before. King Bela IV (1244) and King Stjepan (1263) confirmed these privileges. Before the Turkish period, Vukovar was the greatest *županija* in the Slavon-Srijem region. In church matters, the Archdeacon of Vukovar depended on the bishopric of Peč.

Though the Ottomans had invaded the region earlier, the region of Vukovar was definitively conquered in 1526. They built a bridge in Vukovar that opened the way to the great victory over the Hungarians in Mohacs. Vukovar belonged from then on to the *sandžak* (Turkish province) of Srijem with Osijek (q.v.) as its center. Vukovar got the status of district *(nahija)* and trade center *(kasaba)*. Much of the old Catholic population had perished in the resistance and orthodox Vlasi moved into this frontier area as Turkish companions, especially after the 1670s. The Vlasi were the servants of the Ottomans and retreated together with the Turks when the area was liberated again. Moreover, the remaining Catholics had been decimated by the Calvinists around 1550. All this disrupted the ethnic composition of the region. At the end of the sixteenth century, Vukovar had 202 Muslim houses and only 47 Catholic families. By the beginning of the seventeenth century, only five remained. Vukovar lost its strategic position. When it was liberated in 1687, it only counted 50 houses. At the end of the seventeenth and beginning of the eighteenth century, Vukovar went through important administrative and social changes under the Austrian Empire. The old Catholic Croatian population moved again to the center, as did some Hungarians.

In the last war, Vukovar became the symbol of the aggression of the Serbs on Croatian territory. The town was conquered by the Serbs and completely devastated. The opposition parties criticized the Croatian government that not enough had been done to save the town. Some accusations went as far as to suggest that a horrible showplace had deliberately been created in order to convince the world of the necessity of recognizing at once the independence of Croatia.

VUKOVI. The "Wolves" is an example of a paramilitary organization that arose during the Croatian war against the Yugoslav army (q.v.) and Serbian terrorists. This anti-terrorist group was formed at the end of June 1991 exclusively by volunteers from Zagreb (q.v.). They immediately joined the defensive activities of the regional crisis staff of Banija (q.v.), Posavina and Moslovina. When the struggle escalated with the *četniks* (q.v.) in the region of Sisak (q.v.) during August 1991, a unit of the Wolves was stationed there as a reserve force to the Police Force (MUP). The unit was fighting on the Komarevo-Sunja line and in the region of Hrvatska Dubica and Kostajnica. It was the last to retreat from Petrinja. Then it defended the line on the Kupa (q.v.) and occupied the military barracks in Bjelovar. In a later period of the war, from April 1992, the unit operated in the south.

The group disintegrated on the death of its main commander, Jadranko Garbin, on August 18, 1992. Some members left the battlefield, others joined the MUP or the Croatian army (q.v.). The activity of the unit was at the time officially recognized. President Tuđman (q.v.) personally praised the unit on September 4, 1991, a fact that was reported in the press. Nowadays officials prefer to be more reticent. Joško Morić, assistant of the Minister of the Interior, once praised for his organizational talent and excellent services in the Wolves, denied in September 1993 during the trial of Dobroslav Paraga (q.v.) that he knew anything about the existence of the Wolves.

- W -

WAGES. Real wages have fallen from almost 7,000 dinars in October 1990 (which was then equal to 1,000 DM) to about one-fourth of that level at the end of the last quarter of 1993. The result of this sharp drop in real wages was that many people are living on the edge of the subsistence level. Those who are hit worst by this fall in real wages are people whose only income is wages in the official sector or a pension.

WAR CRIMES TRIBUNAL FOR FORMER YUGOSLAVIA. This Tribunal was created by UN Security Council Resolution 837 of May 25, 1993. It is intended to judge any person presumed responsible for serious violations of international humanitarian law on the territory of former Yugoslavia from January 1, 1991, until a date fixed by a future peace settlement. The Tribunal was created following a proposal of UN Secretary General Boutros Boutros-Ghali under Chapter VII of the UN Charter, i.e., as an international sanction. According to Boutros Boutros-Ghali, the applicable body of international law includes the convention of Geneva on the protection of war victims, the convention on the prevention and repression of the crime of genocide, the convention of The Hague of 1907 on the laws and rules of conduct in case of war, and the Nuremberg principles. The former Yugoslavia has ratified all these conventions on international humanitarian law.

The Tribunal inaugurated its sessions on November 17, 1993, at The Hague. Eleven distinguished judges of so many countries were sworn in to form the three organs of the Tribunal. The Prosecutor of the Court is M. Ramon Escovar-Salom, Attorney-General of Venezuela. Some scepticism about the working of the Tribunal was expressed from the very beginning. There is serious trouble about the selection of files and the procedures. No persons can be judged *in absentia* and it is doubtful whether the countries at war will hand over accused residents. Moreover, some supposed war criminals are still key figures in the negotiation process itself. The work of inquiry commissions on the spot was sometimes made impossible. There were financial difficulties as well.

WAR DAMAGE. According to the State Institute for Macroeconomic Analysis and Forecasting, 590 settlements in Croatia were damaged by the last war and 35 of these were completely levelled. Among them are large cities such as Vukovar, Gospić, Osijek, Dubrovnik, Zadar, Vinkovci (qq.v.), Šibenik, Pakrac and others. There were 210,000 heavily damaged or destroyed housing units (12 percent of all housing units in Croatia). In addition, 11 thermo-electric power plants and 40 high voltage power lines were damaged, and 33 bridges were completely demolished while 24 were damaged. Because of the damages only 67 percent of the railway network was operable, but since the main rail links were cut, the level of rail services was only a quarter of the prewar level. Many industrial plants and agricultural units were destroyed or damaged. Presently occupied are some 25 percent of Croatia's arable land and 38 percent of its forests. There were large losses in livestock as well.

War damage is not easy to quantify. The Agency for Reconstruction estimated war damage up to January 4, 1993, as follows:

Human cost	
Killed	7,642
Wounded	23,062
Missing	13,153
Material costs (bn $)	
Physical damage	22
Settlements destroyed	35
Settlements seriously damaged	34
Settlements badly damaged	590
Hospitals destroyed	9
Churches destroyed	300
Monuments destroyed	200
Bridges destroyed	33
Bridges damaged	22
Industry destroyed (percent of total)	30
Motorways damaged (percent of total)	40
Regional roads damaged (percent of total)	32
Local roads damaged (percent of total)	31
Railway system out of use (percent of total)	63
Post offices out of use (percent of total)	20
Telecommunication out of use (percent of total)	31

WAR ECONOMY. During 1992 gross national product (q.v.) amounted to less than half of the 1990 GNP. War expenses swallowed up one-third of public expenditures and the economy had to take care of about 750,000 refugees by the end of 1992. Public debt amounted to 50 percent of GNP, and foreign obligations to 35 percent. Debt servicing alone consumed 5 percent of gross national product. In 1993 industrial production dropped by another 5.9 percent. The decline continued in the first month of 1994, with a fall of 4.8 percent in January compared with December 1993. (See also WAR DAMAGE)

WHITE CROATIA. The name *White Croatia* has been used in two senses. The first points to the original homeland of the Croatians. According to a passage in *De Administrando Imperio*, written by Constantine Porphyrogenitus (q.v.), the Croats emigrated to Dalmatia from *White Croatia*, a land which lay north of the Carpathians by 30 days' march from the sea. The second use of the term opposes White, Red and Pannonian (q.v.) Croatia. Pannonian Croatia corresponds more or less to the contemporary region. White and Red Croatia stretched along the Adriatic and covered far more land than Dalmatia (q.v.) of today.

White Croatia reached from the Raša River in Istria to the Cetina River south of Split (qq.v.). Red Croatia went as far as the Lake Skutari in Albania. In between lay Zahumlja. These frontiers were not very stable, and some historians assert it had been one region in early times.

Constantine Porphyrogenitus characterized Zahumlja as being Serbian, as is the case with Trebinje (near Dubrovnik [q.v.]) and Dioclea (q.v.) (near Bar and southwards). Croatian historians criticized this characterization. They argue that the Serbian domination was only a temporary situation at the time of the writing of the dissertation.

WOMEN'S INFOTEKA. This institution in Zagreb (q.v.) gathers historical and statistical data about women, including information about the women's movement, medical and other statistics, and women's representation in the media. It also maintains a women's library and publishes a journal.

- Y -

YALTA (CONFERENCE OF). This Conference during January 1945 laid down the order in the Balkans after the Second World War. It insisted on forming a coalition government in Yugoslavia, merging the provisional Belgrade government and members of the Government in Exile in London.

YOUTH TELEVISION/OMLADINSKA TELEVIZIJA (OTV). An independent chain of the official television, bringing youth and alternative programs. It has its own editorial policy and although the Director is a member of Croatian Democratic Union (q.v.), it is not under direct party control.

YUGOSLAV ACADEMY OF ARTS AND SCIENCES/JUGOSLOVENSKA AKADEMIJA ZNANOSTI I UMJETNOSTI (JAZU). The first session of the Yugoslav Academy of Arts and Sciences was solemnly opened on July 28, 1867. One of the greatest supporters of the Yugoslav Academy was Bishop Josip Strossmayer (q.v.). After a quarter of a century, the Academy had produced 241 volumes of scientific work. There were 46 Croats among the 117 active members.

YUGOSLAV COMMITTEE. The Yugoslav Committee was established in Paris on April 30, 1915, and had its seat in London. The leaders were Ante Trumbić (q.v.), Frano Supilo and Ivan Mestrović (q.v.). They acted as the representatives of the Habsburg South Slavs. Frano Supilo pleaded for a union with Serbia on condition that the new state should be a federation of peoples with equal rights. If not, he pleaded for an independent federation of all Slavs living in the former Dual Monarchy. The other members of the Committee did not follow him and opted for unity with Serbia. Supilo left the Committee on June 5, 1916. The Committee began negotiations with the Serb Prime Minister Nikola Pašić on the formation of a coalition. However, about the same time, Serbia undermined the international recognition of the Committee as the representative organ of all Slavs of Austria-Hungary in order to keep its hands free for great-Serbian ambitions. An agreement with the Allies and Italy could yield Serbia a large part of Dalmatia (q.v.) and Bosnia-Hercegovina. In the negotiations with Serbia, the Yugoslav Committee defended the view of postwar Yugoslavia as a federation of peoples. The constitution of the new state should be approved by a two-thirds majority in the Constituent Assembly. The negotiations ended in a not very clear compromise, the 1917 Declaration of Corfu (q.v.).

YUGOSLAVIA (FORMATION OF). It is recognized in the 1990 Constitution (q.v.) of the Republic of Croatia that the formation of Yugoslavia in 1918 contributed to the process of building a long sought national identity of the Croatian nation and the continuity of its statehood, "invoking its historical and natural right as a nation."

The legal formation of the Kingdom of the Serbs, Croats and Slovenes (q.v.) was based on the decisions of the political organs inheriting the state power after the decay of the Dual Monarchy and the military victory of the Western allies. On October 29, 1918, the Croatian-Slavonian Sabor (q.v.) of Zagreb, presided over by Svetozar Pribićević (q.v.), declared the independence of the Triune Kingdom of Croatia, Dalmatia and Slavonia (q.v.) from Austria-Hungary. The Sabor joined the Triune Kingdom with the other South Slavic lands of Austria-Hungary to form the State of Slovenes, Croats and Serbs (SCS). On the same day, the Serbo-Croatian Coalition majority had the Sabor transfer its political authority to the newly created Council of Slovenes, Croats and Serbs of the former South Slavic territories. The President of the Council was the Slovene leader Anton Korošec, the Vice-President was Svetozar Pribićević. With the political power, the Council received the military power. The Council advocated an immediate union of the SCS with the Kingdom of Serbia. The Croatian nationalist deputies of the Croatian People's Peasant Party and the Croatian Party of Rights (qq.v.) protested without result. The Council sent a delegation to Belgrade to unite the SCS with Serbia. On December 1, 1918, Prince Alexander Karađorđević (q.v.) declared the Kingdom of Serbs, Croats and Slovenes.

YUTEL. Yugoslav Television. Commercial Television Station supported by the last Prime Minister of Yugoslavia, the Croat Ante Marković (q.v.). YUTEL was conceived as the replacement of the Jugoslovenski Radio i Televizija (JRT), the Federal Radio and

Television Institute that disintegrated into autonomous republican units. The Croat-Serb war undermined the position of Ante Marković and his project to build a new Yugoslavia on a technocratic basis.

- Z -

ZADAR. Capital of Dalmatia (q.v.) under the Byzantines; it took over this function from Roman Salona (q.v.), which had been destroyed and occupied by the Slavs. In earlier times, Zadar was known under the name of Jadera or Diadora. The old town still possesses beautiful architectural monuments of the early medieval culture in the Adriatic. Among them are the churches Sveti Donat and Sveta Stošija. During the fourth crusade, the town was occupied in 1202 and sacked by the crusaders at the instigation of Venice. Zadar came under the Venetians until the peace of Zadar was concluded in 1358 and it returned to Croatia. In 1409, Ladislas sold Zadar and Dalmatia to the Venetians, whose reign went into effect in 1420 and lasted until the fall of Venetia in 1797. Then Austria took over the city until the end of the First World War, with the exception of eight years under French rule (1805-1813). After the end of the Habsburg reign, Zadar was integrated in the State of Serbs, Croats and Slovenes (q.v.), but was attributed to Italy by the Agreement of Rapallo in 1920. It finally joined Yugoslavia by a decision of the Anti-Fascist Council (q.v.) during the Second World War. Under the communist regime, the immediate vicinity of Zadar developed into a minor industrial center. The center of the town thrived on tourism, sports and cultural activities.

According to the census of 1991, Zadar had 76,343 inhabitants. Zadar suffered heavily from the Serb-Croat war. At least 250 enterprises were affected and more than 20 percent of the labor force was without work. More than 10,000 buildings were damaged. The town received more than 20,000 refugees from the surrounding area. Zadar is the head of a *županija*, which in principle includes the autonomous region of Knin.

ZAGREB. Present capital of Croatia. The early Croatian kingdom centered along the Adriatic coast or the nearby interior (Nin,

Knin, Biograd [qq.v.]). The Turkish and Venetian domination of the Adriatic and the link with Hungary favored the area of Zagreb as the new political center.

Zagreb had its origin in two fortified settlements, Kaptol and Gradec. In 1093, Zvonimir's (q.v.) brother-in-law King Ladislas founded a bishopric in Zagreb, situated on a lower hill of the location, and it was named Kaptol. Gradec, on a separate and slightly higher hill, was granted the rights of a Royal Free City in 1242 by the Golden Bull (q.v.) of Bela IV. This act made Gradec a feudal holding directly responsible to the King. The citizens were given the right to elect their own city judge (the mayor) and to manage their own affairs. The citizens engaged in building defensive walls and towers, fearing a new Tartar invasion. The city had been badly damaged by the Tartar invasion of 1242. In the sixteenth century, Zagreb took upon itself the role of *Antemurale Christianitatis* (bulwark of Christianity) and built further fortifications at the Kaptol location. In 1557, Zagreb was recognized as the metropolis of the Kingdom of Dalmatia, Croatia and Slavonia.

In the nineteenth century, Zagreb was the center of the Illyrian movement (q.v.) and the Croatian national revival. Zagreb assumed the central role in the development of all the arts (opera, drama, novels, poetry, painting, sculpture). The Yugoslav Academy of Arts and Sciences (q.v.) was founded in Zagreb in 1860. Croatia's greatest artists were born or lived in Zagreb, such as A.G. Matoš, T. Ujević and M. Krleža (qq.v.).

Industrial development was stimulated by the construction of a railway to the city in 1862, when the larger factories were also built. Zagreb has now become the major center of industry, business and trade in Croatia, exemplified by the regular exhibitions of the International Trade Fair and the functioning of a World Trade Center.

According to the census of March 31, 1991, Zagreb had 867,717 inhabitants in an area of 1,295 square kilometers. In recent years, the population has expanded due to a large number of refugees from the occupied parts of Croatia and from Bosnia-Hercegovina. (See also ZAGREB UNIVERSITY)

ZAGREB UNIVERSITY. The oldest colleges in Zagreb were the Colleges of Philosophy and Theology established in 1669. Zagreb

University was formally founded by a charter from King Leopold I on September 23, 1669, approved by the Sabor on November 3, 1671. In 1776, a Law School was established.

The University got its real start during the Illyrian (q.v.) period. Strossmayer (q.v.) granted large sums of money to further the institution on a larger scale. The University was then officially opened on October 19, 1874.

Today Zagreb University is made up of 33 colleges with 47,000 students, 3,500 instructors and 2,000 staff members. (See also EDUCATION)

ZAHUMLJANI. Former inhabitants of Hum, now eastern Hercegovina. These people were identified as belonging to an independent Serb tribe by Constantine Porphyrogenitus (q.v.). Their territory was surrounded by the Neretva (q.v.), Bosnia, the Raša and Travunja (q.v.). Ston was Zahumlja's center on the Adriatic.

ZBOR NARODNE GARDE see NATIONAL GUARD

ZDESLAV (878-879). Ban Zdeslav of Dalmatian (q.v.) Croatia recognized the supreme authority of the Byzantine Empire and gave his allegiance to the Greek-Orthodox Church. Zdeslav was deposed by Branimir (q.v.), who chose the side of the Pope. (See also TRPIMIR DYNASTY)

ZEMALJSKO ANTI-FAŠISTIČKO VIJEĆE NARODNOG OSLOBOĐENJA HRVATSKE (ZAVNOH) see ANTI-FASCIST COUNCIL OF THE NATIONAL LIBERATION OF CROATIA

ZEMLJA GROUP. Group of painters and graphic artists in the perriod between the two world wars. Confronted with the dictatorship of January 6, 1934, they immersed themselves in the social problems of Yugoslav society and expressed them in a post-impressionistic style. The activities of the group started in 1929 and were ultimately prohibited in 1935. Members of the group were Krsto Hegedušić (q.v.), Vilim Svečnak, Marijan Detoni and Fedor Vaić.

ZEMUNIK. Airport near Zadar (q.v.). The area came under the fire of the Serbian insurgents of the Kninska Krajina (q.v.). The Croatians tried to regain control over the area through the Maslenica (q.v.) offensive in January 1993. The warring parties then agreed that Zemunik should be placed under the control of UNPROFOR (q.v.). The agreement was not signed by the Serbs and fighting continued on a minor scale.

ŽGOMBIĆ COMPENDIUM. Contains a fifteenth or early sixteenth century version of the legend of John Chrysostom. It is written in Glagolitic čakavian (qq.v.) with some characteristics of Old Church Slavonic (q.v.). The compendium was published in 1931 by Stjepan Ivšić.

The story relates how John Chrysostom - "John with the gold mouth" - was seduced by the devil. An angel asked him which is the minor sin: drinking wine, killing men or raping women? Goldmouth chose drinking wine. In doing so, he committed all three sins.

ŽINEC, OZREN. In the autumn of 1993, with five other Croatian intellectuals he wrote an open letter to President Tuđman (q.v.). They criticized his policy and asked him to resign.

ZRIN. Village in the Banija (q.v.) between the rivers Una and Glina south of Petrinja. The Subić clan found here a second home and name: the Zrinski. On September 9, 1943, the Croatian village was conquered by Serbian partisans and *četniks* and 160 inhabitants died. Fifty years later, on July 26, 1991, the inhabitants of the village had to flee again. (See also ZRINSKI-FRANKOPAN CONSPIRACY)

ZRINSKI-FRANKOPAN CONSPIRACY. The Ban of Croatia, Petar Zrinski (1621-1671), and the big landowner, Krsto Frankopan (1643-1671), rebelled against the Habsburg Monarchy. The conspiracy ended with their beheading on April 30, 1671.

At the end of the Thirty Years War in 1648, the Habsburg state had weakened. Nevertheless, the Croatian Ban Nikola Zrinski (1620-1664) and his brother Petar continued to fight the Ottomans. In August 1651, they defeated a Turkish invading force. Nikola built the fortress of Novi Zrin at the confluence of the

Mur and Drava Rivers. Ahmed Kiuprili directed his army and took the fortress without the intervention of the Habsburg forces. The commander Count Montecuculli defeated the Ottomans on the banks of the Raab and the Habsburgs concluded the Peace of Vasvar (q.v.) in 1664. However, the Ottomans could retain their former Croatian territories and Vienna agreed even to pay a war indemnity. Croatian nobles resented these stipulations and began plotting against the Hungarian-Croatian King Leopold (1556-1705). They planned to throw off the Habsburg rule over the Hungarian-Croatian lands and they decided to start a war against the Ottomans to win back the Croatian and Hungarian territories in Turkish hands.

For this they needed outside help and they decided to offer the Hungarian-Croatian throne to the French. Ban Nikola Zrinski entered secret negotiations with the Venetians, but he unexpectedly died during a boar hunt. His brother Petar took over as leader of the plot. He was appointed Ban by King Leopold. but refused the command over the Karlovac Generality of the Military Border (qq.v.). The King feared with reason a renewed war with the Ottomans. Petar then sought new allies. He contacted Nicholas Bethlen, a Transylvanian prince, and Michael Bori, a confidant of the Hungarian Palatine Count Wesselenyi. Bori communicated with Gremonville, France's diplomat at the Austrian court, who consulted King Louis XIV. The King followed Gremonville's advice not to take the conspiracy seriously. However, some financial support was granted. The circle of conspirators widened. A conference in Wesselenyi's castle brought together Hungarian noblemen. They decided to seek the support of the Turks. France took more interest in the plans and promised full support. The ambiguous Hungarian Wesselenyi did not like the French interference and passed a letter of Gremonville to King Leopold. Vienna set up a secret investigation. In 1669, France concluded a peace treaty with Austria and withheld all help to the conspirators. After broken agreements with the Poles and the Venetians, Zrinski appealed to his old enemies, the Ottomans. He offered to pay a tribute to become the hereditary prince of Croatia. This was soon reported to an Austrian diplomat. On April 7, 1670, Ban Petar sent a letter to Leopold confessing his mistakes. Petar Zrinski and Krsto Frankopan were placed under arrest and sentenced in Vienna. On April 25, 1671, the court found the counts guilty of high treason. A few days later, they were executed.

ZUBAK, KREŠIMIR. Croatian leader of Bosnia. He came to the forefront when Mate Boban (q.v.) was kept out of the international negotiations for the Croatian party. Along with Tuđman (q.v.), he signed the Washington Agreements with Izetbegović on the formation of a Muslim-Bosnian Croatian federation and a confederation of this entity with Croatia.

ŽUJOVIĆ, SRETAN. Revolutionary among Tito's (q.v.) partisans. After the war, he became Minister of Finance and later Minister of Transport. He was closely associated with Andrija Hebrang (q.v.). In May 1948, he was accused of choosing the side of Stalin in the Cominform conflict (q.v.) and eliminated.

ŽUPAN. Head of a family or clan in the old Slavic social structure. It was the old and wise man who led the people. Constantine Porphyrogenitus (q.v.) compared this institution with the *archont* in the more formal Byzantine order, an organizational form that would be taken over later by the Croats.

ŽUPANIJA. In the oldest Croatian tradition the Županj was a local leader of a region called *županija*. These provinces were united into a *banovina*, governed by the Ban and provided with laws by the Sabor (q.v.).

The Tuđman (q.v.) regime acted to respect the tradition and wished to reintroduce the *županije*. They were now by law defined as the units of local administration and local self-government (q.v.). The territory of the *županije* is defined by law and depends on historical and economic factors. The *županije* are supposed to be the natural self-government units within the framework of the Republic. The draft of the Law on the Županije was confirmed by the government on November 19, 1992, and then debated by the Sabor. The law was criticized by the President of the Rijeka Democratic Alliance, Vladimir Smešny. He argued that the division of competences between the central administration and the local *županije* had not been properly defined, so that control ultimately resided in the central government. Similarly, the President of the Croat National Party, Savka Dabčević-Kučar (qq.v.), criticized the proposal because the Župane, the heads of the *županije*, are appointed by the government. The leader of the Social-Democratic Party, Ivo Račan, rejected the whole concept of the law.

The law ultimately reintroduced the administrative *županije* by creating 21 such units, each represented in what may be called the lower house of Parliament, the House of Counties (qq.v.) (Županijski Dom). The *županije* have their seats in the following towns: Zagreb, Split, Rijeka, Osijek, Zadar, Karlovac, Dubrovnik, Sisak, Vukovar (temporarily Vinkovci), Varaždin, Gospić (qq.v.), Slavonski Brod, Čakovec, Šibenik, Požega, Bjelovar, Koprivnica, Virovitica, Krapina and Pazin.

The *županije* are further divided into districts: *kotarevi*. In view of the present situation and the rights of the Serbian minority group, districts with certain self-government powers were created: the district of Glina in the county of Sisak and the district of Knin in the county of Zadar. The Tuđman regime clearly tries to integrate the Serb-dominated towns in the Croatian administrative structure. This solution was vehemently refused by the Serbs.

ŽUPANIJSKI DOM see HOUSE OF COUNTIES

ZVONIMIR, DMITAR (KING) (?-1089). King of the Trpimir dynasty (q.v.). who ruled from 1076 to 1089 after Krešimir IV (q.v.). He belonged to the Latin party and received the crown from the hands of the Pope. His reign was disturbed by a populist and anti-papist movement. Medieval chronicles relate that the King was stoned at the Place of the Five Churches near Kninsko Polje. Zvonimir's son Stjepan ruled only two years from 1089 to 1091.

THE BIBLIOGRAPHY

TABLE OF CONTENTS

INTRODUCTION

The events accompanying the independence of Croatia have led to a discontinuity in information sources. Institutions, publishing houses and editors disappeared or underwent a change in status. New publications began to appear rather slowly given the warlike circumstances. I found it appropriate to cite both publications that appeared in the earlier Republic of Croatia of the Socialist Federation of Yugoslavia and publications appearing under the new regime. The main contents of this bibliography consist of articles published in English after 1989 and books printed after 1980. Exceptions are numerous and motivated by practical purposes, e.g., for basic items in some fields and especially for books on the history of Croatia and literary translations. Some basic material in other languages - mainly Croatian and French - has also been included in this dictionary.

Bibliographies

Of particular interest is a bibliography compiled by the National and University Library of Zagreb containing a list of monographs in Croatian or foreign languages published outside Croatia since 1945. It contains numerous recent items written in English. *Hrvatski Iseljenični Tisak. Katalog Knjiga.* (Croatian Emigrant Publications: Book Catalogue.) Zagreb: Nacionalna i Sveučilišna Biblioteka u Zagrebu, 1992. This monograph was a first step toward integrating emigrant publications in an all-Croatian bibliography. From

1992 onwards, the Croatian Bibliography, Series A (Books) and Series B (Contributions to Journals and Collections) contain publications in other languages whose authors are Croatians. *Hrvatska Bibliografija. Niz A. Knjige.* Zagreb: Nacionalna i Sveučilišna Biblioteka u Zagrebu, 1993. *Hrvatska Bibliografija. Niz B. Prilozi u časopisima i zbornicima.* Zagreb: Nacionalna i Sveučilišna Biblioteka u Zagrebu, 1993.

Furthermore, books published before 1992 will be included in the Croatian retrospective bibliography which is in preparation now. A separate *CIP Bilten* (Cataloguing in Publication Bulletin) gives a monthly list of books in press and contains publications in the English language. *CIP Bilten. Knjige u Tisku.* Zagreb: Nacionalna i Sveučilišna Biblioteka, 1993. There are known to be several earlier bibliographies and general introductions on Croatia, though usually treating it as a part of Yugoslavia.

There are two outstanding, recent bibliographies. One is Horton, John J. *Yugoslavia.* World Bibliographical Series, Vol. 1. Oxford and Santa Barbara, CA: Clio Press, 1990 (Second revised and expanded edition). See especially pp. 54-58 and the index pp. 248-249 on Croatia. This bibliography also gives a short but accurate evaluation of the cited works. The other is Terry, Garth M. *Yugoslav History. A Bibliographic Index to English-Language Articles.* Nottingham: Astra Press, 1990 (Second revised edition). Astra Soviet and East European Bibliographies No. 10. Section 4 covers the Yugoslav Republics; among them Croatia figures on pp. 11-123.

Two older publications focusing specifically on Croatia also contain excellent bibliographical information. One is Prpić, George J. *Croatia and the Croatians: A Selected and Annotated Bibliography in English.* Scottsdale, Arizona: Associated Book Publishers, 1982. The other is Eterovich, Francis H. and Christopher Spalatin (eds.). *Croatia: Land, People, Culture.* Toronto, Ontario: University of Toronto Press. Vol. I, 1964. Vol. II, 1970. In these works the reader will find important references to older sources, not always mentioned in this bibliography.

Statistical Information

The Central Bureau of Statistics in Zagreb publishes theoretical studies regularly and statistical information periodically. The most useful are the *Monthly Statistical Bulletin* and the *Statistical*

Yearbook of Croatia (Bilingual). Publications using data of the latest population census are expected soon. Republika Hrvatska. Republički Zavod za Statistiku. *Popis Stanovništva, Domaćinstava, Stanova i Poljoprivrednih Gospodarstava, 31 ožuljak 1991. Stanovništva prema narodnosti po naseljima.* Zagreb: Republički Zavod za Statistiku, 1992, Dokumentacija 881. This contains a section in English. Republic of Croatia. Central Bureau of Statistics. *Census of Population, Households, Dwellings and Farms. 31st March, 1991.* Zagreb: Central Bureau of Statistics, 1992, Documentation 881.

Considerable statistical data on Croatia in the former Yugoslavia were collected and published by the same Croatian Republic Bureau. Some were also periodically published by the Federal Statistical Office of the Socialist Federal Republic of Yugoslavia, e.g., trade, industry and labor statistics. A translation in English of the introduction and tables of contents of the *Statistical Yearbooks* is available. It also covers most other statistical publications. *Statistical Yearbook of the Socialist Federal Republic of Yugoslavia.* Belgrade: Federal Statistical Office, SFRJ, 1989.

Linguistics and Literature

A comprehensive list of Yugoslav literature and criticism in the English language was provided by two publications of Vasa Mihailovich. Croatian literature and criticism occupy a good deal thereof. Mihailovich, Vasa D. and Mateja Matejić. *A Comprehensive Bibliography of Yugoslav Literature in English 1593-1980.* Columbus, Ohio: Slavica Publishers, 1984. And Mihailovich, Vasa D. *First Supplement to A Comprehensive Bibliography of Yugoslav Literature in English 1981-1985.* Columbus, Ohio: Slavica Publishers, 1988.

Translations of shorter works of contemporary Croatian authors are published by the Croatian Writers' Association in the Journal *Most/The Bridge.* Issue 1-4 of 1989 contains a retrospective bibliography on the years 1966-1988. Issue 6 of 1993, on the occasion of the 59th Congress of the International P.E.N. at Dubrovnik, includes a catalog of publications 1990-1993. It also contains a review of the Croatian Literature and Special Edition Series, as well as other translations of the P.E.N. Center. The Croatian edition of *Lettre Internationale* published until 1993 by the Croatian P.E.N. Center also informed about Croatian literary life.

A considerable though not complete overview of English language contributions to Yugoslav linguistics until 1980 can be found in another publication of Mihailovich. Milivojevich, Dragan and Vasa D. Mihailovich (eds.). *Yugoslav Linguistics in English 1900-1980. A Bibliography*. Columbus, Ohio: Slavica, 1991. A review of each year's work in the Slavonic languages and literatures, including sections on Serbo-Croatian studies and modern Serbo-Croatian, is provided in the volumes of the Modern Humanities Research Association. Mayo, P.J. (ed.). *The Year's Work in Slavonic Languages and Literatures 1989*. London: Modern Humanities Research Association - King's College, n.d., vol. 51, pp. 1047-1062. (Id. 1991, vol. 53, pp. 1070-1077).

The following academic journals regularly publish interesting articles and book reviews on the subject:
Canadian American Slavic Studies (Bakersfield, California State University);
Slavonic and East European Review (London, Modern Humanities Research Association);
Slavic Review (formerly *American Slavic and East-European Review,* edited by the American Association for the Advancement of Slavic Studies, Austin);
Oxford Slavonic Papers (Oxford University Press).

Social Sciences

Political issues concerning Yugoslavia appeared regularly in *Praxis International* (Oxford, Blackwell). It is the international heir of the once famous philosophical journal *Praxis*, published in Zagreb until 1975 when the distribution was blocked by the party. The last issue of *Praxis International* (vol. 13, no. 4, January 1994) was entirely devoted to the disintegration of Yugoslavia.

The Journal *Yugoslav Survey* presented translated articles of party-line social scientists. Another journal even closer to official ideology was *Socialist Thought and Practice*. The more critical journal on social issues *Naše Teme* (Our Themes) has since 1989 had an international edition under the abbreviated title *NT* (Zagreb, Center for Theoretical Studies CC LCC "Vladimir Bakarić").

The current evolution of the Yugoslav crisis - Croatian problems included - is very well covered by the Bulletin of the Institute for War and Peace Reporting: *Balkan War Report - Incorporating the*

Yugoslav Contributions of Yugofax (London). Croatian political science is now published in the *Croatian Political Science Review* (Zagreb).

The Information Department of the Ministry of Foreign Affairs of the Republic of Croatia regularly publishes a *Newsletter* in which official Croatian viewpoints are explained and political events are followed day by day.

The Croatian Section of the Helsinki International Federation regularly presents reports on the human rights situation in Croatia.

Self-Management

A selection of the literature in English on self-management in communist Yugoslavia is contained in the foreign language section of a bibliography of the National Library of Serbia: *Samoupravljanje u Jugoslovenskoj Teoriji i Praksi. Građa za Bibliografiju. Sveska 2.* Belgrade: Narodna Biblioteka Srbije, 1978, pp. 228-244.

Technical research on the economics of self-management can be found in the journal *Economic Analysis and Workers' Management* (Belgrade: Institute of Economic Studies - Prosveta).

Economics

Croatian Economic Trends is a journal edited by the State Institute for Macroeconomic Analysis and Forecasting of Zagreb (Državni Zavod za Makroekonomske Analize i Prognoze). The Institute for Development and International Relations publishes *Razvoj/Development-International,* a journal on the problems of socio-economic development and international relations. The journal has been published quarterly in English, French and Spanish since 1986. The Intelligence Unit of *The Economist* (London-New York) annually publishes authoritative *Country Reports,* as well as quarterly reviews on Bosnia-Hercegovina, Croatia, Macedonia, Serbia-Montenegro and Slovenia.

Philosophy

Since 1986, the Croatian Philosophical Society has been publishing *Synthesis Philosophica,* the international edition of

Filozofska Istraživanja (Zagreb, 1980-). In the academic year 1990-91, the Philosophic Institute of Zagreb University started publication of *Studiae historiae philosophiae Croaticae,* the international edition of *Prilozi za Istraživanje Hrvatske Filozofske Baštine* (Research into the Croatian Philosophical Heritage, 1975-).

Journalism

The Yugoslav newspaper *Politika* (Belgrade) used to publish a weekly English edition.

Medical Science

Current Croatian contributions to medical science are published in the *Croatian Medical Journal* (Zagreb), *Experimental and Clinical Gastroenterology* (Zagreb), *Gynaecologia et Perinatologia* (Zagreb), *Acta Stomatologica Croatica* (Zagreb), *Acta Facultatis Medicae Fluminensis* (Rijeka), *Hrvatski Športskomedicinski Vjesnik* (Zagreb), *Archiv za Zaštitu Majke i Djeteta* (Zagreb) and *Acta Pharmaceutica Jugoslavica* (Zagreb).

Science

Croatian scientific work in the field of physics and chemistry appears in *Fizika* (Zagreb), *Croatica Chemica Acta* (Zagreb) and *Chemical and Biochemical Engineering Quarterly* (Zagreb). Biology, zoology, geology and other natural sciences are covered by the journal *Natura Croatica* (Zagreb). The Natural History Museum of Zagreb initiated this publication in 1992. Older are *Acta Botanica Croatica* (Zagreb), *Periodicum Biologorum* (Zagreb) and *Veterinarski Arhiv* (Zagreb). Human anthropology is represented by *Collegium Antropologicum* (Zagreb). Readers interested in Croatian meteorology should consult *Hrvatski Meteorološki Ćasopis* (Zagreb). Shipbuilding is studied in *Brodogradnja* (Zagreb), contributions on metallurgy appear in *Metalurgija* (Sisak) and technical problems in *Goriva i Maziva* (Zagreb).

Tourism

The war invalidated a lot of earlier information. A recent study on Croatian nature and culture has been provided by Dubravko Horvatić in his attractive and instructive guide on Croatia.

Recent Publications

New publications that are not yet incorporated in this dictionary can be sought in the following databases.
Sociofile Database. It contains references to sociological journals and dissertations.
Econlit. It describes the main economic literature.
Humanities Index. It has mainly items on history, archeology, culture, literature, religion and art.
Social Sciences Citation Index. It has an interesting system of cross-references.
Historical Abstracts. It gives a short description and evaluation of publications on history.
Scad from Eurobases. This is a database of the Commission of the European Community with proposals, decisions and official publications of the Council and the European Parliament. It also contains references to other related documents.

Use of the Bibliography

A last remark concerns the classification of this bibliography. Aspects of reality can only be artificially separated for analytical purposes. History is perceived here as a global process. So, the reader will find references to political and nationality problems under the heading "Historical." Only the most recent period carries a separate label for "Political." The policy of the European Community (EC) towards Yugoslavia and Croatia is mostly classified in the rubric "Economic."

I. GENERAL

1. Bibliographies

Bibliografija Radova Instituta za Razvoj i Međunarodne Odnose 1990-1992. Zagreb: Institut za Razvoj i Međunarodne Odnose, 1993.

CIP Bilten. Knjige u Tisku. Zagreb: Nacionalna i Sveučilišna Biblioteka, 1993.

Građa za bibliografiju Ivana Meštrovića. Zagreb: Fundacija Ivana Meštrovića, 1993.

Horton, John J. *Yugoslavia.* World Bibliographical Series, Vol. 1. Oxford and Santa Barbara, CA: Clio Press, 1990 (Second revised and expanded edition). See especially pp. 54-58 and the index pp. 248-249.

Hrvatska Bibliografija. Niz A. Knjige. (Series A. Books.) Zagreb: Nacionalna i Sveučilišna Biblioteka u Zagrebu, 1993.

Hrvatska Bibliografija. Niz B. Prilozi u časopisima i zbornicima. (Series B. Contributions to Journals and Collections.) Zagreb: Nacionalna i Sveučilišna Biblioteka u Zagrebu, 1993.

Hrvatski Iseljenični Tisak. Katalog Knjiga. (Croatian Emigrant Publications: Book Catalogue.) Zagreb: Nacionalna i Sveučilišna Biblioteka u Zagrebu, 1992.

Ivanović, Snježana. "Research on European Integrations and European Studies in Croatia: Selected Bibliography (1987-1992)." *Razvoj/Development-International,* vol. 7 (1992), no. 1, pp. 175-190.

Maleković, Sanja, Snježana Ivanović and Jagoda Petrić-Kuiš. "Transformation process in the countries of central and eastern Europe: Selected bibliography (1987-1991)." *Razvoj/Development-International,* vol. 6 (1991), no. 2-3, pp. 409-431.

Mihailovich, Vasa D. *First Supplement to A Comprehensive Bibliography of Yugoslav Literature in English 1981-1985.* Columbus, Ohio: Slavica Publishers, 1988.

Mihailovich, Vasa D. and Mateja Matejić. *A Comprehensive Bibliography of Yugoslav Literature in English 1593-1980.* Columbus, Ohio: Slavica Publishers, 1984.

Milivojevich, Dragan and Vasa D. Mihailovich (eds.). *Yugoslav Linguistics in English 1900-1980. A Bibliography.* Columbus, Ohio: Slavica, 1991.

Most/The Bridge. Bibliography. 1966-1988. Zagreb: Most/The Bridge, 1989, no. 1-4.

Most/The Bridge. Catalogue of Publications 1990-1993 on the occasion of the 59th Congress of International P.E.N., Dubrovnik-Zagreb, Croatia. Zagreb: Most/The Bridge, 1993, no. 6.

Prpić, George J. *Croatia and the Croatians: A Selected and Annotated Bibliography in English.* Scottsdale, Arizona: Associated Book Publishers, 1982.

Raus, Đuro and Vukelić, Joso. *Bibliografija Radova Istraživača Zavoda za Istraživanje u Šumarstvu Šumarskog Fakulteta u Zagrebu za Razdoblje 1986-1990/Bibliography of Articles from the Institute for Forestry, Zagreb, over the period 1986-1990.* Zagreb, Sveučilište u Zagrebu, Šumarski Fakultet, 1992.

Stokes, Gale. *Nationalism in the Balkans: An Annotated Bibliography.* New York: Garland, 1984.

Terry, Garth M. *Yugoslav History. A Bibliographic Index to English-Language Articles.* Nottingham: Astra Press, 1990 (Second revised edition). Astra Soviet and East European Bibliographies No. 10. Section 4 covers the Yugoslav Republics; among them Croatia figures on pp. 11-123.

2. General Information and Libraries

Aparac-Gazivoda, Tatjana and Dragutin Katalenac (eds.). *Wounded Libraries in Croatia.* Zagreb: Croatian Library Association, 1993.

Croatia Fact File. Country, History, People, Government, War, Phrases, Useful Data. Zagreb: Ministry of Information, 1992.

Djamić, Anica. "The European Documentation Centre (IRMO-EDOC)." *Razvoj/Development-International,* vol. 6 (1991), no. 1, pp. 129-135.

Dragojević, Sanjin. "The Information System of the Documentation Centre for Cultural Development and Cooperation." *Culturelink*, Special Issue, 1991, pp. 49-70.

________. "The World of Culture and the World of Information." *Razvoj/Development-International*, vol. 7 (1992), no. 1, pp. 95-96.

Five Centuries of Croatian Encyclopaedism - A Catalogue to the Exhibit by the Lexicographic Institute "Miroslav Krleža." Zagreb: Exhibition: Special Edition of the Croatian P.E.N. Center in cooperation with Matica hrvatska for the 59th P.E.N. World Congress, 1993.

Kratofil, Mirko. *Dubrovnik Libraries and Archives.* Translated by Sonia Bićanić. Zagreb: Exhibition: Special Edition of the Croatian P.E.N. Center in cooperation with Matica hrvatska for the 59th P.E.N. World Congress, 1993.

Tudor-Silovic, Neva and Michael W. Hill. *National Surveys and Library Information Services: No. 2: Yugoslavia.* Boston Spa: British Library, 1990.

3. Guides and Yearbooks

Country Reports. Bosnia-Hercegovina, Croatia, Macedonia, Serbia-Montenegro and Slovenia. London, New York: Intelligence Unit of The Economist, 1993.

Croatia 1994. Edited by Milovan Baletić. Zagreb: INA-Konzalting, 1994.

Croatia 1992 Handbook. Zagreb: Ugled, Hrvatsko Novinarsko Društvo, 1992.

Croatian Business Directory '94. Zagreb: Masmedia, 1993.

Directory of Indigenous Non-governmental Organisations and Independent Media in the Former Yugoslavia. Institute for War and Peace Reporting. London: Institute for War and Peace Reporting, 1993. Insert Balkan War Report, October/November 1993, no. 22.

Tko je tko u Hrvatskoj/Who Is Who in Croatia. Edited by Franjo Maletić. Zagreb: Golden Marketing, 1993.

Who's Who in the Socialist Countries of Europe: A Biographical Encyclopedia of More than 12,600 Leading Personalities in Albania, Bulgaria, Czechoslovakia, German Democratic Republic, Hungary, Poland, Romania, Yugoslavia: 1989. Munich, New York: K.G. Saur, 1989 (Second Edition).

Zagreb Economy. Zagreb: Zagrebačka Komora, 1993.

4. Statistics

Census of Population, Households, Dwellings and Farms. 31st March, 1991. Zagreb: Republic of Croatia, Central Bureau of Statistics, 1992, Documentation 881. (English language section of *Popis Stanovništva*)

Monthly Statistical Bulletin. Republic of Croatia. Central Bureau of Statistics (Zagreb).

Popis Stanovništva, Domaćinstava, Stanova i Poljoprivrednih Gospodarstava, 31 ožuljak 1991. Stanovništva prema narodnosti po naseljima. Zagreb: Republika Hrvatska, Republički Zavod za Statistiku, 1992, Dokumentacija 881.

Republika Hrvatska. Državni Zavod za Statistiku. *Program Publiciranja 1933*. Zagreb: Državni Zavod za Statistiku Republike Hrvatske, 1992.

Statistički Godisnjak SFRJ. Statistical Yearbook of the Socialist Federal Republic of Yugoslavia. Belgrade: Socialist Federal Republic of Yugoslavia. Federal Statistical Office. Federal Statistical Office, SFRJ, 1989.

Statistički Ljetopis 1992/Statistical Yearbook of Croatia. Zagreb: Central Bureau of Statistics, 1993. (Bilingual Edition.)

5. *Travel and Description*

Balog, Zvonimir. *Zagreb - Croatian Metropolis: Touristic Guide*. Translated by Beatrice Mićunović. Zagreb: Masmedia, 1993.

Brown, Alec. *Yugoslav Life and Landscape*. London, New York: Elek, 1954.

Bralić, Ivo et al. *Our Lovely Croatia*. Zagreb: Marin Držić, 1992.

Chamberlain, Lesley. "Rebecca West in Yugoslavia." *Contemporary Review,* vol. 248 (1986), May, pp. 262-266.

A Concise Atlas of the Republic of Croatia and of the Republic of Bosnia and Hercegovina. Zagreb: Miroslav Krleža Lexicographical Institute, 1993.

Čorak, Željka and Slobodan P. Novak. *Lokrum*. Translated by Sonja Bašić and Sonia Bićanić. Zagreb: Exhibition: Special Edition of the Croatian P.E.N. Center in cooperation with Matica hrvatska for the 59th P.E.N. World Congress, 1993.

Desin, Marina and Mirko Kratofil. *Konavle-Cavtat-Ćilipi*. Translated by Sonia Bićanić. Zagreb: Special Edition of the Croatian P.E.N. Center in cooperation with Matica hrvatska for the 59th P.E.N. World Congress, 1993.

Dominican Monastery Dubrovnik. Zagreb: Turistkomerc, 1975.

Gattin, Nenad and Igor Zidić. *Dubrovnik*. Translated by Sonja Bašić. Zagreb: Special Edition of the Croatian P.E.N. Center in cooperation with Matica hrvatska for the 59th P.E.N. World Congress, 1993.

Guide to the Archaeological Museum at Split. Split: Archaeological Museum, 1973.

Horvatić, Dubravko. *Croatia*. Translated by Irena Zubčević and Vera Krnajski. Zagreb: Turistkomerc, 1992.

Hrvatska '91. Fotografije. Zagreb: Hrvatske Željenice; Foto Savez Hrvatske, 1992.

Ivelja-Dalmatin, Ana. *Kupari, Srebreno, Mlini, Plat*. Translated by Nikolina Jovanović. Dubrovnik: Turističko Društvo Župa Dubrovačka, 1990.

Jadran. Vodič i Atlas. Zagreb: Jugoslavenski Leksikografski Zavod, 1975 (Treće Izdanje-Third Edition).

Kaplan, Robert D. *Balkan Ghosts. A Journey through History*. New York: St. Martin's Press, 1993.

Lesinger, Darko (ed.). *Slike domovinskog rata/Pictures of the Homeland War*. Zagreb: Azur Journal, 1993.

Marković, A. "The Adriatic Croatia and German Travel Records, by I. Pederin." *Collegium Antropologicum*, vol. 17 (1993), no. 1, pp. 177-179.

Movčan, Josip. *Plitvice*. Translated by Sonja Lovasić. Zagreb: Turistkomerc, 1990.

Museum Networks of Croatia. Zagreb: Croatian Council of Museums, 1990.

Novaković, Josip. "Crossing the Border." *Antaeus*, Autumn 1989, no. 63, pp. 200-205.

Novaković, Marija. *Ćilipi, Konavle: History, Culture, Art, Tourism, Scenery*. Zagreb: Privredni Vjesnik, 1990. Library Tourist Monographs, no. 23.

Obad-Šćitaroci, Mladen. *Castles, Manors and Gardens of Croatian Zagorje*. Zagreb: Školska Knjiga, 1993.

Republic of Croatia and Republic of Bosnia and Hercegovina. *Ethnic Map, Geographic Map, Road Map*. Zagreb: Miroslav Krleža Lexicographical Institute, 1993.

Simović, Anton. *Navigational Guide to the Adriatic*. Zagreb: Miroslav Krleža Lexicographical Institute, 1993.

"Split - Capital of Southern Croatia." *British-Croatian Review*, 1979, Special Issue, no. 16, pp. 1-45.

Split. Croatia. Guidebook. Split: Infografika, 1993.

Split. Illustrated Tourist Guide. Split: Turistički Biro, 1973.

Šulc, Branka. *Museums and Galleries of Croatia*. Zagreb: Ministry of Culture and Education of the Republic of Croatia, 1993. Handbooks of Cultural Affairs, vol. 7.

The Travellers' Guide to Istra. Pula: Suvenir-Dizain, 1990 (1982).

Vojnovich, Louis. *A Historical Saunter through Dubrovnik*. Dubrovnik: Jadran, 1929.

West, Rebecca. *Black Lamb and Grey Falcon. A Journey through Yugoslavia.* New York: Penguin, 1982 (1941).

Yougoslavie. Paris: Hachette, 1979. Les Guides Bleus.

Zadar and Its Surroundings. Zagreb: Turistkomerc, 1975.

Zagreb. Tourist Guide. Zagreb: Quo Vadis, 1993.

II. CULTURAL

1. General

Birnbaum, H. *Aspects of the Slavic Middle Ages and Slavic Renaissance Culture.* New York: Lang, 1991.

Črnja, Zvane. *Cultural History of Croatia.* Zagreb: Office of Information, 1962.

Eterovich, Francis H. and Christopher Spalatin (eds.). *Croatia: Land, People, Culture.* Toronto, Ontario: University of Toronto Press. Vol. I, 1964. Vol. II, 1970.

Kukuljević-Sakcinski, Ivan. *Glasoviti Hrvati prošlih vjekova - Notable Croats of Past Ages.* Zagreb: Croatian P.E.N. Center, Most/The Bridge Literary Series, 1991, no. 5.

Matillon, J. and H. Heger (eds.). *Les Croates et la civilisation du livre.* Symposium international d'études sur l'aire culturelle croate, 1e, Paris, 3 décembre 1983. Paris: PUF, 1986. Croatica Parisiensa no. 1.

Peruško Čulek, Zrinjka. *Broadcasting Environment and Legislature in Croatia: Report for the Bler Study Group.* Zagreb, IRMO, 1992, 14 p.

_______. "The Cultural Dimension of European Studies." *Razvoj/ Development-International,* vol. 7 (1992), no. 1, pp. 118-119.

_______. *Cultural Impacts of the Media Policies in the Croatian Region: Interim Report for Croatia. Project No. 18 of the World Decade for Cultural Development.* Zagreb: IRMO, 1992, 13 p.

_______. "European Cooperation in the Audio-Visual Media: For an Interregional Cultural Policy." *Razvoj/Development-International,* vol. 6 (1991), no. 2-3, pp. 343-356.

_______. "The IRMO Project on International Data Base and Directory for Cultural Policies of the Unesco Member States." *Culturelink,* vol. 2 (1990), no. 3, pp. 43-54.

_______. "Le paysage audiovisuel croate dans la coopération interrégionale européenne," in *Entre Etat et Marché: Audiovisuel et Cinéma en Europe Centrale et Orientale.* Edited by Anna-Marie Autissier and Tristan Mattelart. Paris: Eurocréation, 1993.

Puhar, A. "The Obscenity of TV (The Extremes of Media Freedom in the Former Yugoslavia)." *Index on Censorship,* vol. 22 (1993), no. 2, p. 19.

2. *Literature and Linguistics*

a. Literary Translations and Anthologies

Autobiographies by Croatian Writers. Selected by Nada Šolja, Maja Šoljan and Nikolina Jovanović. Zagreb: Special Edition of Croatian P.E.N. Center in cooperation with Matica hrvatska for the 59th P.E.N. World Congress, 1993.

Cvitan, Dalibor. *Croatian Poetry for Children.* Zagreb: Most/The Bridge, no. 50, 1976.

Dedić, Arsen. *Rain/Kiša.* Zagreb: Special Edition of the Croatian P.E.N. Center in cooperation with Matica hrvatska for the 59th P.E.N. World Congress, 1993.

Desnica, Vladan. "Farewell." Translated by Alan Ferguson. *British-Croatian Review,* 1976, no. 6.

Drakulić, Slavenka. *Holograms of Fear.* New York, London: W. W. Norton and Company, 1992.

________. *How We Survived Communism and Even Laughed.* London: Hutchinson, 1992.

________. "Letter from Croatia." *Partisan Review,* vol. 60 (1993), Summer, pp. 577-586.

Four Yugoslavian Plays. The Black Hole by Goran Stefanovski, The Professional by Dušan Kovačević, The Wall, the Lake by Dušan Jovanović, The Performance of Hamlet in Lower Termwater by Ivo Brešan. Edited by Brenda Walker, introduced by Dragan Klaić. London: Forest Books, 1992.

Gundulić, Ivan. "Dubravka." Translated by E. D. Goy. *British-Croatian Review,* 1976, no. 9.

Harvey, Andrew and A. Pennington. *The Golden Apple: A Round of Stories, Songs, Spells, Proverbs and Riddles.* Chosen and translated by the authors from *Od Zlata jabuka,* compiled by Vasko Popa. London: Anvil Press Poetry, 1980.

Hektorović, Petar. "Fishing and Fishermen's Conversations." Translated by E.D. Goy. *British-Croatian Review,* 1979, no. 15.

Ilin, Dušica (ed.). *The Golden Garland of the Struga Nights of Poetry.* Skopje: Makedonska Kniga, 1986.

Ivšić, Radovan. *King Gordogain.* Translated by Roger Cardinal. Zagreb: Special Edition of the Croatian P.E.N. Center in cooperation with Matica hrvatska for the 59th P.E.N. World Congress, 1993.

Johnson, Bernard (ed.). *New Writing in Yugoslavia.* Harmondsworth: Penguin, 1970.

Kadić, Ante. *Contemporary Croatian Literature*. The Hague: Mouton, 1960.

_______. *Croatian Reader: With Vocabulary*. Berkeley: University of California, 1957.

_______. *Croatian Reader: With Vocabulary*. The Hague: Mouton, 1960.

Kaleb, Vjekoslav. *Glorious Dust*. Translated by Zora G. Depolo. London: Lincolns-Praeger, 1960.

_______. "The Guest." Translated by Alan Ferguson. *British-Croatian Review,* 1976, no. 8.

Koljević, Svetozar (ed.). *Yugoslav Short Stories*. London: Oxford University Press, 1966. (World's Classics, 608.)

Kovačić, Ivan Goran. *The Pit*. Translated by Alec Brown. Zagreb: Matica hrvatska, 1961; Most/The Bridge, 1976, no. 49.

Kovačićek, Miljenko. *Beyond the Song*. Canton, Connecticut: Singular Speech, 1989.

Krleža, Miroslav. *The Cricket Beneath the Waterfall, and Other Stories*. Edited by Branko Lenski. New York: Vanguard, 1973.

_______. *The Golden Garland of the Struga Nights of Poetry,* Edited by Dušica Ilin. Skopje: Makedonska Kniga, 1986, pp. 221-237.

_______. *On the Edge of Reason*. Translated by Zora G. Depolo. New York: Vanguard, 1976.

_______. *The Return of Philip Latinovicz*. Translated by Zora G. Depolo. New York: Vanguard; London: Lincolns-Praeger, 1959.

Krmpotić, Vesna. *Eyes of Eternity: A Spiritual Autobiography.* Translated by Lovett F. Edwards. New York: Harcourt Brace Jovanovich, 1979.

Lavrin, Janko. *An Anthology of Modern Yugoslav Poetry.* London: John Calder, 1962. (Croat Section: pp. 85-135.)

Lenski, Branko (ed). *Death of a Simple Giant, and Other Modern Yugoslav Stories.* New York: Vanguard, 1965.

Marinković, Ranko. "Hands." Translated by Celia Hawkesworth. *British-Croatian Review,* 1977, no. 10.

Marov, Zora. *The Wandering Years.* Translated by Zora Marov. Anaheim: KNI Incorporated, 1984.

Marulić, Marko. "Letter to Pope Adrian VI." Translated by Edo Pivčević. *British-Croatian Review,* 1977, no. 13.

Mihailovich, Vasa D. *First Supplement to A Comprehensive Bibliography of Yugoslav Literature in English 1981-1985.* Columbus, Ohio: Slavica Publishers, 1988.

________(ed.). "Yugoslav Literature." *Southeastern Europe,* vol. 9 (1982), pp. 1-160.

Mihailovich, Vasa D. (ed.) and Gertrud Grauberet-Champe (Introduction). *Contemporary Yugoslav Poetry.* Iowa City: University of Iowa Press, 1977.

Mihailovich, Vasa D. and Mateja Matejić. *A Comprehensive Bibliography of Yugoslav Literature in English 1593-1980.* Columbus, Ohio: Slavica Publishers, 1984.

Mihalić, Slavko. *Atlantis: Selected Poems, 1953-1982.* New York: Greenfield Review Literary Center, 1984.

________. *Black Apples. Selected Poems 1954-1987.* Toronto: Exile Editions, 1989.

_______. "The Grieving of Women." Translated by Charles Simić. *The Literary Review,* vol. 27 (1984), Spring, p. 301.

_______. "The Morning Roar of the City." Translated by Charles Simić. *The Literary Review,* vol. 27 (1984), Spring, p. 300.

_______. "Our Ancient Family Sign." Translated by Charles Simić. *The Literary Review,* vol. 27 (1984), Spring, p. 299.

_______. "Pastoral." Translated by Charles Simić. *The Literary Review,* vol. 27 (1984), Spring, p. 299.

_______. "Under the Microscope." Translated by Charles Simić. *The Literary Review,* vol. 27 (1984), Spring, p. 298.

Mikas, Ivan. "The Certainties of Mr. Marulić - Anno Domini 1500." *British-Croatian Review,* 1977, no. 13.

_______. "A Long Quiet Night." *British-Croatian Review,* 1977, no. 13.

Mikasinovich, Branko (ed.). *Five Modern Plays.* New York: Cyrco, 1977.

_______. *Modern Yugoslav Satire.* Merrick, New York: Cross-Cultural Communications, 1979.

Mikasinovich, Branko and Milivojević, Dragan (eds.). *Yugoslav Fantastic Prose.* Belgrade: Vajat/Proex, 1991.

Mikasinovich, Branko et al. (eds.). *Introduction to Yugoslav Literature. An Anthology of Fiction and Poetry.* New York: Twayne Publishers, 1973.

Milišić, Milan. *Stains.* Translated by Maja Herman. Zagreb: Special Edition of the Croatian P.E.N. Center in cooperation with Matica hrvatska for the 59th P.E.N. World Congress, 1993.

Novak, Slobodan. *Gold, Frankincense and Myrrh.* Translated by Celia Hawkesworth. Most/The Bridge, Croatian Literature Series, 1990, no. 4.

Pantzer, Eugene E. *Antun Gustav Matoš. A Time to Remember.* New York: Twayne, 1981.

Pelegrinović, Mikša. "Jedjupka." Translated by E.D. Goy. *British-Croatian Review,* 1977, no. 13.

Perković, Luka. "The Linen Chest." Translated by Anne Pivčević. *British-Croatian Review,* 1975, no. 3.

Seven Croatian Poets of the 20th Century. Selected by Tonko Maroević. Croatian and English with audio-cassette. Zagreb: Special Edition of Croatian P.E.N. Center in cooperation with Matica hrvatska for the 59th P.E.N. World Congress, 1993.

Šop, Nikola. "Cottages in Space." Translated by Branko Brusar and W.H. Auden. *British-Croatian Review,* 1974, no. 1.

Suško, Mario and Edward J. Czerwinski (eds.). "Alternatives: An Anthology of Slavic and East European Drama." *Slavic and East European Arts (USA),* vol. 2 (1983), no. 1 (Fall).

________. "The Meditative Generation: An Anthology of Younger Yugoslav Poets." *Slavic and East European Arts (USA),* vol. 1 (1982), no. 1 (Spring).

________. "The Mythmakers: An Anthology of Contemporary Yugoslav Short Stories." *Slavic and East European Arts (USA),* vol. 2 (1984), no. 2 (Spring).

Tadijanović, Dragutin. *Izabrane pjesme/Selected poems.* Translated by E. Goy and D. Ward. Zagreb: Croatian P.E.N., 1993.

Ugrešić, Dubravka. *Fording the Stream of Consciousness.* Translated by Michael Henry Heim. London: Virago, 1991.

________. "Fording the Stream of Consciousness." Translated by Michael Henry Heim. *Grand Street,* vol. 10 (1991), no. 3, pp. 11-25.

________. *In the Jaws of Life.* Translated by Celia Hawkesworth and Michael Henry Heim. London: Virago, 1992.

________. "Made in Yugoslavia." *Times Literary Supplement,* July 27, 1990, no. 4556, p. 798.

________. "Parrots and Priests. 'Before' and 'After' in Yugoslavia." *Times Literary Supplement,* May 15, 1992, pp. 12-15.

Vida, Viktor. "The Captive of Time." Translated by E. Pivčević. *British-Croatian Review,* 1977, no. 10.

Vrančić, Antun. *Letter to Hassan-Bey.* Translated by Edo Pivčević. *British-Croatian Review,* 1977, no. 13.

b. Literary Criticism

Barac, Antun. *A History of Yugoslav Literature.* Translated by Petar Mijušković. Ann Arbor: Michigan Slavic Publications, 1973.

Beker, Miroslav (ed.). *Comparative Studies in Croatian Literature.* Zagreb: Zavod za Znanost i Književnost Filozofskog Fakulteta, 1981.

Bogert, Ralph B. *The Writer as Naysayer: Miroslav Krleža and the Aesthetic of Interwar Central Europe.* Columbus, Ohio: Slavica Publishers, UCLA Slavic Studies vol. 20, 1991.

Debeljak, Ales. "Visions of Despair and Hope against Hope: Poetry in Yugoslavia in the Eighties." *World Literature Today,* vol. 66 (1992), Summer, pp. 427-431.

Eekman, Thomas. *Thirty Years of Yugoslav Literature (1945-1975).* Ann Arbor: Michigan Slavic Publications, 1973.

Gruenwald, Oskar. "Yugoslav Camp Literature: Rediscovering the Ghost of a Nation's Past-Present-Future." *Slavic Review,* vol. 46 (1987), Fall-Winter, pp. 513-528; vol. 48 (1989), Summer, pp. 272-281.

"Gundulić, Držić. Dubrovnik." *Most/The Bridge,* 1990, no. 1-2.

Hawkesworth, Celia. "I. Vrkljan: Marina, or About Biography." *Slavonic and East European Review,* vol. 69 (1991), pp. 221-231.

________. "Yugoslav Literature of the Second World War." *Journal of European Studies,* vol. 16 (1986), September, pp. 217-226.

Hayden, Robert N. "Using a Microscope to Scan the Horizon." *Slavic Review,* vol. 48 (1989), Summer, pp. 275-279.

Jurak, Mirko. *Australian Papers: Yugoslavia, Europe and Australia.* Ljubljana: Edvard Kardelj University of Ljubljana, Faculty of Arts and Sciences, 1983.

Kadić, Ante. *Essays in South Slavic Literature.* Columbus, Ohio: Slavica Publishers, 1988.

________. *From Croatian Renaissance to Yugoslav Socialism: Essays.* The Hague: Mouton, 1969.

Kostić, Veselin. *Anglo-Yugoslav Cultural Relations before 1700.* Nottingham, England: Astra, 1989.

Kot, Wlodzimierz. "Croatian and Serbian Modernism. A Comparative Analysis." *Neohelicon,* vol. 2 (1974), pp. 155-183.

Lord, Albert B. (ed.) "The Multinational Literature of Yugoslavia." *Review of National Literatures* (St. John's University, Jamaica), vol. 5 (1974), no. 1 (Spring).

Lukić, Sveta. Edited by Gertrude Joch Robinson and translated by Pola Triandis. *Contemporary Yugoslav Literature. A Sociopolitical Approach.* Urbana: University of Illinois Press, 1972.

Mihailovich, Vasa D. (ed.). *First Supplement to A Comprehensive Bibliography of Yugoslav Literature in English 1981-1985.* Columbus, Ohio: Slavica Publishers, 1988.

_______. "The Karamazov Syndrome in Recent Yugoslav Literature." *World Literature Today,* vol. 65 (1991), Spring, pp. 248-252.

_______. *Yugoslav Literature.* Southeastern Europe, vol. 9 (1982), pp. 1-160.

_______ and Mateja Matejić. *A Comprehensive Bibliography of Yugoslav Literature in English 1593-1980.* Columbus, Ohio: Slavica Publishers, 1984.

Miletich, John S. "Muslim Oral Epic and Medieval Epic." *The Modern Language Review,* vol. 83 (1988), no. 4, pp. 911-924.

Oja, M.F. "Toward a Definition of Camp Literature." *Slavic Review,* vol. 48 (1989), Summer, pp. 272-274.

Simmons, Cynthia. "Croatian Moderna and Russian Modernism." *Slavic and East European Journal,* vol. 28 (1984), pp. 371-382.

Šoljan, Antun. *Two and a Half Years of Croatian P.E.N. Club 1971-1974/Dvije i pol godine Hrvatskoga PEN-CLUBA 1971-1974.* Zagreb: Special Edition of the Croatian P.E.N. Center in cooperation with Matica hrvatska for the 59th P.E.N. World Congress, 1993.

Sujoldzić, A. "The Population Study of Middle Dalmatia. Linguistic History and Current Regional Differentiation of Croatian Dialects." *Collegium Antropologicum,* vol. 15 (1991), no. 2, pp. 309-320.

Torbarina, Josip. *Relations*. Zagreb: Special Edition of the Croatian P.E.N. Center in cooperation with Matica hrvatska for the 59th P.E.N. World Congress, 1993.

Živančević-Sekeruš, Ivana. "Croatian Writers in the Byronic Mould." *The Modern Language Review,* vol. 87 (1992), no. 1, pp. 143-156.

_______. "The Krakowiak in Croatian and Slovene Poetry." *The Slavonic and East European Review,* 71 (1993), no. 2, pp. 278-286.

3. Linguistics

a. Old Croatian and Croatian Slavonic

Auty, R. "Sixteenth-Century Croatian Glagolitic Books in the Bodleian Library." *Oxford Slavonic Papers,* vol. 11 (1978), pp. 132-135.

Barentsen, A. A. et al. (eds.). *Dutch Contributions to the Tenth International Congress of Slavists, Sofia, September 14-22, 1988. Linguistics.* Amsterdam: Rodopi, 1988.

Birnbaum, Hendrik (ed.). *The New York Missal: An Early 15th Century Croato-Glagolitic Manuscript.* Munich: Sagner, 1977.

Birnbaum, Marianna D. *Croatian and Hungarian Latinity in the Sixteenth Century.* Zagreb: Special Edition of Croatian P.E.N. Center in cooperation with Matica hrvatska for the 59th P.E.N. World Congress, 1993.

Budiša, Dražen. *Croatian Books Printed in Venice from 15th to 18th Century.* Exhibition from the Zagreb National Library Treasury. Zagreb: Special Edition of Croatian P.E.N. Center in cooperation with Matica hrvatska for the 59th P.E.N. World Congress, 1993.

Butler, Thomas. *Monumenta Serbocroatica: A Bilingual Anthology of Serbian and Croatian Texts from the 12th to the 19th Century.* Ann Arbor: Michigan Slavic Publications, 1980.

Corin, Andrew R. *The New York Missal: A Paleographic and Phonetic Analysis.* Columbus, Ohio: Slavica, 1991.

Dezsö, Laslo. *Typological Studies in Old Serbo-Croatian Syntax.* Cologne: Böhlau, 1982. Slavistische Forschungen 34.

Foretić, Miljenko. *The Works of Dubrovnik Writers Printed in Europe from 15th to 18th Century.* Translated by Sonia Bićanić. Zagreb: Exhibition: Special Edition of the Croatian P.E.N. Center in cooperation with Matica hrvatska for the 59th P.E.N. World Congress, 1993.

Franolić, Branko. *An Historical Survey of Literary Croatian.* Paris: Nouvelles Editions Latines, 1984.

________. *Language Policy in Yugoslavia: With Special Reference to Croatian.* Paris: Nouvelles Editions Latines, 1988.

Hercigonja, E. "The Place and Role of Croatian Literature in the Literary Development of the Slavonic Middle Ages." In *Comparative Studies in Croatian Literature.* Edited by Miroslav Beker. Zagreb: Zavod za Znanost i Književnosti Filozofskog Fakulteta u Zagrebu, 1981, pp. 9-62.

Jacobson, R. *Slavic Languages. A Condensed Survey.* New York: Columbia Slavic Studies, 1966.

Kadić, Ante. "The Croatian Renaissance." *Slavic Review,* vol. 21 (1962), no. 1, pp. 65-88.

Katičić, Radoslav et al. *Two Thousand Years of Writing in Croatia.* Zagreb: Sveučilišna Naklada Liber, 1987.

Knežević, Anto. "The Cyrillo-Methodian Tradition in Translation into the Contemporary Croatian or Serbian Language." *Synthesis Philosophica,* vol. 5 (1990), no. 1, pp. 313-321.

Mihalječić, Milan. "The Phonological System of the Croatian Redaction of Church Slavonic (with Appendix)." *Slavic and East European Journal,* vol. 36 (1992), Spring, pp. 1-16.

Rječnik crkvenoslavenskoga jezika hrvatske redakcije. (Dictionary of the Croatian Redaction of Church Slavonic.) 1. Uvod - Preface. Zagreb: Staroslavenski Zavod Hrvatskog Filološkog Instituta, 1991.

Rječnik crkvenoslavenskoga jezika hrvatske redakcije. (Dictionary of the Croatian Redaction of Church Slavonic.) 2. A-Antiochiisk. Zagreb: Staroslavenski Zavod Hrvatskog Filološkog Instituta, 1992.

Schmalstieg, W. R. *An Introduction to Old Church Slavic.* Columbus, Ohio: Slavica, 1982 (Second expanded edition).

Vratović, Vladimir. *Croatian Latinity and the Mediterranean Constant.* Zagreb: Special Edition of the Croatian P.E.N. Center in cooperation with Matica hrvatska for the 59th P.E.N. World Congress, 1993.

b. Modern Croatian

Auty, Robert. "Language and Nationality in East-Central Europe 1750-1950." *Oxford Slavonic Papers,* vol. 12 (1979), pp. 52-83.

Babić, Slavna. *Serbo-Croatian Reading Passages with Comments, Exercises, Vocabulary.* Belgrade: Kolarčev Narodni Universitet, 1985 (Drugo Izdanje-Second edition).

Banac, Ivo. *Hrvatsko jezično pitanje. The Croatian Language Question.* Most/The Bridge, Croatian Literature Series, 1991, no. 6.

Belyavski-Frank, Masha. "Narrative Use of Tense Forms in Russian and Serbo-Croatian." *Slavic and East European Journal,* vol. 35 (1991), Spring, pp. 115-132.

Bennett, David C. "Towards an Explanation of Word-Order Differences between Slovene and Serbo-Croat." *The Slavonic and East European Review,* vol. 64 (1986), January, pp. 1-24.

________. "Word-Order Change in Progress: The Case of Slovene and Serbo-Croat and Its Relevance for Germanic." *Journal of Linguistics,* vol. 23 (1987), September, pp. 269-287.

Birnbaum, H. "Language, Ethnicity and Nationalism: On the Linguistic Foundations of a Unified Yugoslavia." In *The Creation of Yugoslavia 1914-1918.* Edited by D. Djordjević. Santa Barbara, Oxford: Clio Books, 1980, pp. 157-182.

Bugarski, Ranko. "Sociolinguistic Issues in Standardizing Linguistic Terminology." *Language in Society,* vol. 12 (1983), no. 1, pp. 65-70.

Dale, Ian R.H. "Digraphia." *International Journal of the Sociology of Language,* no. 26 (1980), pp. 5-13.

Engelsfeld, Mladen. *Croatian through Conversation.* Zagreb: Nakladni Zavod Znanje, 1993 (7th printing).

Filipović, Rudolf (ed.). *Kontrastivna analiza Engleskog i Hrvatskog ili Srpskog jezika/Contrastive Analysis of English and Serbo-Croatian.* Zagreb: University, Institute of Linguistics, 1975.

Grubišić, Vinko. *Bibliography on the Croatian Language.* Norval: HIŠAK-CSAC, 1987. (Priručici za učenje hrvatskog jezika i kulture izvan Hrvatske = Manuals for the study of the Croatian language and culture outside Croatia; vol. 12.)

Gvozdanovic, Jadranka. *Tone and Accent in Standard Serbo-Croatian with a Synopsis of Serbo-Croatian Phonology.* Vienna: Verlag der Österreichische Akademie der Wissenschaften - Philosophisch-Historische Klasse, 1980.

Harris, Jana G. (ed.). *American Contributions to the Tenth International Congress of Slavists, Sofia, September 1988. Literature.* Columbus, Ohio: Slavica, 1988.

Inkelas, Sharon and Draga Zec. "Serbo-Croatian Pitch Accent: The Interaction of Tone, Stress and Intonation." *Language,* vol. 64 (1988), June, pp. 227-248.

Kalogjera, Damir. "Attitudes toward Serbo-Croatian Language Varieties." *International Journal of the Sociology of Language,* no. 52 (1985), pp. 93-110.

Kantor, Marvin. *Aspectual Derivation in Contemporary Serbo-Croatian.* The Hague: Slavistic Printings and Reprintings, 1992.

Karlović, N.L. "Internal Colonialism in a Marxist Society: The Case of Croatia." *Ethnic and Racial Studies,* vol. 5 (1982), no. 3, pp. 276-299.

Levenberg, Joel. "On the Conjugation of Velar Consonant Stems in Serbo-Croatian." *Slavic and East European Journal,* vol. 33 (1989), Winter, pp. 571-592.

Maček, Dora et al. *Relativization in English and Serbo-Croatian.* Zagreb: University, Institute of Linguistics, 1986. Yugoslav Serbo-Croatian-English Contrastive Project. New Studies, no. 3.

Magner, Thomas F. and Ladislav Matejka. *Word Accent in Modern Serbo-Croatian.* London and University Park, Pennsylvania: Pennsylvania State University Press, 1971.

Milivojevich, Dragan and Vasa D. Mihailovich (eds.). *Yugoslav Linguistics in English 1900-1980. A Bibliography.* Columbus, Ohio: Slavica, 1991.

Progovac, L. "Polarity in Serbo-Croatian. Anaphoric Npis and Pronominal Ppis." *Linguistic Inquiry,* vol. 22 (1991), no. 3, pp. 567-572.

Radovanović, Milorad (ed.). *Yugoslav General Linguistics.* Amsterdam, Philadelphia: John Benjamins Publishing, 1989.

Ridjanović, Midhat. "Serbo-Croatian nego (sto) v. od in comparative sentences and nego v. ali in coordinate structures." *Slavic and East European Journal*, vol. 33 (1989), Winter, pp. 571-592.

_______. *A Synchronic Study of Verbal Aspect in English and Serbo-Croatian*. Cambridge, Massachusetts: Slavica, 1976.

Ruzic, R. H. *The Aspects of the Verb in Serbo-Croatian*. Berkeley, California: University of California Press, 1943.

Schmalstieg, W. R. and T.F. Magner (eds.). *Sociolinguistic Problems in Czechoslovakia, Hungary, Romania, and Yugoslavia*. Columbus, Ohio: Slavica, 1978.

Vince, Zlatko. *Putovima hrvatskoga književnog jezika*. Zagreb: Nakladni Zavod Matica Hrvatske, 1990 (Drugo Izdanje-Second Edition).

Vuković, Branislav. "Neither Internal Colonialism nor External Coloniser: A Reply to Karlović." *Ethnic and Racial Studies*, vol. 10 (1987), no. 1, pp. 96-109.

Zovko, C.I. *The Handbook of Croatian Language*. Chicago, Toronto: ZIRAL, 1983.

c. Dictionaries

Boban, Vjekoslav and John Pheby. *The Oxford-Duden Pictorial Serbo-Croat and English Dictionary*. Oxford: Oxford University Press, 1988.

Bogadek, A. *New English-Croatian and Croatian-English Dictionary*. New York: Hafner, 1950 (Third enlarged and corrected edition).

Brozović, Blanka. *Englesko-hrvatski i hrvatsko-engleski džepni rječnik: za osnovnu školu*. Zagreb: Školska Knjiga, 1993.

Bujas, Željko. *Hrvatsko ili sprsko-engleski enciklopedijski rječnik/Croatoserbian-English Encyclopedic Dictionary.* Zagreb: Grafički Zavod Hrvatske, 1983.

Cemerikić, Jovanka, Guy Imart and Victoria Tikhonova-Imart. *Paronymes russo/serbo-croates.* Aix-en-Provence: Université de Provence, Institut d'études orientales et slaves, 1988.

Drvodelić, Milan et al. *Hrvatsko-Engleski rjecnik* (Croatian English Dictionary). Zagreb: Školska Knjiga, 1989 (Sixth edition).

Filipović, Rudolf (ed.). *Engleski-Hrvatski rječnik.* Zagreb: Školska Knjiga, 1992.

Filipović, Rudolf et al. *English-Croatian Dictionary/Englesko-Hrvatski rjecnik.* Zagreb: Zora, 1971.

Franolić, Branko. *A Bibliography of Croatian Dictionaries.* Paris: Nouvelles Editions Latines, 1985.

Glossary of Technical Terms for Market Researchers: English, German, Bulgarian, Czech, Polish, Hungarian, Romanian, Russian, Serbo-Croat. Amsterdam: ESOMAR, 1975.

Jedlićka, Alois. *Slovník Slovanské Lingvistické Terminologie/Dictionary of Slavonic Linguistic Terminology.* Hamburg: Helmut Buske Verlag, 1977.

Novi srpsko-hrvatski-engleski i engleski-srpsko-hrvatski rjecnik: sa tačnim izgovorom i pridatkom/New Serbo-Croatian-English and English-Serbo-Croatian Dictionary: With Correct Pronunciation and Appendix. Chicago: Palandech's, n.d.

Permanent Committee on Geographical Names for British Official Use: Serbo-Croat and Slovene. London: Royal Geographical Society, 1943.

Rječnik crkvenoslavenskoga jezika hrvatske redakcije. (Dictionary of the Croatian Redaction of Church Slavonic.) 1. Uvod - Preface.

Zagreb: Staroslavenski Zavod Hrvatskog Filološkog Instituta, 1991.

Rječnik crkvenoslavenskoga jezika hrvatske redakcije. (Dictionary of the Croatian Redaction of Church Slavonic.) 2. A-Antiochiisk. Zagreb: Staroslavenski Zavod Hrvatskog Filološkog Instituta, 1992.

Spalatin, Krsto. *Peterojezički rječnik europeizama. Kako se prevode hrvatske neprave srodnice na engleski, francuski, njemački, talijanski i druge jezične poteškoće.* (Five-Language Dictionary of Europeanisms. How to Translate Croatian Deceptive Cognates into English, French, German, Italian and Other Language Difficulties.) Zagreb: Nakladni Zavod Matice Hrvatske, 1990.

Williams, Gareth and Karoly Hunyadi. *Dictionary of Weeds of Eastern Europe. Their Common Name and Importance in Latin, Albanian, Bulgarian, Czech, German, English, Greek, Hungarian, Polish, Romanian, Russian, Serbo-Croat and Slovak.* Amsterdam, Oxford, New York: Elsevier, 1987.

4. Music and Theater

Andreis, Josip. *Music in Croatia.* Zagreb: Institute of Musicology, 1974.

________ and Slavko Zlatić. *Yugoslav Music.* Translated by Karla Kunc. Belgrade: Jugoslavija, 1959.

Baker, Clive. "Marshal Godot Goes to War." *New Theatre Quarterly,* vol. 92 (1993), August, pp. 290-292.

Blažeković, Zdravko. "Music in Zagreb between Croatian, Hungarian and Austrian Politics (1860-1883)." *History of European Ideas,* vol. 16 (1993), no. 4-6, pp. 671-676.

Kovačević, Krešimir. *The History of Croatian Music of the Twentieth Century.* Zagreb: Udruženje Kompozitora Hrvatske, 1967.

Majer-Bobetko, Sanja. "Croatian Musical Criticism between the Two World Wars." *International Review of the Aesthetics and Sociology of Music,* vol. 18 (1987), no. 1, pp. 75-95.

_______. *Note on the History of National Ideology in Croatian Music.* International Conference "Folk Music Today." Tallin, 1989, pp. 103-107.

_______. "Unpublished Theoretical Papers of Jozip Hatze." In *Josip Hatze. A Croatian Composer.* Zagreb: Muzički Informativni Centar, 1982, pp. 261-269.

_______. "The Zagreb Philharmonic." In Robert R. Graven (ed.) *Orchestras of the World.* New York: Greenwood Press, 1978.

Stipčević, Ennio. "The Social and Historical Status of Music and Musicians in Croatia in the Early Baroque Period." *International Review of the Aesthetics and Sociology of Music,* vol. 18 (1987), no. 1, pp. 3-17.

Tuksar, Stanislav (ed.). *Zvanstveni skup Glazbeni barok i zapadni Slaveni u kontekstu europskog kulturnog zajedništva/The Musical Baroque, Western Slavs, and the Spirit of the European Cultural Communion: Proceedings of the International Musicological Symposium held in Zagreb, Croatia, on October 12-14, 1989.* Zagreb: Hrvatsko muzikološko društvo, 1993.

5. *Folk Arts*

Kolar, Walter W. (ed.). *The Folk Arts of Yugoslavia.* Pittsburgh, Pennsylvania: Duquesne University Tamburitzans Institute of Folk Arts, 1976.

Radauš Ribarić, Jelka et al. *Croatian Folk Embroidery: Designs and Techniques.* New York: Van Nostrand, 1976.

Salopek, Vladimir. *Folk Costumes and Dances of Yugoslavia.* Translated by Nada Mirković. Zagreb: NIRO Privredni Vjesnik, 1987.

6. Architecture, Sculpture and Painting

Belamarić, Joško. *Nikola Božidarević (1465-1518).* Translated by Sonia Bićanić. Zagreb: Exhibition: Special Edition of the Croatian P.E.N. Center in cooperation with Matica hrvatska for the 59th P.E.N. World Congress, 1993.

Domijan, M., I. Petricoli and P. Vežić. *The Splendour of Zadar Treasuries.* Zagreb, n.p., 1990.

Gabrić, Mijo. *Sacral Institutions on Target: Deliberate Military Destruction of the Sacral Institutions in Croatia and Bosnia-Hercegovina.* Zagreb: Croatian Information Center, 1993.

Gamulin, Grgo. *The Painted Crucifixes in Croatia.* Translated by Ellen Elias Bursac. Zagreb: Udruženi Izdavači, 1983.

Građa za bibliografiju Ivana Meštrovića. Zagreb: Fundacija Ivana Meštrovića, 1993.

"Interim-Report on War Damage Caused on the Cultural Heritage in Croatia." *Collegium Antropologicum,* vol. 16 (1992), no. 1, pp. 19-26.

Ivančević, Radovan (ed.). *Cultural Heritage of Croatia: In the War 1991/92.* Translated by Sonja Bašić. Zagreb: Croatia University Press, 1993.

Karaman, Antun. *Dubrovnik Painting from Brukovac (1855-1922) to Dulčić (1916-1975).* Zagreb: Exhibition: Special Edition of the Croatian P.E.N. Center in cooperation with Matica hrvatska for the 59th P.E.N. World Congress, 1993.

Katalog Galerije Meštrović/Catalogue of Exhibits at the Meštrović Gallery at Split. Zagreb: Turistkomerc, 1983.

Keleman, Boris (ed.). *Ivan Generalić.* Zagreb: Galerija Primitivne Umetnosti, 1976.

________. *Nikola Kovačević.* Zagreb: Galerija Primitivne Umetnosti, 1976.

Meder, F. "War Devastation of the Croatian Cultural Heritage and Means of Its Restoration." *Collegium Antropologicum,* vol. 16 (1992), no. 1, pp. 27-29.

Milinović, D. "Dubrovnik. The Fate of Global Patrimony Due to the Croatian War." *Monuments Historiques,* vol. 182 (1993), pp. 62-64.

Mirth, Karlo. *Mestrović in America: 'Living from the Clod of Croatian Soil Attached to His Roots': From My Memories of Mestrović.* New York: K. Mirth, 1985.

Petricioli, Ivo. *The Cathedral of St. Anastasia - Zadar.* Zadar: Zadar Archbishopric, 1985.

________. *St. Simeon's Shrine in Zadar.* Zagreb: Associated Publishers, 1983.

________. *Thousand Years of Art in Zadar.* Zadar: SICU, 1988.

Tenšek, Ivan and Zvonimir Franić. *Architectural Drawings of Dubrovnik.* Translated by Sonia Bićanić. Zagreb: Special Edition of the Croatian P.E.N. Center in cooperation with Matica hrvatska for the 59th P.E.N. World Congress, 1993.

Twelve Croatian Painters for Croatian Peace Line. Zagreb: Hrvatsko-američko društvo/Croatian-American Society, 1992.

Zidić, Igor. *Đuro Pulitika's Studio.* Translated by Nikolina Jovanović. Zagreb: Special Edition of the Croatian P.E.N. Center in cooperation with Matica hrvatska for the 59th P.E.N. World Congress, 1993.

7. Philosophy

Banić-Pajnić, Erna. "Federicus Grisogono: De divinis mathematicis." *Synthesis Philosophica,* vol. 5 (1990), no. 1, pp. 269-280.

Barbarić, Damir. "The Importance of the University of Padua for the Education of Croatian Humanists." *Studia Historiae Philosophiae Croaticae,* vol. 1 (1991), no. 1, pp. 17-27.

Birnbaum, Marianna D. *Humanists in a Scattered World: Croatian and Hungarian Latinity in the Sixteenth Century.* Columbus, Ohio: Slavica, 1986. UCLA Slavic Studies, vol. 15.

Eekman, Thomas and Ante Kadić (eds.). *Juraj Križanić (1618-1683). Russophile and Economic Visionary: A Symposium.* The Hague: Mouton, 1976.

Filipović, Vladimir. "The Principles of Ethic-Philosophical Orientation of Marko Marulić." *Studia Historiae Philosophiae Croaticae,* vol. 1 (1991), no. 1, pp. 135-155.

Golub, Ivan. *The Slavic Vision of Juraj Križanić. Postcript: Ivo Banac. Friendship with Križanić and Russia.* Translated by Wendy Bracewell. Zagreb: Special Edition of the Croatian P.E.N. Center in cooperation with Matica hrvatska for the 59th P.E.N. World Congress, 1993.

Knežević, Anto. "The Slavic 'Svijet' (World)." *Synthesis Philosophica,* vol. 3 (1988), no. 1, pp. 123-132.

Krstić, Kruno. "The Beginnings of Philosophy in Croatia." *Studia Historiae Philosophiae Croaticae,* vol. 1 (1991), no. 1, pp. 7-16.

Macan, Ivan (ed.). *The Philosophy of Science of Ruder Bošković.* Symposium of the Institute of Philosophy and Theology, S.J., Zagreb, December 11-13, 1986. New York: Fordham University Press, 1987.

Marković, Mihailo and Robert S. Cohen. *Yugoslavia: The Rise and Fall of Socialist Humanism. A History of the Praxis Group.* Nottingham: Bertrand Russell Foundation - Spokeman Books, 1975.

Martinović, Ivica. *Ruđer Bošković (1711-1787).* Translated by Sonia Bićanić. Zagreb: Exhibition: Special Edition of the Croatian P.E.N. Center in cooperation with Matica hrvatska for the 59th P.E.N. World Congress, 1993.

Mikecin, Vjekoslav. "The Ominous Doctrine of a Distinguished Professor. An Answer to Professor Mihailo Marković." *Gaudeamus*, 1991, Fall, no. 4, pp. 21-23.

Pavletić, Vlatko. "A Modern Renaissance Personality: Dr. Ivan Supek." Symposium "From Theoretical Physics to Philosophy of Science and Peace," dedicated to 50 years of work by Ivan Supek, 11.10.1990. *Fizika. A, Atomic and Molecular Physics. Condensed Matter Physics. Plasma Physics*, vol. 1 (1992), no. 1, pp. 3-6.

Schiffler, Ljerka. "The Idea of Encyclopedism and Philosophical Thinking Founders of Croatian Encyclopedic Thought." *Studia Historiae Philosophiae Croaticae,* vol. 1 (1991), no. 1, pp. 83-115.

Stanišić, Ljudmila and Vanja. "Slavic Literary in Slavic Spiritual Culture." *Synthesis Philosophica*, vol. 5 (1990), no. 1, pp. 19-28.

Supek, Ivan. "The Downfall of Ideology." *Encyclopaedia Moderna*, vol. 13 (1992), no. 2, pp. 280-289.

Vereshchagin, Evgenii Mikhailovich. "Cyril and Methodius as the Creators of Theological-Philosophical Terminology in the Slavic Language." *Synthesis Philosophica*, vol. 5 (1990), no. 1, pp. 5-18.

Zenko, Franjo. "Bošković's Absolute Dynamism and Techno(geno)-organogenic Science." *Synthesis Philosophica*, vol. 5 (1990), no. 1, pp. 195-220.

________. "Hermann the Dalmatian (11th/12th Century) - A Sign-post into the Dark Origin of European Science." *Studia Historiae Philosophiae Croaticae,* vol. 1 (1991), no. 1, pp. 117-133.

8. Religion

Alexander, Stella. *The Triple Myth: A Life of Archbishop Alojzije Stepinac.* Boulder, Colorado: East European Monographs, Columbia University Press, 1987.

Bukowski, James B. "The Catholic Church and Croatian National Identity: From the Counter-Reformation to the Early Nineteenth Century." *East European Quarterly,* vol. 13 (1979), no. 3, pp. 327-338.

Eterović, Franjo Hijacint. "Aloysius Cardinal Stepinac - A Spiritual Portrait." N.p., 1970.

Hrvatska kršćanska bibliografija/Bibliographia croatica christiana. Zagreb: Katolički bogoslovni fakultet u Zagrebu, 1977.

Keys, Arthur B. "Yugoslavs Rebuild: Faith and Society." *Christianity and Crisis,* vol. 51 (1991), 18 March, pp. 83-87.

Kordić, Pedrag. *Cosmological Encounter with God.* Norval, Toronto: ZIRAL, 1981.

Korade, Mijo et al. *Jesuits and Croatian Culture.* Zagreb: Croatian Writers' Association, 1992. Most/The Bridge, Croatian Literature Series, vol. 15.

Kristo, Jure. "The Catholic Church in Times of Crisis." In Petra Sabrina Ramet (ed.). *Beyond Yugoslavia.* Boulder, Colorado, and London: Westview Press, 1994.

________. "Catholicism among Croats and Its Critique by Marxists." In Dennis J. Dunn (ed.). Religion and Nationalism in Eastern Europe and the Soviet Union. Boulder, Colorado: Lynne Rienner, 1987.

________. "Marxist Critique of Religion and Croatian Catholic Culture." *Journal of Ecumenical Studies,* vol. 22 (1985), pp. 474-486.

________. "Relations between the State and the Roman Catholic Church in Croatia, Yugoslavia in the 70's and 80's." *Occasional Papers on Religion in Eastern Europe,* vol. 2 (1982), no. 3, pp. 22-33.

Man of God and His People: First Anniversary Commemoration of the Death of Cardinal Stepinac. Cleveland: United American Croatians, 1961.

Mužić, Ivan. *Pavelić i Stepinac.* Split: Logos, 1991.

Nedeljković, Olga. "Two Counter Reformation Views of Eastern Orthodox Slavic Culture. Skarga and Križanić." *Synthesis Philosophica,* vol. 5 (1990), no. 1, pp. 139-160.

O'Brien of Thomond, Anthony Henry. *Archbishop Stepinac: The Man and His Case.* Dublin: The Standard, 1947.

Obrknežević, Miloš. *Development of Orthodoxy in Croatia and the Croatian Orthodox Church.* Barcelona: EGS, 1979.

Okey, R. "Austro-Hungarian Diplomacy and the Campaign for a Slavonic Liturgy in the Catholic Church, 1881-1914." *The Slavonic and East European Review,* vol. 70 (1992), no. 2, pp. 258-283.

Omrčanin, Ivo. *Forced Conversions of Croatians to the Serbian Faith in History.* Washington: Samizdat, 1985. Paper presented to the Third World Congress for Soviet and East European Studies, October 30-Novmber 4, 1985, Washington, D.C.

Ramet, Pedro. "Factionalism in Church-State Interaction: The Croatian Catholic Church in the 1980s." *Slavic Review,* vol. 44 (1985), pp. 298-315.

Raymond, M. *The Man for This Moment. The Life and Death of Aloysius Cardinal Stepinac.* Staten Island, New York: Alba House, 1971.

Sabrina Ramet, Petra. *Balkan Babel: Politics, Culture and Religion in Yugoslavia.* Boulder: Westview Press, 1992.

Sivrić, Ivo. *Bishop J. J. Strossmayer: New Light on Vatican I.* New York: Franciscan Herald Press; Rome: Norval, ZIRAL, 1975.

Slovak, Charles J. "J. J. Strossmayer as a Balkan Bishop." *Balkan Studies,* vol. 18 (1977), no. 1, pp. 121-144.

Thirteen Centuries of Christianity of the Croats: Episcopal Pastoral Letter. Zagreb: n.p., 1976.

Vasilj, Kvirin. *Trinitarian Theories as Judged by Reason: A New Theory.* Translated from Croatian by S.D. Condić. Chicago: ZIRAL, 1987.

Volf, Miroslav. "Exclusion and Embrace: Theological Reflections in the Wake of 'Ethnic Cleansing.'" *Journal of Ecumenical Studies,* vol. 29 (1992), pp. 230-238.

Vrcan, Srđan. "Religion and Irreligion in a Socialist Society: Dilemmas of the Sociological Approach." *Social-Compass,* vol. 19 (1972), no. 2, pp. 245-261.

Zlatar, Zdenko. "Archangel Michael and the Dragon: Slavic Apocrypha, Bogomilism and Dualist Cosmology in the Medieval Balkans." *Encyclopaedia Moderna,* vol. 13 (1992), no. 2, pp. 252-272.

III. ECONOMIC

1. General

Andrljić, Mladen. "The Republic of Croatia." In *La Méditerranée économique. Premier rapport général sur la situation des riverains au début des années 90.* Edited by Ayari, C. et al. Paris: Economica, 1991, pp. 879-909.

________. "The Republic of Croatia." In *Régions et pays Méditerranéens au début des années 90.* Marseille: Centre de Finances Internationales, 1992, pp. 1057-1124.

Anušić, Zoran and Borislav Škegro. "The Economic Outlook for Croatia." LINK Fall Meeting, Ankara, September 14-18, 1992, mimeo.

Barbić, Jakša et al. *Croatian Privatization Fund: Croatian Fund of Privatization Selling the Enterprise and Stocks.* Zagreb: Masmedia, 1993.

"Croatia: Preparing for Peace." *Euromoney,* Supplement May 1992, pp. 1-45.

The Croatian Business Directory '94. Zagreb: Masmedia, 1993.

Čučković, Nevenka (ed.). *Macroeconomic Policy Reform and Private Enterprise in Central and Eastern Europe.* Zagreb: IRMO-ICEG, 1992.

________. "Privatisation in Croatia: What Went Wrong." *History of European Ideas,* vol. 17 (1993), no. 6, pp. 725-735.

________. "Privatization Policy Choice: Is There an Optimal One?" In *Macroeconomic Policy Reform and Private Enterprise in Central and Eastern Europe.* Edited by Nevenka Čučković. Zagreb: IRMO-ICEG, 1992, pp. 40-44.

________. "Privatization Practices in Croatia, Poland, Hungary and Czechoslavakia: Evaluation of Results." In *Macroeconomic Policy Reform and Private Enterprise in Central and Eastern Europe.* Edited by Nevenka Čučković. Zagreb: IRMO-ICEG, 1992, pp. 45-64.

Dubey, Vinod. *Yugoslavia: Development with Decentralization.* Report of a mission sent to Yugoslavia by the World Bank. Baltimore, London: Johns Hopkins University Press, 1975.

Dubravčić, Dinko. "Economic Causes and Political Causes of the Dissolution of a Multinational Federal State." *Communist Economies and Economic Transformation,* vol. 5 (1993), no. 3, pp. 259-272.

________. *The Role of the State in the Processses of Transformation of Social Ownership.* Paper presented at First International Conference on "Restructuring and Privatization of the East-European Economies." Faculty of Economics, Zagreb, 25-26 October 1990.

Dyker, David A. *Yugoslavia: Socialism, Development and Debt.* London, New York: Routledge, 1990.

Estrin, S. *Privatization, Self-Management and Social Ownership.* Paper presented at First International Conference on "Restructuring and Privatization of the East-European Economies." Faculty of Economics, Zagreb, 25-26 October 1990.

Flaherty, D. "Plan, Market und Unequal Regional Development in Yugoslavia." *Soviet Studies,* vol. 40 (1988), no. 1, pp. 100-124.

________. "Self-Management and the Future of Socialism - Lessons from Yugoslavia." *Science and Society,* vol. 56 (1992), no. 1, pp. 92-108.

Gagnon, V.P. "Yugoslavia: Prospects for Stability." *Foreign Affairs,* vol. 70, no. 3 (1991), pp 17-35.

Gapinski, James H. et al. "A Model of Yugoslav Economic Performance." *Journal of Comparative Economics,* vol. 13 (1989), pp. 15-46.

Gelb, Alan H. and Cheryl W. Gray. *The Transformation of Economies in Central and Eastern Europe. Issues, Progress, and Prospects.* Washington: The World Bank, 1991.

Halverson, K. "Privatization in the Yugoslav Republics." *Journal of World Trade,* vol. 26 (1991), no. 6, pp. 43-69.

Hardy, Daniel and Dubravko Mihaljek. "Economic Policymaking in a Federation." *Finance and Development,* vol. 29 (1992), no. 2, pp. 14-17.

Horvat, Branko. *Nationalization, Privatization or Socialization: The Emergence of the Social Corporation.* Paper presented at First International Conference on "Restructuring and Privatization of the East-European Economies." Faculty of Economics, Zagreb, 25-26 October 1990.

________. "Requiem for the Yugoslav Economy. The Politics of Economic Change." *Dissent,* vol. 40 (1993), no. 3, pp. 333-339.

Kalogjera, Dražen. "Privatisation as a World Economic Process." *Razvoj/Development-International,* vol. 6 (1991), no. 2-3, pp. 211-234.

"Law on Transformation of Socially-Owned Enterprises." In Jurković, Pero (ed.). *Investierungen in Kroatien/Investment in Croatia. All Rights and Obligations of Foreign Investors/Ulaganje u Hrvatsku.* Translated into English by Beatrice Mićunović and Jelena Peternal, with a foreword by Franjo Gregurić. Zagreb: Masmedia, 1992, Second edition, pp. 149-161.

Lydall, Harold. *Yugoslavia in Crisis.* Oxford: Clarendon Press, 1989.

Maleković, Sanja and Mario Polić. *Regional Development and the Development of Small and Medium-Sized Enterprises in an Economy in Transition to the Market System.* Report to the Conference: "The Local and International in the Twenty-first Century, the Importance of Collaboration in Networks." Bilbao, February 28 - March 1, 1991. Zagreb: IRMO, 1991, 9 p.

________, Snježana Ivanović and Jagoda Petrić-Kuiš. "Transformation Process in the Countries of Central and Eastern Europe: Selected Bibliography (1987-1991)" *Razvoj/Development-International,* vol. 6, no. 2-3, pp. 409-431.

Milanović, Branko. "Pattern of Regional Growth in Yugoslavia: 1952-83." *Journal of Development Economics,* vol. 25 (1987), no. 1, pp. 1-19.

Miller, R.F. "The Pitfalls of Economic Reform in Yugoslavia." *Australian Journal of International Affairs,* vol. 45 (1991), no. 2, pp. 213-222.

Ottolenghi, Daniel and Alfred Steinherr. "Yugoslavia: Was It a Winner's Curse?" *The Economics of Transition,* vol. 1 (1993), no. 2, pp. 209-244.

Perić, Željko (ed.). *A Business Portrait of Croatia.* Zagreb: Ministry of Foreign Affairs, 1992.

Pitter, Laura and Vince Beiser. "Reforms under Siege." *Business Central Europe,* vol. 1 (1993), no. 4, pp. 22-23.

Salay, Jurgen. "An Economic Survey of Slovenia and Croatia." *EFTA Occasional Papers,* 1992, no. 42, pp. 1-39.

Samardžija, Višnja. "Mediterranean Policy of the EEC." In *1992. Europe and the Mediterranean Countries.* Edited by Yilmaz Ozkan. Ankara: University of Ankara, Center for Mediterranean Studies, 1990, pp. 15-23.

________. *The Role of the European Community in the Economic Transformation of Croatia.* Zagreb: IRMO, 1992, 7 p.

Štajner, Rikard. "The Pacific Experience and Its Lessons." *Razvoj/ Development-International,* vol. 6 (1991), no. 2-3, pp. 235-268.

Staničić, Mladen. "How to Transform the Economies Which Were Devastated by the Voluntaristic Socialism." *Razvoj/Development-International,* vol. 5 (1990), no. 1, pp. 9-68.

Švob-Đokić, Nada. *Characteristics and Trends in Development Research in Croatia/Yugoslavia.* Report to the Conference: "Sustaining Development Research in a Changing Europe: The Need for New Priorities and Resources at National and Supra-

National Levels." Antwerp, November 7-8, 1991. Zagreb: IRMO, 1991, 4 p.

Uvalić, Milica. "The Disintegration of Yugoslavia: Its Costs and Benefits." *Economist Economies and Economic Transformation,* vol. 5 (1993), no. 3, pp. 273-294.

Vujčić, Boris. "Economic Situation in Croatia: Facts and Prospects." Zagreb: Faculty of Economics, 1993, mimeo.

Vukmir, Branko. "Privatization in Croatia. Thematic Issues: Privatization in Reforming Socialist Economies." *Public Enterprise,* vol. 11 (1991), no. 2-3, pp. 163-174.

Young, B. "With Axes in Their Eyes - Rentierism and Market Reform in Yugoslavia." *Studies in Comparative Communism,* vol. 25 (1992), no. 3, pp. 274-286.

Žižmond, E. "The Collapse of the Yugoslav Economy." *Soviet Studies,* vol. 44 (1992), no. 1, pp. 101-112.

2. *Agriculture*

EC Community. *The Current Situation, Evolution and Future Prospects for Agriculture in Yugoslavia.* Luxembourg: Publications EC, 1992.

EC Council. *Council Regulation (EEC) No. 548/92 of 3 February 1992 complementing Regulation (EEC) No. 3587/91 extending into 1992 the application of Regulation (EC) No. 3833/90 applying generalized tariff preferences for 1991 in respect of certain agricultural products originating in developing countries with the view of re-establishing the benefit of these preferences in respect of the Republics of Croatia and Slovenia and the Yugoslav Republics of Bosnia-Hercegovina, Macedonia and Montenegro.* OJL63/7.03.1992.

Hoffler, A. "Efficiency in Social versus Private Agricultural Production - The Case of Yugoslavia." *Review of Economics and Statistics*, vol. 75 (1993), no. 1, pp. 153-157.

3. Finance, Credit and Banking

Koveos, Peter E. et al. *Financial Analysis of Firms: Selected Topics.* Syracuse, New York: School of Management, Syracuse University; Zagreb: School of Management, 1992. New Emerging Market Economies Series.

Kraft, E. and M. Vodopivec. "How Soft Is the Budget Constraint for Yugoslav Firms." *Journal of Comparative Economics,* vol. 16 (1992), no. 3, pp. 432-455.

Lahiri, A.K. "Money and Inflation in Yugoslavia." *International Monetary Fund Staff Papers,* vol. 38 (1991), no. 4, pp. 751-788.

Mates, Neven. "Measurement of Government Budget Deficit, Losses of Central Banks and the Impact of Aggregate Deficit of the Public Sector on Inflation." *Economic Analysis and Workers' Management,* vol. 25 (1991), no. 3, pp. 197-232.

Schönfelder, Bruno. "Croatia between Reform and Post-Communist Populism." *Communist Economies and Economic Transformation,* vol. 5 (1993), no. 3, pp. 317-330.

Woodward, Susan L. "Reforming a Socialist State. Ideology and Public Finance in Yugoslavia." *World Politics,* vol. 41 (1989), pp. 266-305.

4. Foreign Aid, Trade and Investment

Andrlić, Mladen. "Export Orientation and Market Transformation of the Croatian Economy." *Razvoj/Development-International,* vol. 6 (1991), no. 2-3, pp. 269-281.

Bombelles, J.T. "Federal Aid to the Less Developed Areas of Yugoslavia." *East European Politics and Societies,* vol. 5 (1991), no. 3, pp. 439-465.

EC Commission. *Commission Regulation (EEC) No. 343/92 of 22 January 1992 on the definition of the concept of originating products and methods of administrative cooperation applicable to imports into the Community of products originating in the Republics of Croatia and Slovenia and the Yugoslav Republics of Bosnia-Hercegovina and Macedonia.* OJL38/14.02.1992.

________. *Commission Regulation (EEC) No. 3660/2 of 18 December 1992 amending Regulations (EEC) No. 693/88, (EEC) No. 809/88 and (EEC) No. 343/92 on the definition of the concept of originating products and methods of administrative cooperation with regard to imports into the Community of products originating in developing countries, in the Occupied Territories and in the Republics of Bosnia-Herzegovina, Croatia and Slovenia and the former Republic of Macedonia.* OJL370/19.12. 1992.

________. *Proposal for a Council Regulation (EEC) amending Council Regulation (EEC) No. 545/92 of 3 February 1992 concerning the arrangements applicable to imports into the Community of products originating in the Republics of Bosnia-Hercegovina, Croatia and Slovenia and the Yugoslav Republic of Macedonia.* COM/92/393/Fin, 14/09/1992.

EC Council. *Council Regulation (EEC) amending Council Regulation (EEC) No. 547/92 of 3 February 1992 opening and providing for the administration of Community tariff quotas for certain products originating in the Republics of Croatia and Slovenia and the Yugoslav Republics of Bosnia-Hercegovina, Macedonia and Montenegro.* OJL63/7.03.1992.

________. *Council Regulation (EEC) No. 3567/91 of 2 December 1991 concerning the arrangements applicable to the import of products originating in the Republics of Bosnia-Hercegovina, Croatia, Macedonia and Slovenia.* OJL342/12.12.1991.

________. *Council Regulation (EEC) No. 3953/92 of 21 December 1992 concerning the arrangements applicable to the import into the community of products originating in the Republics of Bosnia-Herzegovina, Croatia and Slovenia and the territory of the former Republic of Macedonia.* OJL400/31.12.1992.

________. *Decision of the representatives of the governments of the member states, meeting within the Council of 3 February 1992, concerning the arrangements applicable to the import into the community of products covered by the ECSC Treaty and originating in the Republics of Croatia and Slovenia and the Yugoslav Republics of Bosnia-Hercegovina, Macedonia and Montenegro.* OJL63/7.03.1992.

________. *Protocols to the EEC-Yugoslavia Cooperation Agreement and other basic texts.* Luxembourg: Publications EC, 1992.

EC Representatives of the Governments of Member States. *Decision of the Representatives of the Governments of the Member States, meeting within the Council, of 21 December 1992, concerning the arrangements applicable to the import into the Community of products covered by the ECSC Treaty and originating in the Republics of Bosnia-Herzegovina, Croatia, Slovenia and in the territory of the former Yugoslav Republic of Macedonia.* OJL406/31.12.1992.

European Parliament. *Legislative Regulation (EEC) embodying the opinion of the European Parliament on the Commission Proposal for a Council Regulation (EEC) amending Regulation No. 3906/89 in order to extend economic aid to include Croatia and Slovenia.* OJC241/21.9.1992.

________. *Report by the Committee on External Economic Relations on the Commission Proposal for a Council Regulation (EEC) amending Regulation (EEC) No. 3906/89 in order to extend economic aid to include Croatia and Slovenia.* COM/92/156 Fin.

"Foreign Investment in Croatia." *Central European* (London), September 1993, no. 25, pp. 50-61.

Jurković, Pero (ed.). *Investierungen in Kroatien/Investment in Croatia. All Rights and Obligations of Foreign Investors/Ulaganje u Hrvatsku.* Translated into English by Beatrice Mićunović and Jelena Peternel, with a foreword by Franjo Gregurić. Zagreb: Masmedia, 1992 (Second Edition).

Štajner, Rikard. "On the Issues of Comparative Advantages and on the Policy of Cooperation with Developing Countries." *Razvoj/Development-International,* vol. 5 (1990), no. 1, pp. 163-164.

Staničić, Mladen. *European Integration and Structural Changes in the World Economy. Report to the Conference:* "VI. Generalna konferencija EADI-a. Oslo, June 1990." Zagreb: IRMO, 1990.

________. "On Economic Interests for Cooperation with the Developing Countries." *Razvoj/Development-International,* vol. 5 (1990), no. 1, pp. 162-163.

Tomašić, Vjekoslav. "The Effects of Foreign Direct Investments on the Balance of Payments in Industrial Ventures in SR Croatia." *Economic Analysis and Workers' Management,* vol. 18, no. 4 (1984), pp. 333-341.

5. Mining, Industry, Commerce and Communication

Bićanić, I. and M. Škreb. "Measurement of the Private Sector's Contribution. Country Study: Yugoslavia." Part of the World Bank Project: Accounting for CPEs in Transition: System-Related Issues in Measuring Economic Performance, 1991, mimeo.

Dubravčić, Dinko and Željka Kordelj-De Villa. "A Note on Adjustment Processes in Croatian Industry during the Eighties." *Economic Analysis and Workers' Management,* vol. 25 (1991), no. 3, pp. 311-321.

Gapinski, J.H. "Sectoral Inflation in Yugoslavia." *Journal of Developing Areas,* vol. 27 (1992), no. 1, pp. 33-48.

How to Do Business with Croatia? Basic Information on Croatian Economy, Activities of the Croatian Chamber of Commerce, and Digest Regulations Governing Foreign Investments and Economic Regulations with Foreign Countries. Zagreb: Croatian Chamber of Commerce, 1992.

Škreb, Marko. "Business Interest Associations in Croatia." Paper Prepared for the Conference on Business Interest Associations in Eastern Europe and Russia, Warwick, September 11-12, 1992, mimeo.

Svarc, J. "An Empirical Analysis of the Utilization of Sti in the Industry of Croatia. A Marketing Approach." *Journal of Information Science,* vol. 17 (1991), no. 6, pp. 373-383.

Vodopivec, M. "Determination of Earnings in Yugoslav Firms - Can It be Squared with Labor Management?" *Economic Development and Cultural Change,* vol. 41 (1993), no. 3, pp. 623-632.

Vujčić, Boris. "Growth of Service Sector Employment in Croatia." Zagreb: Faculty of Economics, 1992, mimeo.

________. "Some Supply-side Determinants of Rising Female Employment in Croatia." *Economic Analysis and Workers' Management,* vol. 25 (1991), no. 3, pp. 233-248.

IV. HISTORIC

1. General

Banac, Ivo. "Historiography of the Countries of Eastern Europe. Yugoslavia." *The American Historical Review,* vol. 97 (1992), no. 4, pp. 1084-1104.

________. *The National Question in Yugoslavia. Origins, History, Politics.* Ithaca, New York: Cornell University Press, 1984.

Bonifačić, Antun F. and Clement S. Mihanovich (eds.). *The Croatian Nation in Its Struggle for Freedom and Independence.* A Symposium by Seventeen Croatian Writers. Chicago, Illinois: Croatia Cultural Publishing Center, 1955.

Castellan, Georges. *History of the Balkans. From Mohammed the Conqueror to Stalin.* Boulder, Colorado: East European Monographs, no. 325, 1992. Distributed By Columbia University Press, New York.

Cesarich, George. *Croatia and Serbia. Why Is Their Peaceful Separation a European Necessity?* Chicago, Illinois: Croatia Cultural Publishing Center, 1954.

Darby, Henry C. "Croatia." In *A Short History of Yugoslavia from Early Times to 1966.* Edited by Stephen Clissold. Cambridge: Cambridge University Press, 1966.

Dedijer, Vladimir et al. *History of Yugoslavia.* Translated by Kordija Kveder. New York: McGraw-Hill, 1974.

Enciklopedia Hrvatske Povijesti i Kulture. Zagreb: Školska Knjiga, 1980.

Gaži, Stjepan. *A History of Croatia.* New York: Philosophical Library, 1973.

Hefer, Stjepan. *Croatian Struggle for Freedom and Statehood.* Buenos Aires: Croatian Information Service, 1956.

Historical Maps of Croatia from the Penguin Atlas of World History. Zagreb: Croatian Information Centre, 1993.

Knežević, Antun. *A Short History of the Croatian Nation.* Translated by Rudolph J. Hraščanec. Philadelphia: Croatian Catholic Union, Lodge "Croatia," 1983.

Kostelski, Z. *The Croats.* Floreffe, Pennsylvania: Kolo, 1950.

Macan, Trpimir. *Povijest Hrvatskog Naroda. (*History of the Croats.) Zagreb: Nakladni Zavod Matice Hrvatske - Školska Knjiga, 1992.

Macan, Trpimir and Josip Šentija, with an introduction by Ivo Banac. *A Short History of Croatia.* Zagreb: Special Edition, Most/The Bridge - Journal of Croatian Literature, 1992.

Omrčanin, Ivo. *Diplomatic and Political History of Croatia.* Philadelphia, Pennsylvania: Dorrance, 1972.

________. *Holocaust of Croatians.* Washington: Samizdat, 1986.

________. *Military History of Croatia.* Philadelphia: Dorrance, 1984.

________. *Sacred Crown of the Kingdom of Croatia.* Philadelphia: Dorrance, 1976.

Pandžić, Basil and Stephen Pandžić. *A Review of Croatian History.* Chicago: Croatia, 1954.

Pavlowitch, Stevan K. *Yugoslavia.* New York, Washington: Praeger, 1971.

Preveden, Francis R. *A History of the Croatian People.* New York: Philosophical Library, 1955-1962.

Pušić, Eugen. "The Objectivity of the Historical Process." *Croatian Political Science Review,* vol. 1 (1992), no. 1, pp. 10-19.

Seton-Watson, Hugh. *Nations and States. An Enquiry into the Origins of Nations and the Politics of Nationalism.* London: Methuen, 1977.

Singleton, Fred. *A Short History of the Yugoslav Peoples.* New York: New York University Press, 1985.

Šišić, Ferdo. *Pregled Povijesti Hrvatskog Naroda.* (Review of the History of the Croats.) Zagreb: Matica hrvatska, 1962.

Šuljak, Dinko N. *Croatia's Struggle for Independence: A Documentary History*. Arcadia, California: Croatian Information Service, 1977.

Vitez, Vladimir. *History of the Croatian Coast*. Melbourne, Australia: Richmond, 1970.

_______. *In the Defence of Justice: An Answer to Dr. J. Cairns*. Melbourne: Richmond, 1970.

Vujica, Stanko M. *Croatia's Struggle for Independence*. New York: Croatian National Council in Exile, 1965.

Zdunić, Drago (ed.). *Croatia*. Zagreb: Spektar, 1974.

2. *Archeology*

Bezeczky, Tamás. *Roman Amphorae from the Amber Route in Western Pannonia*. Osney Mead, Oxford: BAR, 1987.

Chapman, J.C. (ed.). *Recent Developments in Yugoslav Archaeology*. Osney Mead, Oxford: BAR, 1988.

_______ and Johannes Muller. "Early Farmers in the Mediterranean Basin: The Dalmatian Evidence." *Antiquity,* vol. 64 (1990), March, pp. 127-134.

_______ et al. "New Absolute Dates for Prehistoric and Roman Dalmatia." *Vjesnik za Arheologiju i Historiju dalmatinsku,* vol. 83 (1990), pp. 29-46.

"Crisis in Yugoslavia." *Archaeology*, vol. 45 (1992), no. 2, pp. 20-21.

Evans, M.A. *The Early Medieval Archaeology of Croatia A.D. 600-900.* Osney Mead, Oxford: BAR, 1989.

3. Settlement of the Croats and the Early Kingdoms

Barada, M. "The Social Structure of Vinodol." *British-Croatian Review,* 1978, no. 14, pp. 12-24.

Constantine Porphyrogenitus. *De Administrando Imperio.* Greek and English, translated by R.J.H. Jenkins, edited by G. Moravczik. Budapest, 1949.

Ferjančić, Božidar. *Bizantiski izvori za istoriju naroda Jugoslavije.* (Byzantine Sources on the History of Yugoslavia.) Vol. II. Belgrade: Naučno Delo, 1959.

Fine, John V.A. *The Early Medieval Balkans: A Critical Survey from the Sixth to the Twelfth Century.* Ann Arbor: University of Michigan Press, 1983.

Guldescu, Stanko. *History of Medieval Croatia.* The Hague: Mouton, 1964.

Matijević-Sokol, Mirjana (ed.). *Branimirova Hrvatska u Pismima Pape Ivana VIII/Branimir's Croatia in the Letters of Pope John VIII.* Translated by Karmela Vlahović, foreword by Mate Zekan. Split: Književni Krug, 1990 (Second Edition).

Ostrogorski, Georgije. *Bizantiski izvori za istoriju naroda Jugoslavije.* (Byzantine Sources on the History of Yugoslavia.) Vol. I. Belgrade: Naućno Delo, 1955.

Pivčević, Edo (ed.). *The Cartulary of the Benedictine Abbey of St. Peter of Gumay (Croatia) 1080-1187.* Bristol: David Arthur and Sons, 1984.

________. *Two Medieval Croatian Statutes.* Bristol: BC Review Publications, 1978.

"The Statute of Polica." Translated by Alan Ferguson. *British-Croatian Review,* 1977, no. 11-12.

"The Statute of Vinodol." Translated by Alan Ferguson. *British-Croatian Review,* 1978, no. 14.

4. Under Hungary and Habsburgs

Aleksić, Lucija. *Vlaho Bukovac (1855-1922).* Translated by Maja Šoljan. Zagreb: Exhibition: Special Edition of the Croatian P.E.N. Center in cooperation with Matica hrvatska for the 59th P.E.N. World Congress, 1993.

Bakisian, Nina. "An Unrealized Reality: Some Views on Danubian Federation." *Balkan Studies,* vol. 33 (1992), pp. 99-110.

Baletić, Zvonimir. "Križanić between Russia and Europe." *International Social Science Review,* vol. 62 (1987), no. 4, pp. 147-150.

Bracewell, Catherine Wendy. *The Uskoks of Senj. Piracy, Banditry and Holy War in the Sixteenth Century Adriatic.* Ithaca: Cornell University Press, 1992.

Fine, John V.A. *The Late Medieval Balkans: A Critical Survey from the Late Twelfth Century to the Ottoman Conquest.* Ann Arbor: University of Michigan Press, 1987.

Guldescu, Stanko. *The Croatian-Slavonian Kingdom 1526-1792.* The Hague: Mouton, 1970.

Jaszi, Oscar. "Croatia versus Hungary." In *The Dissolution of the Habsburg Monarchy.* Chicago: University of Chicago Press, 1961.

Jelavich, Barbara. *History of the Balkans.* Cambridge: Cambridge University Press, 1983.

Kann, Robert A. *The Multinational Empire. Nationalism and National Reform in the Habsburg Monarchy, 1848-1918.* New York: Columbia University Press, 1950.

Longworth, Philip. "The Senj Uskoks Reconsidered." *Slavonic and East European Review,* vol. 57 (1979), no. 3, pp. 348-368.

Prlender, Ivica. *All the Sieges of Dubrovnik/Sve Opsade Dubrovnika.* Zagreb: Special Edition of the Croatian P.E.N. Center in cooperation with Matica hrvatska for the 59th P.E.N. World Congress, 1993.

Rothenberg, Gunther E. "The Croatian Military Border and the Rise of Yugoslav Nationalism." *Slavonic and East European Review,* vol. 43 (1964), no. 100, pp. 34-45.

Sondhaus, L. "Croatians in the Habsburg Navy, 1797-1918." *East European Quarterly,* vol. 26 (1992), no. 2, pp. 149-161.

Sugar, Peter F. *Industrialization of Bosnia-Hercegovina, 1878-1918.* Seattle: University of Washington Press, 1963.

Vasiliev, A.A. *History of the Byzantine Empire 324-1453.* Madison, Milwaukee: University of Wisconsin Press, 1964.

Walters, Eurof. "Aehrenthals Attempt in 1907 to Re-group the European Powers." *Slavonic and East European Review,* vol. 30 (1951), no. 74, pp. 213-251.

Zlatar, Zdenko. *Between the Double Eagle and the Crescent.* New York: Columbia University Press, 1992. East European Monographs 348.

________. *Our Kingdom Come. The Counter-Reformation, the Republic of Dubrovnik, and the Liberation of the Balkan Slavs.* New York: Columbia University Press, 1992. East European Monographs 342.

5. First World War and Creation of Yugoslavia

Banac, Ivo. "Emperor Karl Has Become a Comitadji: The Croatian Disturbances of Autumn 1918." *Slavonic and East European Review,* vol. 70 (1992), no. 2, pp. 284-305.

Barac, Franjo. *Croats and Slovenes Friends of the Entente in the World War.* Paris: South Slav Committee, 1919.

Dragnich, Alex N. *Serbs and Croats. The Struggle in Yugoslavia.* San Diego: Harcourt Brace, 1992.

Gow, J. "Deconstructing Yugoslavia." *Survival,* vol. 33 (1991), July-August, pp. 291-311.

Jelavich, Charles and Barbara Jelavich. *The Establishment of the Balkan National States, 1804-1920.* Seattle: University of Washington Press, 1977.

Karakostanoglou, Veniamin. "The Right to Self-determination and the Case of Yugoslavia." *Balkan Studies,* vol. 32 (1991), pp. 335-362.

Lederer, Ivo J. *Yugoslavia at the Paris Peace Conference. A Study in Frontiermaking.* New Haven, Connecticut, London: Yale University Press, 1963.

Sovera-Latuada, G. "Giuseppe Sovera-Latuada's Role in the Inception of d'Annunzio's Raid on Fiume." *Modern Language Review,* vol. 87 (1992), no. 2, pp. 335-341.

Taylor, A.H.E. *The Future of the Southern Slavs.* London: Fisher, 1917.

Trifković, S. "The 1st Yugoslavia and Origins of Croatian Separatism." *East European Quarterly,* vol. 26 (1992), no. 3, pp. 345-370.

Živojinović, Dragan R. *America, Italy and the Birth of Yugoslavia (1917-1919).* Boulder, Colorado: East European Monographs, 1972.

6. Between the Two World Wars

Dragnich, Alex N. *The First Yugoslavia: Search for a Viable Political System.* Stanford, California: Hoover Institution Press, 1983.

Đuretić, Veselin. *Razaranje Srpstva u XX-Veku. Ideološka Upotreba Istorije.* (The Demolition of Serbianism in the XXth Century. The Ideological Use of History.) Belgrade: Srpska Akademija Nauka i Umetnosti, 1992.

Good, Marie Sapowitch. "International Diplomacy and the Perception of the Croatian Problem: 1921-1924." Buffalo: State University of New York, 1978. PhD Thesis.

Graham, Stephen. *Alexander of Yugoslavia. The Story of the King Who Was Murdered at Marseilles.* New Haven: Yale University Press, 1939.

Ivanović, Vane. *LX: Memoirs of a Yugoslav.* New York: Harcourt Brace, 1977.

Kerner, Robert Joseph and Harry Nicolas Howard. *The Balkan Conferences and the Balkan Entente 1930-1935: A Study in the Recent History of the Balkan and Near Eastern Peoples.* Berkeley, California: University of California Press, 1936.

Macadams, C. Michael. *Allied Prisoners of War in Croatia 1941-1945.* Arcadia: Croatian Information Service, 1980.

Maček, Vladko. *In the Struggle for Freedom.* Translated by Elizabeth and Stjepan Gaži. University Park: Pennsylvania State University Press, 1957. Reprinted 1968.

Sadkovich, James J. *Italian Support for Croatian Separatism, 1927-37.* New York: Garland, 1987.

Šentija, Josip. *Croatia from 1941 to 1991.* Zagreb: Ministry of Information, 1992 (Second Edition).

Seton-Watson, Hugh. *Eastern Europe between the Wars 1918-1941.* Cambridge: Cambridge University Press, 1946.

Sraka, Anthony Mirko. "'Peasant Concord' between the Wars: An Examination of the Cultural Wing of the Croatian Peasant Party with Special Reference to the 1920s." Montreal: McGill University, 1992. Thesis.

Vrbanić, George Franz. *The Failure to Save the First Yugoslavia: The Serbo-Croatian Sporazum of 1939.* Chicago: ZIRAL, 1991.

7. Second World War

Boban, Ljubo. "Jasenovac and the Manipulation of History." *East European Politics and Societies,* vol. 4 (1990), no. 3, pp. 580-592.

________. "Still More Balance on Jasenovac and the Manipulation of History." *East European Politics and Societies,* vol. 6 (1992), no. 4, pp. 213-217.

Bulajić, Milan. *Tuđman's "Jasenovac Myth". Ustaša Crimes of Genocide.* Belgrade: Ministry of Information of the Republic of Serbia, 1992.

Deroc, M. *British Special Operations Explored: Yugoslavia in Turmoil 1941-1943 and the British Response.* Boulder, Colorado: East European Monographs; New York: Columbia University Press, 1988.

Garcia, Eduardo Augusto. *La tragedia de Bleiburg: documentos sobre las matanzas en masa de los Croatas en Yugoeslavia comunista en 1945.* Buenos Aires: Studia Croatica, 1963.

Hayden, Robert M. "Balancing Discussion of Jasenovac and the Manipulation of History." *East European Politics and Societies,* vol. 6 (1992), no. 4, pp. 207-212.

________. "Recounting the Dead: The Rediscovery and Redefinition of Wartime Massacres in the Late- and Post-Communist Yugoslavia." In *Memory and Opposition under State Socialism.* Edited by Rubie S. Watson. Santa Fe, New Mexico: School of American Research, 1993.

Hećimović, Josip. *In Tito's Death Marches.* Translated by John Prcela. Chicago: Croatian Franciscan Press, 1961.

Irvine, Jill A. *The Croat Question. Partisan Politics in the Formation of the Yugoslav Socialist State.* With a foreword by Ivo Banac. Boulder, Colorado: Westview Press, 1992.

________. "Tito, Hebrang and the Croat Question, 1943-1944." *East European Politics and Societies,* vol. 5 (1991), no. 2, pp. 306-340.

Italian Genocide Policy against the Slovenes and Croats: A Selection of Documents. Belgrade: International Politics and Economics, 1954.

Kaplan, Robert D. *Balkan Ghosts. A Journey through History.* New York: St. Martin's Press, 1993.

Kljakić, Slobodan. *A Conspiracy of Silence: Genocide in the Independent State of Croatia and Concentration Camp Jasenovac.* Belgrade: Nebojsa Jerković, 1991.

Pavlowitch, Steven K. *Unconventional Perceptions of Yugoslavia 1940-1945.* Boulder, Colorado: East European Monographs, 1985.

Peter II. *A King's Heritage: The Memoirs of King Peter II of Yugoslavia.* London: Cassell, 1955.

Petrović, Rastislav. *The Extermination of Serbs on the Territory of the Independent State of Croatia.* Belgrade: Nebojsa Jerković, 1991.

Supek, Ivan. *Crown Witness against Hebrang: A History of the Time and a Biographical Novel of One Man's Journey to the Promised Jugoslav Utopia: A Docu-Novel.* Translated by N.N. Gill. Chicago: Markanton Press, 1983.

The War Diaries of Vladimir Dedijer. Ann Arbor: University of Michigan Press, 1990.

Wheeler, Mark. "White Eagles and White Guards: British Perceptions of Anti-Communist Insurgency in Yugoslavia in 1945." *Slavonic and East European Review,* vol. 66 (1988), July, pp. 46-61.

Whittam, J.R. "Drawing the Line: Britain and the Emergence of the Trieste Question, January 1941-May 1945." *English Historical Review,* vol. 106 (1991), April, pp. 346-370.

8. Communist Regime

Allcock, John B, John J. Horton and Marko Milivojević (eds.). *Yugoslavia in Transition: Choices and Constraints. Essays in Honour of Fred Singleton.* New York: Berg, 1992.

Bakarić, Vladimir. *Theoretical Foundations of Social Reproduction in Socialism.* Belgrade: Socialist Thought and Practice, 1975.

Banac, Ivo. *With Stalin against Tito: Cominformist Splits in Yugoslav Communism.* Ithaca, New York: Cornell University Press, 1988.

Bilandžić, Dušan. "Key Factors in the 'Memorandum' of 1986. The Document of the Serbian Academy of Arts and Sciences - SANU." *Gaudeamus,* 1991, Fall, no. 4, pp. 19-21.

Blum, Robert M. "Surprised by Tito: The Anatomy of an Intelligence Failure." *Diplomatic History,* vol. 12 (1988), Winter, pp. 39-57.

Bose, S. "Yugoslavia. Crisis of the Titoist State." *Economic and Political Weekly,* vol. 27 (1992), no. 18, pp. 938-941.

Botić, Ivan and Stjepan Djureković. *Yugoslavia in Crisis. The Political and Economic Dimensions.* New York: Croatian National Congress, 1983.

Campbell, J.C. "Nationalism and Federalism in Yugoslavia, 1962-1991, 2d Edition, by S.P. Ramet." *American Historical Review,* vol. 98 (1993), no. 3, pp. 907-908.

Cichock, Mark A. "The Soviet Union and Yugoslavia in the 1980s: A Relationship in Flux." *Political Science Quarterly,* vol. 105 (1990), no. 1, pp. 53-74.

Cohen, Lenard J. *The Socialist Pyramid: Elites and Power in Yugoslavia.* Oakville, Ontario: Mosaic Press, 1989.

Cuvalo, Ante. *The Croatian National Movement 1966-1972.* New York: Columbia University Press, 1990.

Cviić, Christopher. "Tito's Land, Tito's Legacy: Myths and Counter-Myths (review article)." *Encounter,* vol. 66 (1986), April, pp. 53-59.

Denitch, Bogdan. *The Crisis of Yugoslav Socialism and State Socialist Systems.* Minneapolis: University of Minnesota Press, 1990.

Đilas, Aleksa. *The Contested Country: Yugoslav Unity and Communist Revolution, 1919-1953.* Cambridge, Massachusetts: Harvard University Press, 1991.

Dragnich, Alex N. "The Anatomy of a Myth: Serbian Hegemony." *Slavic Review*, vol. 50 (1991), Fall, pp. 659-671.

Ferfila, Bogomil. "Yugoslavia: Confederation or Disintegration?" *Problems of Communism,* vol. 40 (1991), July-August, pp. 18-30.

Floyd, David. "On Failing to Get Along with the Russians: Yugoslav Testimony." *Encounter,* vol. 66 (1986), March, pp. 69-72.

Gow, James. *Legitimacy and the Military. The Yugoslav Crisis.* London: Pinter, 1992.

________. *Yugoslav Endgames: Civil Strife and Inner-State Conflict.* London: Brassey's for the Centre of Defence Studies, 1991.

Hayden, Robert M. *The Beginning of the End of Federal Yugoslavia: The Slovenian Amendment Crisis of 1989.* Pittsburgh: Center for Russian and East European Studies, University of Pittsburgh, 1992. Carl Beck Papers in Russian and East European Studies, no. 1001.

Horvat, Branko et al. *Self-Governing Socialism.* New York: International Arts and Sciences Press, 1975.

Katich, Boris. *So Speak Croatian Dissidents.* Toronto: ZIRAL, 1983.

Kostunica, Vojislav and Kosta Čavoški. *Party Pluralism or Monism: Social Movements and the Political System in Yugoslavia 1944-49.* Boulder, Colorado: Social Science Monographs, 1985.

Lajtman, Ivo (ed.). *War Crimes against Croatia.* Zagreb: Večerni List, 1991.

Lane, Ann J. "Putting Britain Right with Tito: The Displaced Persons Question in Anglo-Yugoslav Relations 1946-47." *European History Quarterly,* vol. 22 (1992), April, pp. 217-246.

Maclean, Fitzroy. *Josip Broz Tito. A Pictorial Biography.* Maidenhead, England: McGraw-Hill, 1980.

Meier, Viktor. "Yugoslavia's National Question." *Problems of Communism,* March-April 1983, pp. 47-60.

Mičunović, Vukašin et al. *Handbook on Yugoslavia.* Translated by Margot and Boško Milosavljević. Belgrade: Federal Secretariat for Information - NIRO Export Press, 1987.

Miller, R.F. "Theoretical and Ideological Issues of Reform in Socialist Systems: Some Yugoslav and Soviet Examples." *Soviet Studies,* vol. 41 (1989), no. 3, pp. 430-448.

Nakarada, R. "The Mystery of Nationalism - The Paramount Case of Yugoslavia." *Millennium-Journal of International Studies,* vol. 20 (1991), no. 3, pp. 369-382.

Naked Island = Goli Otok: Part of Yugoslav Gulag. Toronto: Croatian Information Agency, 1978.

Pavlović, S.K. *Yugoslavia's Great Dictator. Tito. A Reassessment.* London: Hearst and Co., 1992.

Pederin, Ivan. "The Collapse of Yugoslav Communism. On the Background to the Present Crisis." *Planet. The Welsh Internationalist,* October/November 1991, pp. 9-17.

Perlman, F. *Revolt in Socialist Yugoslavia. June 1968.* Detroit, Michigan: Black and Red, 1973. (First printed as *Birth of a Revolutionary Movement in Yugoslavia,* 1969.)

Plestina, Dijana. *Regional Development in Communist Yugoslavia: Success, Failure and Consequences.* Boulder, Colorado: Westview Press, 1993.

Sabrina Ramet, P. *Nationalism and Federalism in Yugoslavia, 1962-1991.* Bloomington, Indiana: Indiana University Press, 1992 (Second Enlarged Edition).

Schopflin, George. "Power, Ethnicity and Communism in Yugoslavia (A chapter from the forthcoming book on Nationalism)." *New Hungarian Quarterly,* vol. 33 (1992), no. 128, pp. 3-32.

Sekulić, Duško. "Nationalism versus Democracy: Legacies of Marxism." *International Journal of Politics, Culture and Society,* vol. 6 (1992), no. 1, pp. 113-132.

Seroka, J. "Nationalism and the New Political Compact in Yugoslavia." *History of European Ideas,* vol. 15 (1992), no. 4-6, pp. 577-581.

Shoup, Paul. *Communism and the Yugoslav National Question.* New York: Columbia University Press, 1968.

Sudar, Drago. *Coming of Age in Tito's Prisons.* Translated by Tihomil Milas. Los Angeles: Mosor, 1987.

Tuđman, Franjo. *Croatia on Trial.* London: United Publishers, 1981.

________. *Croatia on Trial: The Case of the Croatian Historian Dr. F. Tuđman.* Translated by Zdenka Palić-Kušan. London: United Publishers, 1981.

________. *Nationalism in Contemporary Europe.* New York: Columbia University Press, 1981.

Vanek, Jarovlav. *Self-management: Economic Liberation of Man. Selected Readings.* Harmondsworth: Penguin, 1975.

Veselica, Marko. *The Croatian National Question - Yugoslavia's Achilles' Heel.* London: United Publishers, 1981.

Yavuz, M.H. "Nationalism and Federalism in Yugoslavia, 1962-1991, by S.P. Ramet." *Millennium. Journal of International Studies,* vol. 22 (1993), no. 1, pp. 115-117.

9. War and New Regime

Altmann, Franz-Lothar. "Ex-Yugoslavia's Neighbours: Who Wants What?" *World Today,* vol. 48 (1992), no. 8-9, pp. 163-165.

Antić, Ljubomir and Franjo Letić. *Serbian Terrorism and Violence in Croatia 1990-1991.* Zagreb: Ministry of Information, 1992.

Arato, Andrew and Seyla Benhabib. "The Yugoslav Tragedy." *Praxis International,* vol. 13 (1994), no. 4, pp. 325-331.

Banac, Ivo. "The Fearful Asymmetry of War: The Causes and Consequences of Yugoslavia's Demise." *Daedalus,* vol. 121 (1992), pp. 141-172.

Beljo, Ante et al. (eds.). *Greater Serbia: From Ideology to Aggression. Croatia in Yugoslavia 1918-1991.* Zagreb: Croatian Information Center, 1993.

Bilandžić, Dušan et al. *Croatia between War and Independence.* Zagreb: Zagreb University and OKC Zagreb, 1991 (Second Edition).

Breakdown: War and Reconstruction in Yugoslavia. London: Yugofax - War Report and the Helsinki Citizens Assembly, 1992.

Buj, Lorenzo. "Yugoslavia and the Press." *Artforum*, vol. 30 (1992), May, pp. 84-85.

Cohen, L.J. "The Disintegration of Yugoslavia." *Current History,* vol. 91 (1992), no. 568, pp. 369-375.

"Croat Cleansing." *New Statesman and Society,* vol. 6 (1993), no. 252, p. 6.

Cviić, Chris. *Remaking the Balkans.* London: Pinter, Chatham House Papers, 1991.

Denitch, Bogdan. "Reform and Conflict in Yugoslavia." *Dissent,* vol. 37 (1990), no. 2, pp. 151-153.

Doder, Duško. "Yugoslavia: New War, Old Hatreds." *Foreign Policy,* Summer 1993, pp. 3-23.

Dragnich, Alex N. "The Anatomy of a Myth: Serbian Hegemony." *Slavic Review,* vol. 50 (1991), pp. 659-671.

Foretić, Mijenko (ed.). *Dubrovnik in War.* Dubrovnik: Matica hrvatska, 1993.

Glenny, Misha. *The Fall of Yugoslavia. The Third Balkan War.* Harmondsworth: Penguin, 1992.

Golubović, Zagorka. "The Conditions Leading to the Breakdown of the Yugoslav State: What Has Generated the Civil War in Yugoslavia?" *Praxis International,* vol. 12 (1992), no. 2, pp. 129-144.

Gow, J. "The Use of Coercion in the Yugoslav Crisis." *World Today,* vol. 48, no. 11, pp. 198-202.

Grmek, Mirko, Marc Gjidara and Neven Šimac. *Le Nettoyage Ethnique.* Paris: Fayard, 1993.

Hayden, Robert M. "Yugoslavia's Collapse. National Suicide with Foreign Assistance." *Economic and Political Weekly,* vol. 27 (1992), no. 27, pp. 1377-1382.

James, Alan. "The UN in Croatia: An Exercise in Futility?" *World Today,* vol. 49 (1993), no. 5, pp. 93-96.

Jegen, Mary Evelin. "In the Shelter of Each Other." *Parabola,* vol. 18 (1993), Fall, pp. 54-58.

Kaldor, Mary. "Yugoslavia and the New Nationalism." *New Left Review,* 1993, January-February, no. 197, pp. 96-112.

Kaplan, R.D. "The Latest Balkan Ugliness - Croatianism." *New Republic,* 1991, vol. 205 (1991), no. 22, p. 16.

Kasriel, K. "A Little Bit Pregnant (the Media at War in Croatia)." *Index on Censorship,* vol. 22 (1993), no. 2, pp. 18-19.

Katz, Lee Michael. "Danger Zone." *Quill,* vol. 80 (1992), October, pp. 46-47.

Kearns, Ian. "Croatia: The Politics behind the War." *World Today,* vol. 49, no. 4, pp. 62-64.

Kirka, Danica. "Caught in the Crossfire." *Columbia Journalism Review,* vol. 30 (1992), January-February, pp. 10-12.

Knežević, Anto. *An Analysis of Serbian Propaganda. The Misrepresentation of the Writings of the Historian Franjo Tuđman in Light of the Serbian-Croatian War.* Zagreb: Domovina TT, 1992.

Kostović, Ivica and Milos Judaš (eds.). *Mass Killing and Genocide in Croatia 1991/92: A Book of Evidence (Based upon the Evidence of the Division of Information, the Ministry of Health of the Republic of Croatia).* Zagreb: Hrvatska Sveučilišna Naklada, 1992.

Magas, Branka. *The Destruction of Yugoslavia: Tracking the Break-Up 1980-1992.* London, New York: Vaso, 1993.

Marković, A. "War in Croatia. A Visit to Lipik." *Collegium Antropologicum,* vol. 16 (1992), no. 2, pp. 241-246.

McAdams, C. Michael. *Croatia - Myth and Reality.* Sacramento, California: CIS Monographs, 1992.

Murray Seymour, Jack. "The Yugoslav Idea: Will It Die with Yugoslavia?" *History of European Ideas,* vol. 18 (1994), no. 2, pp. 199-213.

Neller, M. "The International Response to the Dissolution of the SFRJ." *American Journal of International Law,* vol. 86 (1992), no. 3, pp. 569-607.

Novakovich, Josip. "Shrapnel in the Liver: The Third Balkan War." *Massachusetts Review,* vol. 34 (1993), Spring, pp. 144-160.

One Hundred Eyewitnesses. Reports of Croatian Refugees and Prisoners of Concentration Camps. Edited by Ljerka Fulgosi and Vlasta Vince-Ribarić. Zagreb: INA Commerce, 1993.

Parlement Européen. *La crise dans l'ex-Yougoslavie.* Luxembourg: Direction Générale des Etudes, Série Politique 18, 1993.

Pavić, Radovan. "Balkanic and Intra-Yugoslav Position of Croatia and Slovenia." *Gaudeamus,* 1991, Fall, no. 4, pp. 12-14.

Ricchiardi, Sherry. "Covering Carnage in the Balkans." *WJR,* vol. 14 (1992), November, pp. 18-23.

________. "Exposing Genocide...for What? (Interview with R. Gutman)." *American Journalism Review,* vol. 15 (1993), June, pp. 32-36.

________. "Kill the Reporters!" *WJR,* vol. 14 (1992), January-February, pp. 33-35.

Rusinow, Dennison. *To Be or Not to Be: Yugoslavia as Hamlet.* N.p.: Field Staff Reports, no. 18, 1991.

Sušac, Mate. *Croatia - Vukovar.* Zagreb: Hrvatska kršćanska demokratska stranka, 1992.

Thompson, Mark. *A Paper House. The Ending of Yugoslavia.* London: Hutchinson/Radius, 1992.

Tomac, Zdravko. *The Struggle for the Croatian State: Through Hell to Democracy.* Zagreb: Profikon, 1993.

The United Nations and the Situation in the Former Yugoslavia. New York: United Nations, Department of Public Information, 1993.

U.S. Department of State. *Material relating to the London Conference (August 26-27, 1992) and the crisis in the former Yugoslavia.* Bureau of Public Affairs, Dispatch Supplement, September 1992, vol. 3, Supplement No. 7.

Vejvoda, Ivan. "Yugoslavia and the Empty Place of Power." *Praxis International,* vol. 13 (1994), no. 4, pp. 346-353.

Wiberg, H. "Yugoslavia War, by T. Kuzmanić and A. Truger." *Journal of Peace Research,* vol. 30 (1993), no. 1, pp. 121-122.

Wolfframm, Gunther. *The Implications for Yugoslav Borders of the Dissolution of the Yugoslav State.* Carlisle, Pennsylvania: U.S. Army War College, 1992.

V. JURIDICAL

Akhavan, P. "Punishing War Crimes in the Former Yugoslavia - A Critical Juncture for the New World Order." *Human Rights Quarterly,* vol. 15 (1993), no. 2, pp. 262-289.

Anatomy of a Fraud. The Affidavit of Bajro Avdic: A Case Study of Fraudulent Evidence Used in an OSI Extradition: Report of the Attorney General of the United States. N.p., 1988.

Bujošević, D. "Constitutional Court Decision: Republics Testing Strength." *Politika: The International Weekly,* vol. 1 (1990), April 7-13, p. 6.

________. "Declaration against Law." *Politika: The International Weekly,* vol. 1 (1990), no. 16, July 7-14, p. 1.

Castro, E. "The Conflict in Former Yugoslavia (Message Delivered at the Special Session of the UN Commission on Human Rights, August 13-14, 1992)." *Sobornost Incorporating Eastern Churches Review,* vol. 14 (1992), no. 2, pp. 53-55.

Cohen, Lenard J. "Post-Federalism and Judicial Change in Yugoslavia: The Rise of Ethno-Political Justice." *International Political Science Review,* vol. 13 (1992), no. 3, pp. 301-319.

"The Constitutional Law of Human Rights and Freedoms and the Rights of National and Ethnic Communities or Minorities in the Republic of Croatia." *Croatian Political Science Review,* vol. 1 (1992), no. 1, pp. 136-155.

Čulek, Zrinjka Peruško. *Broadcasting Environment and Legislature in Croatia. Report for the BLER Study Group.* Zagreb: Institute for Development and International Relations, September 1992.

Degan, Vladimir Đuro. "Yugoslavia in Dissolution: Opinion no. 1 of the Arbitration Commission of 7 December, 1991." *Croatian Political Science Review,* vol. 1 (1992), no. 1, pp. 20-32.

Deren-Antoljak, Štefica. "The Croatian Electoral Model: Its Most Important Elements. *Croatian Political Science Review,* vol. 1 (1992), no. 1, pp. 100-124.

Djamić, Anica. "On the New Constitution of the Republic of Croatia." *Razvoj/Development-International,* vol. 6 (1991), no. 1, pp. 107-110.

Doimi, Ingrid. "Croatia and Independence. The International Law Aspects." *Gaudeamus* (Association of Alumni and Friends of Croatian Universities), 1991, no. 4, p. 3.

Đurković, D. and D. Kusar. "The Opinion of the Constitutional Court of Yugoslavia on Conflicts between Amendments on the Constitutions of the Republics and Autonomous Provinces and the Constitution of the SFRY." *Yugoslav Survey,* vol. 31 (1990), no. 2, pp. 59-70.

Ferguson, A. "The Statute of Vinodol from 1288." *B.C. Review,* no. 14 (1978), pp. 12-24.

________. "Vinodol and Medieval Croatia." *B.C. Review,* no. 14 (1978), pp. 3-6.

Fisk, W. "The Constitutional Movement in Yugoslavia: A Preliminary Survey." *Slavic Review,* 1971, June, pp. 277-297.

Hayden, Robert M. "Constitutional Nationalism in the Former Yugoslav Republics." *Slavic Review,* vol. 51 (1992), no. 4, pp. 654-673.

________. "Human Rights and the Civil War in Yugoslavia - Morality of Liberal Absolutism." *Economic and Political Weekly,* vol. 27 (1992), pp. 1252-1254.

________. *Social Court in Theory and Practice: Yugoslav Workers' Courts in Comparative Perspective.* Philadelphia: University of Pennsylvania Press, 1990.

Headlam-Morley, Agnes. *The New Democratic Constitutions of Europe: A Comparative Study of Postwar European Institutions with Special Reference to Germany, Czechoslovakia, Poland, Finland, the Kingdom of the Serbs, Croats and Slovenes and the Baltic States.* London: Oxford University Press, 1928.

Kayal, A.Z., P.L. Parker and D. Weisenbrodt. "The 44th Session of the UN Sub-Commission on Prevention of Discrimination and Protection of Minorities and the Special Session of the Commission on Human Rights on the Situation in the Former Yugoslavia." *Human Rights Quarterly,* vol. 15 (1993), no. 2, pp. 410-458.

Marko, Joseph and Tomislav Borić (eds.). *Slovenien-Kroatien-Serbien. Die neue Verfassungen.* Studien zu Politik und Verwaltung. Vienna, Cologne, Graz: Böhlau, 1991.

Meron, T. "The Case for War-Crime Trials in Yugoslavia." *Foreign Affairs,* vol. 72 (1993), no. 3, Summer, pp. 122-135.

Omrcanin, Ivo. *L'influence du droit canonique sur le droit coutumier croate.* Washington: Ivor Press, 1990.

Pallua, Emilio. "A Survey of the Constitutional History of the Kingdom of Dalmatia, Croatia and Slovenia." *Canadian American Slavic Studies,* vol. 24 (1990), no. 2, pp. 129-154.

Pusić, Vesna. "Constitutional Politics in Croatia." *Praxis International,* vol. 13 (1994), no. 4, pp. 389-404.

Rodin, Davor. "Political War and Total War." *Croatian Political Science Review,* vol. 1 (1992), no. 1, pp. 5-9.

Smerdel, Branko. "The Republic of Croatia: Three Fundamental Constitutional Choices." *Croatian Political Science Review,* vol. 1 (1992), no. 1, pp. 60-78.

Srzentić, N. *The Constitutional Judiciary in Yugoslavia.* Belgrade: Jugoslovenski Pregled, 1984.

Štrbac, D. "The Court Assesses and Rules." *Politika: The International Weekly,* 1990, April 14-21, p. 3.

Valković, Ljubomir. *The Constitution of the Republic of Croatia.* Zagreb: Sabor Republike Hrvatske, 1991.

Varady, T. "Collective Minority Rights and Problems in Their Legal Protection - The Example of Yugoslavia." *East European Politics and Societies,* vol. 6 (1992), no. 3, pp. 260-282.

Warbrick, C. "Human Rights, Realities and Possibilities - Northern Ireland, the Republic of Ireland, Yugoslavia and Hungary, by L.J. Macfarlane." *International Affairs,* vol. 68 (1992), no. 1, pp. 157-158.

VI. POLITICAL

1. Domestic

Arday, L. "The Historical Background of the Crisis in Former Yugoslavia." *Aussen Politik,* vol. 44 (1993), no. 3, pp. 253-260.

Banac, Ivo. "The Fearful Asymmetry of War: The Causes and Consequences of Yugoslavia's Demise." *Daedalus,* vol. 121 (1992), pp. 141-172.

Bebler, A. "Yugoslavia's Variety of Communist Federalism and Her Demise." *Communist and Post-Communist Studies,* vol. 26 (1993), no. 1, pp. 72-76.

Carević, Olga. "Why I Raise My Voice." *Gaudeamus,* 1991, Fall, no. 4, pp. 25-26.

Cohen, Lenard and Paul Warwick. *Political Cohesion in a Fragile Mosaic. The Yugoslav Experience.* Boulder, Colorado: Westview Press, 1983.

Dević, Ana. "The Limits of Ethno-National Analysis." *International Journal of Politics, Culture and Society,* vol. 6 (1992), no. 1, pp. 133-138.

Đukić, Milan. "Serb Homeland." *Gaudeamus,* 1991, Fall, no. 4, pp. 24-25.

"Europe Cannot Be Built on Dubrovnik's Ruins." *Gaudeamus,* 1991, Fall, no. 4, pp. 27-29.

Grdešić, Ivan. "Nineteen Hundred and Ninety Elections in Croatia." *Croatian Political Science Review,* vol. 1 (1992), no. 1, pp. 91-99.

Job, C. "Yugoslavia's Ethnic Furies." *Foreign Policy,* 1993, no. 92, pp. 52-74.

Kaldor, N. "Yugoslavia and the New Nationalism." *New Left Review,* 1993, no. 197, pp. 96-112.

Kaplan, R.D. "The Latest Balkan Ugliness - Croatianism." *New Republic,* 1991, vol. 205 (1991), no. 22, p. 16.

Kearns, I. "Croatia. The Politics behind the War." *World Today,* vol. 49 (1993), no. 4, pp. 62-64.

Kovačević, Božo. "A View on the Proposals for the Solution of the Serb Question in Croatia." *Gaudeamus,* 1991, Fall, no. 4, pp. 21-24.

Lovric, Jelena. "Croatia: Edging towards a One-Party State?" *Balkan War Report,* December 1992, no. 16, pp. 3-4.

Maleković, Sanja and Zlatan Frölich. "Regional/Local Government Situation in Yugoslav Republics." Report to the Conference: "Meeting of the Ouverture Expert Advisory Group," Brussels, March 14, 1991. Zagreb: IRMO, 1991. 9 p. + Annex.

Melčić, Dunja. "Communication and National Identity: Croatian and Serbian Pattern." *Praxis International,* vol. 13 (1994), no. 4, pp. 354-372.

Novak, Slobodan Prosperov. *59th P.E.N. World Congress Dubrovnik, Croatia 19-25 April, Place and Destiny.* Zagreb: Special Edition of the Croatian P.E.N. Center in cooperation with Matica hrvatska for the 59th P.E.N. World Congress, 1993.

Pavić, Radovan. "The Knin Pass - A Link or Barrier?: History, Natural and Ethnic Features." *Croatian Political Science Review,* vol. 1 (1992), no. 1, pp. 125-135.

Puhowski, Žarko. "UN Protectorate a Pre-Requisite for a Political Solution." *Balkan War Report,* October 1992, no. 15, p. 15.

Pusić, V. "A Country by Any Other Name. Transition and Stability in Croatia and Yugoslavia." *East European Politics and Societies,* vol. 6 (1992), no. 3, pp. 242-259.

Rady, Martyn. "Minority Rights and Self-Determination in Contemporary Eastern Europe." *Slavonic and East European Review,* vol. 71 (1993), no. 4, pp. 716-728.

Rieff, D. "Croatia, a Crisis of Meaning." *World Policy Journal,* vol. 10 (1993), no. 2, pp. 41-45.

Schaaf, R.W. "United Nations Peacekeeping in Yugoslavia." *Government Publications Review,* vol. 19 (1992), no. 5, pp. 537-543.

Tax, Meredith. "Croatia's 'Witches'. Five Women Who Won't Be Silenced." *Nation,* vol. 256 (1993), no. 18 (May 10), pp. 624-627.

Tuđman, Franjo. *Nationalism in Contemporary Europe.* New York: East European Monographs/Columbia University Press, 1981.

Zakošek, Nenad. "Choosing Political Institutions in Post-Socialism and the Formation of the Croatian Political System." *Croatian Political Science Review,* vol. 1 (1992), no. 1, pp. 79-90.

2. Foreign Relations

Altmann, Franz-Lothar. "Ex-Yugoslavia's Neighbours: Who Wants What?" *World Today,* vol. 48 (1992), no. 8-9, pp. 163-165.

Béhar, Pierre. *L'Autriche-Hongrie. Idée d'Avenir. Permanences Géopolitiques de l'Europe Centrale et Balkanique.* Paris: Editions Desjonquères, 1991.

Big Europe - Small Nations: The Book of Abstracts/Zagrebački književni razgovori, Museum Mimara, Zagreb, October 1-3, 1992. Zagreb: Croatian Writers' Association and Croatia P.E.N. Center, 1992.

Blackburn, R. "The Break-up of Yugoslavia and the Fate of Bosnia." *New Left Review,* 1993, no. 199, pp. 100-119.

Blitz, M. "United States Interests in Yugoslavia - A Symposium." *Policy Review,* vol. 62 (1992), Fall, pp. 37-40.

Doder, Duško. "Yugoslavia: New War, Old Hatreds." *Foreign Policy,* 1991, no. 91, pp. 3-23.

Đokić, Nada Svob. "The International Community and the Case of Croatia and Slovenia." *International Spectator* (Rome), vol. 27 (1992), no. 4, pp. 81-94.

European Parliament. *Joint Resolution on the Decision by the Council to Recognize Croatia and Slovenia.* OCJ39/17.02.1992.

________. *Resolution on the Death Sentences on Croatian Citizens in Belgrade* (B3-1047/92). Session of July 1992. OJC241/21.9.1992.

Fenske, John. "The West and 'The Problem from Hell.'" *Current History,* vol. 92 (1993), no. 577, pp. 353-356.

Gauthier, Xavier. *L'Europe à l'épreuve des Balkans.* Paris: Bertoin, 1992.

Goodby, James E. "Peacekeeping in the New Europe." *Washington Quarterly,* vol. 15, no. 2 (1992), pp. 153-171.

Gow, James. "The Use of Coercion in the Yugoslav Crisis." *World Today,* vol. 48 (1992), no. 11, pp. 198-202.

Higgins, R. "The New United Nations and Former Yugoslavia." *International Affairs,* vol. 69 (1993), no. 3, pp. 465-483.

Horsley, William. "United Germany's Seven Cardinal Sins: A Critique of German Foreign Policy." *Journal of International Studies,* vol. 21, no. 2 (1992), pp. 225-241.

"Interview with David Owen on the Balkans." *Foreign Affairs,* vol. 72 (1993), no. 2, Spring, pp. 1-9.

James, A. "The UN in Croatia. An Exercise in Futility." *World Today,* vol. 49 (1993), no. 5, pp. 93-96.

Lopandić, Duško. "Un exemple de sanctions économiques de la CEE: Suspension/dénonciation de l'accord de coopération entre la CEE et la Yougoslavie." *Revue des Affaires Européennes,* 1992, no. 2, pp. 67-72.

Lytle, P.F. "United States Policy towards the Demise of Yugoslavia - The Virus of Nationalism." *East European Politics and Societies,* vol. 6 (1992), no. 3, pp. 308-318.

Melčić, Dunja. "The Balkans and Europe - A Philosophical Problem?" *Praxis International,* vol. 13 (1994), no. 4. pp. 332-338.

Mey, H.H. "View from Germany - Germany, NATO, and the War in the Former Yugoslavia." *Comparative Strategy,* vol. 12 (1993), no. 2, pp. 239-245.

Mullerson, R. "The Continuity and Succession of States, by Reference to the Former USSR and Yugoslavia." *International and Comparative Law Quarterly,* vol. 42 (1993), July, pp. 473-493.

Nel, Philip. "Underestimating Insecurity. The International Community and Yugoslavia." *Review of International Affairs,* vol. 43 (1993), nos. 1012-1013, pp. 3-6, pp. 23-26.

Neller, M. "The International Response to the Dissolution of the Socialist Federal Republic of Yugoslavia." *American Journal of International Law,* vol. 86 (1992), no. 3, pp. 569-607.

Omrčanin, Ivo. *Anglo-American Croatian Rapprochement.* Washington, D.C.: Samizdat, 1989.

Pfaff, William. "Invitation to War." *Foreign Affairs,* vol. 72 (1993), no. 3, Summer, pp. 97-109.

Salmon, T.C. "Testing Times for European Political Cooperation - The Gulf and Yugoslavia, 1990-1992." *International Affairs,* vol. 68 (1992), no. 2, pp. 233-253.

Švob-Đokić, Nada. *Croatia and Slovenia: New Interlocutors in the International Order.* Zagreb: IRMO, 1992, 35 p.

________. "The International Community and the Case of Croatia and Slovenia." *International Spectator,* vol. 29 (1992), no. 4, pp. 383-387.

VII. SCIENTIFIC

1. Information Science and Communication

Cabrajec, L. and Z. Dukic. "Communication Practices of Croatian Scientists." *International Library Review,* vol. 23 (1991), no. 3, pp. 237-253.

Crnjaković, Marta and Dragan Bukovec. "Museum Inventory Using a Personal Computer and the PC-Museum Program. On the Example of Micro-Samples." *Natura Croatica,* vol. 1 (1992), pp. 115-118.

Jokić, M. "Information Value of Papers Written in Slavonic Languages in the Medline Database." *Online Review,* vol. 6 (1992), no. 1, pp. 17-27.

Maleković, Sanja. "The Local and the International in the Twenty-first Century: The Importance of Collaboration Networks (Bilbao, 26 February-2 March 1991)." *Razvoj/Development-International,* vol. 6 (1991), no. 1, pp. 121-123.

Pifat-Mrzljak, Greta. *Nobel Laureates for Peace in Croatia.* Zagreb: Hrvatska Sveučilišna Naklada, 1992.

________. *Scientists against the War in Croatia. World Responses to the Ruđer Bošković Institute's Endeavour for Peace in Croatia.* Zagreb: Hrvatska Sveučilišna Naklada, 1992.

Pravdić, Nevenka. "In Search of a 'Non-Citation Index' Indicator for Scientific Activity Assessment in Less Developed Countries. Case Study of Croatia/Yugoslavia." *Scientometrics,* vol. 14 (1988), no. 1-2, pp. 111-125.

Pravdić, Nevenka and Vesna Oluić-Vuković. "Dual Approach to Multiple Authorship in the Study of Collaboration/Scientific Output Relationship." *Scientometrics,* vol. 10 (1986), no. 5-6, pp. 259-280.

2. *Environment*

Bašić, F., A. Vranković and A. Butorac. *Dynamics of Redox Potential in Hydromorphic Soils of Disturbed Pedunculate Oak Ecosystems in Croatia.* Kyoto, Japan: Fourteenth International Congress of Soil Science, 1990.

Biškup, J. *The Philosophy and Methods of Sociology of Forestry.* Ljubljana: 18th IUFRO Congress, Div. 6, 1986, pp. 346-358.

Bojanin, S., S. Nikolić and F. Penzar. *Harvesting and Processing of High Value Slavonian Oak - A Complex Approach in Treatment of Forests.* Zagreb: Knjiga-vodič za IUFRO ekskurziju, 1986.

Branica, Marko (ed.). *Lead in the Marine Environment: Proceedings of the International Experts Discussion on Lead Occurrence, Fate and Pollution in the Marine Environment, Rovinj, Yugoslavia, 18-22 October 1977.* Oxford: International Experts Discussion on Lead Occurrence, 1980.

Cerjan-Stefanović, Štefica, Felicita Briški and Marija Kaštelan-Macan. "Separation of Silver from Waste by Ion-Exchange Resins and Concentration by Microbial Cells. Silver Uptake by Microbial Cells from Treated Waste Waters after Ion Exchange." *Fresenius' Journal of Analytical Chemistry,* vol. 339 (1991), pp. 636-639.

Cerjan-Stefanović, Štefica, Marija Kaštelan-Macan and Tugomir Filipan. "Ion Exchange Characterisation of Modified Zeolite." *Water Science and Technology,* vol. 6 (1992), pp. 2269-2272.

Cerjan-Stefanović, Štefica, Marija Kaštelan-Macan and Mira Petrović. "TLC, Separation of m- and p-amino-phenols by Metal-Ion Addition to the Chromatographic Layer." *Fresenius' Journal of Analytical Chemistry,* vol. 340 (1991), pp. 784-785.

Fisher, Duncan. "The Environmental Movement in Central and Eastern Europe: Its Emergence and Role in the Political Changes of 1989." *Associations Transnationales/Transnational Associations,* vol. 45 (1993), no. 4, pp. 207-216.

Jancar, Barbara. *Environmental Management in the Soviet Union and Yugoslavia.* Durham, North Carolina: Duke University Press, 1987.

Kaštelan-Macan, Marija, Štefica Cerjan-Stefanović and Darko Jalšoveć. "TLC Determination of Aquatic Humid Acids." *Water Science Technology,* vol. 26 (1992), pp. 2567-2570.

Klepac, D. *The Management of Forest Ecosystems where Ecological and Social Functions Predominate.* Zagreb: Anali za šumarstvo JAZU, 1990.

Raus, Đuro i Joso Vukelić. *Bibliografija Radova Istraživača Zavoda za Istraživanje u Šumarstvu Šumarskog Fakulteta u Zagrebu za Razdoblje 1981-1985/Bibliography of Articles from the Institute for Forestry, Zagreb over the Period 1981-1985.* Zagreb: Sveučilište u Zagrebu, Šumarski Fakultet, 1986.

________. *Bibliografija Radova Istraživača Zavoda za Istraživanje u Šumarstvu Šumarskog Fakulteta u Zagrebu za Razdoblje 1986-1990/Bibliography of Articles from the Institute for Forestry, Zagreb over the Period 1986-1990.* Zagreb: Sveučilište u Zagrebu, Šumarski Fakultet, 1992.

Rose, J. "Croatia. Environmental Effects of War." *Environmental Science and Technology,* vol. 27 (1993), no. 6, pp. 1010-1011.

Tomanić, S. "Twenty Years of Forest Work Study in Yugoslavia." Thessaloniki, Greece: IUFRO Symposium on the Measurement of Productivity in Forest Operations, 1988.

Vukina, Tomislav. *Energy and the Environment: Some Key Issues.* EDI Working Papers, Energy Series. Washington, D.C.: World Bank, 1992, 82 p.

3. Geography

Boban, Ljubo. *Croatian Borders 1918-1992.* Translated by Želko Novačić. Zagreb: Školska Knjiga, 1993.

Bognar, Andrija (ed.). *Proceedings of the International Symposium "Geomorphology and Sea" and the Meeting of the Geomorphological Commission of the Carpatho-Balkan Countries, Mali Lošinj, September 2-26, 1992.* Zagreb: Geografski odjel Prirodnoslovno-matematičkog fakulteta, Sveučilište u Zagrebu, 1993.

The Creation and Changes of the Internal Borders of Yugoslavia. Belgrade: Ministry of Information of the Republic of Serbia, n.d.

Danforth, Kenneth. "Yugoslavia. A House Much Divided." *National Geographic,* vol. 178 (1990), no. 2, pp. 92-123.

Feil, L. et al. "Determination of the Vertical Crustal Movements in Croatia." Vienna: Twentieth General Assembly IUGG, Symposium "General Geodynamics," 1991.

Geopolitical and Demographical Issue of Croatia. Zagreb: Zagreb University, Department of Geography, 1991.

Hayden-Bakić, Milica and Robert M. Hayden. "Orientalist Variations on the Theme 'Balkans' - Symbolic Geography in Recent Yugoslav Cultural Politics." *Slavic Review,* vol. 51 (1992), no. 1, pp. 1-15.

Miloš, Višnja et al. "Quantities Characteristics for the Gravity Field in Yugoslavia." Vienna: Twentieth General Assembly IUGG, Symposium "General Geodynamics," 1991.

Mršić, Zdravko. "New Strategies." *Gaudeamus,* 1991, Fall, no. 4, pp. 17-19.

Pavić, Radovan. "Commentary of the Map of Croatia and Its Geopolitical Surrounding." *Gaudeamus,* 1991, Fall, no. 4, pp. 14-15.

Pejin, Jovan. "How Baranja Was Seized in 1945 and Annexed to Croatia." In *The Creation and Changes of the Internal Borders of Yugoslavia*. Belgrade: Ministry of Information of the Republic of Serbia, n.d., pp. 57-69.

Permanent Committee on Geographical Names for British Official Use: Serbo-Croat and Slovene. London: Royal Geographical Society, 1943.

Republic of Croatia and of the Republic of Bosnia and Hercegovina. Ethnic Map. Geographic Map. Road Map. Zagreb: Leksikografski Zavod Miroslav Krleža, 1993.

Sellier, André and Jean. *Atlas des Peuples d'Europe Centrale*. Paris: La Découverte, 1991.

Zečević, Miodrag and Bogdan Lekić. *Frontiers and Internal Territorial Division in Yugoslavia*. Belgrade: Ministry of Information of the Republic of Serbia, 1991.

4. Physics and Chemistry

Alaga, Gaja et al. *Problems of Vibrational Nuclei: Proceedings of the Topical Conference on Problems of Vibrational Nuclei, Zagreb, Croatia, Yugoslávia*. Amsterdam: North-Holland, 1975.

Barnes, A.J. "Molecular Spectroscopy and Molecular Structure 1991: Proceedings of the 20th European Congress on Molecular Spectroscopy, Which Should Have Been Held in Zagreb, Croatia, 25-30 August 1991." Amsterdam: Elsevier, 1992. *Journal of Molecular Structure*. Special issues 266/267.

Colombo, L. (ed.). *State of the Art in Vibrational Spectroscopy*. Zagreb: Vjesnik, 1988. Croatica chimica acta.

Feretić, Danilo. "Nuclear Power: Its Present Status and Trends." *Encyclopaedia Moderna*, vol. 13 (1992), vol. 2, pp. 321-324.

Ljolje, Krunoslav. "Reminiscences of My Work with Professor Supek." Symposium "From Theoretical Physics to Philosophy of Science and Peace," dedicated to 50 years of work by Ivan Supek, 11.10.1990. *Fizika. A, Atomic and Molecular Physics. Condensed Matter Physics. Plasma Physics,* vol. 1 (1992), no. 1, pp. 37-47.

Martinis, M. and I. Andrić. *Superstrings, Anomalies and Unification: 5th Adriatic Meeting on Particle Physics, Dubrovnik, Croatia, Yugoslavia, June 16-28, 1986.* Singapore: World Scientific, 1987.

Pavletić, Vlatko. "A Modern Renaissance Personality Dr. Ivan Supek." Symposium "From Theoretical Physics to Philosophy of Science and Peace," dedicated to 50 years of work by Ivan Supek, 11.10.1990. *Fizika. A, Atomic and Molecular Physics. Condensed Matter Physics. Plasma Physics,* vol. 1 (1992), no. 1, pp. 3-6.

Peierls, Rudolf. "People in the Early Days of Quantum Mechanics." Symposium "From Theoretical Physics to Philosophy of Science and Peace," dedicated to 50 years of work by Ivan Supek, 11.10.1990. *Fizika. A, Atomic and Molecular Physics. Condensed Matter Physics. Plasma Physics,* vol. 1 (1992), no. 1, pp. 11-30.

Točan, Lojze and UNCTAD Secretariat. *The Diffusion of Electronics Technology in the Capital Goods Sector: The Yugoslav Case.* New York: United Nations, 1986.

Tadić, Dubravko. "Ivan Supek and Theoretical Physics in Zagreb." Symposium "From Theoretical Physics to Philosophy of Science and Peace," dedicated to 50 years of work by Ivan Supek, 11.10.1990. *Fizika. A, Atomic and Molecular Physics. Condensed Matter Physics. Plasma Physics,* vol. 1 (1992), no. 1, pp. 111-119.

Whyte, L.L. (ed.). *Roger Joseph Boscovich, S.J., F.R.S., 1711-1785 - Studies of His Life and Work on the 250th Anniversary of His Birth.* London: George Allen and Unwin, 1961.

Žubrinić, Darko. *Faculty of Electrical Engineering: With a Short Survey of the History of Croatia.* Zagreb: Faculty of Electrical Engineering, 1992.

5. Natural History and Biology

Balabanić, Josip. "Natura Croatica. Editorial." *Natura Croatica,* vol. 1 (1992), pp. 1-6.

Jurišić-Polšak, Zlata, Zlatan Bajraktarević and Stjepan Bahun. "Spiridion Brusina's Miocene Freshwater and Pleistocene Marine Fossils from Sinjsko Polje." *Natura Croatica,* vol. 1 (1992), pp. 19-26.

Kučinić, Mladen. "The Noctuidae (Insecta, Lepidoptera) of Lička Plješevica Mountain (Croatia)." *Natura Croatica,* vol. 1 (1992), pp. 71-80.

Lukač, Gordan et al. "Characteristics of Habitat and Distribution of Sitta Neumayer Mich. (Aves) in Croatia and Neighbouring Areas." *Natura Croatica,* vol. 1 (1992), pp. 81-91.

Sakac, Krešimir. "Discoptychites Oenensis N. SP. and the Accompanying Ammonite Fauna from Anisian Deposits in Brotinja, Lika, Central Croatia." *Natura Croatica,* vol. 1 (1992), pp. 27-40.

Štamol, Vesna. "The Significance of Quantitative Fluctuations in Eurivalent Land Snails (Mollusca: Gastropoda Terrestria) in Malacocoenoses." *Natura Croatica,* vol. 1 (1992), pp. 105-114.

Sušić, Goran and Milan Mestrov. *Ornitologija u Hrvatskoj/Ornithology in Croatia.* Zagreb: Jugoslovenska Akademija Znanosti i Umjetnosti, 1988.

Trinajstić, Ivo and Mirjana Vrbek. "Association Oleo-Euphorbietum Dendroidis Trinajstić 1973 (Oleo-Ceratonion) in the Vegetation of the Island of Dugi Otok, Croatia." *Natura Croatica,* vol. 1 (1992), pp. 7-12.

VIII. SOCIAL

1. Anthropology and Ethnology

Andrić, Jasna. "On the Custom of Burial in Hollowed-out Tree Trunks." *Studia Ethnologica*, vol. 3 (1991), pp. 80-83.

Belaj, Vitomir. "An Argument for Ethnology as a Historical Science Concerning Ethnic Groups." *Studia Ethnologica*, vol. 1 (1989), pp. 13-17.

Brožek, J. "In and from Croatia: A Retrospect." *Collegium Antropologicum*, vol. 17 (1993), no. 2, pp. 355-357.

Čapo, Jasna. "Croatian Ethnology, the Science of Peoples or the Science of Culture." *Studia Ethnologica*, vol. 3 (1991), pp. 17-25.

Černelić, Milana. "Role of the Starješina Svatova among the Bunjevci." *Studia Ethnologica*, vol. 3 (1991), pp. 181-191.

Domaćinović, Vlasta and Vera Tadić. *Human Relationship with Bees and Sheep in Yugoslavia. Animal Welfare. Proceedings of the Animal Welfare Sessions Twenty-fourth World Veterinary Congress, Rio de Janeiro 1991*. London: Animal Welfare Committee of the World Veterinary Association, pp. 223-227.

Fear, Death and Resistance: An Ethnography of War: Croatia 1991-1992. Zagreb: Institute of Ethnology and Folklore Research, 1993.

Korčula-Moreška. Zagreb: Exhibition: Special Edition of the Croatian P.E.N. Center in cooperation with Matica hrvatska for the 59th P.E.N. World Congress, 1993.

Krader, Barbara. "Slavic Folk Music: Forms of Singing and Self-Identity." *Ethnomusicology*, vol. 31 (1987), Winter, pp. 9-17.

Lopašić, Alexandar (ed.). *Mediterranean Societies: Tradition and Change.* Zagreb: Croatian Anthropological Society, 1993.

Petrović, Tihana. "Women's Individual Property in South Slavic Zadrugas." *Studia Ethnologica,* vol. 3 (1991), pp. 193-200.

Prpić, George. J. *Croatian Folk Art and Folklore.* N.p., 1984.

Rheubottom, David B. "'Sisters First': Betrothal Order and Age at Marriage in Fifteenth-Century Ragusa." *Journal of Family History,* vol. 13 (1988), no. 4, pp. 359-376.

Svirac, Manda. "Croatian Ethnology." *Gaudeamus,* Winter 1992-1993, no. 7-8, p. 19.

_______. "International Folklore Festival and Zagreb." Zagreb: Twenty-third Međunarodna smotra folklora, 1988.

_______. "On the Occasion of the Silver Jubilee of the International Folkore Festival." Zagreb: Twenty-fifth Međunarodna smotra folklora, 1990, pp. 7-9.

_______. "The Symbolics of Bread on Special Occasions." *Studia Ethnologica,* vol. 3 (1991), pp. 173-179.

Vince-Pallua, Jelka. "Ethnological Reflections of Petar Nižetić (Pietro Nisiteo)." *Ethnologia Slavica,* vol. 22 (1990), pp. 253-264.

2. *Demography*

Hammel, E. A. "Short-Term Demographic Fluctuations in the Croatian Military Border of Austria, 1830-1847." *European Journal of Population,* vol. 1 (1985), no. 2-3, pp. 265-290.

Marković, A. "Depopulation in Croatia - Causes, Traits, Implications, by I. Nejasmic, 1991." *Collegium Antropologicum,* vol. 16 (1992), no. 1, pp. 223-224.

Milišević, G. "Croatian National Growth and Development Study. 1. Descriptive Statistics for Zagreb Pubertal Population - Girls, 11-15 Years of Age." *Collegium Antropologicum,* vol. 17 (1993), no. 1, pp. 67-78.

Sujoldžić, A. "Isonymy and Population Structure of the Island of Korčula (Croatia)." *Collegium Antropologicum,* vol. 17 (1993), no. 1, pp. 17-24.

Zivičnjak, M. et al. "Croatian National Growth and Development Study. 2. Descriptive Statistics for Zagreb Pubertal Population - Boys, 11-15 Years of Age." *Collegium Antropologicum,* vol. 17 (1993), no. 1, pp. 79-89.

3. Education

The Development of Education in the Republic of Croatia. National Report from Croatia. Zagreb: Ministry of Education, 1994.

Ivančević, N. "University Educational System and Scientific Institutions in the Republic of Croatia." *Collegium Antropologicum,* vol. 17 (1993), no. 1, pp. 383-386.

Maleković, Sanja. "On the Need to Introduce Regional Studies at the University of Zagreb." *Razvoj/Development-International,* vol. 7 (1992), no. 1, pp. 113-118.

Mihaljević, Jelena. "Attitudes Towards the Teacher as a Factor in Foreign Language Learning." *Studia Romanica et Anglica Zagrabiensia,* vol. 36-37 (1991-1992), pp. 143-152.

Peruško Čulek, Zrinjka. "European Diploma in Cultural Management: A New Training Opportunity in Europe." *Razvoj/Development-International,* vol. 7 (1992), no. 1, pp. 135-138.

Samardžija, Višnja. "Development of European Studies at the University of Zagreb in the Light of Ongoing Programmes in Different Countries of Europe." *Razvoj/Development-International,* vol. 7 (1992), no. 1, pp. 15-34.

________. "Overview of the Topics Discussed During the Workshop (Tempus Workshop on European Studies)." *Razvoj/Development-International,* vol. 7 (1992), no. 1, pp. 119-122.

________. "Workshop on the Management of Joint European Projects, Vienna, 29 June - 1 July 1992." *Razvoj/Development-International,* vol. 7 (1992), no. 1, pp. 139-142.

Švob-Đokić, Nada. "Trends in Development Research in Croatia. What Thematic, Geographical and Institutional Changes Are Occurring in Eastern and Western Europe? The Viewpoint of Research Institutions." In *EADI Seminar Report, Sustaining Development Research in a Changing Europe: The Need for New Priorities and Resources at National and Supra-National Levels,* Antwerp, 7-8 November 1991, p. 22 and p. 37. Edited by J. Rodgers.

Vrbetić, Marta. "Report on the Workshop on Introducing European Studies at the University of Zagreb." *Razvoj/Development-International,* vol. 7 (1992), no. 1, pp. 123-129.

4. *Health and Medical Science*

Acheson, D. "Health, Humanitarian Relief, and Survival in Former Yugoslavia." *British Medical Journal,* vol. 307 (1993), no. 6895, pp. 44-48.

Begovac, J. et al. "Health Status of 1,458 Croatian Prisoners of War, 1991-1992." *Journal of the American Medical Association,* vol. 270 (1993), no. 5, pp. 574-575.

Belicza, Biserka. "A Brief Review of Croatian Medical History until the Nineteenth Century: part 1." *Acta Medica Croatica,* vol. 46 (1992), no. 2, pp. 69-73.

Borot, N. et al. "GM and KM Immunoglobulin Allotypes in Populations on the Island of Pag - Croatia." *Collegium Antropologicum*, vol. 15 (1991), no. 2, pp. 247-255.

Bosanac, Vesna. "The Suffering of Children in Vukovar." Special Issue on "Diseases, Injuries and Sufferings of Children in the War against Croatia." *Archiv za Žaštitu Majke i Djeteta*, vol. 36 (1992), no. 2-3, pp. 105-106.

Bulat, M. (ed.). *Pharmacological Communications: Proceedings of the First Croatian Congress of Pharmocology, Zagreb, October 6-8, 1993*. Zagreb: Croatian Pharmacological Society, 1993.

Cvetnić, Vladimir (ed.). *Atlas of Ultrasonography in the Diagnosis of Head and Neck Diseases*. Zagreb: Vladimir Cvetnić, 1993.

Duraković, Z. and M. Marinković. "Deterioration of Dilatative Cardiomyopathy as a Result of Therapy Withdrawal in the Prisoner's Camp in Serbia." *Collegium Antropologicum*, vol. 17 (1993), no. 2, pp. 359-361.

Hiršl-Hečej, Vlasta and Ivan Fattorini. "The Suffering of Children in the War against Croatia." Special Issue on "Diseases, Injuries and Sufferings of Children in the War against Croatia." *Archiv za Žaštitu Majke i Djeteta*, vol. 36 (1992), no. 2-3, pp. 83-96.

Jefferson, T. "Public Health Aspects of the War in Yugoslavia." *Public Health*, vol. 107 (1993), no. 2, pp. 75-78.

Johnson, R.G. "War in Croatia." *Journal of Trauma*, vol. 33 (1992), no. 4, pp. 643-645.

Jureša, Vesna et al. "School Children in Wartime." Special Issue on "Diseases, Injuries and Sufferings of Children in the War against Croatia." *Archiv za Žaštitu Majke i Djeteta*, vol. 36 (1992), no. 2-3, pp. 165-174.

Mimica, N., J. Skavić and B. Žeželj. "Fatal Traffic Accidents in the Area of Zagreb (Croatia) in the Period 1940-1981." *Collegium Antropologicum*, vol. 17 (1993), no. 1, pp. 91-101.

Novosel, Marija and Robert Kohn. "Physician and Society. A Study of People's Perception of the Social Role of Physicians in a Region of Yugoslavia." *Journal of Science and Medicine,* vol. 13A (1979), no. 1, pp. 73-80.

Perinic, J. "Adult Dento-Oral Health Survey as a Part of Anthropological Investigations (the Island of Brač, Croatia)." *Collegium Antropologicum,* vol. 15 (1991), no. 2, pp. 257-269.

Smolej-Narančić, N. and M. Mustac. "Lung Volumes in Healthy Teenage Boys and Girls of North Dalmatia (Croatia)." *Collegium Antropologicum,* vol. 16 (1992), no. 2, pp. 377-381.

Turek, S. "War in Croatia. Witness of the Crime." *Collegium Antropologicum,* vol. 16 (1992), no. 1, pp. 13-17.

Vorkojović, A. and F. Jović. "Macro Model Prediction of Elderly People's Injury and Death in Road Traffic Accidents in Croatia." *Accident Analysis and Prevention,* vol. 24 (1992), no. 6, pp. 667-672.

5. *Psychology and Psychiatry*

Ajduković, M., O. Petak and S. Mršić. "Assessment of Professionals and Professionals' Attitudes toward Child Abuse in Croatia." *Child Abuse and Neglect,* vol. 17 (1993), no. 4, pp. 549-556.

Ekblad, S. "Psychosocial Adaptation of Children while Housed in a Swedish Refugee Camp - Aftermath of the Collapse of Yugoslavia." *Stress Medicine,* vol. 9 (1993), no. 3, pp. 159-166.

Folnegović, Z. and V. Folnegović-Smalc. "Schizophrenia in Croatia - Interregional Differences in Prevalence and a Comment on Constant Incidence." *Journal of Epidemiology and Community Health,* vol. 46 (1992), no. 3, pp. 248-255.

Kapor, S. N. "Adolescent Reproductive Behavior in Yugoslavia." *International Journal of Psychology,* vol. 27 (1992), no. 3-4, p. 183.

Knežević, A. "Trends in Mental Health Care in Yugoslavia - Difficulties in Achieving Comprehensive, Continuous Care." *International Journal of Mental Health,* vol. 20 (1992), no. 4, pp. 77-82.

Kozarić-Kovačić, D., V. Folnegović-Smalc and A. Marušić. "Psychological Disturbances among 47 Croatian Prisoners of War Tortured in Detention Camps." *Journal of the American Medical Association,* vol. 270 (1993), no. 5, p. 575.

Lorković, Hrvoje, Antun Pinterović and Mladen Schwartz. *Das Kroatische Trauma. Kulturpsychologisches über ein Volk am Rande der Vernichtung.* Koblenz: Verlag Siegfried Bublies, 1991.

Manenica, I. "A Study of Job Satisfaction and Work Values in Three Different Industries." *Contemporary Ergonomics.* Edited by E.D. Megaw. London: Taylor and Francis, 1988, pp. 363-367.

Marinković, K. "The History of Psychology in Former Yugoslavia - An Overview." *Journal of the History of the Behavioral Sciences,* vol. 28 (1992), no. 4, pp. 340-351.

Padgett, D.K. "Socio-Demographic and Disease-Related Correlates of Depressive Morbidity among Diabetic Patients in Zagreb." *Journal of Nervous and Mental Disease,* vol. 181 (1993), no. 2, pp. 123-129.

Psychology and Psychiatry of War. Zagreb: University of Zagreb, Faculty of Medicine, 1992.

Živčić, I. "Emotional Reactions of Children to War Stress in Croatia." *Journal of the American Academy of Child and Adolescent Psychiatry,* vol. 32 (1993), no. 4, pp. 709-713.

6. Sociology

Allcock, John B. "Tourism and Social Change in Dalmatia." *Journal of Development Studies*, vol. 21 (1983), no. 1, pp. 34-55.

Ceso-Zanić, Jasmina. "Family Placement Legislation and Experience in the Socialist Republic of Croatia." *Community Alternatives*, vol. 1 (1989), no. 2, pp. 31-39.

Darville, R.L. and J.B. Reeves. "Social Inequality among Yugoslav Women in Directorial Positions." *Sociological Spectrum*, vol. 12 (1992), no. 3, pp. 279-292.

First-Dilić, Ruža. "The Life Cycle of the Yugoslav Peasant Farm Family." *Journal of Marriage and the Family*, November 1974, pp. 819-826.

Meštrović, Stjepan G., Slaven Letica and Miroslav Goreta. *Habits of the Balkan Heart: Social Character and the Fall of Communism*. Houston, Texas: University of Texas Press, 1993.

Meznarić, Silva. "A Neo-Marxist Approach to the Sociology of Nationalism. Doomed Nations and Doomed Schemes." *Praxis International*, vol. 7 (1987), no. 1, pp. 79-89.

Model, Suzanne, W. "Constructing Ethnic Identity." *Sociological Forum*, vol. 1 (1986), no. 2, pp. 388-393.

Obradović, Josip and William N. Dunn. *Workers' Self-Management and Organizational Power in Yugoslavia*. Pittsburgh: University Center for International Studies, University of Pittsburgh Press, 1978.

Schierup, C.U. "Quasi-Proletarians and a Patriarchal Bureaucracy - Aspects of Yugoslavia's Reperipheralization." *Soviet Studies*, vol. 44 (1992), no. 1, pp. 77-79.

7. *Urbanization and Internal Migration*

Begović, B. "Industrial Diversification and City Size. The Case of Yugoslavia." *Urban Studies,* vol. 29 (1992), no. 1, pp. 77-88.

Mihovilović, Miro A. "Leisure and Tourism in Europe." *International Social Science Journal,* vol. 32 (1980), no. 1, pp. 99-113.

Spoljarvrzina, S.M. "Estimation of the Population Structure through Temporal Migration Analysis - Example from the Island of Korčula (Croatia)." *Collegium Antropologicum,* vol. 17 (1993), no. 1, pp. 7-16.

Stambuk, M. "Agricultural Depopulation in Croatia." *Sociologia Ruralis,* vol. 31 (1991), no. 4, pp. 281-289.

8. *Emigration and Croatian Culture Abroad*

Bonutti, Karl and George J. Prpić. *Selected Ethnic Communities of Cleveland: A Socio-Economic Study.* Cleveland, Ohio: Cleveland State University, 1977.

Croatian Response to the Serbian National Program. Saddle River, New Jersey: The Croatian National Congress, 1988.

Dabrowski, Irene. "Ecological Determinants of 'White Ethnic' Identity in St. Louis, Missouri." *Human Mosaic,* vol. 16 (1992), no. 1, pp. 11-32.

Day, Robert D. "Ethnic Soccer Clubs in London, Canada: A Study in Assimilation." *International Review of Sport and Sociology,* vol. 16 (1981), no. 1, pp. 37-52.

Horvatić, Dubravko. *The Contribution of Croatians to Western Culture.* Translated by Maja Šoljan. Zagreb: Hrvatski P.E.N., 1992.

Ifković, Edward. "South-Slavic American Autobiography: Three Variations." *Melus,* vol. 10 (1983), Summer, pp. 49-55.

Jodlbauer, Ralph et al. *Die Deutschen in Südtirol und die Kroaten in Burgenland: Untersuchungen zu ihren Sprachgebrauch.* Hamburg: Buske, 1986.

Jutronjić-Tihomirović, Dunja. "A Contribution to the Study of Syntactic Interference in Language Contact." *Folia Slavica,* 1986, no. 6, pp. 310-321.

_______. "Language Maintenance and Language Shift of the Serbo-Croatian in Steelton, Penna." In R.L. Lenček and T.F. Magner (eds.). *The Dilemma of the Melting Pot.* University Park, Pennsylvania: Pennsylvania State University Press, 1974, pp. 166-186.

_______. "Linguistic Accommodation on the Morphological Level." In R. Filipović and M. Bratanić. *Languages in Contact.* Zagreb: Institute of Linguistics, 1991.

_______. "The Serbo-Croatian Language in Steelton." *General Linguistics,* 1974, no. 1, pp. 15-34.

Milivojević, Dragan. "Language Maintenance and Language Shift among Yugoslavs of New Orleans, Louisiana - Ten Years After." *Slavic and East European Journal,* vol. 34 (1990), Summer, pp. 208-223.

Mohl, Raymond A. et al. "The Immigrant Church in Gary, Indiana: Religious Adjustment and Cultural Defense." *Ethnicity,* vol. 8 (1981), no. 1, pp. 1-17.

Pfaff, Carol W. "Sociolinguistic Problems of Immigrants: Foreign Workers and Their Children in Germany." *Language in Society,* vol. 10 (1981), no. 2, pp. 155-158.

Polić, M. et al. "Refugee Perception of Their Situation. The Case of Croatian Refugees in Slovenia." *International Journal of Psychology,* vol. 27 (1992), no. 3-4, pp. 314-315.

Rowley, A. R. "Minority Schools in the South Tyrol and in the Austrian Burgenland. A Comparison of Two Models." *Journal of Multilingual and Multicultural Development,* vol. 7 (1986), no. 2-3, pp. 229-251.

Smolicz, J. J. "Minority Languages and the Core Values of Culture: Changing Policies and Ethnic Response in Australia." *Journal of Multilingual and Multicultural Development,* vol. 5 (1984), no. 1, pp. 23-41.

Stepanović, Predrag. "A Taxonomic Description of the Dialects of Croats in Hungary: The Stokavian Dialect." Cologne: Bohlau, 1986.

Tollefson, J. W. "Language Policy and Power - Yugoslavia, the Philippines and Southeast-Asian Refugees in the United States." *International Journal of the Sociology of Language,* vol. 103 (1993), pp. 73-95.

ABOUT THE AUTHORS

Robert Stallaerts is researcher at the Centre for Ethics of UFSIA (University of Antwerp). He is a member of a team, working on a project called "Ethics and Economics." His main research interests include the interaction of economics and ethics in economic doctrines and the economics of self-management and participation. His principal contributions are on the economics and politics of former Yugoslavia, e.g., in *Economic Analysis and Workers' Management* (Belgrade) and Afscheid van Joegoslavië. Achtergronden van de crisis (Leuven: Garant, 1992). He is currently working on a collection presenting translations of the poetry from the peoples of former Yugoslavia.

Jeannine Laurens did post-graduate work at the Institute for Economic Studies in Belgrade and has published on the Yugoslav trade unions, self-management and delegate system.